D1268604

Immigrant Vulnerability and Resilience

Series Editors:
Peter Li and Baha-Abu-Laban

The series publishes original scholarly books that advance our understanding of international migration and immigrant integration. Written by academic experts and policy specialists, each volume addresses a clearly defined research question or theme, employs critical analysis and develops evidence-based scholarship. The series includes single- or multi-authored monographs, volumes and edited collections.

The scope of the series is international migration and integration research. Topics include but are not limited to thematic and current issues and debates; comparative research of a regional, national or international nature; the changing character of urban areas in which migrants or refugees settle; the reciprocal influence of migrants/refugees and host communities; issues of integration and social inequality as well as policy analysis in migration research.

For further volumes:
http://www.springer.com/series/8811

María Aysa-Lastra • Lorenzo Cachón

Editors

Immigrant Vulnerability and Resilience

Comparative Perspectives on Latin American Immigrants During the Great Recession

Springer

Editors
María Aysa-Lastra
Department of Sociology
  and Anthropology
Winthrop University
Rock Hill, SC, USA

Lorenzo Cachón
Departamento de Sociología I
Universidad Complutense de Madrid
Madrid, Spain

ISSN 2214-9805   ISSN 2214-9813 (electronic)
ISBN 978-3-319-14796-3 ISBN 978-3-319-14797-0   (eBook)
DOI 10.1007/978-3-319-14797-0
Springer Cham Heidelberg New York Dordrecht London

Library of Congress Control Number: 2015935670

© Springer International Publishing Switzerland 2015
This work is subject to copyright. All rights are reserved by the Publisher, whether the whole or part of
the material is concerned, specifically the rights of translation, reprinting, reuse of illustrations, recita-
tion, broadcasting, reproduction on microfilms or in any other physical way, and transmission or information storage and retrieval, electronic adaptation, computer software, or by similar or dissimilar methodology now known or hereafter developed. Exempted from this legal reservation are brief excerpts in
connection with reviews or scholarly analysis or material supplied specifically for the purpose of being
entered and executed on a computer system, for exclusive use by the purchaser of the work. Duplica-
tion of this publication or parts thereof is permitted only under the provisions of the Copyright Law of
the Publisher's location, in its current version, and permission for use must always be obtained from
Springer. Permissions for use may be obtained through RightsLink at the Copyright Clearance Center.
Violations are liable to prosecution under the respective Copyright Law.
The use of general descriptive names, registered names, trademarks, service marks, etc. in this publication does not imply, even in the absence of a specific statement, that such names are exempt from the
relevant protective laws and regulations and therefore free for general use.
While the advice and information in this book are believed to be true and accurate at the date of publication, neither the authors nor the editors nor the publisher can accept any legal responsibility for any errors
or omissions that may be made. The publisher makes no warranty, express or implied, with respect to the
material contained herein.

Printed on acid-free paper

Springer is part of Springer Science+Business Media (www.springer.com)

B3558907

Preface

The Great Divide Between Spain and the United States

During times of recession, immigrants are especially vulnerable because they are over-represented in the secondary sector of the labor market, in jobs that are unstable, poorly paid, and carry few benefits even during good economic times; and those fortunate enough to be working in the primary sector often hold peripheral positions that are at greater risk of elimination during lean economic times. As a result, immigrants generally experience higher rates of unemployment than natives during downturns. Immigrants are resilient, of course, and adapt in creative ways, but even when they find new employment it is often for lower pay and fewer hours.

Although natives may not suffer as much as immigrants when the economy goes bad, recessions necessarily increase their feelings of insecurity. As human beings often do when faced with threatening circumstances beyond their control, natives all-to-often look for scapegoats and project their fears and apprehensions onto immigrants, blaming them for their poor economic prospects. The demonization of immigrants as threatening "others" is unfortunately a common side effect of economic downturns.

These observations apply on both sides of the Atlantic, and to some extent Latin American immigrants in both Spain and the United States have suffered increased discrimination and exclusion in the years since 2008, especially those of African or Indigenous origins who are subject to systematic processes of racialization in which negative attributes are tied to their physical characteristics (Massey 2014). In general, however, the degree of racialization and exclusion has not been as pronounced in Spain as in the United States. For one thing, Latin Americans in Spain speak the same language as native Spanish citizens and come with cultures that have obvious Spanish roots.

A greater contrast, however, is the massive prevalence of illegality among Latino immigrants living in the United States. According to the latest estimates, around 60 % of Mexican and two-thirds of Central American immigrants living in the United States are unauthorized (cf. Hoefer et al. 2011; Acosta and de la Cruz 2011). Although many Latin American migrants to Spain overstayed their tourist visas and began working without authorization, over the years the Spanish government undertook a series of regularizations to grant them legal status. As a result, relatively few Latin American migrants are undocumented. Whatever the problems and vulnerabilities they experience in Spain because of the Great Recession, they do not have them compounded by mass illegality, a peculiarly American condition (Massey 2013).

Illegality is not an intrinsic characteristic of immigrants in the United States, but one manufactured by U.S. policies (De Genova 2004). The roots of mass illegality can be traced back to 1965 when the U.S. Congress unilaterally terminated a 22-year-old guest worker treaty with Mexico and passed legislation to place numerical limits on immigration from the Western Hemisphere for the first time in history. Prior to that date the Bracero Program had liberally issued permits to Mexicans for temporary labor in the United States, and there was no limit on the annual number of Mexicans admitted for legal permanent residence. In the late 1950s, some 450,000 Mexicans crossed the border each year with temporary work permits and another 50,000 entered as permanent residents (Massey et al. 2002).

During the early 1960s, however, the Bracero Program was scaled back and ultimately ended in 1965 while in that same year a new cap of 120,000 residence visas was imposed on the Western Hemisphere. In the ensuing years the separate hemispheric cap was eliminated in favor of a single worldwide cap of 290,000 and a new annual limit of 20,000 visas per country was imposed throughout the Americas. Whereas in the late 1950s Mexico was legally sending half a million migrants to the United States each year, 90 % as temporary workers, by the late 1970s the guest worker program was gone and permanent resident entries were capped at 20,000. Although U.S. policies toward Mexican migration had changed, the economic conditions promoting and sustaining it had not, and the annual inflow of workers quickly reestablished itself under undocumented auspices (Massey and Pren 2012b).

From 1965 to 1979 the number of border apprehensions steadily rose as migrants who formerly had circulated with documents continued to migrate without them, and by the latter date the undocumented flow had reached the rough equivalent of where it had been back in the late 1950s, except now of course the migrants were all unauthorized. The fact that the migrants were now "illegal" offered a golden opportunity to politicians seeking to mobilize voters and bureaucrats seeking more resources for their agencies. Illegal migrants were by definition "lawbreakers" and "criminals" who could easily be portrayed as a grave threat to the nation, and the 1970s and 1980s witnessed a rise of a "Latino threat narrative" in the mass media (Chavez 2001, 2008).

The Latino threat was initially framed using marine metaphors which portrayed Mexican migration as a flood in which the border was being hit by a "tidal wave" of migrants who would "inundate" U.S. society and "drown" American culture; but over time, martial metaphors became more prominent (Santa Ana 2002). Illegal migrants increasingly became "alien invaders" who launched "banzai charges" at the border which was "defended" by outgunned agents who sought to "hold the line" to keep the invaders from "occupying" the United States. From 1965 to 1979 newspaper mentions of Mexican immigration as a crisis, flood, or invasion steadily increased (Massey and Pren 2012a).

During the Cold War these "invaders" were commonly portrayed as communist infiltrators, especially after the Sandinistas came to power in Nicaragua and the U.S. launched its Contra Intervention while providing political support and military aid to right-wing regimes in El Salvador, Guatemala, and Honduras. The resulting wave of civil violence and political turmoil in the region generated huge waves of Central American refugees heading northward to the United States. Fleeing a left-wing regime, those from Nicaragua were welcomed as political refugees and granted an easy path to permanent U.S. residence. Those from El Salvador, Guatemala, and Honduras, however, had the misfortune of fleeing right-wing regimes allied with the United States and were labeled economic refugees, forcing them to enter principally as undocumented migrants. Once across the border, they joined Mexicans as the second largest segment of the unauthorized population (Baker and Rytina 2013).

After the end of the Cold War, undocumented immigration was increasingly conflated with the "War on Terror." Even during the Cold War, President Reagan warned Americans that "terrorists and subversives are just two days' driving time from [the border crossing at] Harlingen, Texas" (Kamen 1990). The continuing conflation of immigration is indicated by the press conference given recently by Texas Governor Rick Perry, who alleged that terrorists were likely entering from Mexico, noting that "because of the condition of the border from the standpoint of it not being secure and us not knowing who is penetrating across that individuals from ISIS or other terrorist groups could be" (Huetteman and Montgomery 2014).

The rhetoric of crisis and invasion ultimately brought about the progressive militarization of the Mexico-U.S. border, beginning with the Immigration Reform and Control Act of 1986 and continuing through the 1990 Amendments to the Immigration Act, the 1996 Illegal Immigration Reform and Immigrant Responsibility Act, the 2001 USA Patriot Act, and the 2010 Border Security Act. From 1986 to 2012 the number of Border Patrol Officers increased by a factor of six and the Border Patrol Budget grew 23 times. Given economic conditions on both sides of the border, however, the massive increase in border enforcement did not prevent migrants from entering the United States, but it did raise the costs and risks of border crossing to the point where it discouraged them circulating back and forth (Massey et al. 2002).

According to Massey and Singer (1995), from 1965 to 1985 around 85 % of undocumented entries were offset by departures, and even among legal immigrants, return migration was common. Jasso and Rosenzweig (1982) estimate that at least 56 % of legal permanent residents who entered the United States in 1970 returned to

Mexico by 1979. Warren and Kraly (1985) estimate that out-migration among Mexican legal residents in any given year averaged about 20 % of in-migration during the 1970s. With the militarization of the border, this circulation stopped and the probability of returning from any given undocumented trip plummeted (Massey et al. 2009).

With in-migration continuing apace and out-migration falling to record low levels, the net rate of undocumented increased and undocumented population growth accelerated through the 1990s and early 2000s to peak at a size of around 12 million in 2008. Although the number of undocumented residents declined in the aftermath of the Great Recession, it appears to have stabilized at around 11 million, around 60 % from Mexico and 15 % from Central America (Baker and Rytina 2013). Having spent many years in the United States and acquired U.S.-born children, jobs, property, and lives north of the border, these migrants show no sign of returning, despite the challenges of being undocumented and post-2008 economic dislocations.

Mass illegality could be easily solved by a legalization program, an option supported by a majority of U.S. citizens according to surveys and enacted in legislation passed by the U.S. Senate. Unfortunately, the political stalemate in the House of Representatives has ended all hope for immigration reform, at least for the time being. Indeed, rather than enacting policies to promote the integration of Latino immigrants, the thrust of U.S. actions in recent decades has been to render immigrant integration less likely. Legislation passed in 1996 stripped away civic and social rights from all non-citizens regardless of legal status, expanded the grounds for deportation, streamlined the removal process, and limited the rights of apprehended immigrants to judicial proceedings, actions that were only strengthened by the 2001 USA PATRIOT Act (Zolberg 2006). Deportations consequently surged from just 30,000 in 1990 to 419,000 in 2012 with bipartisan support from Presidents Clinton, Obama, and both Bushes.

As the undocumented population grew, therefore, those without documents came under ever greater pressure from federal authorities, putting downward pressure on the wages and working conditions of all immigrants, including legal immigrants (Massey and Gentsch 2014). After 2000, anti-immigrant policies targeting undocumented migrants spread to the state and local levels (Hopkins 2010) though with more limited effects (Parrado 2012). With the prospects for immigration reform dim, mass illegality has become a semi-permanent condition for Latino immigrants in the United States, and given the negative effects of current enforcement efforts, illegality has become the single greatest barrier to the social and economic integration of immigrants in the United States. Mass illegality thus represents the greatest divide separating Latin Americans in Spain from their counterparts in the United States and the implications of this fact must always be borne in mind when considering their prospects in each nation.

Princeton University   Douglas S. Massey
Princeton, NJ, USA

References

Acosta, Y. D., & De la Cruz, G. P. (2011). *The foreign born from Latin America and the Caribbean: 2010*. American Community Survey Brief 10–15. Washington, DC: U.S. Bureau of the Census.

Baker, B., & Rytina, N. (2013). *Estimates of the unauthorized immigrant population residing in the United States: January 2012*. Washington, DC: U.S. Office of Immigration Statistics.

Chavez, L. R. (2001). *Covering immigration: Population images and the politics of the Nation*. Berkeley: University of California Press.

Chavez, L. R. (2008). *The Latino threat: Constructing immigrants, citizens, and the nation*. Stanford: Stanford University Press.

De Genova, N. (2004). The legal production of Mexican/immigrant 'illegality.' *Latino Studies, 2*, 160–185.

Hoefer, M., Rytina, N., & Baker, B. (2011). *Estimates of the unauthorized immigrant population residing in the United States: January 2010*. Washington, DC: U.S. Office of Immigration Statistics.

Hopkins, D. J. (2010). Politicized places: Explaining where and when immigrants provoke local opposition. *American Political Science Review, 104*, 40–60.

Huetteman, E., & Montgomery, D. (2014, August 22). Perry says terrorists could be entering the U.S. from Mexico. *New York Times*, p. A17.

Jasso, G., & Rosenzweig, M. R. (1982). Estimating the emigration rates of legal immigrants using administrative and survey data: The 1971 cohort of immigrants to the United States. *Demography* 19(3):279–290.

Kamen, A. (1990, October 21). Central America is no longer the central issue for Americans. *Austin American Statesman*, p. 1.

Massey, D. S. (2013). America's immigration policy fiasco: Learning from past mistakes. *Daedalus, 142*(3), 5–15.

Massey, D. S. (2014). The racialization of Latinos in the United States. In M. Tonry & S. Bucerius (Eds.), *The Oxford handbook on ethnicity, crime, and immigration* (pp. 21–40). New York: Oxford University Press.

Massey, D. S., & Gentsch, K. (2014). Undocumented migration and the wages of Mexican immigrants in the United States. *International Migration Review, 48*(2), 482–499.

Massey, D. S., & Pren, K. A. (2012a). Origins of the new Latino underclass. *Race and Social Problems, 4*(1), 5–17.

Massey, D. S., & Pren, K. A. (2012b). Unintended consequences of US immigration policy: Explaining the post-1965 surge from Latin America. *Population and Development Review, 38*, 1–29.

Massey, D. S., & Singer, A. (1995). New estimates of undocumented Mexican migration and the probability of apprehension. *Demography, 32*, 203–213.

Massey, D. S., Durand, J., & Malone, N. (2002). *Beyond smoke and mirrors: Mexican immigration in an age of economic integration*. New York: Russell Sage Foundation.

Massey, D. S., Durand, J., & Pren, K. (2009). Nuevos Escenarios de la Migración México-Estados Unidos: Las Consecuencias de la Guerra Antiinmigrante. *Papeles de Población, 61*, 101–128.

Parrado, E. A. (2012). Immigration enforcement policies, the economic recession, and the size of the local Mexican immigrant populations. *Annals of the American Academy of Political and Social Science, 641*, 16–37.

Santa Ana, O. (2002). *Brown tide rising: Metaphors of Latinos in contemporary American public discourse*. Austin: University of Texas Press.

Warren, R. & Kraly, E. P. (1985). The elusive exodus: Emigration from the United States. Population Trends and Public Policy Occasional Paper No. 8. Washington DC: Population Reference Bureau.

Zolberg, A. R. (2006). *A nation by design: Immigration policy in the fashioning of America*. New York: Russell Sage Foundation.

Contents

Chapter 1
Introduction: Vulnerability and Resilience of Latin American Immigrants During the Great Recession

María Aysa-Lastra and Lorenzo Cachón

The Great Recession is the deepest economic crisis faced by capitalist economies since the Great Depression in the 1930s. The consequences of the Great Recession are visible in many areas of people's lives. Inequality has increased as millions of jobs have been eliminated and unemployment rates have dramatically risen. Even considering a positive outlook, recovery of employment to pre-recession levels is still several years away in some countries. The crisis occurred at the height of a Latin American migration to regions around the world, with main destinations being North America and Europe, particularly the United States and Spain. The impact of the Great Recession on the immigrant population has been notable. This volume seeks to describe some of these consequences on Latino immigrants by comparing their experiences on both sides of the Atlantic using multiple disciplinary lenses.

1.1 Latin Americans in the United States and Spain

When the Great Recession began, there were approximately 214 million migrants worldwide (UN 2009). Of those, 38 million lived in the United States and about 6 million in Spain. Latin American immigrants comprised about 38 % of the immigrant population in Spain and 53 % in the United States. The U.S. and Spain are the two countries among the Organization for Economic Co-operation and

M. Aysa-Lastra (✉)
Department of Sociology and Anthropology, Winthrop University, Rock Hill, SC, USA
e-mail: aysalastram@winthrop.edu

L. Cachón
Departamento de Sociología I, Universidad Complutense de Madrid, Madrid, Spain
e-mail: lcachonr@ucm.es

© Springer International Publishing Switzerland 2015
M. Aysa-Lastra, L. Cachón (eds.), *Immigrant Vulnerability and Resilience*,
International Perspectives on Migration 11, DOI 10.1007/978-3-319-14797-0_1

Development members (OECD) that received the most immigrants in the period from 2004 to 2008: 5.5 and 3.7 million, respectively (OECD 2010). Spain is the country of the EU with the highest proportion of foreign born population (12.3 % in 2010; Eurostat 2011). In addition, the U.S. and Spain have the highest number of immigrant workers from Latin America and the Caribbean: 11.3 million in the U.S. and 1.7 million in Spain in 2011.

Most emigrants from the Americas (82 %) in 2010–2011 resided in the United States; notably, 99 % of Mexican emigrants resided in the U.S. during that time period. However, there was a greater likelihood for migrants from South America to reside in Europe than in the United States. Spain accounted for most of the Southern American immigrants in Europe in 2011(57 %) (OAS 2012). The large presence of Latino immigrants sets the stage for the emergence of the "New Latin Nation" (Portes 2006) in the U.S. and Latin American communities in the European Union. We refer as "Latinos" those citizens born in Latin America and the Spanish speaking Caribbean. Massey (1993: 454) has pointed out that under the term "Hispanic" or "Latino" "are a disparate collection of national origin groups with heterogeneous experiences of settlement, immigration, political participation, and economic incorporation". Nonetheless, there are also signs of convergence. Diverse mutually-reinforcing forces tend to group all Latinos into an ethnic group (Portes 2006). First, there is a common culture, grounded on language and religion. Moreover, the power of the state is bent on turning Hispanics into a "real" ethnic minority. Nagel (1986) demonstrated long ago that the state can manufacture ethnicities and even races by the simple expedient of cataloguing and treating people "as if" they belonged to the same group. Something of the sort is happening with Latin American immigrants and their descendants in U.S. and also in Spain. Younger immigrant generations (1.5 and second generations) tend to identify themselves with this ethnic label more than with their parents national origins. It is then "quite possible that what started as a label of convenience used by Census officials to group together diverse Spanish-speaking groups becomes a sociological reality" (Portes 2006: 74).

There are notable differences in the processes that led to the concentration of Latino immigrants in the U.S. and Spain. We identify differences in at least four areas: (1) historical and contemporary Latin American migration flows to the U.S. and Spain; (2) development and implementation of diverse immigration policies; (3) proximity of the destination country to Latin America; and (4) characteristics of migrant populations such as sex composition, level of education, labor force activity rates, and sector of employment.

The United States has a longstanding tradition of immigration; in contrast, immigration is a recent phenomenon in Spain. As a consequence of the diverse development of immigration flows over time to both countries there are large cohorts of second and third generation descendants of Latino immigrants in the United States, but not in Spain. The presence of settled co-ethnic networks in the host country has an impact on labor market integration of new immigrants (affecting job search strategies, creating co-ethnic niches that lead to segregation in some industries, etc.). Immigrants from Latin America have been a key component of U.S. immigration since the late nineteenth century (Massey 1995). Latin American immigrants were mainly Mexican workers responding to changes in the American economy that demanded large amounts of unskilled workers who could be hired at low wages (Portes and Bach 1985). They were followed by other groups of Caribbean migrants (e.g., Puerto Ricans, Cubans, and Dominicans among others), and later, during the 1970s, by more Mexicans as well as other Latinos (Durand and Massey 2010). This migration flow, especially among Mexicans, developed migration specific social capital, which facilitates the subsequent migration of members belonging to a social network (Massey and Aysa-Lastra 2011; Flores and Aysa-Lastra 2011).

By contrast, Latin American immigration to Spain is relatively recent. It starts in the late 1990s. The total volume of immigration increased almost fourfold from 1.1 million in 2001 to 5.3 million in 2011. The proportion of the immigrant population went from 2.7 % in 2001 to 11.4 % in 2011. Immigrants with Latin American citizenship numbered 344,700 in 2001 and 2,029,200 in 2011, which means that the Latino immigrant population in Spain multiplied almost six times in the first decade of the century. In 2001, 32 % of immigrants were Latino, and this figure grew to 39 % in 2011. This immigrant growth is explained by an increased demand for low skilled workers in the construction sector (mostly for men) and in personal care services (mostly for women).

The U.S. and Spain have implemented different migration policies in the last decade. Until late 2004, Spain did not have a suitable policy device for managing immigrant flows. The result was clear: there was a boom in unauthorized immigration. Estimates of unauthorized immigrants in early 2005 approximated 1.2 million people, which accounted for about 40 % of total immigration in Spain (Cachón 2009: 143). The Foreigner Regulation (*Reglamento de Extranjería*), approved in late 2004, launched a set of mechanisms to manage the flows and marked the beginning of a change in the migration management model (ibid: 161–198). It was complemented by a process that allowed more than 565,000 regularizations of unauthorized immigrants. As a result, Spain experienced a substantial change in the traditional model of strong and irregular immigration typical of Southern Europe (Laparra and Cachón 2008). By January 2011, there were approximately 250,000 undocumented immigrants, equivalent to 5 % of all foreigners in Spain. The United States presents a different picture. While, there has been no overall change in immigration policy in the U.S. since 1986 when the Immigration Reform and Control Act (IRCA) was passed, we have witnessed an increase in state and local anti-immigrant legislation that escalates surveillance and racial profiling of immigrants, particularly Latin American immigrants, which account for a large percentage of the estimated 11.7 million unauthorized immigrants residing permanently in the U.S. (Passel et al. 2013). In 1986, IRCA included an amnesty for undocumented aliens which was carried out as a regularization process (CBO 2006). But there have been substantial changes in the 1990s and 2000s, as a period of increasing restrictive regulations centered on national security and border enforcement. In addition, administrative changes have drastically modified the way the State has shaped the public discourse and the dynamics of the Latin American migrant flow to the United States (Massey and Pren 2012). Moreover, differences in immigration policies between both countries are reflected in the modes of entry of unauthorized immigrants. In Spain Latino immigrants usually enter as tourists (with or without a visa) and then overstay working as irregular immigrants until they apply for regularization. Several extraordinary regularization processes were carried out until 2005. Thereafter, there is a permanent individual regularization process by settlement (*arraigo*). In the U.S., although there are a number of visa overstayers, the majority of undocumented immigrants has crossed the border without authorization and has stayed in irregular status.

Access to citizenship through naturalization processes differs in Spain and the United States. In the U.S., there are different categories and time requirements. The general regime specifies that immigrants (green card holders) can apply for citizenship after 5 years of continuous legal residency in the United States; spouses of U.S. citizens, after 3 years; and immigrants who serve in the military can apply sooner. A large proportion of immigrants to the United States from Latin America are granted permanent residency based on the principle of family reunification. In 2010, there were approximately 40 million foreign born persons living in the United States. Of those, 21.2 million were from Latin America; notably, 32.1 % (6.8 million) of the Latin American immigrants were naturalized citizens. Between 2007 and 2011, 3,764,837 naturalizations and 5,395,024 legal permanent residencies were granted in the U.S. About 40 % of naturalizations and legal permanent residencies were granted to Latin American immigrants. In Spain, the general regime requires 10 years of continuous legal residency in the country to apply for citizenship. However, there is a special regime for Latin Americans and for immigrants from countries or groups to which Spain has had relations in the past (e.g., Philippines, Equatorial Guinea, etc.). Latin American immigrants can apply for Spanish citizenship after 2 years of continuous legal residency in Spain. Between 2007 and 2011, 473,897 naturalizations were granted through continuous legal residency, which is equivalent to 10 % of the average annual number of immigrants for the period. Eighty-two percent of the naturalizations were granted to Latin American immigrants.

Another difference is the "proximity" of the U.S. and Spain to the region. The U.S. has both geographical and historical proximity to Latin America. For example, Mexico shares a border with the U.S. and a long history with the country dating back centuries. As with the U.S., Latino immigrants to Spain have historical proximity, but most importantly, cultural proximity, as the Spanish language helps facilitate the integration of Latino immigrants into Spanish society. In the U.S., English poses a barrier, to the economic and social integration of Latino immigrants (Connor and Massey 2010).

Latino immigrants to Spain and the U.S. differ by their national origin, sex composition, and educational levels. Most Latino immigrants in the United States were born in Mexico (57 %), Central American (17 %) or Caribbean (14 %) countries. In contrast, most Latin Americans residing in Spain are from South American countries; individuals from Ecuador, Colombia, Bolivia, Peru, and Argentina account for two thirds of Latino immigrants in Spain (see Table 1.1). Differences in the sex composition of Latino immigrant populations in both

Table 1.1 Distribution of Latin American immigrants in Spain and the United States by country of origin (2011)

Country of origin	Spain		United States	
	% Latin American	Growth rate in the last decade (2001–2011)	% Latin American	Growth rate in the last decade (2001–2011)
Countries	1,650,243	289.6 %	12,086,358	24.5 %
Ecuador	21.8	158.3	1.1	30.5
Colombia	16.5	211.6	1.6	16.0
Bolivia	12.0	2,889.8	0.2	31.4
Peru	8.0	277.1	0.9	38.5
Argentina	7.3	270.1	0.4	35.8
Brazil	6.5	526.0	0.9	62.6
Dominican Republic	5.5	190.9	2.4	8.9
Paraguay	5.3	N.A.	0.0	N.A.
Venezuela	3.6	259.3	0.4	48.5
Cuba	3.3	121.8	1.9	9.4
Uruguay	2.6	523.6	0.1	92.1
Chile	2.5	257.3	0.3	8.4
Honduras	1.9	N.A.	1.1	52.7
Mexico	1.5	236.7	38.3	23.1

Source: Spain: INE, Municipal population register, January 1st 2011; United States Census Bureau, American Community Survey 2009; own estimations

countries as recently as 2011 are striking. In Spain, 54.8 % of Latino immigrants are female versus 31.5 % in the U.S. The educational level of economically active Latino immigrants in Spain is somewhat higher than in the U.S. In Spain, Latino immigrants have an average of 11.3 years of schooling, compared to 12.5 years among the native Spanish population; Latino immigrants in the U.S. have an average of 10.9 years of schooling, compared to 14.3 years among Americans (Aysa-Lastra and Cachón 2012).

The labor force activity rates of native and Latino immigrant populations differ between the two countries as well. In 2011, 57.4 % of the Spanish population ages 16–64 participated in the labor force while 63.7 % of Americans did. Latino immigrants have higher activity rates than native populations in both countries but with notable differences. In the U.S., their labor force activity rate is 70.5 % (and has remained stable over the last decade), while in Spain, it is 83.3 % (and increased five points between 2001 and 2011). The higher activity rate of Latino immigrants in Spain is due to the very different behavior of Latino immigrant women, as immigrant men have similar rates in both countries (approximately 86–87 %). While Latina immigrants in the U.S. have a participation rate of 50 % (lower than American women), in Spain, their rate reached 81 % (30 points higher than Spanish women). This high activity rate among Latinas in Spain shows that their migration trips are consistent with their own labor projects; and, that they found opportunities in sectors that have traditionally been occupied by women, such as services and domestic service specifically. Latina immigrants' lower participation in the labor market in the U.S. compared to Spain might be explained by their role as tied migrants (most coming for family reunification) and having young children in the household, among other barriers (Granberry and Marcelli 2011).

In both countries the activity rates of Latinos have a positive relation with education: higher educational levels result in higher activity rates. In addition, in the case of Spain, the activity rates of Latinos are high at all educational levels. The difference in the global activity rates for Latino immigrants in the U.S. and Spain are partially explained by two factors: first, the higher educational levels of Latino immigrants in Spain versus Latino immigrants in the U.S.; and second, the higher levels of female Latino immigrant participation in the Spanish labor market.

The sectorial and occupational distribution of Latino immigrants in both countries is quite different; but in both countries, there is a concentration of Latino immigrants in low-skilled jobs. Before the 2008 crisis in the U.S., Latino men worked primarily in construction (26 %), services (27 %), production (12 %), and transportation (11 %) jobs, while Latino women were employed in services (48 %) and production (15 %). Also, about 5 % of Latino men and women worked in agriculture. The arrival of Latinos to nontraditional settlement areas in the U.S. has diversified their presence in different sectors (López-Sanders 2012). In Spain, Latino men were concentrated in construction (27 %), services (56 %), and industrial (10 %) sectors, while Latinas were employed almost exclusively in the service sector (93 %). Moreover, due to the important Latino immigrant growth in the last decade, their presence is increasing in a growing and diverse number of occupations (Cachón 2009).

1.2   Great Recession and Immigration

The roots of the Great Recession, which still many economies continue to face 6 years after the onset of the financial crisis, are linked to the deregulation of the financial markets implemented during the years of flourishing neoliberalism in the developed world.. We can also link the crisis to the increasing income and wealth inequalities that are produced in parallel to the implementation of neoliberal policies (Bonica et al. 2013; Pfeffer et al. 2013). Moreover, from the standpoint of international labor migration legislation, the Great Recession takes place at a time of restrictive policies on both sides of the Atlantic and produces what Hollifield (1992) has termed the "liberal paradox": times of increasing demand of immigrant workers in destination countries, but in a period of restrictive immigration policies that limit the entry of new labor migrants.

The years before the crisis set the conditions leading to the perfect storm: a deep transformation of the structure, size, and significance of the housing finance sector in the U.S. and the real estate boom in other parts of the world (Fligstein and Goldstein 2012) as well as changes in the global financial system (Stiglitz 2009).

The economic crisis that began in 2007 is the deepest since World War II and the Great Depression (Elsby et al. 2010; Elwell 2013). The collapse of housing and mortgage-backed securities (subprimes) markets in the U.S. produced a financial earthquake that threatened global financial markets. The onset of the crisis is marked by the Lehman Brothers bankruptcy filing in September 2008. Banks and other financial institutions panicked and months later, the U.S. government rescued (i.e., "bailed out") "too big to fail" financial institutions and large banks (Blinder 2013a). Remarking on the need to bail out financial institutions, Ben Bernanke, the Federal Reserve Chairman, said "in our judgment, the failure of AIG would have been basically the end" (Madrick 2013). Despite the bailouts to major financial institutions, consumers and businesses significantly diminished spending. This created a downward spiral in the economy, and the most severe crisis in global capitalism took hold (Fligstein and Goldstein 2012). These negative events were followed by the burst of the housing market bubble in several European countries (Ireland, Greece, Portugal, and Spain), which was generated by low interest rates associated with the adoption of the euro in 2002.

We can say that the Great Recession is an economic phenomenon that is mutating: in the words of Robert Zoellick (2009), President of the World Bank, "What started as a financial crisis, became an economic crisis, is now becoming an unemployment crisis – and to what degree does it become a human and social crisis?" Castles and Miller (2010) point out that the changing character of the Great Recession has influenced immigrant laborers in different ways. The initial focus of the crisis was on the *real estate crisis* as a result of the U.S. housing market collapse in 2006–2007; over the course of 2007–2008, the crisis mutated into a general *financial crisis*, with banks in critical situations, many requiring bailouts financed by the State in order to survive. By late 2008, the core sectors of the economy started to weaken and the world was confronted with an *employment crisis*. We stress that these episodes are now being followed by anti-immigrant times and increasing discrimination toward immigrants, particularly those identified as undocumented migrants. Despite some signs of recovery, many regions have so far experienced a jobless recovery.

Although there are diverse opinions on governments' responses to the Great Recession, for us public policy responses to these important changes in the economy have been "too little, too late" (Madrick 2013) and ill designed. Some of the implemented policies have deepened the effects of the Great Recession (Krugman 2009, 2012; Hetzel 2012). However, we can distinguish the different paths followed by the U.S. (under the Obama Administration) and in the European Union (under the leadership and pressure from Germany's Angela Merkel) (Blinder 2013b). Key differences emanate from the policies adopted by the Central Banks and the absence of policies aimed at economic growth: the Federal Reserve in the United States has implemented limited expansionary monetary policies and the government approved an economic stimulus (ARRA), while in Europe the monetary policies have been restrictive for the entire euro zone and there have not been substantial and significant stimulus policies (at least until the last months of 2014). Moreover, the problems in the structure of European Union political institutions

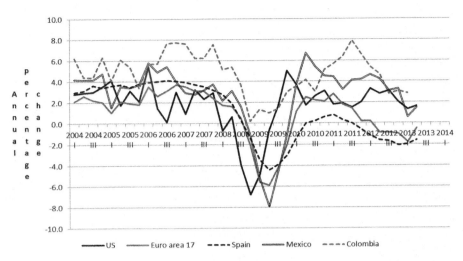

Fig. 1.1 GDP Growth Rates for the U.S., Euro zone, Spain, Mexico, and Colombia (2004–2014) (Source: National BLS, INEGI, DANE and Eurostat)

and the resulting lack of governance regarding the euro are needed to be addressed (Habermas 2013).

The implementation of different monetary policies has determined the different trajectories of growth in both economies in recent years. In the U.S. and other regions of the world, the growth rate over time follows a V shape; in the European Union, the growth rate over time follows a W shape (see Fig. 1.1) (Roubini 2009). In other words, as a consequence of restrictive fiscal policies, after 2010 we can observe for the EU economy the W shaped recovery defined by Arpaia and Curci (2010: 38) as: "episodes in which output growth resumes after a sharp contraction, but for few quarters only, and falls back into recession before the recovery takes hold". For Spain, this decline in GDP is even more important. To put these trends in perspective, it is important to note that some immigrants' countries of origin (e.g. Mexico) suffered an important decline in GDP caused by the decline in the U.S. but have experienced a notable recovery. Colombia, as many other South American countries, never registered absolute declines in GDP (or negative growth), however, the rate of GDP growth diminished during the crisis and, currently, has again increased.

It is important to underscore that this crisis differs in important ways from many other recent economic downturns (Castles and Miller 2010; Tilly 2011). It is the first crisis of a global scale (Martin 2009) and consequently it has affected every country in different ways. These two characteristics are important for our analysis of the Great Recession on international migration and Latin American immigrants. The global character of this crisis is particularly significant in migration because migrants were particularly burdened with difficulties in finding alternative destinations. Another relevant aspect regarding international migration is that this is the first time we observe a combination of high international migration and a global economic downturn. Therefore, the comparisons with earlier economic crises must be tempered by the recognition that twenty-first century international migration has certain novel characteristics (Rogers 2009).

The consequences of the Great Recession go beyond increasing unemployment, the destruction of family wealth and patrimony (Wolff et al. 2012), and the resulting increasing inequality and poverty among those in the weakest tiers of societies (Card and Raphael 2013). It has triggered structural and cultural changes (Grusky et al. 2012; Hall and Lamont 2013; Danziger 2013), prompted grass roots movements voicing social concerns and discontent with the current situation and the implemented restrictive social policies (e.g., Occupy Wall Street in U.S., or 15 M demonstrations in Spain); and, promoted financial regulations (Dodd-Frank Wall Street Reform and Consumer Protection Act –HR 4173) and improvements in the financial architecture of a unique currency in regions with economies of diverse size such as the euro zone.

The Great Recession is having a large impact on international migration. We believe that we are only beginning to observe the important structural changes that this global recession has set off. However, several studies have shown that although Latino marginality was exacerbated during the Great Recession, the negative effects of this economic shock are additional to longer trends in declining in earnings, worsening of health conditions, increasing gaps in education, growing residential segregation, and rising poverty rates. Illegality and marginality, resulting in increasing racialization and criminalization of Latino immigrants are potent barriers to their integration (Massey 2012: 6).

1.3 Immigrant Vulnerability and Resilience During Economic Downturns

The aim of this volume is to present studies that analyze how Latino immigrants have responded to the Great Recession. The Great Recession has imposed constraints and challenges on almost all social segments in several countries. However, its effects on Latino immigrant populations in the U.S. have been more palpable due to the deterioration of the labor market, U.S. immigration policy in the twentieth century, rising anti-immigrant sentiment and increasing racialization of Latinos in their host communities (Massey 2013; Menjívar and Kanstroom 2014).

A basic feature of most immigrant groups is their subordinate position in the social structure and the fact that their placement in this position tends to socially construct them as subjects with "objective vulnerability" (Portes 1978). This ascribed vulnerability creates conditions in which immigrants are more easily exposed to acts of discrimination and stigmatizing processes. However, from these objectively subordinate positions within the social structure of host societies, immigrants individually and collectively act, not only looking for "exits" or paths to escape from their current vulnerable position, but also they look for "voice" in an attempt to improve their situation (Hirschman 1970). As an example and in contrast to vulnerability, it is important to underscore the visibility of immigrant ethnic resilience, especially during crises such as the Great Recession.

Vulnerability and resilience are not antagonistic concepts within migration studies. In other areas such as disaster or environmental studies, vulnerability and resilience are placed at the ends of a spectrum aimed at evaluating conditions within a structure. Moreover, the use of vulnerability and resilience in developmental psychology also differs. Resilience within this framework is conceived as an outcome: that is, as the individual accomplishment of a goal, even if risk conditions of failure were present. In this sense, being at risk, or experiencing a series of negative conditions, is related to one's vulnerable condition.

In the field of immigration studies, resilience should be considered as the capacity of individuals, and not of social systems or institutions; it is a capacity that derives from the social capital defined as "those expectations for action within a collectivity that affect the economic goals and goal-seeking behavior of its members, even if these expectations are not oriented toward the economic sphere" (Portes and Sensenbrenner 1993: 1321). Social Capital can adopt different forms: value introjection, reciprocity transactions, bounded solidarity, or enforceable trust (ibid), and all of these are relevant in migration studies.

Moreover, resilience should be conceived as a process, a reaction, and a form of resistance exercised by the actors within a "field of possibilities" that are marked by the social structure that tend to construct vulnerable subjects. There is an "ambivalence" (Simmel 1950) in which immigrants and immigrant communities are placed: vulnerable subjects (discriminated and stigmatized) according to their position in the social structure (class, race and ethnic perception and identification, gender and any other social characteristic) that responds to the diverse strategies in which they exercise their resilience, their expectations, and their capacity for action to protect themselves or minimize the effects of their vulnerable condition. The ambivalence that triumphs in the relations between the "foreigner," and the majority group in the host society "is the mirror of an asymmetric power relation in which none of the parties is not totally destituted of power, neither can it exercises it without limits" (Tabboni 1997: 241).

1.3.1 Roots of Immigrant Vulnerability

The vulnerability of individuals or social groups has its foundation in the "holy trinity" of inequality (Massey 2007): class, race and ethnicity, and gender. Frequently, these inequalities are combined and create additional interactive and multiplicative negative effects. Moreover, the ways in which these inequalities operate change over time. Immigrants and natives face vulnerabilities caused by these inequalities, but immigrants have an additional constraint: the discrimination suffered as a result of their immigrant condition; immigrants crossed a border and entered a State in which they are not citizens, making them a more fragile social subject. Immigrants are socially constructed as vulnerable subjects, as powerless agents. This is the origin of what we have denominated the "discriminatory institutional framework" (Cachón 1995): the exercise of the State to establish borders and "manage" (recognize, guarantee, or deny) individual rights and distinguish between the insiders and the outsiders.

In short, the "discriminatory institutional framework" shows a series of institutional constraints that delineate paths, place barriers, and establish preferences for some groups over others. In addition to these institutional constraints, the market and the host societies offer different opportunities, which vary over time, to different groups. Immigrants take into account these constraints and opportunities in conforming their strategies or resilient behaviors, individually and collectively, to value their different forms of "capital" (human, social, etc.) and to confront discrimination (Cachón 2009).

The vulnerability of a person or group, such as immigrants, is determined by the absolute or relative deprivation of symbolic, social, emotional, or material resources or the difficulty or impossibility to use them in a specific historical context due to institutional, political, economic, social, or cultural constraints. This effective lack of resources is what makes some groups of immigrants more vulnerable than others. Causes and circumstances for migration also impose vulnerabilities on immigrants. Forced migrants or those who were obligated to leave their countries of origin due to threats to their lives, physical integrity or freedom, and victims of human trafficking are at additional disadvantage. The former is likely to be deprived of social networks in destination that facilitate their integration; and in addition the latter is deprived of fundamental rights. In general, immigrant vulnerability decreases over time with acculturation and integration progress. However, these processes follow a "segmented assimilation" (Portes and Zhou 1993; Haller et al. 2011) that traps immigrants in the lower social tiers. In summary, the condition of being an immigrant makes them "categorically unequal" citizens (Massey 2007).

In addition to their immigrant condition, another fundamental feature that defines immigrant vulnerability is the class component, as immigrants are concentrated in the lower segments of the working class. The immigrants' working condition, although not common among all immigrants, is a key element to understanding immigration and immigrant vulnerability. The concentration of immigrants in lower occupational categories shows this trait among the majority of immigrants in destination countries. In many cases, this working character is a consequence of having crossed a border, thereby becoming an immigrant. Immigrants experience downward social mobility by working occupations with lower prestige that require less qualifications than employment in their countries of origin (Chiswick 1978; Aysa-Lastra and Cachón 2013).

Capitalism, in all its stages, always requires supplies of vulnerable and disadvantaged workers (Sassen 1988). Hicks's argument is clear: "the commodity economy has never been able to do without servants" (see Moulier-Boutang 1998). Consequently, there are growing segments in the labor market that are more flexible, cheaper, and docile. Massey (2007, 2009) points out, for example, that in the United States, Mexicans are being socially constructed as a "better underclass." We could argue something similar regarding any other immigrant recipient country: its government looks for certain characteristics in particular immigrant groups, builds a discourse, and implements policies that result in the construction of a "better underclass" (Telles and Ortiz 2008).

Several authors from different perspectives have recognized the labor segmentation of the immigrant labor market (Piore 1979). This labor market segmentation has produced, in the long run, the marginalization of specific immigrant groups. Although in general there are no rigid barriers based on race, ethnicity, or nationality, certain groups are overrepresented in disadvantaged positions. In the case of immigrants, their marginalization is not entirely explained by specific factors such as education, length of stay at destination, or labor market experience.

We argue that the Great Recession deepened existing immigrant vulnerabilities due to the deterioration of the labor market, and also exacerbated discrimination practices and stigmatization of immigrant communities through the implementation of restrictive immigration laws accompanied by austerity measures adopted from the neoliberal economic framework prevalent since the 1980s.

1.3.2 Immigrant Resilience During the Great Recession and Anti-immigrant Times

In an adapted and malleable notion of resilience (Brand and Jax 2007), we noted its relation to social capital and the need of defining it as a process, as a reaction, or as an act of resistance of the agents within a "field of possibilities" delimited by their position in the social structure. Resilience and its corresponding strategies can be included within Hirschman's definition of "voice": "any attempt at all to change, rather than to escape from, an objectionable state of affairs, whether through individual or collective petition to the management directly to change, through appeal to a higher authority with the intention to forge a change in management, or through various types of actions and protests, including those that are meant to mobilize public opinion" (Hirschman 1970: 30). As Lamont et al. (2013) point out, "Responses to stigmatization can be individual or collective and they take a variety of forms such as confronting, evading or deflating conflict; claiming inclusion; educating/reforming the ignorant; attempting to conform to majority culture or affirming distinctiveness; wanting to 'pass' or denouncing stereotyping; and engaging in boundary work toward undesirable 'others' when responding to stigmatization." Lamont and his colleagues show that responses from those who are stigmatized are related to cultural myths about national belonging. In our case, we must ask ourselves how cultural myths about national belonging are built and how ethnic, specifically Latino, belonging is built in different contexts like the U.S. and Spain.

Immigrants are active agents that build their identity in a negotiation process with the social context in which they place themselves and are placed by others (Barth 1969), a process referred to as "boundary-brokering" (Massey and Sánchez 2010). In many cases, immigrants develop reactive identities. Because they face barriers through stigmatization and discrimination, instead of trying to "blend" into their host communities with the mainstream culture, they develop identities that associate themselves with "their" group and belong to a "new" community. Portes and Rumbaut (2001: 248) highlight the growth and effects of reactive ethnicity: "The discourses and self-images that it creates develop as a situational response to present realities. Even when the process involves embracing the parent, original national identities, this is less a sign of continuing loyalty to the home country than a reaction to hostile conditions in the receiving society". If the State does not support the emergence of selective acculturation, then these resources will come from the assets and social capital of families and communities. "The irony of the situation is that many immigrant families are doing for American society what it will not do for itself: raising law-abiding, achievement-oriented, and bilingual citizens in the teeth of the obstacles steaming from intransigent nativism and forceful assimilation" (ibid: 276).

These reactive processes bring a base for collective action (both to show solidarity to a cause and to increase visibility and gain leverage in the political arena), although the effects of reactive processes at the individual level might be less visible. However, at the individual level, there are exceptional cases of selective assimilation, as observed in the cases of Marta Tienda, Raquel Torres, Luis Donato Esquivel, or Dan-el Padilla (see Portes et al. 2009). We can gather hundreds of similar histories that show how individual and family resilience and the capacity of immigrants to overcome obstacles and achieve goals in adverse contexts and situations. Nevertheless, even in these exceptional cases we can identify the vulnerability of their initial position in the social structure, in terms of class and perceived ethnicity in the destination countries.

Crosnoe (2005) has shown that the children of Mexican immigrants who develop certain forms of resilience based on closer ties to their families and communities overcome the limitations of educational resources and contextual risk factors imposed by the stratified U.S. public education system. Resilient undocumented immigrant students face many stressors and barriers, but many overcome these obstacles, become academically successful role models, and continue to make a difference in many lives (Coronado 2008; Perez et al. 2009). We can even point out that even some behaviors that are seen as marginal or deviant are in fact acts of resilience (Rios 2012). "Resilience keeps people energized and helps them maintain their commitment and overcome difficult situations" (Bhagat and London 1999: 360). And this shared energy and commitment might be a precursor for collective action.

Collective action is the most fertile field for ethnic resilience. A central argument in the studies of social capital is the importance of cross-ethnic ties. In other words, one's social network can serve as a resource for action, and for racial minorities, social ties to Whites are a form of social capital (Telles and Ortiz 2008). Social capital arguments imply that there should be mobilization benefits to having cross-cutting ties: providing information, normative expectations, and motivations that encourage political participation. As shown by Santoro et al. (2012: 228), "Mexican Americans are more likely to be active across both cultural and political dimensions if they have cross-cutting ties."

We can enhance our understanding of social resilience by "considering whether and how stigmatized groups may be empowered by potentially contradictory contextual forces—more specifically, by cultural repertoires that enable their social inclusion" (Lamont et al. 2013: 129–130). Paradoxically, neo-liberalism may encourage stigmatized groups to make claims based on human rights (Kymlicka 2013). Moreover, it has been shown that societies that adopt multicultural perspectives do not hinder immigrant engagement with society and government; multicultural societies not only provide recognition to immigrants, but also foster their emotional and cognitive engagement, as manifested in their greater political participation (Wright and Bloemraad 2012).

There are historic experiences that illustrate how social resilience channeled through collective action movements has led to beneficial 'turning-points.' The movement led by Dolores Huerta and Cesar Chávez with the creation of the National Farmworkers Association in the 1970s (right at the moment in which civil rights laws were being passed) is one of those turning-points. Chavez's famous phrase *"Sí se puede"* still resonates in today's Latino demonstrations. The key moment for the revival of collective resilience is the announcement on December 16, 2005 of Law HR4437 (The Border Protection, Anti-terrorism, and Illegal Immigration Control Act) in California. This stringent anti-immigrant proposal, presented by Congressman J. Sensenbrenner (R-WI), denied immigrants any possibility of legal integration into American society. This law triggered an unprecedented mobilization and the sudden and massive politicization of the Latino community (Santamaría 2007). A variety of grass roots organizations participated in these national demonstrations, including Latino organizations, immigrant rights defense organizations, and human rights organizations. A significant, novel feature of these demonstrations is that students and unauthorized immigrants were active participants in the marches.

The mobilization of Latino immigrant students did not received enough support in Congress for the approval of the DREAM Act (Development, Relief, and Education for Alien Minors), but it has achieved an Executive order from President Obama in 2012 that delays the deportation of 850,000 unauthorized young Latino immigrants (Passel et al. 2014). Several groups supporting immigrant rights continue to support comprehensive immigration reform in the U.S. While a bipartisan proposal for immigration reform was being negotiated and prepared in March 2012, 350 organizations concentrated before the United States Capitol and claimed "the time for immigration reform is now," and assembled a demonstration in Washington later that month under the slogan "March for America. Change Takes Courage." March 21st 2010 is a day to remember in the history of immigrant rights in the United States. At the time of this writing (October 2014), immigration reform is included on the legislative agenda. However, it is likely to be blocked by the

Republican Party in the U.S. House of Representatives. President Obama has promised, once again, to issue executive orders on immigration policy before the end of 2014, if the Immigration Reform is not passed by Congress. Latino demonstrations in favor of immigration reform and immigrant rights will continue to be the "voice" of millions of marginalized and stigmatized Latinos immigrants.

1.4 Structure of This Volume

This volume presents research that examines the effects of the Great Recession on Latin American immigrants. To this end, our team of American and European colleagues, using an array of disciplinary approaches, has taken into account changes in the labor markets and social contexts in the two main destination countries for Latin American immigrants and considered developments in these immigrants' countries of origin. We emphasize immigrant vulnerabilities and describe immigrants' strategies to cope during the Great Recession and use a comparative perspective to identify the similarities and differences that are being produced in the Latino immigrant population on both sides of the Atlantic.

The volume is divided into three parts. The first part, titled "Effects of the Great Recession on Latin American Immigrant Labor," begins with two chapters examining labor market trends for Latino immigrants during the Great Recession in the U.S. and Spain. These chapters, authored by María Aysa-Lastra and Lorenzo Cachón, compare employment and unemployment data among naturalized citizens born in Latin America, Latin American immigrants and natives. The analysis shows immigrants' employment sensitivity to labor market contractions and underscores the significant impact of the Great Recession on male Latino immigrants and their flexibility to maintain employment status even if forced to accept jobs of lower quality. In Spain, the deep and very long employment crisis has provoked many Latin American immigrants to return to South America.

These two chapters are followed by an analysis on Latina women employment in both countries. Sonia Parella (Chap. 4), using an intersectional approach, shows the role of Latino women during the Great Recession. The Great Recession largely affected sectors in which males were predominantly employed. For women the loss of employment was less severe -in some cases, they even became the main sources of income for their households. However, the informality and conditions of their employment, particularly domestic employment, are still of concern, especially in the case of undocumented migrants at risk of deportation.

In Chap. 5, Cristina Bradatan and Neeraja Kolloju study labor trends of highly skilled Latin American immigrants during the economic decline. They compared data from the labor surveys in both countries before and during the Great Recession. Their analysis of Latin American immigrants and natives with bachelor's degrees and advanced professional education shows that although higher education serves as a risk premium against unemployment, Latin American highly skilled immigrants faced higher unemployment rates in both countries relative to natives.

In the closing chapter of this first part of the volume, Cecilia Menjívar and María Enchautegui (Chap. 6), provide data on the confluence of economic recession and restrictive immigration laws focusing on the salient case of the state of Arizona. They focus on employment and daily routines of Latino Immigrant workers. They complement their quantitative analysis with qualitative interviews on how stricter law enforcement (e.g. SB 1070, 287(g) and LAWA) and internal border control, criminalization, insecurity and limited opportunities in the labor market further increased undergroundness and vulnerability of Hispanic foreign born non-citizens in undocumented niche occupations (e.g., housekeepers, maids, cooks, farm workers and construction helpers). The chapters in Part I shed light on the diversity of Latino immigrant experiences during this period.

The second part of the book, "Understanding Immigrant Adaptation in Difficult Times," aims to explore how Latin American immigrants adapt and develop social mechanisms in times of high unemployment, increasing discrimination (Massey 2009), and changing host societies' perceptions towards immigrants. It begins in Chap. 7, authored by María Ángeles Cea D'Ancona and Miguel Valles Martínez. They analyze changes in the perception of Latin American immigrants in receiving societies during the Great Recession and discuss how material interests (economic and material position) and ethnocentrism shape the opinion of Americans and Spaniards towards immigrants in the U.S. and Spain, before and during the economic downturn. Their results show that immigrants who are perceived as having indigenous roots or poor, (i.e., "class-based racism") rank lower in natives' perceptions. This trend is more pronounced in the U.S. than in Spain.

Continuing our investigation of the effects of the Great Recession on attitudes towards Latino immigrants, in Chap. 8, Meghan Conley examines the impact of the Great Recession and criminalization on Latin American immigrant identity building and malleability. Her analysis focuses on the effects of law HB 56 in Alabama in 2011. She argues that immigrant scapegoating is predictable during periods of economic insecurity and, as a consequence, restrictionist state legislation proliferated in the absence of federal immigration reform. She describes how the majority of these state laws and local efforts to regulate immigration required law enforcement officers to determine citizenship and immigration status of individuals. These practices evolved in the racialization of Latinos as "those not belonging." She argues that the implementation of Alabama HB 56 resulted in the harassment of Latinos and their constant fear of what she calls the "enforcement lottery," but that Latinos' resilient strategies as a response to their imposed vulnerability resulted in acts of resistance and civil disobedience, organized trainings on immigrants' rights across the state, and the formation of people's committees.

To continue studying the importance of immigrant organization as channels for voicing immigrant resilience and fostering immigrant integration in Chap. 9 Héctor Cebolla-Boado and Ana López-Sala compare the Spanish and American approaches to immigrant organizations. Based on survey data, they studied the impact of the Great Recession on immigrant organizations in Spain. Their argument centers on the stability of these organizations, because many of them are the product of a top-down policy on immigrant integration. The Spanish government during the economic and immigration boom, as part of its immigrant integration policies, financed and fostered immigrant organizations. However, during the Great Recession, the government imposed fiscal austerity policies. These measures resulted in reduced budgets in all areas, but particularly in those deemed not basic or strategic for economic recovery. In this scenario, Cebolla and López-Sala observe that many organizations disappeared and those still providing services to immigrants have changed their scope from immigrant integration in Spain to programs that support the return of immigrants to their countries or origin.

Once we have presented how the Great Recession has affected immigrants' opportunities in the labor market, and how immigrants responded to the economic and social challenges imposed, we then turn to the third part of the volume, which focuses on the effects of the economic downturn on transnational practices and remittances, and the voluntary and forced return of Latin American migrants to their countries of origin. In this section the authors present data on the economic and social conditions in Latin American countries, remittance sending patterns, and how the prevailing anti-immigrant climate in the U.S. and some European countries can be counterproductive for the maintenance and further development of transnational practices in a global society. In Chap. 10, Jorge Durand and María Aysa-Lastra critically examine variations in the development rankings among Latin American countries, changes in the demographic structure leading to population aging, employment and wage trends, and the interrelation of these factors to future prospects for intra-regional migration as well as international migration to traditional destinations.

In Chap. 11, Manuel Orozco provides new evidence on the temporal impact of the Great Recession on remittances to Latin America. Moreover, he explores the current financial position and remitting behaviors of migrants living in the U.S. using data from three cross-sectional national surveys. His analysis indicates that in 2013, migrant recovery from the economic downturn was modest and that Latino immigrants' financial and economic vulnerability is still high. Despite this modest recovery and their vulnerable position, Latin American and Caribbean immigrants were able to increase their remitting capacity between 2009 and 2013.

One of the core elements in the literature on transnational practices is immigrants' remitting behavior; however, immigrants' maintenance of regular engagement with their communities of origin also depends on immigration policies. In Chap. 12, Ninna Nyberg Sørensen carries out an analysis of pre and post-recession contexts for migratory projects. She argues that the negative effects of the Great Recession coupled with the intensification and diversification of migration control have limited the opportunities of development for vulnerable communities whose migrants remain undocumented. She brings a broad vision of historical migration patterns and places the Great Recession in the context of neoliberal changes in the political economy that are shaping current migration trends from Latin America. She claims that pre-recession patterns of migrant recruitment, remittances and return migration, have been transformed due to the hardening of U.S. and European immigration policies in practices characterized by danger, debt and deportation for many migrants.

The concluding chapter provides a comparative analysis of the effects of the Great Recession on Latin American immigrants and their responses and problematizes immigration and immigrant integration in uncertain times and under uncertain circumstances.

References

Arpaia, A., & Curci, N. (2010). *EU labor market behaviour during the Great Recession*. MPRA: http://mpra.ub.uni-muenchen.de/22393/. Accessed 4 Oct 2014.

Aysa-Lastra, M., & Cachón, L. (2012). Latino immigrant employment during the great recession: A comparison between the United States and Spain. *Norteamérica, 7*(2), 7–45.

Aysa-Lastra, M., & Cachón, L. (2013). Segmented occupational mobility: The case of non-EU immigrants in Spain. *Revista Espaola de Investigaciones Sociológicas, 144*, 23–47.

Barth, F. (1969). *Ethnic groups and boundaries: The social organization of culture difference*. Boston: Little, Brown and Company.

Bhagat, R. S., & London, M. (1999). Getting started and getting ahead: Career dynamics of immigrants. *Human Resource Management Review, 9*(3), 349–365.

Blinder, A. S. (2013a). *After the music stopped: The financial crisis, the response, and the work ahead*. London: Penguin.

Blinder, A. S. (2013b). The macroeconomic policy paradox: Failing by succeeding. *The ANNALS of the American Academy of Political and Social Science, 650*, 26–46.

Bonica, A., McCarty, N., Poole, K. T., & Rosenthal, H. (2013). Why hasn't democracy slowed rising inequality? *Journal of Economic Perspectives, 27*(3), 103–124.

Brand, F. S., & Jax, K. (2007). Focusing the meaning(s) of resilience: Resilience as a descriptive concept and a boundary object. *Ecology and Society, 12*(1), 23.

Cachón, L. (1995). Marco institucional de la discriminación y tipos de inmigrantes en el mercado de trabajo en España. *Revista Española de Investigaciones Sociológicas, 69*, 105–124.

Cachón, L. (2009). *La "Espapa inmigrante": marco discriminatorio, mercado de trabajo y políticas de integración*. Barcelona: Anthropos.

Card, D., & Raphael, S. (2013). Introduction. In D. Card & S. Raphael (Eds.), *Immigration, poverty, and socioeconomic inequality* (pp. 1–26). New York: Russell Sage Foundation.

Castles, S., & Miller, M. J. (2010). *Migration and the global economic crisis: One year on*. www.age-of-migration.com/na/financialcrisis/update1.html. Accessed 21 July 2012.

Chiswick, B. R. (1978). The effect of Americanization on the earnings of foreign-born men. *The Journal of Political Economy, 86*(5), 897–921.

Congressional Budget Office (CBO). (2006). *Immigration policy in the United States*. Washington, DC: The Congress of the United States.

Connor, P., & Massey, D. S. (2010). Economic outcomes among Latino migrants to Spain and the United States: Differences by source region and legal status. *International Migration Review, 44*(4), 802–829.

Coronado, H. M. (2008). Voices of courage and strength: Undocumented immigrant students in the United States. Activist Scholarship: 2006 Chicana/o Graduate Student Conference, Chicano Studies Institute, UC Santa Barbara.

Crosnoe, R. (2005). Double disadvantage or signs of resilience? The elementary school contexts of children from Mexican immigrant families. *American Educational Research Journal, 42*(2), 269–303.

Danziger, S. (2013). Evaluating the effects of the great recession. *The ANNALS of the American Academy of Political and Social Science, 650*, 6–24.

Durand, J., & Massey, D. S. (2010). New world orders: Continuities and changes in Latin American migration. *Annals of the American Academy of Political and Social Science, 630,* 20–52.

Elsby, M. W., Hobijn, B., & Sahin, A. (2010, May). The labor market in the great recession. NBER working paper, 15979.

Elwell, C. K. (2013). Economic recovery: Sustaining U.S. economic growth in a post-crisis economy. Congressional research service report R41332, www.crs.gov. Accessed 27 Feb 2014.

EUROSTAT. (2011). *Database. Population by citizenship and by country of birth.* Luxembourg: Eurostat.

Fligstein, N., & Goldstein, A. (2012). The roots of the great recession. In D. B. Grusky, B. Wertern, & C. Wimer (Eds.), *The great recession* (pp. 21–55). New York: Russell Sage Foundation.

Flores, N., & Aysa-Lastra, M. (2011). Place of origin, types of ties, and support networks in Mexico-U.S. Migration. *Rural Sociology, 76*(4), 481–510.

Granberry, P. J., & Marcelli, E. A. (2011). Social capital is associated with earnings among foreign-born Mexican men but not women in Los Angeles county. *International Migration, 49*(6), 113–128.

Grusky, D. B., Western, B., & Wimer, C. (Eds.). (2012). *The great recession.* New York: Russell Sage Foundation.

Habermas, J. (2013, August 20). Cuando las élites fracasan. El País

Hall, P. A., & Lamont, M. (2013). Introduction. Social resilience in the neoliberal era. In P. A. Hall & M. Lamont (Eds.), *Social resilience in the neoliberal era* (pp. 1–31). New York: Cambridge University Press.

Haller, W., Portes, A., & Lynch, S. M. (2011). Dreams fulfilled, dreams shattered: Determinants of segmented assimilation in the second generation. *Social Forces, 89*(3), 733–762.

Hetzel, R. L. (2012). *The great recession. Market failure or policy failure?* New York: Cambridge University Press.

Hirschman, A. O. (1970). *Exit, voice and loyalty: Responses on decline of firms, organizations and states.* Cambridge: Harvard University Press.

Hollifield, J. F. (1992). *Immigrants, markets and states: The political economy of postwar Europe.* Cambridge: Harvard University Press.

Krugman, P. (2009). *The return of the depression economics and the crisis of 2008.* New York: W.W. Norton.

Krugman, P. (2012). *End this depression now.* New York: W.W. Norton.

Kymlicka, W. (2013). Neoliberal multiculturalism? In P. A. Hall & M. Lamont (Eds.), *Social resilience in the neoliberal era* (pp. 99–125). New York: Cambridge University Press.

Lamont, M., Welburn, J. S., & Fleming, C. M. (2013). Responses to discrimination and social resistance under neoliberalism. The United States compared. In P. A. Hall & M. Lamont (Eds.), *Social resilience in the neoliberal era* (pp. 129–157). New York: Cambridge University Press.

Laparra, M., & Cachón, L. (2008). Sistema migratorio, mercado de trabajo y régimen de bienestar: el nuevo modelo del sur de Europa. In L. Cachón & M. Laparra (Eds.), *Inmigración y políticas sociales* (pp. 19–50). Barcelona: Bellaterra.

López-Sanders, L. (2012). Bible belt immigrants: Latino religious incorporation in new immigrant destinations. *Latino Studies, 10,* 128–154. doi:10.1057/lst.2012.9.

Madrick, J. (2013, March 7). Too little, too late: Why? *The New York Review of Books,* pp. 14–16.

Martin, P. (2009). Recession and migration: A new era for labor migration? *International Migration Review, 43*(3), 671–691.

Massey, D. S. (1993). Latinos, poverty, and the underclass: A new agenda for research. *Hispanic Journal of Behavioral Sciences, 15,* 449–475.

Massey, D. S. (1995). The new immigration and ethnicity in the United States. *Population and Development Review, 21*(3), 631–652.

Massey, D. S. (2007). *Categorically unequal: The American stratification system*. New York: Russell Sage Foundation.

Massey, D. S. (2009). Racial formation in theory and practice: The case of Mexicans in the United States. *Race Social Problems, 1*, 12–26.

Massey, D. S. (2012). *Immigration and the great recession*. Stanford: Stanford Center on Poverty and Inequality.

Massey, D. S. (2013). Immigration enforcement as a race making institution. In D. Card & S. Raphael (Eds.), *Immigration, poverty, and socioeconomic inequality* (pp. 257–281). New York: Russell Sage Foundation.

Massey, D. S., & Aysa-Lastra, M. (2011). Social capital and international migration from Latin America. *International Journal of Population Research, 2011*, Article ID 834145.

Massey, D. S., & Pren, K. A. (2012). Origins of the New Latino underclass. *Race Social Problems, 4*, 5–17.

Massey, D. S., & Sánchez, M. (2010). *Brokered boundaries. Creating immigrant identity in anti-immigrant times*. New York: Russell Sage Foundation.

Menjívar, C., & Kanstroom, D. (Eds.). (2014). *Constructing immigrant "illegality": Critiques, experiences, and responses*. New York: Cambridge University Press.

Moulier-Boutang, Y. (1998). *De l'esclavage au salariat*. Paris: PUF.

Nagel, J. (1986). The political construction of ethnicity. In J. Nagel & S. Olzak (Eds.), *Competitive ethnic relations* (pp. 93–112). Orlando: Academic.

OECD. (2010). *International migration outlook SOPEMI 2010*. Paris: OECD.

Organization of American States (OAS). (2012). International migration in the Americas. Second Report on the Continuous Reporting System on International Migration in the Americas. http://www.oecd.org/els/mig/G48952_WB_SICREMI_2012_ENGLISH_REPORT_LR.pdf. Accessed 25 Feb 2014.

Passel, J. S., Cohn, D.'. V., & González-Barrera, A. (2013). *Population decline of unauthorized immigrants stalls, may have reversed*. Washington, DC: Pew Hispanic Center.

Passel, J. S., Lopez, M. H., Cohn, D.'. V., & Rohal, M. (2014). *As growth stalls, unauthorized immigrant population becomes more settled*. Washington, DC: Pew Hispanic Center.

Perez, W., Espinoza, R., Ramos, K., Coronado, H. M., & Cortes, R. (2009). Academic resilience among undocumented Latino students. *Hispanic Journal of Behavioral Sciences, 31*(2), 149–181.

Pfeffer, F. T., Danziger, S., & Schoeni, R. F. (2013). Wealth disparities before and after the great recession. *The ANNALS of the American Academy of Political and Social Science, 650*, 98–123.

Piore, M. J. (1979). *Birds of passage: Migrant labor and industrial societies*. New York: Century University Press.

Portes, A. (1978). Introduction: Toward a structural analysis of illegal (undocumented) immigration. *International Migration Review, 12*(4), 469–484.

Portes, A. (2006). La nueva nación latina. Inmigración y la población hispana en los Estados Unidos. *Revista Española de Investigaciones Sociológicas, 116*, 55–96.

Portes, A., & Bach, R. L. (1985). *Latin journey: Cuban and Mexican immigrants in the United States*. Berkeley: University of California Press.

Portes, A., & Rumbaut, R. G. (2001). *Legacies: The story of the immigrant second generation*. Berkeley: University of California Press/Russell Sage Foundation.

Portes, A., & Sensenbrenner, J. (1993). Embeddedness and immigration: Notes on the social determinants of economic action. *American Journal of Sociology, 98*(May), 1320–1350.

Portes, A., & Zhou, M. (1993). The new second generation: Segmented assimilation and its variants. *Annals of the American Academy of Political and Social Sciences, 530*, 74–96.

Portes, A., Fernández-Kelly, P., & Haller, W. (2009). The adaptation of the immigrant second generation in America: A theoretical overview and recent evidence. *Journal of Ethnic and Migration Studies, 35*(7), 1077–1104.

Rios, V. M. (2012). Stealing a bag of potato chips and other crimes of resistance. *Contexts, 11*, 48–53.

Rogers, A. (2009). *Recession, vulnerable workers and immigration: Background report.* Oxford: COMPAS.

Roubini, n. (2009, August 23). The risk of a double-dip recession is rising. *Financial Times.*

Santamaría, A. (2007). El movimiento de los inmigrantes indocumentados en Estados Unidos. *Política y Cultura, 27*(primavera), 99–120.

Santoro, W. A., Vélez, M. B., & Keogh, S. M. (2012). Mexican American protest, ethnic resiliency and social capital: The mobilization benefits of cross-cutting ties. *Social Forces, 91*(1), 209–231.

Sassen, S. (1988). *The mobility of labor and capital: A study in international investment and labor flow.* Cambridge, UK: Cambridge University Press.

Simmel, G. (1950). *The sociology of Georg Simmel.* Glencoe: Free Press.

Stiglitz, J. E. (2009, June). *Interpreting the causes of the great recession of 2008.* Lecture delivered at BIS conference, Basel.

Tabboni, S. (1997). Le multiculturalisme et l'ambivalance de l'étranger. In M. Wieviorka (Ed.), *Une société fragmentée? La multiculturalisme en débat* (pp. 227–250). Paris: La Découverte & Syros.

Telles, E. E., & Ortiz, V. (2008). *Generations of exclusion. Mexican Americans, assimilation, and race.* New York: Russell Sage Foundation.

Tilly, C. (2011). The impact of the economic crisis on international migration: a review. *Work, Employment and Society, 25*(4), 675–692.

UN (United Nations). (2009). International migrant stock: The 2008 revision. http://esa.un.org/migration/. Accessed 27 Feb 2014.

Wolff, E. N., Owens, L. A., & Burak, E. (2012). How much wealth was destroyed in the great recession? In D. B. Grusky et al. (Eds.), *The great recession* (pp. 127–158). New York: Russell Sage Foundation.

Wright, M., & Bloemraad, I. (2012). Is there a trade-off between multiculturalism and socio-political integration? Policy regimes and immigrant incorporation in comparative perspective. *Perspectives on Politics, 10*(1), 77–95.

Zoellick, R. (2009, February 19). Zoellick calls for a global response to crisis. *Financial Times.*

Part I
Effects of the Great Recession on Latin American Immigrant Labor

Chapter 2
Native and Latino Employment During the Great Recession in the US and Spain

Lorenzo Cachón and María Aysa-Lastra

2.1 Introduction

The Great Recession (GR) is still producing deeper and more extensive effects on employment than any other economic downturn since the Great Depression in 1930 (Hout et al. 2011). The US economy lost 8.5 million jobs between its peak of 138.1 million jobs in December 2007 and its nadir of 129 million jobs in February 2010, which represents a decline of 6.2 %. The unemployment rate more than doubled in 26 months, from 5.0 % to 10.4 %. Spain lost 18 % of available jobs between the third quarters of 2007 and 2013, and the unemployment rate went from 8 % to 26 % in the period. The state of the labor market in Spain can be described as "catastrophic." This deep but unequal deterioration of the labor market in both countries has had notable effects on immigrants and more importantly on Latino immigrants. The United States has faced previous crises while hosting large foreign born populations, but this is the first large-scale recession Spain has experienced while hosting a large foreign born population (see Chap. 1).

The effects of the GR on employment have three common characteristics in both countries: this recession is the deepest after the Great Depression, the longest, and it has been followed by a slow, weak recovery. The GR has been more deep than previous recessions: during a typical post-World War II recession in the US, about 3 % of all jobs were lost, whereas job loss during the GR has occurred at twice that rate (Freeman 2013); Spain lost 14 % of employment during the long crisis in the 1970–1980s and 7 % in the short but deep recession in the 1990s; however, during

L. Cachón (✉)
Departamento de Sociología I, Universidad Complutense de Madrid, Madrid, Spain
e-mail: lcachonr@ucm.es

M. Aysa-Lastra
Department of Sociology and Anthropology, Winthrop University, Rock Hill, SC, USA
e-mail: aysalastram@winthrop.edu

© Springer International Publishing Switzerland 2015   25
M. Aysa-Lastra, L. Cachón (eds.), *Immigrant Vulnerability and Resilience*,
International Perspectives on Migration 11, DOI 10.1007/978-3-319-14797-0_2

the 6 years of the GR, 18 % of employment has been lost. The GR is on a path to becoming the longest recession in recorded history; Freeman (2013) has shown that in previous crises, job recovery has been faster than in the GR. In Spain, only until the third quarter of 2014 indicators suggest a weak and unstable recovery of the labor market. Moreover, the recovery period in the US is occurring with an employment growth that is "slow and anemic" (ibid: 9) and below GDP growth. For this reason, analysts characterized the conclusion of the GR in the US as a "jobless recovery" (Rampell 2012) and even argue that the "great US jobs machine failed to live up to expectations in the crisis" (Freeman 2013). This seems to be the path that Spain will follow when the recovery arrives: job growth that is weak and below GDP growth. Greenstone and Looney (2013) suggest that the calendar will read 2020 before the American and Spanish economies regain the number of jobs they had before the GR, and Danziger (2013: 23) points out that it is likely that a "lost decade of economic progress" may become "two lost decades." This pace of improvement is too slow to restore security for American and Spanish, and immigrant workers anytime soon (Hout et al. 2011: 78). The worst legacy of the GR is the generation of a large and persistent job gap (OECD 2013).

The US and Spain are countries with labor markets structured into different logics and frameworks. Using Freeman's (2008) characterization, we can say that the US labor market is a driven labor system, while the Spanish labor market is a European institution-driven labor system. European labor markers are more regulated than US labor markets, and widely covered by collective bargaining contracts. Two indicators show these differences. First, according to the Fraser Institute, the US scores 9 in economic freedom in "labor market regulation" and ranks second among 152 countries. Spain scores 5.4 and ranks 112th (Gwartney et al. 2013). Second, in the US, 14 % of workers are covered by collective contracts (and ranks 24th among 25 countries); in Spain, more than 80 % of workers are covered by bargaining agreements (and ranks 6th) (OECD 2004). Other labor market regulations show these different organizational principles (OECD 2013). However, inspired by the types of welfare states (Esping-Andersen 1990), it could be said that Spain (as other Southern European countries) has a "Mediterranean institution-driven labor system." Three main features differentiate this system from other labor systems in Europe and partially explain observed trends during the GR. First, Southern-European countries have labor institutions that favor labor market dualism (strong protections for permanent jobs and great flexibility for temporal contracts) (OECD 2004). Second, the informal economy plays an important role on the labor demand (Andrews et al. 2011) and it weighs on specialized sectors such as tourism, construction and domestic services for private households. Third, a mismatch between labor demand and supply that results in high unemployment levels even in periods of economic growth. This labor mismatch attracted numerous migrants during the regional economic boom before the GR (Cachón 2009).

More flexible institutions allow market-driven economies to do better than institution-driven systems in periods of economic change (Freeman 2008: 24). But not only institutions matter, financial, monetary, and economic stimulus policies implemented in both countries as responses to the GR also explain their different outcomes. The US is undergoing a recovery period; although, there are still concerns about a second round of recession, this time without supporting stimulus from policy actions (Elwell 2013: 9). By the end of 2013, after four quarters of continuous and smooth declines, the unemployment rates in the US were similar to those observed before the crisis. However, Spain was still at the end of 2013 witnessing continuous job losses.

The impact of the GR on immigrants is likely to vary across countries according to economic and political conditions (Papademetriou et al. 2010). Here, we show the different effects in the US and Spain, countries with different institutional frameworks, migration histories, and labor structures. Although all demographic groups have experienced job losses, some groups have been more adversely affected than others. Repeating the pattern of most previous downturns, the GR's impact has been worst for low educated and minority workers (Orrenius and Zavodny 2010: 316). One group in which the negative effects have been felt the strongest is Latino immigrants in the US and in Spain, in the next sections we describe their increased vulnerability during the period, and as well as their resilient behavior in the labor market.

2.2 Vulnerability and Resilience in the Labor Market During the Great Recession

It is a well-documented fact that foreign workers appear to be relatively more vulnerable than natives during cyclical downturns (Chiswick et al. 1997; OEDC 2009; Orrenius and Zavodny 2009; Papademetriou and Terrazas 2009; Enchautegui 2012). The vulnerability of immigrants derives from their immigrant condition given the discriminatory institutional framework and their class condition as workers. The segmented assimilation that is produced in their process of integration to the recipient country is reflected in their occupations and positions in the segmented labor markets (Aysa-Lastra and Cachón 2013a, b). These barriers and conditions result in the creation of categorically unequal social subjects (see Chap. 1). Some key elements in the labor market, either from the supply or demand side, could explain this increased immigrant employment vulnerability during economic downturns.

A key structural factor, particularly important during the GR, is the overrepresentation of immigrants in sectors sensitive to economic cycles, including construction and related industries and parts of the manufacturing and service sectors (OEDC 2009). This overrepresentation is associated to worsening labor conditions in these sectors. As a consequence, these are among the least desirable sectors among native workers (Cachón 1997). During the GR in countries where construction had been the engine of growth in recent years such as Spain and the US, migrant workers employed in the sector have paid the highest price in terms of loss of employment (Awad 2009: 55).

There are other factors in the labor market that might produce a significant and differential negative effect on immigrant employment relative to native employment. One, the overrepresentation of immigrants in nonstandard employ-ments—it is well known that temporary employment falls rapidly in the early stages of economic crises (Holmlund and Storrie 2002; European Commission 2011). Two, the overrepresentation of immigrants among workers who have spent less time in their current job. The last-hired, first-fired phenomenon is unfavorable to immigrants. The OECD (2009: 25) recalls how "countries with the highest share of recent immigrants [...] are therefore more likely to witness a strong deterioration of immigrant labor market outcomes"; the OECD expressly included Spain among these countries. Three, the overrepresentation of immigrants in the population of workers that experience selective layoffs and discriminatory acts. Evidence of discrimination based on race or ethnic origin is supported by numerous studies. The OECD (2008: 184) synthesizes the effects of discrimination stating that "available evidence suggests that gender and racial discrimination in the labor market is still significant in a number of OECD countries." In the case of the US, the racial and ethnic classification system has consequences for Latino immigrants. Those with darker skin tones face greater discrimination in the labor market, and their annual revenue is, on average, lower than those with lighter skin (Frank et al. 2010). In addition, numerous studies point to the increasing criminalization and victimization of immigrants (Fussell 2011; Menjívar and Kanstroom 2014). These factors explain the additional decline of employment and job deterioration for Latino immigrants during the GR.

Another important question in the labor market is the overrepresentation of immigrants and Latino immigrants in the informal economy (OEDC 2009). Reyneri (1998) argues that as in the case of Italy—an argument that is applicable to countries like Spain and the US—"the informal economy has important and strong national roots to the point that it exerts a pull factor on immigrants from less developed countries, when the local labor pool does not accept work in marginal occupations." The informal economy attracts a large number of unauthorized immigrants (Tapinos 1999). In Spain a 10 % points increase in the share of immigrants at the regional level generated between 3 % and 8 % points increase in unregistered employment between 2000 and 2009 (Bosh and Farre 2013). In the US, Cebula and Feige (2011) argue that as unemployment increases the under-ground economy increases (proxy by tax evasion). Moreover, the GR coincides with increasing border and internal controls for immigrant employment (e-Verify and raids), which are also associated with increases in the informal economy among unauthorized immigrants. The impossibility to participate in the formal economy due to the lack of legal status, and a growing informal sector during the GR might have attracted a large number of unauthorized immigrants into the informal econ-omy (see Chap. 6). As Castles and Miller point out (2009: 232–342), irregular migration and employment are the result of the emergence of a 'new economy' in which workers are treated differently because of their ethnicity, race, origins, and legal status.

From a labor market supply perspective, immigrants are overrepresented in groups with certain sociodemographic characteristics that increase their vulnera-bility in the job market. Especially important is the predominance of low educational attainment among un-skilled immigrant workers, because education determines access to good jobs or bad jobs, workers with relatively low skills and education—such as non-whites, the foreign-born, and older workers—are more vulnerable than others to structural changes (Kalleberg 2011: 57). Nonetheless, it is also relevant that immigrants are overrepresented in groups such as women, youth, and those less likely to speak a country's predominant language. Immigrants in these groups are likely to lose their jobs during economic downturns (Orrenius and Zavodny 2010; Papademetriou et al. 2010; European Commission 2011). Immigrants' increased vulnerability resulting from the deterioration of the labor market has provoked a larger erosion of employment for them relative to native employment during the crisis (Aysa-Lastra and Cachón 2012). Additionally, there are other vulnerability factors such as the lower participation in unions among immigrants in the US (Rosenfeld and Kleykamp 2009) and Spain.

Other institutional factors are significant sources of vulnerability in the labor market. The additional institutional requirements that migrant workers face (visas, work permits, certifications, etc.) motivate disparities in the job search strategies between immigrants and natives. For example, the higher institutional pressure on immigrants is associated to continuous employment among authorized immigrants (Cachón 2009). Another factor is remittances: immigrants often send part of their income to family members still living in the country of origin who depend on these resources to lead a decent life and to raise their children. In addition, immigrants often pay for the trip related debts and migration expenses of other family members. Lower relational social capital among immigrants compared to natives, also decreases their possibilities in the job market because it is a vital resource when searching for employment (Granovetter 1974). Moreover, their limited relational social capital can become a barrier, inhibiting their opportunities (Portes 1998; Aysa-Lastra and Cachón 2013b). Immigrants also have less access to social protections (unemployment insurance, health care, conditions for claiming labor rights when employers need to reduce their workforce, etc.) (TUC 2008) or health insurance in US (Krogstad and Lopez 2014).

Immigrants' resilience, from their position as vulnerable subjects, emerges as a form of resistance within the field of possibilities in which they are placed. It is expected that different forms of resilience surface because migration is a selective process. It is important to remember that one of the standard propositions in the international economic migration literature is self-selection. Economic migrants are described as more able, ambitious, aggressive, and entrepreneurial than similar individuals who opt to remain in their countries of origin (Chiswick 1999; Borjas 1995). This is key to explaining their economic success, even in a segmented process of economic integration (Aysa-Lastra and Cachón 2013a). Sisk and Donato (2013) argue that one possible explanation for the relatively strong outcomes among low-skill Mexican immigrant workers is that they possess more resilience—and the ability to recover from adverse life events—than low-skill US-born whites. After facing a difficult and long multidimensional process, such as uprooting oneself from the home/country of origin to migrate to the US or Spain, it is expected that immigrants show strong resilience in the labor market. Their need to reduce their level of "acceptability" linked to their increased vulnerability forces them to accept precarious jobs that natives reject. Their vulnerability pushes them, when unemployed, to accept the first (frequently bad) job they find, exchanging unemployment for underemployment (underemployment exists when a worker work less hours, earn less income or use their occupational skills incompletely). As Papademetriou and Terrazas argue (2009: iii), immigrants "may be able to adjust more quickly than native-born workers to changing labor market conditions because they are more amenable to changing jobs and their place of residence for work-related reasons."

Another element to consider regarding immigrant resilience relates to their more vulnerable bargaining position—relative to natives—in the labor market. Some employers might prefer to hire vulnerable immigrants because they are more flexible, docile, and less likely to complain about the working conditions, (or, in the employers' terms—more motivated and productive) and for this reason, they are subject to jobs of inferior quality with lower salaries (Waldinger 1997; Donato and Bankston 2008).

Some of these resilience strategies improve immigrants' condition in the labor market, as observed in their higher geographical and occupational mobility relative to natives. Return migration to their country of origin or migration to a new destination are also resilience strategies that improve their employment possibilities; these strategies also increase the chances that other immigrants will find jobs, as the number of similar workers competing for jobs diminishes.

2.3 Methods

Our work focuses on a comparative analysis of the US and Spain, the two countries with the largest Latino immigrant communities. Although comparative studies have a long tradition in international migration studies, there are few comparative analyses of the GR on immigrant employment in destination countries. The exceptions are the articles published by Papademetriou and colleagues (Papademetriou and Terrazas, 2009; Papademetriou et al. 2010), Awad (2009), and Tilly (2011) and the book edited by Higley et al. (2011) comparing the US and Australia.

To compare Latino immigrants in the US and Spain, we used data from two national labor force surveys: the Current Population Survey (CPS) for the US and the Economically Active Population Survey (*Encuesta de Población Activa*, EPA) for Spain. Both surveys collect demographic information characterizing the citizenship status and country of birth of different population groups residing in the respective countries. Therefore, this information allows us to know the employment status of different populations at different points in time. The CPS in the US collects information every month on a representative sample of about 60,000 households. The CPS questionnaire includes sociodemographic variables (e.g., education, race and ethnicity, age, etc.), a long battery of questions on employment characteristics including wages and earnings, union affiliation, length of stay for the foreign born, and citizenship status (BLS 2006). The EPA collects information on sociodemographic characteristics and labor market conditions (except wages, affiliation to social security, or unions) on a national representative sample of about 65,000 households every 3 months (INE 2008). We selected the samples corresponding to the CPS March supplement and to the second trimester (April-June) from EPA for the period 2007 to 2013.

This article focuses on labor market outcomes; therefore, our universe is the adult civilian population—those who are 16 and older at the time of the survey. The term "immigrant" is used differently in Europe and in the US. In order to create comparable groups for our analysis, we divided the population into three categories: natives,[1] naturalized citizens born in Latin America, and non-naturalized immigrants born in Latin America, we will refer to this last group as immigrants throughout the chapter. Immigrants and naturalized citizens not born in Latin America are not considered in the analysis. Natives for the Spanish case are defined as those who have Spanish citizenship only, regardless of their place of birth. In the US, natives are those born in the US or born abroad of American parents. It is important to remember that people born in Spain to nationals of other countries are not Spanish citizens. Naturalized Spanish citizens of Latin American origin are those who hold Spanish citizenship at the time of the survey, most of them also hold citizenship from a Latin American country. Moreover Latin American immigrants in Spain can request citizenship by naturalization after 2 years of legal residence in Spain. Immigrants from other regions must hold legal residency for at least 10 years before they can request citizenship. The naturalization process in the US on average takes longer than in Spain: 3 years after becoming a permanent resident under family reunification criteria and 5 years under employment criteria.[2] Our third group is immigrants from Latin America. In Spain these are foreigners who hold citizenship from a Latin American country. In the US, Latino immigrants were defined as those who are not US citizens at the time of the survey and were born in Latin America.

We must be aware that there are potential sources of bias in analyzing data on immigrants at destination, such as changes in the composition of the immigrant flow over time (Borjas 1985, 1995), return or transit migration to a third country (Constant and Massey 2003), or fluctuations in the characteristics of immigrants entering the labor force (Aslund and Rooth 2007). As in other studies (Reyneri and Fullin 2011), we assume that the unobserved characteristics of migrants do not change significantly over time.

---

[1] This group includes native citizens of all races. Although racial disadvantages are observed for non-whites in both countries, we kept all natives in one group to keep our analytical focus on immigration and ease the comparison among natives, naturalized citizens, and immigrants.

[2] Van Hook and Bachmeier (2013) found that citizenship status is inaccurately reported on U.S. Surveys among long-term foreign born residents from Mexico.

2.4   Latino Immigrant Labor Force in United States and Spain

In 2013, there were about 14 million people of Latin American origin among the workforce population in the US. Five million of them were naturalized citizens and more than nine million were immigrants, which respectively accounted for 3.2 % and 6 % of the total workforce. In Spain, there were about 400,000 Spanish citizens who were born in Latin America and more than one million Latin American immigrants, which accounted for 1.6 % and 5.2 % of the total workforce, respectively. Overall, workers from Latin American countries accounted for 9.2 % of the workforce in the US and 6.8 % in Spain.

The GR had a different impact among the Latino population in both countries. In the US, there was a notable decrease (of about 600,000 workers) in the first 2 years of the recession (2008 and 2009), and even further declines between 2011 and 2013. However, the trend in the relative size of the Latino workforce has slightly increased. According to Toossi (2002), in 2002 Hispanic origin workers may reach 16 % of the workforce in 2020 and their presence will continue to grow. In Spain, the effect of the GR among Latino immigrant workers is different for three main reasons that mark dissimilarities with the US experience. First, immigration to Spain is a relatively recent phenomenon; second, the institutional immigration framework; and, third, Spain's lower capacity for economic and labor recovery (see Chap. 1). In the first years of the GR, the immigrant Latino workforce continued to grow at a rate similar to that found in the years before the crisis (about 350,000 more workers in 2008 and 2009); in 2010, Latinos accounted for 8.2 % of the workforce in Spain. Nonetheless, since then there has been a rapid and accelerated decline in which 440,000 have left the labor force and their presence is reduced to 6.8 % of the workforce in Spain in 2013 (see Table 2.1). We anticipate that this decline will continue in the coming years, then stabilize at around 6 % in 2020, but with a higher number of naturalized citizens, and a lower proportion of immigrants born in Latin America (Cachón 2014).

An important feature of the working Latino immigrant population in the US and Spain is their gender composition. Males are predominant in the US, but women are predominant in Spain (see Chap. 4). In 2013, 60 % and 67 % of the Latino workforce is concentrated among young adults (ages 25–44) respectively in the US and Spain. During the crisis, this group has lost some relative size in favor of those aged 45 and older. The educational level of the immigrant Latino native population has slightly improved since 2007, but in 2013 it is still substantially lower than the educational level among natives. There is a significant proportion of Latino immigrants with elementary education or less: 21 % in the US and 17 % in Spain. The proportion of Latino immigrants with college education is lower than that found among natives (see Table 2.1). It seems that there is a convergence in the age structure of Latino and native workforce, but there remains a significant difference by educational level.

Table 2.1 Latin American workforce and economic activity rates in the United States and Spain (2007, 2010, and 2013)

	USA				Spain			
	Total	Natives	Citizens LA[a]	Immigr. LA[a]	Total	Natives	Citizens LA[a]	Immigr. LA[a]
Workforce								
N (thousands) (2013)	155,468	130,145	4,969	9,292	22,761	19,089	365	1,173
2007	100.0	84.4	2.6	6.4	100.0	84.9	0.7	6.7
2010	100.0	84.4	3.0	6.0	100.0	82.8	1.2	7.0
2013	100.0	83.7	3.2	6.0	100.0	83.9	1.6	5.2
Distribution by gender (2013)								
Males	53.2	52.3	51.7	64.6	54.0	54.6	42.8	43.4
Females	46.8	47.7	48.3	35.4	46.0	45.4	57.2	56.6
Distribution by age (2013)								
16–25	13.3	14.5	4.0	11.0	7.3	6.9	10.7	9.5
25–44	43.0	41.4	40.0	59.7	54.7	52.8	55.4	67.3
45–64	38.4	38.6	50.3	27.8	37.3	39.6	32.8	22.6
65+	5.3	5.5	5.7	1.5	0.7	0.7	1.1	0.5
Distribution by educational level (2013)								
Elementary and less	1.8	0.2	7.4	21.4	11.5	9.8	13.6	17.4
Middle school	7.9	6.6	14.1	26.6	29.6	30.5	22.7	26.8
High school	27.1	27.5	28.2	29.6	23.2	21.5	38.1	36.5
College and higher	63.2	65.7	50.2	22.5	35.7	38.2	25.6	19.3
Economic activity rates								
2007	66.0	65.6	69.1	72.1	58.9	56.6	79.7	82.8
2010	64.9	64.3	68.7	71.0	60.1	57.5	81.5	84.0
2013	63.2	62.7	66.0	69.6	59.5	57.4	80.4	80.0

(continued)

Table 2.1 (continued)

	USA				Spain			
	Total	Natives	Citizens LA[a]	Immigr. LA[a]	Total	Natives	Citizens LA[a]	Immigr. LA[a]
Gender (2013)								
Males	69.4	67.8	75.6	85.1	66.1	64.2	82.2	81.5
Females	57.4	57.9	58.2	52.2	53.3	50.9	79.1	78.9
Age groups (2013)								
16–25	53.2	53.5	50.3	57.8	40.9	39.6	49.1	44.0
25–44	81.8	82.7	81.7	76.3	88.6	89.2	92.4	90.1
45–64	72.9	72.5	77.2	71.5	70.4	69.4	87.9	89.3
65+	19.0	18.9	19.3	20.1	1.9	1.8	20.2	15.2
Educational level (2013)								
Elementary and less	46.8	18.7	43.8	65.2	24.8	19.9	70.3	69.7
Middle school	38.0	32.8	58.3	65.1	66.7	65.9	74.3	76.1
High school	60.0	59.1	65.3	73.3	69.0	66.7	84.9	86.4
College and higher	71.5	71.5	74.9	75.7	81.5	81.9	86.7	85.5

Source: United States: BLS, CPS (March); Spain: INE, EPA (second quarter); own estimations
[a]Latin America

Economic activity rates (the ratio of the labor force to the working age population, expressed in percentages) are key indicators of the different generations participating in the labor market. In the US, the activity rate at the beginning of the GR was 66 %, a high level among OECD countries; however it declined to 63.2 % in 2013. In Spain, in 2008 the activity rate was 58.9 % and it continued to grow, reaching 60 % in 2010, then slightly declining over the last 3 years.

In the case of naturalized Latino citizens and Latino immigrants, the activity rates reflect diverse institutional aspects of their migration histories. Before and after the GR, in the US, the economic activity rates of Latin American origin citizens were around 3 % points higher than those of natives; the activity rates of Latino immigrants were 7 points higher. Before the crisis and until 2010, the activity rates for Spanish citizens born in Latin American countries were 23 % points above the rate for natives and 26 points in the case of Latino immigrants. Since 2010, this difference has decreased by 3 points. The large differential between the activity rates of Latino immigrants and natives in Spain is partially explained by the implementation of immigration policies classified as "labor oriented" (Cachón 2009) in contrast to "family reunification" policies (Kalleberg 2011) in the US. Another indicator of the effects of immigration policies is reflected in the activity rates for Latino immigrant women, their rates are 5 points above rates for native women in the US; and 28 points above in Spain, reaching an activity rate of 79 %, which is similar to the rate for Latino immigrant men. The trends of the activity rates in Spain are common among Southern European countries due to the labor market orientation of their policies and the age structure of the labor force concentrated among the most active groups (ages 25–64) and because Latino immigrants, among all immigrants, are incorporated more frequently into the labor market.

The analysis on educational level reveals significant differentials between natives and Latino immigrants. At the lowest educational level, in both countries, natives with elementary education or less have very low activity rates, particularly among women. However, the activity rates for Latino naturalized citizens and Latino immigrants are high, 50 % points above the rates for natives (see Table 2.1).

2.5 Latin American Immigrant Employment During the Great Recession

The third quarter of 2008 marks the starting point for the decline in employment in the United States and Spain. In the fourth quarter of 2010, five quarters after GDP began its recovery, employment grew again in the US, although this growth was "slow and anemic" (Freeman 2013: 9). In March 2013, the number of employed workers in the US was still 2 % lower than that of March 2008. In Spain, the decline in employment lasted 25 quarters because in the third quarter of 2014, employment stopped its continuous decline. In the second quarter of 2013, employment was

18 % lower than that of 2008. If we compare both labor markets, we must reserve the term "catastrophic," which has been used to describe the US case (Rothstein 2012), for the Spanish case.

The last decade can be divided into two distinct periods: expansion until 2007 and crisis starting in 2008 (not to mention the brief crisis of 2002). In the expansion period, between 2000 and 2008, the US employed population grew at an average annual rate of 0.8 % (or 1.1 million people each year); in Spain, it grew at an annual average of 4.4 % (or 0.7 million people each year). Employment among Latino immigrants, in particular, in the US grew on average 3.9 % annually (a high figure for a country with an initial high level of immigration). In Spain, the volume of Latino immigrants employed grew at an average annual rate of 145 %. The case of Spain is exceptional among developed countries in recent decades. Its increase in immigration responds to an expansive phase of the economic cycle as this increase is closely linked to important growth in the construction sector and other sectors such as domestic service and tourism. There was a mismatch in the Spanish labor market: the native labor force had higher educational levels and skills but the labor market demanded unskilled workers (Cachón 2002). Moreover, this period coincides with political and economic crisis in some migrant origin countries (e.g., Colombia and Ecuador).

The GR followed different patterns in both countries in terms of its duration and in the negative effects on employment, but in both countries, Latino immigrant employment was sensitive to changes in the economic cycle. In 2007, before the crisis, Latino employment grew more than native employment in the US and Spain. These patterns changed in 2008 in the US as Latino immigrant employment shows a significant setback vs. the still positive growth of employment among natives. In Spain, native employment started to decline in 2008, while employment of Latino immigrants increased by 8 %. In 2009, the conditions of the labor market for Latino immigrants in Spain changed dramatically; the decline of employment is generalized and began to have negative effects for all, but particularly for Latinos. In 2010, employment trends in the US and in Spain branched away: the US started a slow employment recovery; but in Spain, employment continued its significant decline. The employment trends of Latinos in both countries differ. In the US, Latino employment recovers at a faster pace than native employment but in an uneven fashion because there is a notable increase in underemployment and great sensitivity to further declines in economic growth. In Spain, the Latino immigrants' job losses are "catastrophic" as they amount to 25 % over the last 2 years (see Fig. 2.1 and Table 2.2). Job losses resulted in the substantial return migration of Latino immigrants from Spain to their countries of origin, or to third countries (see Chap. 13).

Latino employment was more sensitive to the sudden change in the economic cycle in the US (maybe due to the weakening of the construction sector, which started in 2006) that led to a rapid process of return to their origin countries and to the observed declines in the workforce (Massey 2012). In Spain, Latino immigrants who lost their employment during the first year of the crisis looked for jobs with more intensity than natives because they had pressing needs and, due to their

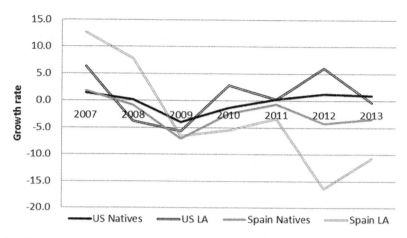

Fig. 2.1 Employment annual growth rates for natives and foreign born Latinos for the US and Spain (2007–2013) (Source: Own elaboration based on BLS, CPS for the United States; INE, EPA for Spain)

Table 2.2 Latin American employed population in the US and Spain (2007, 2010, and 2013)

	USA				Spain			
	Natives	Citizens LA	Immigr. LA	Total	Natives	Citizens LA	Immigr. LA	Total
Employed population (thousands)								
2007	123,072	3,929	9,242	145,879	17,426	140	1,308	20,367
2010	117,129	4,165	8,125	138,690	15,680	201	1,179	18,477
2013	119,976	4,630	8,390	143,367	14,417	238	759	16,784
Absolute average annual change (thousands)								
2007–2010	−5,943	236	−1,117	−7,189	−1,746	61	−130	−1,890
2010–2013	2,847	465	265	4,677	−1,263	37	−418	−1,693
Average annual percentage change (%)								
2007-2010	−4.8	6.0	−12.1	−4.9	−10.0	43.3	−9.9	−9.3
2010-2013	2.4	11.2	3.3	3.4	−8.1	18.3	−35.6	−9.2

Source: United States, BLS, CPS (March); Spain: INE, EPA (second quarter); own estimations
Note: Totals for the US and Spain include immigrants and citizens not born in Latin America

willingness to accept part-time and lower quality jobs, they found jobs more easily—which is a feature of Latino immigrants' resiliency. There are some factors that explain why immigrant employment was more resilient during the initial stage of the crisis. Vulnerable workers, like Latino immigrants in Spain, are often employed in labor-intensive work. Their lower "social bargaining power" (Cachón 2002) make it difficult for them to resist employers' pressure to increase hours and otherwise intensify work. For this reason, they are preferred in certain sectors. However, this ability to resist is correspondingly lower during periods of rising unemployment (Rogers 2009) as has been the case since 2009. Another factor that may explain this delayed response in Spain is the mismatch between qualifications and jobs held by immigrants. This mismatch facilitates their occupational mobility and the search of jobs different from the jobs they held before the crisis. A third factor is the increased willingness to migrate to other towns and cities, especially during the early years of immigration. Their flexibility and mobility enables them to search widely for employment opportunities in different sectors. Nonetheless, these search strategies have limits, such as the lack of employment opportunities during a long period of time, as in the case of Spain. The severity and length of the Spanish crisis resulted in a substantial return migration in 2012 and 2013.

The effects of the GR differ by gender because employment losses are more prevalent among traditionally male occupations than among female occupations, and this pattern is similar for natives and Latino immigrants in both countries (see Chap. 4). We can call the GR a "man-cession" (Hout et al. 2011) in terms of gender, but also a Latin-cession in terms of Latin American immigration.

The GR has produced a significant shift in the age patterns of workers. Six years after the start of the recession, employment decreased for those younger than 45 years of age and it increased for those 45 and older in the US and in Spain. We observe this trend among natives and Latino immigrants. However, among the latter, the proportion is much higher. This once again shows the higher sensitivity of Latino employment; those younger than 45 faced higher declines in employment than natives in the same age group. In both countries those older than 45 experienced increases in employment in larger proportions.

The impact of the GR by educational level is different among natives and Latinos. In the US, Latino immigrants without college education fared better than their native counterparts in the first phase of the GR (until 2010). In the second phase (until 2013), they also coped better, regardless of their level of education. Latino immigrants who did not graduate from high school lost fewer jobs than their native counterparts and Latino immigrants with high school or higher education experienced an increase in employment compared to natives in the same educational category. In Spain, the patterns are different: Latino immigrants with lower levels of education (not higher than high school) fared relatively better than their native counterparts; however, for those with higher education (higher than high school) the outcomes are worse. It seems that the recovery after the GR is allowing Latino immigrants with lower levels of education to improve their position relative to their native counterparts in the US, while in Spain, the long duration of the GR is further worsening their position in the labor market.

The negative and substantial impact of the GR on Latino employment in both countries is also reflected in the deterioration of their labor conditions and in increasing unemployment among immigrants (see Chap. 3).

2.6   Sectorial Changes

The evolution of employment by sector has been uneven in both countries during the first (2007–2010) and the second (2011–2013) phases of the GR. Employment declined during the first phase in all sectors but public administration in both countries, agriculture in the US, and transportation in Spain. During this phase, the most notable decline was in the construction sector, which lost 23 % of employment in the US and 37 % in Spain. Moreover, due to the multiplier effect in related sectors, the true impact of the housing bubble burst is larger than what is reflected by these figures. In addition to the employment losses in the construction sector, we must consider collapses in branches of industry and services related to the building industry, such as suppliers and vendors. In the second phase of the GR employment started its slow recovery in all sectors in the US, with the exception of construction, and, food and clothing. Meanwhile, in Spain the decline in employment worsened and declines in all sectors were occurring faster than in the first phase of the GR. Moreover, during the second phase the construction sector suffered an additional employment decline of 42 % (see Table 2.3). As it has been noted, "the construction industry and the manufacturing firms that support [the economy] were ground zero for this recession" (Hout et al. 2011: 69). The negative impact of its collapse on employment has been very strong both in the US and in Spain.

Latino employment, either for naturalized citizens or for immigrants, has followed these general patterns but changes for this group have been more pronounced: in the first phase of the GR, they lost employment in construction and related industries in both countries (by one-third in the US and almost 50 % in Spain). This is a fundamental change, because construction was the mainstay of job growth for Latino workers, especially those who are immigrants both in the US (Kochhar 2008) and Spain (Cachón 2009). Latino immigrant employment also decreased in manufacturing sectors in the US and even by a larger share in Spain. Latino immigrant employment in agriculture increased in the US, but in Spain, employment in this sector declined. In the second phase of the GR, the evolution of employment differs in both countries: in Spain there is a steep and generalized decline in Latino employment in all sectors, and most notably in construction where Latinos lost about 70 % of jobs between 2010 and 2013. This decline is less significant in agriculture. Meanwhile in the US, Latino employment recovers in many sectors, especially agriculture, commerce, and financial services (See Fig. 2.2).

Latino immigrant employment in agriculture in the US and Spain is a special case. Both the US and Spain are among the developed countries in which immigrants are overrepresented in this sector. Moreover, it is the only sector where employment contraction in the GR is different: in Spain, employment (and especially Latino immigrant employment) contracted in both periods of the GR, but in the second period the contraction is lower relative to other sectors; while in the US it slightly increases (especially for Latino immigrants). Agriculture has been an

Table 2.3 Employment of immigrants and naturalized citizens born in Latin America by industry in the US and Spain, 2007–2013

	United States						Spain					
	Change in employment (%)		Relative distribution[a]		Participation of Latino immigrants[b]		Change in employment (%)		Distribution of Latino immigrants[a]		Participation of Latino immigrants[b]	
	2007–2010	2010–2013	2007	2013	2007	2013	2007–2010	2010–2013	2007	2013	2007	2013
Total	**−5.3**	**3.1**	**100**	**100**	**8.8**	**9.0**	**−9.3**	**−11.0**	**100**	**100**	**7.1**	**6.1**
Agriculture	3.1	1.6	5.7	6.7	18.5	20.7	−17.6	−6.1	4.2	4.7	7.0	7.1
Food, clothing, etc.	−14.5	−1.8	7.6	6.7	13.0	13.5	−23.6	−10.5	3.5	3.2	4.8	4.5
Extractive industr.	−14.4	10.7	3.8	3.3	7.5	6.9	−15.4	−15.3	3.2	1.7	3.9	2.0
Machine construct.	−17.0	9.1	3.5	3.0	6.3	5.8	−20.9	−13.1	2.5	1.4	3.7	2.1
Construction	−22.8	−2.1	19.9	14.1	16.9	15.6	−37.4	−42.4	22.0	5.4	12.0	5.6
Trade	−2.2	3.6	26.8	29.1	9.8	10.4	−8.2	−6.3	26.1	28.6	8.3	7.3
Transportation	−5.7	0.3	4.5	4.9	8.4	9.6	17.5	−8.6	3.8	5.1	4.6	4.0
Financial services	−5.4	9.8	9.0	11.2	6.4	7.6	−9.1	−7.3	8.6	9.5	4.9	4.4
Public administrat.	3.5	0.5	13.3	14.7	4.8	5.0	10.5	−6.3	3.9	9.5	1.6	2.6
Others	−2.8	3.1	5.9	6.3	8.1	8.5	−4.7	−8.7	22.2	30.8	18.4	20.1

Source: United States: BLS, CPS (March); Spain: INE, EPA (second quarter); own estimations

[a]Relative distribution of workers who are Latin American immigrants or naturalized citizens by industry

[b]Relative weight of workers who are Latin American immigrants or naturalized citizens out of all workers in each specific industry

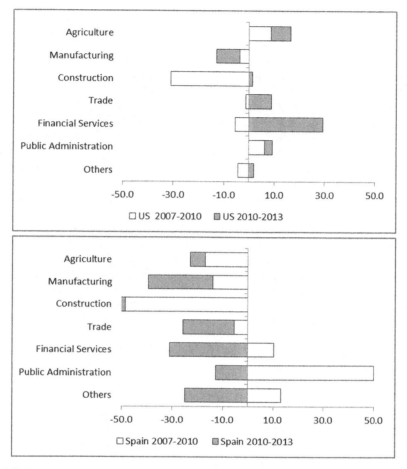

Fig. 2.2 Employment growth rates for natives and Latino immigrants by industry in the US and Spain (2007–2010 and 2010–2013) (Source: United States: BLS, CPS (March); Spain: INE, EPA (second quarter); own estimations)

"entry sector" for Latino immigrants in both countries and during the GR it has been a "shelter sector" for a share of Latino immigrants who lost their employment in other sectors, and above all, for low educated and unskilled immigrants who worked in construction.

The evolution of Latino employment relative to native employment in diverse branches of the service sector in the US and Spain has followed opposite patterns. In the US, Latinos have been more resilient than natives in the first phase of the GR in the service sector and have experienced an increase in the number of jobs in trade, transportation, financial services, and public administration faster than natives (this might be explained by their still relatively low presence in these sectors). On the other hand, in Spain, although Latino immigrants fared better than natives in the first phase, Latinos have lost much more employment (in relative terms) than natives in the service sector during the second phase.

The evolution of employment during the GR has produced a significant reconfiguration of Latino employment among sectors following a similar pattern in both countries: industrial and construction sectors lost weight among occupied Latinos and to the contrary, there are gains in agriculture and among all branches, the service sector. The percentage of Latino employees in construction decreased by 5 % points between 2007 and 2013 in the US, and by 17 % points in Spain the same period. In 2013, in the US the trade sector employed the largest number of Latino workers (29 %), followed by public administration (15 %) and construction (14 %). In Spain, the largest concentration of Latino employees is in private households and the "other" category (31 %, which are mainly women), followed by trade (29 %), public administration (10 %), and financial services (10 %). Construction only represented 5 % of Latino employed workers in 2013, after the massive erosion of jobs in this sector (see Table 2.3). There is only one masculin- ized sector, agriculture, which gains weight among Latino immigrants after the GR. All other sectors that gain relative weight have a substantial presence of women.

The GR did not changed the concentration of workers among the four sectors with a large Latino immigration presence, three of which are common to the US and Spain: agriculture, construction, and trade (which according to the relative number of Latino workers ranked first, second, and fourth in the US and third, fourth, and second in Spain, respectively). The third-ranked group of occupations for Latino immigrant employment in the US is manufacturing of food, clothing, and other goods. In Spain, the first-ranked occupation is services in private households, or domestic work. The trends indicate that the GR accentuated the sectorial segrega- tion of Latino immigrants in sectors such as agriculture and trade in the US and in domestic work in Spain. In other sectors, such as construction, the GR reduced their presence.

2.7   Conclusions

The data reviewed in this article show that Latino employment became more vulnerable than native employment during the GR in the US and Spain. Despite the differences between both economies, their labor market structures and dynam- ics; the historical differences in immigration from Latin America to both countries; the diverse types of "proximity" between Latin America and the US and Spain; and, the marked differences in the demographic characteristics of Latino immigrants, the effects of the Great Recession on immigrant Latino employment have some similar features that indicate increasing employment vulnerability during the current eco- nomic downturn.

The increased immigrant vulnerability derives from their immigrant condition given the "discriminatory institutional framework" and their working class status.

The segmented assimilation that rises from their unequal integration into the host society is mirrored in their occupations and positions in the segmented labor markets, which ultimately results in immigrants being "categorically unequal." This condition is produced by a diversity of factors. A key factor during the GR has been Latino immigrant overrepresentation in sectors most sensitive in the event of economic crisis, such as construction. But there are other factors that exacerbate their vulnerability such as their overrepresentation in temporary and non-tenure jobs; selective and discriminatory layoffs; participation in the informal economy; overrepresentation among the young population and among those with lower educational level; institutional factors, including the additional requirements from the "institutional discriminatory framework"; additional demands from their families in countries of origin; and some differences in access to social protection.

The GR has followed different patterns in both countries, not only in the severity of its impact on employment but also in the duration of its negative impact. In Spain, the severity of the effects has been catastrophic and the effects still continue without any signs of recovery at the end of 2013. The lack of flexibility of the "Mediterranean institution-driven labor market" produced substantial negative outcomes for the labor market in Spain.

The Latino workforce has a substantial role in the labor markets of both countries. As a result of the GR, there is an increase in the relative importance of Latinos in the US workforce, but it has started to decrease in Spain, as a consequence of the number of returnees who have traveled to their countries of origin in the last 3 years. The flow of returnees increased from 2011 to 2013 and as of this writing (last quarter 2014) it is still positive. The Latino immigrant population in both countries has higher activity rates than natives and this difference is more pronounced in Spain, and even more notable among women. This is partially the result of institutional factors such as labor market oriented policies, the younger structure of the Latino population, and the higher propensity among Latinos to participate in the labor market relative to other groups.

In both countries, Latino employment has shown a greater sensitivity to changes in the economic cycle in comparison to natives. It increases more during economic expansions and declines substantially more during economic declines. Before the crisis, Latino employment grew at a faster pace than native employment. During the crisis, this tendency reverses and Latino immigrants' situation in the labor market worsened relative to natives. In the US, this trend is observed from the start of the GR and the Latino employment disadvantage lasts while employment declines. As the "slow and anemic" employment recovery starts, Latino employment recovers more rapidly than native employment. In Spain, the decline in Latino immigrant employment is delayed until the second year of the GR, but in 2009, the catastrophic decline in employment begins and is stronger for Latino immigrants than for natives.

The effects of the GR on Latino immigrants have two main features in both countries. They have affected more immigrant men than immigrant women, and for this reason we can talk about a "Latino man-cession", and have particularly affected youth and young adults (younger than age 45). On the contrary, the effects of the

GR have been different by education level in both countries. In Spain, it has more negatively affected those with lower education, but this has not been the case in the US.

The collapse of the construction sector has been a key factor in explaining the acute impact of the GR on Latino immigrant employment. Relative loss of jobs in this sector is four times higher than the relative loss of jobs in the labor market. Conversely, agriculture serves as a "shelter sector" for Latino immigrants countries in the initial phase of the crisis.

After analyzing the evolution of employment during the Great Recession for Latino immigrants in relation to natives in the US and Spain, we conclude that the GR indeed has large, negative impacts on employment for this population. In general, we can say that the effects varied by education level, gender, and sector, and that Latino immigrant employment as of this writing has experienced a reconfiguration in the US, but is declining without sign of recovery as return migration is underway in the case of Spain.

References

Andrews, D., Caldera, A., & Johansson, A. (2011). *Towards a better understanding of the informal economy*. Paris: OECD Economics Department Working Papers No. 873.

Aslund, O., & Rooth, D. O. (2007). Do when and where matter? Initial labour market conditions and immigrant earnings. *The Economic Journal, 117*, 422–448.

Awad, I. (2009). *The global economic crisis and migrant workers: Impact and response*. Geneva: ILO.

Aysa-Lastra, M., & Cachón, L. (2012). Latino immigrant employment during the great recession: A comparison between the United States and Spain. *Norteamerica, 7*(2), 7–45.

Aysa-Lastra, M., & Cachón, L. (2013a). Segmented occupational mobility: The case of non-EU immigrants in Spain. *Revista Espapola de Investigaciones Sociológicas, 144*, 23–47.

Aysa-Lastra, M., & Cachón, L. (2013b). Determinantes de la movilidad ocupacional segmentada de los inmigrantes no comunitarios en Espapa. *Revista Internacional de Sociología, 71*(2), 383–413.

Borjas, G. (1985). Assimilation, changes in cohort quality, and the earnings of immigrants. *Journal of Labor Economics, 3*(4), 463–489.

Borjas, G. (1995). Assimilation and changes in cohort quality revisited: What happened to immigrant earnings in the 1980s? *Journal of Labor Economics, 13*(2), 201–245.

Bosh, M., & Farre, L. (2013). Immigration and the informal labor market. Institute for the Study of Labor (IZA) discussion paper no. 7843.

BLS (Bureau of Labor Statistics). (2006). *Design and Methodology. Current Population Survey* (Technical Paper 66). Washington, DC: US Department of Labor.

Cachón, L. (1997). Segregación sectorial de los inmigrantes en el mercado de trabajo en Espapa. *Cuadernos de Relaciones Laborales, 10*, 49–74.

Cachón, L. (2002). La formación de la 'Espapa inmigrante': mercado y ciudadanía. *Revista Espapola de Investigaciones Sociológicas, 97*, 95–126.

Cachón, L. (2009). *La "Espapa inmigrante": marco discriminatorio, mercado de trabajo y políticas de integración*. Barcelona: Anthropos.

Cachón, L. (2014). La inmigración en Espapa tras el fin de 'El Dorado'. In G. Moreno (Coord.), *Anuario de la inmigración en el País Vasco 2013* (pp. 545–553). Bilbao: Universidad del País Vasco.

Castles, S., & Miller, M. J. (2009). *The age of migration: International population movements in the modern world*. Basingstoke: Palgrave-Macmillan.

Cebula, R., & Feige E. L. (2011). America's underground economy: Measuring the size, growth and determinants of income tax evasion in the US. Social Systems Research Institute Working Paper Series, University of Wisconsin-Madison.http://www.ssc.wisc.edu/econ/archive/wp2011-1.pdf. Accessed 30 Sept 2014.

Chiswick, B. R. (1999). Immigration policy and immigrant quality. Are immigrants favorably self-selected?*American Economic Review, 89*(2), 181–185.

Chiswick, B. R., Cohen, Y., & Zach, T. (1997). The labor market status of immigrants: Effects of the unemployment rate at arrival and duration of residence. *Industrial and Labor Relations Review, 50*(2), 289–303.

Constant, A., & Massey, D. S. (2003). Self-selection, earnings, and out-migration: A longitudinal study of immigrants to Germany. *Journal of Population Economics, 16*, 631–653.

Danziger, S. (2013). Evaluating the effects of the great recession. *The ANNALS of the American Academy of Political and Social Science, 650*, 6–24.

Donato, K. M., & Bankston, C. L. (2008). The origins of employer demand for immigrants in a new destination: The salience of soft skills in a volatile economy. In D. S. Massey (Ed.), *New faces in new places: The changing geography of American immigration* (pp. 99–123). New York: Russell Sage Foundation.

Elwell, C. K. (2013). Economic recovery: Sustaining US economic growth in a post-crisis economy. Congressional Research Service Report R41332

Enchautegui, M. E. (2012). *Hit hard but bouncing back: The employment of immigrants during the great recession and recovery*. Washington, DC: Urban Institute.

Esping-Andersen, G. (1990). *The three worlds of welfare capitalism*. London: Polity Press.

European Commission. (2011). *Employment in Europe 2010*. Brussels: European Commission.

Frank, R., Akresh, I., & Lu, B. (2010). Latino immigrants and the US racial order: How and where do they fit in? *American Sociological Review, 75*(3), 378–401.

Freeman, R. B. (2008). *America works: Critical thoughts on the exceptional US labor market*. New York: Russell Sage Foundation.

Freeman, R. B. (2013). Failing the test? The flexible US job market in the great recession. *The ANNALS of the American Academy of Political and Social Science, 650*, 78–97.

Fussell, E. (2011). The deportation threat dynamic and victimization of Latino migrants: Wage theft and robbery. *The Sociological Quarterly, 52*(4), 593–615.

Granovetter, M. (1974). *Getting a job: A study of contacts and careers*. Cambridge, MA: Harvard University Press.

Greenstone, M., & Looney, A. (2013). Shrinking job opportunities: The challenge of putting Americans back to work. The Hamilton Project. http://www.hamiltonproject.org/papers/shrinking_job_opportunities/. Accessed 28 Nov 2013.

Gwartney, J., Lawson, R., & Hall, J. (2013). *Economic freedom of the world annual report 2013*. Vancouver: Fraser Institute.

Higley, J., Nieuwenhuysen, J., & Neerup, S. (Eds.). (2011). *Immigration and the financial crisis: The United States and Australia compared*. Northampton: Edward Elgar.

Holmlund, B., & Storrie, D. (2002). Temporary work in turbulent times: The Swedish experience. *The Economic Journal, 112*, F245–F269.

Hout, M., Levanon, A., & Cumbreworth, E. (2011). Job loss and unemployment. In D. B. Grusky, B. Wertern, & C. Wimer (Eds.), *The great recession* (pp. 59–81). New York: Russell Sage Foundation.

INE (Instituto Nacional de Estadística). (2008). *Encuesta de Población Activa Metodología 2005*. Madrid: INE.

Kalleberg, A. L. (2011). *Goob jobs, bad jobs. The rise of polarized and precarious employment systems in the United States, 1970s to 2000s*. New York: Russell Sage Foundation.

Kochhar, R. (2008). *Latino labor report, 2008: Construction reverses job growth for Latinos.* Washington, DC: Pew Hispanic Center. http://pewhispanic.org/files/reports/88.pdf. Accessed 10 Dec 2013.

Krogstad, J. M., & Lopez, M. H. (2014). *Hispanic immigrants more likely to lack health insurance than U.S.-born.* Washington, DC: Pew Hispanic Center.

Massey, D. S. (2012). *Immigration and the great recession.* Stanford: Stanford Center on Poverty and Inequality.

Menjívar, C., & Kanstroom, D. (Eds.). (2014). *Constructing immigrant "illegality": Critiques, experiences, and responses.* New York: Cambridge University Press.

OECD. (2004). *Employment outlook 2004.* Paris: OECD.

OECD. (2009). *International migration outlook SOPEMI 2009.* Paris: OECD.

OECD. (2008). *Employment outlook 2008.* Paris: OECD.

OECD. (2013). *Employment outlook 2013.* Paris: OECD.

Orrenius, P. M., & Zavodny, M. (2009). *Tied to the business cycle: How immigrants fare in good and bad economic times.* Washington, DC: Migration Policy Institute.

Orrenius, P. M., & Zavodny, M. (2010). Mexican immigrant employment outcomes over the business cycle. *American Economic Review, 100*(2), 316–320.

Papademetriou, D. G., & Terrazas, A. (2009). *Immigrants and the current financial crisis: Research evidence, policy challenges, and implications.* Washington, DC: Migration Policy Institute.

Papademetriou, D. G., Sumption, M., & Terrazas, A. (2010). *Migration and immigrants two years after the financial collapse: Where do we stand?* Washington, DC: Migration Policy Institute.

Portes, A. (1998). Social capital: Its origins and applications in modern sociology. *Annual Review of Sociology, 24*, 1–24.

Rampell, C. (2012). Hiring picks up in July, but data gives no clear signal. *The New York Times,* August 3. http://www.nytimes.com/2012/08/04/business/economy/us-added-163000-jobs-in-julyjobless-rate-ticked-up.html. Accessed 25 Apr 2013.

Reyneri, E. (1998). Immigrazione ed economia sommersa. *Stato e Mercato, 53*, 287–313.

Reyneri, E., & Fullin, G. (2011). Labour market penalties of new immigrants in new and old receiving West European countries. *International Migration, 49*(1), 32–57.

Rogers, A. (2009). *Recession, vulnerable workers and immigration: Background report.* Oxford: COMPASS.

Rosenfeld, J., & Kleykamp, M. (2009). Hispanics and organized labor in the United States, 1973 to 2007. *American Sociological Review, 74*, 916–937.

Rothstein, J. (2012). The labor market four years into the crisis: Assessing structural explanations. *Industrial and Labor Relations Review, 65*(3), 467–500.

Sisk, B., & Donato, K. M. (2013). *Weathering the storm? Employment transitions of the low-skill Mexican immigrants 2005–2011.* Unpublished manuscript.

Tapinos, G. (1999). Illegal immigrants and the labour market. *OECD Observer, 219.* http://www.eacdobserver.org. Accessed 30 Sept 2014.

Tilly, C. (2011). The impact of the economic crisis on international migration: A review. *Work, Employment and Society, 25*(4), 675–692.

Toossi, M. (2002, May). A century of change: The U.S. labor force 1950–2050. *Monthly Labor Review, 125*, 15–28.

TUC (Trade Union Confederation). (2008). *Hard work, hidden lives. The full report of the commission on vulnerable employment.* London: TUC.

Waldinger, R. (1997). Black/immigrant competition re-assessed: New evidence from Los Angeles. *Sociological Perspectives, 40*(3), 365–386.

Van Hook, J., & Bachmeier, J. D. (2013). How well does the American community survey count naturalized citizens? *Demographic Research, 29*(1), 1–32.

Chapter 3
Unemployment and Nonstandard Employment Among Natives and Latinos in the US and Spain

María Aysa-Lastra and Lorenzo Cachón

3.1 Introduction

The Great Recession (GR) left "a large and persistent job gap" (OECD 2013), a persistent high level of unemployment and a significant (and likely durable) deterioration of working conditions for those employed.

As a result of the large decline in employment, the GR qualifies as the longest and deepest recession, and the slowest to show signs of recovery, since the Great Depression. The GR's most significant and persistent effect has been the decimation of employment: the US lost more than 6 % of its jobs between 2007 and 2010. Since then, the data has shown a "slow and anemic" (Freeman 2013) employment recovery. The Spanish case is truly catastrophic because since 2007 the number of jobs has declined by 18 %, and still in 2013, there were no signs of job recovery (see Chap. 2). Only until the second semester of 2014 the data showed a weak and unstable job recovery.

The first consequence of the GR's substantial impact on employment has been the increase of unemployment to very high levels, along with all the social consequences that this has for workers and their families. The long duration of the GR has produced another effect: a considerable increase in long term unemployment which exacerbates the social consequences of a weak labor market. In the US, this was not significant until the GR, but today it is one of the country's most acute problems. In Spain, long term unemployment is a persistent problem that has worsened considerably (OECD 2013; European Commission 2013).

M. Aysa-Lastra (✉)
Department of Sociology and Anthropology, Winthrop University, Rock Hill, SC, USA
e-mail: aysalastram@winthrop.edu

L. Cachón
Departamento de Sociología I, Universidad Complutense de Madrid, Madrid, Spain
e-mail: lcachonr@ucm.es

© Springer International Publishing Switzerland 2015
M. Aysa-Lastra, L. Cachón (eds.), *Immigrant Vulnerability and Resilience*,
International Perspectives on Migration 11, DOI 10.1007/978-3-319-14797-0_3

The high rates of unemployment have been slow to recede in the US. This has led many to conclude that structural changes have occurred in the labor market or that structural impediments have appeared (e.g., labor supply disincentives due to conditional transfers such as unemployment insurance, or geographic immobility due to housing market frictions) which might indicate that the economy will not return to the low rates of unemployment that prevailed in the recent past prior to the GR. However, the evidence does not support these claims. Rothstein argues that "nothing in the data indicates that employers with jobs to fill are having trouble filling them, except perhaps in a few isolated and small submarkets" (2012: 496). Neither industrial nor demographic shifts, nor a mismatch of skills and job vacancies, are behind the increased rates of unemployment (Lazear and Spletzer 2012). Labor demand shortfalls continue to be an important feature of the labor market and the primary determinant of labor market performance.

But the crisis has not only affected the quantity dimension of unemployment but also a quality dimension of employment. For labor market researchers, job quality is a fundamental concern (Osterman 2013). It requires looking at the characteristics of the employment: compensation (earnings), substance of work (skills, autonomy, and intensity), the employment contract (temporary or part time employments), unionization, fringe benefits, job tenure, job schedules, etc. There is no standard or agreed definition of quality in work in the academic literature (European Commission 2001). Kalleberg (2011) points out that most people would agree that the job quality depends heavily on economic compensation such as earning and fringe benefits, job security and opportunities for advancement, employees' control over their work activities, employees' feeling that their jobs are interesting, time at work, and employee's control over their work schedules. Not all dimensions of job quality are easy to measure. Therefore, there are no widely accepted synthetic indicators of job desirability (Jencks et al. 1988) or decent work (Ghai 2003). However, we can assume, as in the theories of labor market segmentation, that a variety of job quality aspects covaries such that certain indicators share similar trends over time (Tilly 2011). The erosion of the dimensions of the social contract for workers (wages, pension coverage, job satisfaction) started in the 1980s (Kochan 2013), but it was accentuated during the GR.

The polarization of jobs is not new (Edward et al. 1975), duality between primary and secondary labor markets has increased along with dwindling traditionally middle class jobs. "The labor force has become increasingly polarized into those with more education and marketable skills and those without these human capital attributions" (Kalleberg 2011: 15). In countries where labor market institutions have been inadequate to protect workers' interests (like the US) or where workers' security have more recently been weakened (as in Spain), "the result has been a deterioration in the quality of jobs that did not require a university degree, an increase in the incidence of low-wage work, and a widening of the earning gap between high- and low-paid workers" (Applebaum 2010: 186). By comparing these contrasting cases, it could be said that in the US case these are the results of a liberal market economy; and in the Spanish case, these are the outcomes of a

"Mediterranean institution-driven labor system" (see Chap. 2), heightened by the fiscal conservative policies that have been adopted to counteract the economic crisis.

Workers in the secondary labor market are more vulnerable than others. This labor market segment is where the majority of Latino immigrants are concentrated in the US and Spain. As Sassen (1998) explains, synthetizing previous labor market segmentation theories, a large supply of low-wage jobs in services, construction, and agriculture has attracted a large contingent of economic immigrants, among them Latinos, to both countries. Once this labor force is available, the process has feedback effects because their presence stimulates the development of sectors with low-wage jobs (Piore 1979).

Immigrants in general and Latino immigrants in particular are more vulnerable subjects in the labor market. Given their conditions and position as vulnerable subjects, they develop resilient strategies as a form of resistance within the "field of possibilities" to which they are objectively subjected. Immigrants are more likely to show their resilience in the job market than other workers because migration is an self-selective process (Borjas 1995), their selectivity is one of the key aspects to explain their relative economic success, even if many of them are reproducing positions in the secondary labor market in countries of destination (Aysa-Lastra and Cachón 2013a, b). The motivation that immigrants have to reduce their "job acceptability" threshold is linked to their higher vulnerability which leads to their constant search for jobs, their efforts to have short periods of unemployment, and their willingness to accept precarious jobs, part time jobs, or other forms of underemployment that natives are not willing to accept. Moreover, some employers prefer hiring vulnerable immigrants rather than native workers because immigrants are more flexible, more docile, and they can be subjected to the worst jobs and lowest salaries (Waldinger 1997; Donato and Bankston 2008) (see Chap. 2).

This chapter analyzes how the GR has affected the volume and characteristics of unemployment and working conditions of Latino immigrants and natives in the US and Spain. We provide data on trends indicating deterioration in the relative quality of jobs held by Latino immigrants vs. natives, unemployment trends and probabilities, and long term unemployment trends.

3.2   Methods

To compare Latino immigrants' employment conditions and unemployment trends in the US and Spain, we used data from two national labor force surveys: the Current Population Survey (CPS) for the US and the Economically Active Population Survey (*Encuesta de Población Activa*, EPA) for Spain. In addition to extensive data on employment both surveys collect demographic information on citizenship status and country of birth. This information allows us to know the employment and unemployment status of different populations at different points in time. The CPS in the United States collects information every month on a representative sample of about 60,000 households. The CPS questionnaire includes sociodemographic variables (e.g., education, race and ethnicity, age, etc.) and a long battery of questions on employment characteristics including wages and earnings, union affiliation, and length of stay for the foreign born (BLS 2006). Every 3 months, the EPA collects information on sociodemographic characteristics and labor market conditions (except on wages, affiliation to social security, and unions) on a national, representative sample of about 65,000 households (INE 2008). We selected samples corresponding to the CPS March supplement and to the second trimester (April-June) from EPA for the period 2007–2013.

In order to create comparable groups for our analysis, we divided the population into three categories: natives, naturalized citizens born in Latin America, and immigrants born in Latin America (we do not consider immigrants or naturalized citizens born in other world regions) (see Chap. 2).

In this chapter we describe different trends in job quality indicators such as, real median weekly wages, earnings gap, poverty, part time work, and involuntary part time work, as well as trends in unionization and benefits, and access to pension systems. We then continue our analysis with unemployment trends as well as changes in the estimated adjusted probabilities of unemployment. To estimate the probabilities of unemployment by group, we estimate separate logistic models for each group and included as control variables gender, educational level, age group, and previous occupation.

3.3   The Decline of Job Quality Among Latinos During the GR

The GR accelerated the erosion of job quality that began in the 1980s. Data on a variety of aspects on the quality of the jobs held by Latino immigrants in both countries indicate this trend. We even point out that, although employment began its recovery in the US in 2010, the effects of the GR on job quality are still worsening. Data from CPS and EPA show the following:

1. The real median weekly wages for full time workers in the fiscal year 2012 was 2 % less than in the 2007 fiscal year. This is the most relevant and generalized devaluatory effect of the GR. For natives and immigrants, the loss in purchasing power has been close to 3 %, and in the case of non-Latino naturalized citizens, it has been lower (about 1.5 %). This contrasts with the increase in real wages of Latino naturalized citizens whose salaries have increased by around 5 %.

2. During the GR, the median weekly salary gap—for full time employees—between Latinos and natives remained almost constant: the median weekly salary for Latino immigrants and naturalized citizens was 58 % and 83 % of natives' median weekly salary, respectively. This wage gap is mostly explained by the differences in human capital and the occupations for each group, as well as by discrimination and exclusion against some Latino immigrants. Massey and

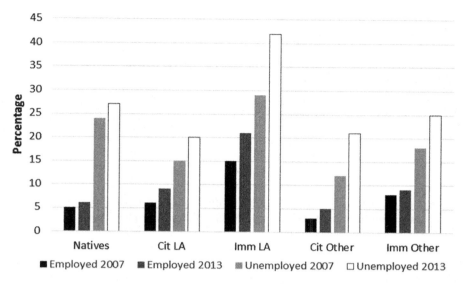

Fig. 3.1 Proportion of population in poverty by group in US (2007 & 2013) (Source: United States: BLS, CPS March)

Gelatt (2010) present evidence of a systematic decline in the returns of human capital for Mexicans and Donato and Sisk (2012) show how earnings of Mexican immigrants have fallen behind those of the US labor market as a whole after the implementation of the Immigration Reform and Control Act (IRCA).

3. Given the aforementioned wage differentials, it is not surprising that the proportion of Latino immigrants in poverty, which was already three times the proportion for natives before the crisis, had notably increased since 2007 (see Fig. 3.1). The proportion of Latino immigrants under the poverty line reached 42 % in 2013.

4. Part time employment for economic reasons increased during the GR in the US, for Latino immigrants: among natives part time employment for economic reasons increased by 98 % between 2007 and 2009; among immigrants this figure was 158 %. Since then, there has been a slow decline in part time employment due to the growth of full time employment. Nonetheless, in 2007 Latinos worked 16 % of part time jobs, a figure that increased to over 20 % in 2013. In 2007, 6 % of those who were employed part time for economic reasons were Latino immigrants. This is twice the rate of natives who were employed part time for economic reasons (3 %). These proportions have increased in 2013, further expanding the gap (11 % vs 6 %). The patterns are very similar in Spain, where in general part time employment is lower than in the US, but has significantly increased its share in total employment over the six years of the GR.

5. The reasons for which workers hold part time jobs despite desiring full time jobs show the unfavorable conditions for Latino immigrants. Forty-five percent of Latinos are in slack work (face a reduction in hours in response to the GR) vs.

21 % of natives; 20 % of Latinos were not able to find a full time job vs. 13 % of natives. In contrast, only 20 % of Latinos reported that they wanted part time job compared to 40 % of natives. Latino naturalized citizens occupy an intermediate position in these indicators. In Spain, 86 % of Latino immigrants (and almost the same proportion of Latino naturalized citizens) had a part time job because they did not find a full time job, as 58 % of natives did. Only 1 % of Latino immigrants, 4 % of Latino naturalized citizens, and 7 % of natives who had part time jobs did not want a full time job. This high level of involuntary part-time employment is an example of the vulnerability of Latino immigrants and, to a lesser extent, of Latino naturalized citizens, but also an indicator of their resilience in the labor market: they work jobs of lower quality or below their expectations.

6. In the US, the proportion of Latino members in labor unions is very different among immigrants and naturalized citizens: the former have membership rates below that of natives, but the later have rates higher than natives. In 2007, the proportion of native labor union members was 13 % and it has been stable at this level during the GR. However, among Latino immigrants it has changed: 8 % were labor union members in 2007, and 5 % in 2009. Since then, it has not recovered to the pre-recession level (Catron 2013). This trend contrasts sharply with unionization rates of Latino naturalized citizens: while in the first 2 years of the GR, their membership was reduced from 19 % in 2007 to 11 % in 2009, in subsequent years, membership has recovered reaching 16 % in 2013 (see Fig. 3.2). This group may represent the contribution of Latinos to the revitalization of US labor unions (Rosenfeld and Kleykamp 2009). Although some key factors for union membership are the substantive effects of positional variables like the characteristics of the job or the firm (Rosenfeld and Kleykamp 2013), the low unionization of Latino immigrants is a reflection and a factor of vulnerability and the unionization of Latino naturalized citizens can be considered an element of their resilience.

7. In the US, only 40 % of employees benefit from participating in a pension plan at work. As in other job quality indicators, Latinos face limitations in their access to a pension system: Only 22 % of Latino immigrant workers have access to a pension plan vs. 55 % of natives (and 42 % of Latino naturalized citizens). These trends were stable during the GR. In Spain, all employees must participate and contribute to the Social Security system, which results in benefits upon retirement and other social benefits (e.g., unemployment insurance). Most employees pay their contributions to Social Security; however, this is not the case among the immigrants. In 2007 only 55 % of Latino immigrants were covered under social security; this figure declined slightly during the first 4 years of the crisis but increased between 2011 and 2013 to reach 65 % coverage for this population.

In the analysis of these data, we have not taken into account the legal status of Latino immigrants. It is a well-studied fact that unauthorized immigrants face acute vulnerability (see Sisk and Donato 2013). At the beginning of the GR, Passel (2006) pointed out that undocumented immigrants accounted for about 5 % of the US labor

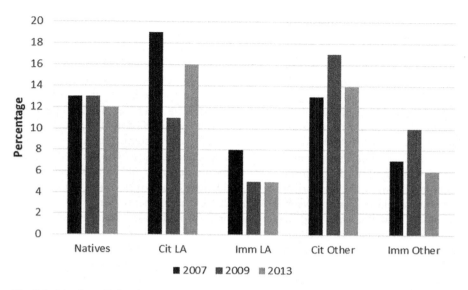

Fig. 3.2 Member of labor union of different groups in US (2007, 2009 & 2013) (Source: United States: BLS, CPS March)

force and about one-third of the foreign-born labor force. Most undocumented immigrants were from Latin American countries, with those from Mexico accounting for about 55 % of the total (Kochhar 2008). The Great Recession produced "the first pause in growth [of the undocumented immigrant population in the US] in approximately a quarter-century" (Massey 2012: 5)—as a consequence of the weakening in labor demand, the number of undocumented immigrant declined until 2010 to 11.3 million. The onset of the slow job market recovery in 2010 produced an increase in temporary immigrant workers (Massey 2012) as well as undocumented immigrants, particularly non-Mexican Latinos. In 2012, there were about 11.7 million undocumented immigrants in the US (Passel et al. 2013). These changes suggested an increase in the diversity of undocumented immigration (Donato and Armenta 2011).

Despite the historical importance of irregular immigration to Southern European countries, such as Spain, the volume of undocumented immigrants has drastically changed during the years of the GR. Although estimates of the number of undocumented immigrants are not available for Spain, as in the case of the US, by applying residual estimation techniques (Jandl 2004) and comparing data of authorized immigrants from immigration statistics with data from the population registry,[1] we can surmise this figure. In spite of all the problems arising from comparing

---

[1] Registration in municipal records does not require any legal status for immigrants and being registered in the administrative municipal records offers significant advantages for undocumented immigrants (e.g. access to education).

these two sources (Cachón 2009), we can state that Spain entered the GR in 2007 with a high volume of undocumented immigrants, about one million, which accounted for 33 % of the immigrant population. In 2013, this figure dropped to about 100,000 undocumented immigrants or only 2 % of total immigrants. A large decline in the undocumented Latino immigrant population is observed between 2007 and 2013. A variety of institutional aspects, as well as the deterioration of the labor market, contributed to this phenomenon. Among them are: (1) the implementation of an extraordinary immigrant regularization in 2005 that resulted in the authorization of 565,000 immigrants; (2) the entry of Eastern European countries into the European Union (particularly Romania in 2007) which allowed for the regularization of all illegal immigrants from these new member states; and (3) the system of individual regularization by residence (*arraigo*) that resulted in about 400,000 regularizations between 2008 and 2013. Among the former group, we must point out that the rapid and acute deterioration of the labor market, especially among Latinos, has produced a significant flow of return migrants to their countries of origin from 2011 onwards. The literature on return migration argues that the first wave of return/circular migrants is composed of those with freedom to travel back and forth across international borders. However, the loss of jobs in the Spanish labor market has been so acute that even those who know they would not be able to return are leaving the country after waiting unsuccessfully for the labor market to recover (see Chaps. 10 and 13).

3.4 Unemployment Trends for Latino Immigrants During the GR

3.4.1 Unemployment Trends

In 2007, the US unemployment rate was 4.7 %—very close to its lowest unemployment rate in the last 30 years (which was 4 % in 2000). In Spain, the unemployment rate was 8.0 %, the lowest it had been in the last 30 years, and closest to the unemployment rate in Germany. Spain was experiencing a labor market close to full employment; its rate of unemployment almost matched the Non-Accelerating Wage Rate of Unemployment (European Commission 2008). Only the young, women, and immigrants had unemployment rates above 10 %. For the first time in Spain's modern history we observed "quasi-ideal conditions" in the labor market coupled with rapidly growing and high immigration.

The economic blackout produced by the GR has dramatically increased unemployment figures (see Table 3.1). Unemployment levels before the GR were different in the US and Spain (4.7 vs 8.0 respectively), but the evolution of unemployment rates in both countries was similar in the period 2007–2010. The rates multiplied by a 2.2 factor in the US (to reach 10.2 % in January 2010) and by 2.5 in Spain (reaching 20.1 in 2010). From 2010 to 2013, the evolution of

Table 3.1 Unemployment rate of Latino American and natives in the US and Spain 2007, 2010, and 2013

	United States				Spain			
	Natives	Latino citizens	Latino immigrants	Total	Natives	Latino citizens	Latino immigrants	Total
2007	4.8	3.0	5.9	4.7	7.3	11.1	11.2	8.0
2010	10.2	9.9	12.9	10.2	18.1	27.2	26.9	20.1
2013	7.8	6.8	9.7	7.8	24.5	34.8	35.3	26.3
Changes in unemployment rate by period								
2007–2010	5.4	6.9	7.0	5.5	10.8	16.1	15.7	12.1
2010–2013	−2.4	−3.1	−3.2	−2.4	6.4	7.6	8.4	6.2
2007–2013	3.1	3.8	3.8	3.1	17.2	23.8	24.1	18.3

Note: Totals for US and Spain include citizens and immigrants from other non-Latin American countries
Source: United States: BLS, CPS (March); Spain: INE, EPA (second quarter); own estimations

unemployment rates in both countries followed opposite patterns: the rate decreased in the US to 7.8 in 2013, and in Spain the rate continued to increase, reaching 26.1 % in 2013. Both countries still had unemployment rates higher than at the beginning of the GR: in the US this rate is 1.7 times higher and in Spain it is 3.3 times higher than in 2007. Spain is the most extreme case of unemployment during this period among OECD countries (Guichard and Rusticelli 2010; European Commission 2013).

Like in most developed countries (Aysa-Lastra and Cachón 2012), Latino immigrants in the US and Spain entered the crisis with unemployment rates significantly higher than natives. In the US, the unemployment rate of Latino immigrants was 0.9 points higher than the rate of the natives, but the rate of the Latino naturalized citizens was 1.8 points lower than the rate for natives. In Spain, the unemployment rate for Latino naturalized citizens and immigrants was 3.8 points higher than the unemployment rate of natives.

Between 2007 and 2010, the unemployment rates for Latino naturalized citizens in the US grew very rapidly and this group lost its advantage over the natives' unemployment rate. The unemployment rate for Latino immigrants grew very fast during the first year of the crisis but afterward it follows the same pattern as the unemployment rate for the native population.

In the US from 2010 to 2013, unemployment rates for the three groups show a similar decreasing pattern. The unemployment rate gaps between Latino immigrants and naturalized citizens relative to natives are larger after the GR. Latino naturalized citizens lost their comparative advantage and Latino immigrants faced increases in their comparative disadvantage.

The growth of unemployment from 2007 to 2009 in Spain is dramatic (between 140 % and 150 %). From 2010 to 2013, unemployment rates continued increasing

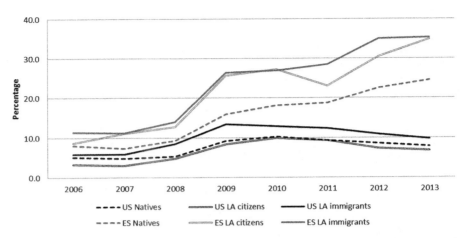

Fig. 3.3 Unemployment rates for Latinos and natives in the US and Spain. 2006–2013 (Source: BPS (CPS) and INE (EPA); own calculations)

but at a slower pace (about 30 % for all groups). Unemployment rate differentials among the groups increased in the first period (2007–2009), but these gaps have slightly decreased in the second period (2009–2010) due to the increasing unemployment of natives (see Fig. 3.3).

In order to explain the patterns of unemployment among Latin American immigrants in Spain, we consider the employment contraction during the first 6 years of the GR, and the dynamics of the economic migration flow. The arrival of Latino immigrants to Spain remained high—although the pace of growth declined—during the early years of the GR (2007–2010). The arrival of new immigrants as the labor market began to contract explains about 64 % of the increase in unemployment among Latino immigrants. This trend started to change in 2012. Data from population registration systems show a significant return migration to Latin American countries, due to high and sustained contraction of the Spanish labor market (see Chap. 13). Return migration then contributes to decreasing unemployment trends among Latino immigrants in Spain (Cachón 2014).

Our analysis of unemployment trends by gender revealed different patterns in the US and in Spain before and after the GR. In the US before the GR males registered higher unemployment rates than women (5.2 vs. 4.2 respectively), while in Spain, and in Europe, the unemployment rate for women was almost double that of males (10.5 vs. 6.1 respectively). After 6 years from the onset of the Great Recession, the gender gap is still observed in the US: the unemployment rate for women is 7.3 %, one point below the unemployment rate for men. In Spain female unemployment rates were 27.1 %, one point above that of males. The gender gap remained stable in the US, while in Spain, the large gap observed before the GR has practically disappeared. In Spain, the pattern results from the historical growth of sectors that require female labor force and the fact that during the GR, the most heavily affected sectors employed a higher proportion of males (see Chap. 4).

Observed trends on unemployment by gender among Latino immigrants show that male employment was most affected during the GR. Latino immigrant women started the crisis with an unemployment rate slightly lower than their male counterparts (5.5 vs. 6.0, respectively) in the US, and with a rate five points higher than males in Spain (13.4 vs. 8.7, respectively). This gap reversed 6 years after the onset of the GR. In 2013, unemployment rates for Latino women were four points higher than for Latino males in the US (12.1 vs. 8.4, respectively). On the contrary, in Spain, female unemployment rates were seven points lower than for males (32.3 vs. 39.2, respectively). In the US, job sectors with a high presence of Latino immigrant male workers have started to grow, but this has not happened yet in Spain, where the loss of employment in sectors with a large presence of male immigrants has been dramatic and uninterrupted as of this writing (March 2014). Unemployment trends among Latino immigrant males shows that the GR can be characterized as a "man-Latino-recession" (see Chap. 2).

Unemployment rates by age groups before the crisis showed a well-known negative association between age and unemployment. The GR has not changed this pattern but we observe a relative growth of unemployment among adult Latino immigrants. The unemployment gap between Latino immigrants and natives show two common patterns in both countries. One, the unemployment gap increases with age: the older the Latino workers, the more likely they are to face unemployment relative to natives of the same age. Two, the unemployment gap widened during the GR. However, there are two significant exceptions: in the US, Latinos (both immigrants and natives) under age 25 have unemployment rates lower than natives; and, Latino naturalized citizens over age 25 have unemployment rates similar to natives.

According to human capital theories, as education rises, the risk of unemployment diminishes. The Spanish case clearly shows this relation. Before and during the GR, we observe that the higher the education level, the lower the unemployment rate. In 2013, the unemployment rate for workers with elementary education was 40 %, for those with high school was 33 %, and for college graduates was 16 %. In the US, we also observe this pattern but only in categories above high school. Workers without high school diplomas have an unemployment rate lower than high school graduates (10 % and 18 % respectively in 2013). This "anomaly" is explained by the composition of this group. In 2013, Latino immigrants accounted for 77 % of the working population with elementary education. The resilience strategies with which Latino immigrants counterbalance their vulnerability force them to accept low quality jobs rather than being unemployed. Other recent studies have also found a lower probability of unemployment for low-skilled Mexican immigrants relative to natives (Sisk and Donato 2013). The educational gap in unemployment widened in the first stage of the GR (until 2010), but it slightly decreased due to the relative increase of unemployment (or absolute increase in the case of Spain) for those holding college degrees, for whom the college employment risk premium has declined (see Chap. 5). We observe these trends for all groups in both countries.

Beyond the explanations provided by human capital theories, several studies have shown that racial and ethnic groups are differently affected by unemployment, controlling for educational level. Latino immigrants and naturalized citizens with low education, had lower unemployment rates than natives in 2007 but higher after the GR. Before the crisis, immigrants with elementary education held jobs with low wages—wages and jobs that natives were not willing to accept. But during the GR, the number of low wage jobs diminished and the competition for these low quality jobs increased, resulting in a higher unemployment rate for Latinos even at this educational level.

We observe differences on the patterns of unemployment for Latino immigrants in both countries. In Spain, Latino immigrants as well as Latino naturalized citizens have higher unemployment rates than natives at all educational levels, before and during the GR. In the US, natives with elementary education have higher unemployment rates than Latinos before the GR but lower rates during the crisis (there is a high proportion of African American among the natives with elementary education); native high school graduates or those with some college have higher unemployment rates than Latino immigrants before and during the recession. Among college graduates, Latino immigrants and citizens have higher rates than natives before and during the recession. These patterns suggest declining returns on education for Latino immigrants, a factor corroborated in other studies since the late 1980s (Donato and Massey 1993; Donato and Sisk 2012).

3.4.2   Unemployment Probabilities

Our analysis of unemployment trends during the GR shows that there are large variations across groups and by sociodemographic characteristics. We calculated probabilities of unemployment for Latino immigrants, Latino citizens and natives during the periods 2007–2008, 2009–2010, and 2011–2013 in both countries. We estimated 18 logistic regression models on the probability of unemployment for each group, country and period, controlling for age, sex, level of education and sector of previous employment.

Our estimations shown in Table 3.2 indicate that in the first period there are no statistically significant differences in the probability of unemployment among Latino immigrants, Latino citizens and natives in the US net of the aforementioned controls. However, we find statistically significant differences across groups in the 2008–2009 and 2010–2013 periods. During and after the recession Latino immigrants had lower probabilities of unemployment than natives and Latino citizens.

In Spain we observe increasing probabilities of unemployment over time for all groups. This outcome is expected, Spain (along with Greece) experience the largest increase of unemployment of any OECD country during the GR. Over the period 2007–2013, the disadvantaged condition of Latinos—as they have higher

Table 3.2 Unemployment probabilities[a]

	2007–2008			2009–2010			2011, 2012, & 2013		
	Mean	95 % CI		Mean	95 % CI		Mean	95 % CI	
		Lower bound	Upper bound		Lower bound	Upper bound		Lower bound	Upper bound
United States									
Natives	0.0666	0.0617	0.0716	0.1584	0.1505	0.1663	0.1260	0.1199	0.1320
Cit LA	0.0621	0.0383	0.0859	0.1631	0.1259	0.2003	0.1116	0.0852	0.1380
Imm LA	0.0708	0.0546	0.0870	0.1263	0.1045	0.1480	0.0861	0.0709	0.1013
Spain									
Natives	0.0432	0.0392	0.0473	0.1274	0.1193	0.1355	0.1529	0.1449	0.1608
Cit LA	0.0803	0.0274	0.1332	0.3101	0.1867	0.4336	0.2590	0.1737	0.3444
Imm LA	0.1221	0.0849	0.1593	0.2878	0.2297	0.3460	0.3397	0.2736	0.4059

Source: Own estimations based on BLS (CPS) for US and INE (EPA) for Spain

[a]Reference category: male, age 25–44, with some college education and with work experience in trade. Definitions for control variables are shown on Tables 2.1 and 2.3 in Chap. 2

probabilities of unemployment—worsened as the unemployment gap between natives and immigrants increased.

The conditions in Spain show the increasing vulnerability of Latinos and the process of exclusion they faced, as the unemployment gap between Latinos and natives increased regardless of their citizenship status during a long period of very high unemployment. The data from the US at the end of the GR show the resilience of Latinos in the labor market, and the resilience of Latino immigrants in particular. Latino immigrants responded to their vulnerability by working in nonstandard jobs that allowed them to face the increasing competition in the labor market, but that placed them in worse conditions of employment. In addition, the presence of a large undocumented immigrant population might explain this increased acceptability of low quality jobs. In Spain, the conditions of a depressed and rigid labor market did not allow Latino immigrants access even to low quality jobs.

3.4.3   Long Term Unemployment

Traditionally, the big difference between unemployment in the United States and in other advanced countries was that the United States had a much lower incidence of long-term unemployment (LTU; i.e., a situation in which persons without a job have been continuously looking for employment in the last 12 months). Underlying this low incidence of LTU are exceptionally high rates of transition from unemployment to employment and from employment to unemployment in the US (Freeman 2013). The American experience with LTU changes dramatically during the GR (see Fig. 3.4). In 2008 less than 6 % of the unemployed had been looking for a job for more than 1 year. However, since 2008 LTU increased rapidly and reach 24 % in 2011. Although some scholars have argued that this is a convergence to the typical European experience, the average LTU rate in the European Union was 42 % in 2011. Although Spain had reduced LTU's share of unemployment at the beginning of the GR to "only" 28 % in 2007, by 2013 it was 60 %. The core elements responsible for the LTU trend in Spain are persistent aggregate demand shocks and institutional factors. The former seems to explain a larger part of the increase in the LTU rate during the GR (European Commission 2013). As shown in Fig. 3.4, although there is an increase in LTU in the US, in Spain it is three times higher in 2013.

At the start of the GR in the US, only 3 % of Latino immigrants, 4 % of Latino naturalized citizens, and 6 % of natives were long-term unemployed. In Spain, these figures were more than double for all groups (14 %, 12 %, and 26 %, respectively). The data shows that the proportion of Latinos immigrants in long-term unemployment was lower by about 50 % relative to natives. The low proportion of Latinos in long-term unemployment is an indicator of their resilience against unemployment, even in the Spanish context. Nonetheless, the GR has changed this pattern as it has accentuated the incidence of LTU among low-skilled workers and construction sector workers (European Commission 2013). It is not surprising that the proportion

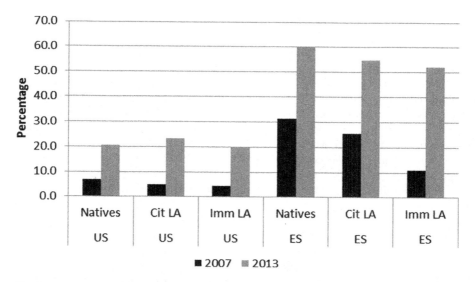

Fig. 3.4 Distribution of the population in long term unemployment for Latino immigrants, Latino naturalized citizens, and natives in the US and Spain (2007, 2013) (Source: BPS (CPS) and INE (EPA); own calculations)

of LTU among Latinos multiplied during the GR. In 2013 the LTU for Latinos is similar to natives in the US (about 20 %) and in Spain is (about 60 %).

3.5 Conclusions

The vulnerability of Latino American immigrants during the GR is reflected in their unemployment rates and in the deterioration of their working conditions. Both countries started the recession at very different levels of unemployment but Latino unemployment rates were higher than that of natives (with a small gap in the US but a larger gap in Spain). Between 2007 and 2010 general unemployment rates have more than doubled both in Spain and the US and reached 10 % and 20 % respectively in 2010. Since then, unemployment has slowly decreased in the US to 7.8 % in 2013. However, unemployment in Spain is still growing (26 % in 2013). The unemployment rate for Latino immigrants reached 9.7 % in the US in 2013 and 35.3 % in Spain. During the GR, the disadvantages for Latino immigrants widened as the unemployment gap between Latin American immigrants and natives increased (Aysa-Lastra and Cachón 2012). However, during the last years of the crisis, there is a slight decrease in the unemployment gap resulting from the relative increases of unemployment among natives in the US; moreover, in Spain there is a radical change produced by migration flows—from positive net migration flows until 2010 to negative net migration flows starting in 2012. This is evidenced by the large return migration flow of Latinos to their countries of origin. Many of them were unemployed before their return (see Chap. 13).

The GR changed the unemployment gap by gender among Latinos. At the start of the crisis, Latino immigrant women had unemployment rates slightly lower than their male counterparts in the US, and five points higher in the case of Spain. The GR reverses this pattern. In 2013 unemployment rates for Latino women in the US were higher than for Latino males; and in Spain, Latino female unemployment rates were lower than for Latino males. These changing patterns show the increasing participation of Latino women in the US workforce and the impact of severe employment loss in the construction sector on the Latino male unemployment rate in Spain.

The tenet that higher educational level leads to lower unemployment is true in Spain, both before and during the recession. In the US, this is true only for workers in education-level categories above high school. In the US workers without high school diplomas have lower unemployment rates than those with higher education. The strong presence of Latino immigrants, and their resilience, among those without high school diplomas (about 77 % of the total population in this educational category) explains the lower rate of unemployment. Latino immigrants respond to the conditions that increased their vulnerability (e.g., unemployment) by holding low quality jobs rather than not having any job.

The estimated probabilities of unemployment suggest a somewhat different perspective for both countries. In Spain, where unemployment reached very high levels, both natives and Latino immigrants saw increases in the likelihood of losing their jobs since 2007. In particular, Latino immigrants had higher probabilities of unemployment during the periods considered in the analysis. In the US, the data suggest a different pattern. In 2009–2010, only Latino immigrants had lower probabilities of unemployment than natives, and in the period 2011–2013, Latino immigrants and naturalized citizens had lower probabilities of unemployment than natives. The conditions in Spain show the increased vulnerability of Latinos in a long and deep employment crisis. However, data from the US indicate that at the end of the GR, Latinos exercise their resilient strategies in the labor market.

Latino resilience to unemployment is also shown by the lower proportion of LTU for Latinos vs. natives before and after the GR in both countries. But, after 6 years of the GR, the proportion of Latinos in LTU has almost equaled that of natives. The causes lie in the large and lasting impact that the GR has had on low-skilled workers and those who have previously worked in the construction industry.

However, the effects of the GR result not only in increased unemployment and LTU, but on worsening working conditions. Some of the data shown in this chapter describe deterioration in job quality for Latinos in the US and their disadvantages in the labor market. These conditions were present before the GR, but the crisis has exacerbated some of them significantly. Some of these disadvantages are: (1) Latino real median weekly wages of full time employment in the tax year 2012 decreased by 1.52 % compared to 2007 (a decline similar to natives). (2) The gap of median weekly wages for full time employment between Latinos and natives remains practically constant in this period: the median wages of Latino immigrants is 58 % of natives' median wages, and the median wage of Latino naturalized citizens is 83 % of natives' median wages. This gap is largely explained by education and occupational differences. (3) The poverty rate for Latinos before the crisis was three times that of natives, and it has increased since 2007. In 2013, 21 % of employed Latino immigrants, and 42 % of unemployed Latino immigrants, were living below the poverty line. (4) Part-time employment for economic reasons increased in the GR especially among Latinos, who accounted for 20 % of all these jobs in 2013. (5) A larger proportion of Latinos compared to natives work part-time despite wanting a job full time job. (6) The proportion of Latino members in labor unions varies depending on citizenship status. Immigrants have lower unionization rates than natives but Latino naturalized citizens have higher unionization rates than natives. Although the crisis has reduced the level of unionization, immigrants have not recovered to their pre-crisis levels, but Latino naturalized citizens did recover.

As Osterman (2013), Kalleberg (2011) and Kochan (2013) have argued the US and Spain need new approaches to address the effects of the GR. There is a need for policies that promote a new social contract to support the creation of quality jobs to escape from the unemployment trap, and especially from devastating long term unemployment. The growth of the latter has been one of the distinctive features of the GR, and the risk remains that its mark will persist over time. Gangl (2006) showed that the unemployed, especially those just starting their careers, bear a "scar of unemployment" that will last for many years. Both the US and Spain need social and labor policies to help combat inequality and inequality affecting Latino immigrants in particular. It is not only a matter of social justice but also of economic efficiency.

From a labor market perspective it is necessary that the US passes a comprehensive immigration reform and that Spain stabilizes the immigration management instruments approved in 2004. Changes in immigration policies and programs will facilitate the economic and social integration of Latino immigrants in both countries.

References

Applebaum, E. (2010). Institutions, firms, and the quality of jobs in low-wage labor markets. In J. Gautié & J. Schmitt (Eds.), *Low-wage work in the wealthy world* (pp. 185–210). New York: Russell Sage.

Aysa-Lastra, M., & Cachón, L. (2012). Latino immigrant employment during the great recession: A comparison between the United States and Spain. *Norteamérica, 7*(2), 7–45.

Aysa-Lastra, M., & Cachón, L. (2013a). Segmented occupational mobility: The case of non-EU immigrants in Spain. *Revista Española de Investigaciones Sociológicas, 144*, 23–47.

Aysa-Lastra, M., & Cachón, L. (2013b). Determinantes de la movilidad ocupacional segmentada de los inmigrantes no comunitarios en España. *Revista Internacional de Sociología, 71*(2), 383–413.

Borjas, G. (1995). Assimilation and changes in cohort quality revisited: What happened to immigrant earnings in the 1980s? *Journal of Labor Economics, 13*(2), 201–245.

BLS (Bureau of Labor Statistics). (2006). *Design and methodology. Current population survey* (Technical Paper 66). Washington DC: US Department of Labor.

Cachón, L. (2009). *La "España inmigrante": Marco discriminatorio, mercado de trabajo y políticas de integración.* Barcelona: Anthropos.

Cachón, L. (2014). La inmigración en España tras el fin de 'El Dorado'. In G. Moreno (Ed.), *Anuario de la inmigración en el País Vasco* (pp. 545–553). Bilbao: Universidad del País Vasco.

Catron, P. (2013). Immigration unionization through the great recession. *American Sociological Review, 78*(2), 315–332.

Donato, K. M., & Armenta, A. (2011). What we know about unauthorized migration. *Annual Review of Sociology, 37*, 529–543.

Donato, K. M., & Bankston, C. L. (2008). The origins of employer demand for immigrants in a new destination: The salience of soft skills in a volatile economy. In D. S. Massey (Ed.), *New faces in new places: The changing geography of American immigration* (pp. 99–123). New York: Russell Sage.

Donato, K. M., & Massey, D. S. (1993). Effect of the immigration reform and control act on the wages of Mexican migrants. *Social Science Quarterly, 74*(3), 523–541.

Donato, K. M., & Sisk, B. (2012). Shifts in the employment outcomes among Mexican migrants to the United States, 1976–2009. *Research in Social Stratification and Mobility, 30*(1), 63–77.

Edward, R., Reich, M., & Gordon, D. M. (1975). *Labor market segmentation.* Lexington: D.C. Heath.

European Commission. (2001). *Communication on Employment and social policies: A framework for investing in quality, COM 2001, 313.* Brussels: European Commission.

European Commission. (2008). *Employment in Europe 2008.* Brussels: European Commission.

European Commission. (2013). *Employment in Europe 2012.* Brussels: European Commission.

Freeman, R. B. (2013). Failing the test? The flexible US job market in the great recession. *The ANNALS of the American Academy of Political and Social Science, 650*, 78–97.

Gangl, M. (2006). Scar effects of unemployment: An assessment of institutional complementarities. *American Sociological Review, 71*, 986–1013.

Ghai, D. (2003). Decent work: Concept and indicators. *International Labour Review, 142*(2), 113–145.

Guichard, S., & Rusticelli, E. (2010). *Assessing the impact of the financial crisis on structural unemployment in OECD countries.* OECD economics department working papers, N° 767. Paris: OECD.

INE (Instituto Nacional de Estadística), (2008). *Encuesta de Población Activa Metodología 2005.* Madrid: INE.

Jandl, M. (2004). The estimation of illegal migration in Europe. *Migration Studies, 41*(153), 141–155.

Jencks, C., Perman, L., & Rainwater, L. (1988). What is a good job? A new measure of labor-market success. *American Journal of Sociology, 93*(6), 1322–1357.

Kalleberg, A. L. (2011). *Good jobs, bad jobs. The rise of polarized and precarious employment systems in the United States, 1970s to 2000s.* New York: Russell Sage.

Kochan, T. (2013). The American jobs crisis and its implication for the future of employment policy: A call for a new jobs compact. *Industrial and Labor Relations Review, 66*(2), 291–314.

Kochhar, R. (2008). *Latino labor report 2008: Construction reverses job growth for Latinos.* Washington, DC: Pew Hispanic Center. http://pewhispanic.org/files/reports/88.pdf. Accessed 10 Dec 2013.

Lazear, E. P., & Spletzer, J. R. (2012). *The United States labor market: Status Quo or a new normal?* NBER working paper 18386. http://www.nber.org/papers/w18386. Accessed 5 Dec 2013.

Massey, D. S. (2012). *Immigration and the great recession.* Stanford: Stanford Center on Poverty and Inequality.

Massey, D. S., & Gelatt, J. (2010). What happened to the wages of Mexican immigrants? Trends and interpretations. *Latino Studies, 8*(3), 328–354.

OECD. (2013). *Employment Outlook 2013*. Paris: OECD.

Osterman, P. (2013). Introduction to the special issue on job quality: What does it mean and how might we think about it? *Industrial and Labor Relations Review, 66*(4), 739–752.

Passel, J. S. (2006). *Size and characteristics of the unauthorized migrant population in the U.S.* Washington, DC: Pew Hispanic Center. http://www.pewhispanic.org/2006/03/07/size-andcharacteristics-of-the-unauthorized-migrant-population-in-the-us/. Accessed 10 Dec 2013.

Passel, J. S. Cohn, D., & Gonzalez-Barrera, A. (2013). *Population decline of unauthorized immigrants stalls, may have reversed.* Washington, DC: Pew Hispanic Center. http://www.pewhispanic.org/2013/09/23/population-decline-of-unauthorized-immigrants-stallsmay-have-reversed/. Accessed 10 Dec 2013.

Piore, M. (1979). *Birds of passage: Migrant labour and industrial societies.* Cambridge: Cambridge University Press.

Rosenfeld, J., & Kleykamp, M. (2009). Hispanics and organized labor in the United States, 1973 to 2007. *American Sociological Review, 74*, 916–937.

Rosenfeld, J., & Kleykamp, M. (2013). Immigration, organization, and the great recession: Structural change or continuity? *American Sociological Review, 78*, 333–338.

Rothstein, J. (2012). The labor market four years into the crisis: Assessing structural explanations. *Industrial and Labor Relations Review, 65*(3), 467–500.

Sassen, S. (1998). *The globalization and its discontents.* New York: The New Press.

Sisk, B., & Donato, K. M. (2013). *Weathering the storm? Employment transitions of the low-skill Mexican immigrants 2005–2011.* Unpublished manuscript

Tilly, C. (2011). The impact of the economic crisis on international migration: A review. *Work, Employment and Society, 25*(4), 675–692.

Waldinger, R. (1997). Black/immigrant competition re-assessed: New evidence from Los Angeles. *Sociological Perspectives, 40*(3), 365–386.

Chapter 4
Latin American Women During the Great Recession in the US and Spain

Sonia Parella

4.1 Introduction

The economic crisis has caused similar effects among different countries; although certainly, the intensity and the type of impacts depend on the different character-istics of the economic structures and on previous growth trends. Although migrant labour force is highly vulnerable to destruction of employment, research has shown that the effects of the Great Recession on unemployment for migrant workers have been prominent both in United States and in UE, (see Chap. 3). In spite of the "common challenges" that migrants must face on both sides of the Atlantic, we can distinguish different impacts in the two contexts. Apart from the differences related to structural factors given by the contexts of reception (migration policies, the labour market characteristics, etc.), it must be considered that the degree of economic integration available for migrants varies substantially with immigrant workers' education and skill levels, language ability, length of residence and the type of entry route.

Both in Spain and the United States (see Chap. 1), despite all the differences, an important common trend is the fact that the composition of international migration flows by the late twentieth century is extremely diverse regarding national origins, educational level, race, ethnicity and gender. As far as gender differences are concerned, migration itself is a gendered phenomenon and whatever type of migration, the conditions facing women migrants and the implications for their lives are very different from those of their male counterparts (Mahler and Pessar 2006; Ghosh 2009). Over the last decades, there is a consensus of thought among social scientist based on the need to advance in a greater visibility of migrant women and to introduce the gender perspective for a better and more holistic

S. Parella (✉)
Departmento de Sociología, GEDIME/CER-Migracions, Universidad Autónoma de Barcelona, Barcelona, Spain
e-mail: sonia.parella@uab.cat

© Springer International Publishing Switzerland 2015
M. Aysa-Lastra, L. Cachón (eds.), *Immigrant Vulnerability and Resilience*,
International Perspectives on Migration 11, DOI 10.1007/978-3-319-14797-0_4

understanding of international migration issues (Oso and Parella 2012). During the present economic crisis, migrant women have faced multiple challenges in terms of employment and job losses, but also from the growing informalisation of employment, lower wages and the disproportionate and increasing burden of care-responsibilities (Frank and Spehar 2010).

In both countries, the development of immigration flows over time shows growth and increasing national diversity of Latino immigrant population. Unlike the United States, where the flows from Mexico and Central America are predominant; in the Spanish case, there is a pattern of 'latinoamericanization' of flows mainly from Andean countries (Ecuador, Colombia, Bolivia and Perú as the main national origin groups). Latino women have gained increasing prominence in migratory movements in both cases. In comparative terms, in United States these flows consisted at the beginning mainly of men and progressively women have increased their participation. In Spain, by the contrary, Latin American immigration has been predominantly composed by *women* since the early 1990s, when increasing numbers of female migrants, both single and married, have started moving on their own to take up jobs mainly in domestic service (Oso and Parella 2012).

For many immigrant women, crossing a border represents a positive experience, since they can obtain a vital source of income for them and their families – as well as for those left behind. But it is also an opportunity to change oppressive gender relations and to escape from abusive marriage or family relationships due to the influence of a traditional social reproduction model (Arias 2013). In that regard, Sassen (1991) argues that the main cause of the 'feminization of migration' is the development of service-based economies in postindustrial nations that favors the international migration of women laborers. Besides, according to the comparative research coordinated by Sánchez and Serra (2013), Latin American female migration is not a homogeneous phenomenon. They argue that among migrant women there is great variety of profiles, experiences and migratory and settlement processes.

This chapter assesses the effects of the Great Recession on Latin American women in United States and Spain. I have considered the analysis of potential differences by sex and national origin, by adopting an intersectional approach (Crenshaw 1995; Landivar 2012). According to McCall (2005), the intersectional analysis is focused on what she defines as an "intracategorical" approach, which takes into account the differences of experience for subgroups within a category, by considering a unified intersectional core – a single social group, event, or concept.

For the study of the specific case of migrant Latin American women, the adoption of this theoretical approach allows the incorporation of the multiple disadvantages faced by these women in the labor market. This analytical framework serves to identify barriers and improve intervention strategies to minimize their effects (Expósito 2012). Race, class, and gender remain closely intertwined and provoke forms of stratification that need to be studied in relation to each other, using a nonadditive way of understanding social inequality (Choo and Marx 2010). This is what, according to Choo and Marx (2010), different scholars conceptualize as a "matrix of domination" (Collins 1990), "intersectional perspective" (Crenshaw

1995), "integrative approach" (Glenn 1999), or "race-class-gender approach" (Pascale 2007).

This chapter is structured in three main sections. First, a general overview on the effects of Great Recession on immigrant's employment is provided from a gender perspective. Second, I describe in more detail the consequences for Latin American women in both countries, based on an analysis of statistical data using the same classification as defined in Chaps. 2 and 3 to compare women immigrants, as well as research findings on the topic. I conclude with a brief reflexion on the common patterns shared by Latin American women in both contexts, as well as the most important observed differences. Implications for theory and for improving intervention strategies are discussed at the end of the chapter.

4.2 The Effects of Great Recession on Employment in the US and Spain from a Gender Perspective: An Overview

The current crisis has caused a dramatic rise in unemployment in Europe and the US, although the South European countries tended to be affected more severely. According to the comparative analysis by Papademetriou et al. (2010), states such as Greece, Portugal, Spain and Italy – that had a rapidly growing immigrant population prior to recession – particularly Spain, now face devastating increases in their unemployment rates in general, but particularly for immigrant men and for youth. By contrast, female unemployment has increased more slowly, as we will see later. Part of the explanation for this distinctive pattern is that most migrants were mainly concentrated in sectors such as construction, agriculture, hotel and restaurants, domestic service and other services which require low levels of education and specialization (Papademetriou et al. 2010). In each of these sectors, jobs are the lowest paid and have the worst working conditions (OCDE 2009; Reyneri and Fullin 2011; Cachón 2013). That is to say, this tendency was the result of the kind of demand for un-skilled labor that Spain generated prior to the crisis, due to strong growth in low-skilled and labor-intensive sectors.

In the United States, according to Papademetriou et al. (2010: 28), unemployment is more cyclical among immigrants than among natives. But in contrast to many European countries, US immigrant and native unemployment track each other very closely. In spite of this, we must consider that a significant portion of the immigrant population in United States is particularly vulnerable to job losses during economic downturns, due to the concentration in low skilled and the most unprotected sectors. It's important to note the bias of the current US immigration system, which shows a "bimodal distribution" and favors both the admission of well-educated immigrants through legal channels and the entrance of a large number of less-skilled immigrants through informal channels – particularly from Mexico and Central America (Terrazas 2011).

Certainly, contrary to expectations, in Spain there has not been a massive return of migrants to their countries of origin in spite of the dramatic rise in unemployment. Since 2012, although many migrants have adopted a 'wait and see' approach, hoping for improvements in the labor market, the available indicators show a significant increase of return migration to Latin American countries, due to the length and the severity of the crisis in Spain, specially among irregular migrants (Fundación Encuentro 2011; Parella and Petroff 2014). Although in United States there is some evidence of a significant reduction in irregular flows since 2009, mainly from Mexico to United States (Terrazas 2011; Castles 2011); there are predictions pointing to an increase in irregular migration in the medium-term if informal labor markets expand (Koser 2009).

All these effects observed within the context of the current crisis, present certain characteristics, constraints and challenges that are specific to female migrants, as we will see below. Gender plays a crucial role in both countries in defining access to employment, the kind of jobs (sectoral gender segregation) and employment conditions. Data from the Bureau of Labor Statistics (for the case of USA) and from the Active Population Survey (EPA) (for the case of Spain) show that an important feature of the working Latino population in both countries is their gender composition. While males predominate in the US, there are two males for every three Latino immigrants; in Spain, women account for 58 % of the Latino working population in 2012. In spite of this, since 2007 there is an increase in the presence of females among the Latin American workforce in both countries and notably this is partly caused because a number of Latino men have left the workforce or have returned to their countries of origin.

In the case of Spain, three main regulatory elements generate gendered patterns among migrant women. All of these elements operate under the umbrella of the welfare state defined by different scholars as "conservative southern" welfare regime (Kofman 2008) or "implicit familism model" (Leitner 2003). One of the characteristics of the model of South-European countries is the insufficient development of social services for families, while the demand for care is growing due to longstanding low fertility and a resulting rapid population aging. Furthermore, whereas the family exercises the function of the provision of welfare (the state is residual or subsidiary), a new work division between family, market and state emerges and replaces the "family" care model by the "migrant woman to the family" model. The latter operates in an extremely deregulated market (Bettio et al. 2006). Given the diverse needs for family care across European countries, the absolute number and relative relevance of female migrants, and their consequent contribution to host societies, are very different. Labour force participation rates for migrant women tend to be higher in Southern European countries, where migrant women are largely represented among domestic workers (Frank and Spehar 2010).

The available *statistical* data from the National Immigrant Survey for 2007 (Encuesta Nacional de Inmigrantes, ENI-2007) in Spain, one of the first targeted migrant surveys carried out in Europe, show important differences in the occupational trajectories between men and women (Grande et al. 2013). A total of 15,465 individuals were interviewed, all born outside of Spain. Latin American women make up 44.4 % of the sample of women, with Ecuador, Colombia, Argentina, Bolivia and Peru being, in that order, the main countries of origin. By using the same source, Parella et al. (2013) show the marked concentration of surveyed women in unskilled jobs (which include paid domestic work), with the exception of women from Argentina. They analyze the mobility patterns of the workers occupational history, through the comparison between the first and current employment in Spain. They identified that the sector where immigrant women got their first job in Spain becomes a determinant factor of mobility. It was particularly noteworthy that women who worked in the domestic service (together with agriculture) experience less upward mobility than those who describe labor market trajectories from other unskilled sectors (Parella et al. 2013). This influence is even stronger than that of the length of stay in Spain and the legal status. The type of family structure and the number and age of dependent children, undoubtedly condition the amount and intensity of needs derived from domestic and care work. Therefore, these variables condition the availability of time and flexibility that women have when they decide on joining the workforce, what type of job to take and the type of occupations that they will perform. Sallé et al. (2009) found similar results using data from the Active Population Survey (EPA) and Social Security Registration.

In United States, certain immigrant groups, particularly Hispanics, are much more likely to be less educated and, as a result, have suffered disproportionate job losses during the recession, in comparative terms (see Chaps. 3 and 5). Besides, Hispanic immigrants are more likely than other groups to enter without authorization, or without employment-based visas; so their flexibility is a form of resilience due to their increasing vulnerability during the economic cycle ups and downs (Terrazas 2011). The jobs they perform are among the most dangerous, with generally low wages. Besides, these jobs do not often provide health insurance and other benefits for workers or their families (Castañeda and Ruiz 2011). Signs of a slight increase in employment and a decline in unemployment among Hispanic immigrants are visible in United States after 2009. Unfortunately, this situation differs in Spain, where the labor market outcomes of migrants continue to deteriorate not only among immigrants from Latin America countries, but among migrants from elsewhere (OAS 2012) (see Chap. 2).

In the United States, as in the Spanish case, there are growing numbers of foreign women serving as nannies and housekeepers in private households. In both countries, migration from Latin America accounts for the largest share of women employed in domestic work, although a very large share of women domestic workers is most probably still unaccounted for, due to their irregular migration and employment status (Frank and Spehar 2010). In both labor markets, the domestic service sector shows a pattern that has been resilient in terms of destruction of jobs (OAS 2012).

According to Hill-Maher (2004), employers in United Sates prefer *Latina* immigrant women as housekeepers and nannies, due to stereotypical images as a result of the interrelationship between gender, ethnicity and social class. The turn toward foreign women to provide social reproduction labor in private households is strongly related to the growing economic opportunities for middle-class women, with needs that are mainly covered by a global market in line with the proliferation of low-wage services in major cities (Solé and Parella 2005: 250). The State does not provide services aimed at reconciling work and family for its citizens. For this reason, the market emerges as the means of satisfying these needs, through an unregulated market that generates precarious jobs and provokes invisibility and exploitation for immigrant women.

Exploring the US Census 2006, Castañeda and Ruiz (2011) argue that more Mexican immigrant women worked nationally as housekeepers (310,000) than in any other occupation, and that another large percentage were employed as child care providers. In both countries, United States and Spain, there is a great incongruence between the high demand for care workers, on the one hand, and low annual immigration quotas for unskilled workers on the other; which has produced significant cohorts of irregular domestic workers who become vulnerable to abuse and exploitation and, who of course, are at the risk of deportation. Spain has intermittently opened its gates to low-skilled workers, through controversial 'regularization programs' – in 1986, 1991, 1996, 2000–2001 and the last one in 2005 – which offer those migrants who are in a country without authorization the opportunity to legalize their status ('amnesty') (Levinson 2005a, b). The 2005 regularization program has several noteworthy components that favoured domestic workers (31.7 % of the 690,679 applications received), when compared to earlier programs (Arango and Jachimovich 2005; Kostova 2006)[1] But, in the case of United States, in spite of the famous temporary worker programs of the past (e.g. the Bracero Program in the 1940s) and the amnesty contained in the Immigration Reform and Control Act (IRCA) of 1986, it has not recently developed any regularization program for unauthorized migrant care workers present in the country (Michel 2011).

4.3   The Effects of Great Recession on Latin American Women

4.3.1   The Spanish Case

In this section I analyze available data from the Active Population Survey (Encuesta de Poblacion Activa). According to these data, the Great Recession has meant a general reduction of labor force participation rate for all national groups, except for Latina women. Economic activity rate for Latin American immigrant women is nearly 30 points higher than for native women in 2012. Differences

---

[1] Domestic workers employed in more than one home were eligible for regularization, together with 'live-in' domestic workers. In doing so, the government recognized the often clandestine nature of the various types of domestic work (Arango and Jachimovich 2005).

Table 4.1 Employment status of the civilian labor force by sex and nationality (2007 and 2012)[a]

	Participation rate		Employed (thousands)		Unemployment rate	
	2007	2012	2007	2012	2007	2012
Total						
16 years and over	59.0	60.0	20,356.0	17,282.0	8.8	25.8
Men	69.3	67.0	11,987.2	9,432.3	6.7	25.4
Women	49.0	53.4	8,368.8	7,849.7	10.8	26.2
National (Spaniards)						
16 years and over	56.7	57.6	20,356.0	17,282.0	7.9	24.1
Men	67.2	64.7	11,987.2	9,432.3	6.2	23.4
Women	46.6	50.9	8,368.8	7,849.7	10.3	24.8
Foreigners						
16 years and over	75.9	75.1	2,785.1	2,189.2	12.4	36.5
Men	85.2	82.1	1,576.7	1,106.8	11.4	38.2
Women	66.9	68.7	1,208.4	1,082.4	13.7	34.7
Foreigner: Latin American countries						
16 years and over	82.8	82.5	1,346.0	872.9	10.9	28.5
Men	88.7	84.9	661.6	363.6	9.2[b]	31.1[b]
Women	78.0	80.6	684.4	509.3	12.5[b]	26.3[b]

Source: Encuesta de Población Activa (EPA), INE, and Colectivo IOE (2012)
[a]Fourth quarter *EPA data* and author's own calculations
[b]2011, fourth quarter EPA Micro data from Colectivo IOE (2012: 74)

between male and female participation rates have narrowed for all groups, particularly for Latin American immigrants, who have seen how women have reached an activity rate that exceeds the rate of men (by two points) (see Table 4.1). Possible explanations include the mobilization of women's labour market participation due mostly to male unemployment.

The destruction of employment has had a strong impact on male-dominated jobs. In contrast, service sector jobs in which immigrant women predominated (mainly domestic service) were less affected (Maguid and Cerrutti 2012; Colectivo 2012). Certainly, this economic downturn continues to influence the loss of employment between 2007 and 2012. Job losses occurred throughout all groups: 14.8 % of the total population, 21.4 % of the foreign population and 35.1 % of immigrants from Latin American countries. As can be appreciated from the data, gender differences are notorious in all the cases; since the biggest decreases have always occurred among men. Specifically concerning migrants from Latin America, there is a larger loss of employment in absolute terms among men than among women (45 % and 25.6 %) (see Table 4.1). The fact that men are more affected than women by the reduction of employment is clear if we take into account data from the affiliations to the Social Security System. The higher intensity (compared with data from EPA) is due to the fact that Social Security only considers the formal labor market.

In the last two columns of Table 4.1 it is shown that unemployment rates increased for all national groups between 2007 and 2012. Whilst people with Spanish nationality were less likely to be unemployed than immigrants, among foreigners, Latino American were the group who experienced lower levels of unemployment. The unemployment rate increased more for men than women during the period; although in 2012 women continued to have higher employment *rates than men*; except for Latin Americans, for whom men's unemployment exceeds women's unemployment by nearly five points in 2011 (31.1 % vs. 26.3 %, respectively). According to the statistical analysis on EPA data, released by Muñoz Comet (2012), women have more benefits from education than men. Besides, it's important to realize that there is no significant association between the previous labor market experience in Spain and unemployment resilience (Muñoz Comet 2012).

We must consider that since 2008, when the crisis began, the impact of unemployment has become stronger for Latin American immigrants, in comparison to other national origin groups. For example, Moroccans and Romanians had higher unemployment rates before 2007 (Pajares 2009). Among Latin American immigrants, the national groups with higher rates of unemployment are Bolivians, Paraguayans, Hondurans, Brazilians and Nicaraguans. These groups, unlike immigrants from Ecuador, Colombia, Argentina and Peru, all reached Spain in the last few years. The most recent arrival explains their higher incidence among those with irregular status and the fact that they were beneficiaries to a lesser extent of the last *regularization procedure* in Spain, in 2005 (Actis 2009; Esteban 2011).

Since many unemployed people had an occupation before, the rise of unemployment is not connected with an increase of active population, but with loss of *jobs* (Esteban 2011). But for the case of immigrant women from African countries, their high rate of unemployment (55.7 %) has to do with the increasing participation of women in labor force, due to the crisis and the loss of jobs by male household members. That means that the much higher proportion of African women in the working population is certainly one important factor explaining the upward trend in their unemployment rate (Colectivo 2012; Maguid and Cerrutti 2012). Obviously, we must consider gender segregation in labor market in order to interpret the gender gap in unemployment rates (Maguid and Cerrutti 2012).

Regarding the impact of the crisis on wages, data from the Annual Wage Structure Survey (EAES) show three relevant features (see Table 4.2): (1) Spaniards show average annual earnings above the average for immigrants and the gap has widened during the crisis. (2) Non-European migrants, including Latin Americans, earned lower wages before and during the crisis, compared to migrants from Europe. (3) The data indicate that the median annual earnings for Latin American women have grown faster than earnings for Latin American males (14.5 % and 5.7 %), which explains the relatively smaller gender wage gap (see Fig. 4.1).

In sum, as the data have shown, immigrant women, and particularly women from Latin America, have experienced less job losses during the economic downturn of 2007–2012, due to their concentration in labor market segments less *sensitive* to economic fluctuations and to sociodemographic factors associated with unavoidable and long-term needs (aging of population). Nevertheless, it's important to take into account that the degree of employment protection that can be found in female-dominated jobs (such as domestic service) considerably reduces their *power* to *negotiate* employment conditions. In this vein, there is no doubt that the recession

Table 4.2 Real median annual earnings of full-time wage and salary workers by sex and nationality (Euros)

Groups	2007	2011	% change 2011–2007
Total	20,390.3	22,899.3	12.3
Men	22,780.3	25,667.9	12.7
Women	16,943.9	19,767.6	16.7
National (Spaniards)	20,876.8	23,429.4	12.2
Men	23,399.2	26,361.3	12.7
Women	17,292.1	20,166.4	16.6
European Union	17,137.2	17,893.0	4.4
Men	18,556.0	20,160.9	8.6
Women	14,920.2	15,165.3	1.6
Latin American	13,494.3	14,713.4	9.0
Men	15,246.1	16,115.9	5.7
Women	11,403.1	13,059.2	14.5
Rest of the World[a]	14,140.9	14,732.7	4.2
Men	14,918.2	15,640.9	4.8
Women	10,609.8[b]	11,957.4[b]	12.7

Source: Annual wage structure survey (EAES), INE
[a]Data from "Rest of Europe" countries are not included, because the number of respondents is too low
[b]Data from "Rest of the World" are included, because the number of respondents allows for statistical significant estimations of wages

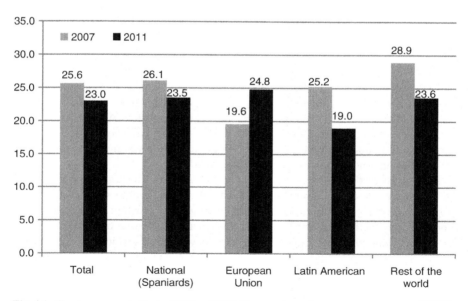

Fig. 4.1 Gender pay gap in Spain, 2007 and 2011 (Source: Annual wage structure survey (EAES), INE and own's calculation)

reports the worsening of labor market conditions for immigrant female workers, concerning wages, working time conditions, social security protection and job instability (Oso and Parella 2012).

In order to further examine the specific legal status of domestic service in Spain, attention must be drawn here to a new regulation to protect workers employed in private households. This regulation was established by Royal Decree 1620/2011 and entered into force on 1 January 2012. Although all these measures have been positive and affected approximately 700,000 workers, most of whom are women, the context of economic crisis has not contributed to substantial improvements regarding their status, terms and working conditions, contrary to what was expected. An exploratory study of Briones et al. (2014) identifies important legal and economic barriers regarding social security coverage of domestic workers under the new Decree. He argues that employers face important difficulties to afford the social security contributions of their domestic employees. Thus in turn, this policy has negative impacts on the possibility of migrant women achieving legal status because they remain in the informal labor market.

Moreover, we must highlight the situation of growing vulnerability to abuse and violence of migrant women engaged as sex workers – both voluntary and forced – because of their illegal and precarious economic status. The economic crisis has reduced both the number of services and their rates. According to Oliveira (2012), due to the fact that migrant sex workers are simultaneously immigrants and sex workers, they are perceived as a threat to social order and a sign of moral disorder. Because of this, they experience processes of rejection, exclusion and stigmatization more significantly than local sex workers, particularly the street-based ones. *At the same time*, they are suffering more *persecution* from the police in public spaces and this fact increases their risk and pushes them to work into the clubs, where conditions are sometimes even worse and where they can lose the power to make decisions about their own labor (Juliano 2012: 534).

Pedone et al. (2012) discuss how job losses, worsening of social security benefits and lack of a coherent housing policy have impacted female migrants and their families. They argue that there is an increasing trend at restricting family oriented migration regulations. Furthermore, due to the crisis, currently there are more practical and financial obstacles to family reunification, given the requirement for sufficient economic resources and housing conditions.

As a result of the crisis and the housing bubble burst of 2008, housing prices started falling and many families, both Spaniards and immigrants, could no longer pay their mortgage. Consequently, banks relying on existing legislation have proceeded to evictions (Spanish mortgage loans are not non-recourse debt). Many immigrants, who planned to return home once they lost their job and their house, are still responsible for debt on a property they no longer own. In such dramatic scenario, Latin American migrants (both low-income and medium-income) have become one of the worst *affected* groups. Many Latin Americans bought a *house* since it was easier in the early 2000s for an *immigrant* to buy than to rent. Latin American immigrants faced both, statistical discrimination and the rigidities of the

Spanish property market. In addition, many of them were not satisfactory informed about the economic risk they assumed (Vizán Rodríguez 2011).

Because of the above mentioned situation, Pedone et al. (2012) identify important changes in migration patterns of Latino American families in Spain produced by Great Recession, including return migration to home countries and reemigration trends to other European cities, as London or Berlin. Certainly, both decisions depend on the economic and social opportunities that family members perceive, on their social resources and migrant networks. Their qualitative research has identified what they have named 'processes of family un-reunification', consistent with a selective and partial return to home country of only some members of the family group (those without employment or even just kids in order to reduce expenses in Spain) (Pedone et al. 2012). As Juliano (2012) indicates, there are situations in which Latin American families decide it is better that women remain in Spain, since she is the only member of the family with a source of income.

In general terms, return migration from Spain has been lower than it was expected. There is a consensus among experts that most of them resist to return due to the precarious and difficult economic conditions in certain home countries (Tobes Portillo 2011). True, the difference in the quality of living standards between Spain and their countries of origin is a determinant factor in their decision to stay or return (see Chap. 10). Even if immigrants have experienced job losses and notorious income reductions, upon return they loose access to social protection (education and health) and potential loss of personal security in some places of origin due to increasing urban and political violence (Tobes Portillo 2011). In spite of this, return migration increased during the period 2007–2012. According to *Residential Variation Statistics* (RVS), estimated from municipal population registers, there were 198,974 immigrant unsubscriptions in 2007 and 320,657 in 2012. For all Latin American groups, the majority of unsubscriptions indicate that more *men than women* were *returning* to their home countries. Such is the case of Bolivia (61.9 % of males), Ecuador (58.2 % of males), Colombia (55.4 % of males) and, to a lesser extent, Argentina (53.5 % of males).

4.3.2 The Case of United States

In this section I analyze available data from the Current Population Survey in order to consider the behavior of Latin American immigrant *women* in the *job* market. According to the Table 4.3, there is a drop in participation rate among men between 2007 and 2012, which is slightly higher for naturalized citizens born in Latin American countries (−4.3 points) compared with the rest of the groups. Immigrant males born in Latin American countries show the highest participation rate, both in 2007 and 2012, despite the declining rates. Even though there was a remarkable increase of unemployment for both men and women between 2007 and 2012, the unemployment rate in the United States is lower than the appalling and widespread joblessness in Spain (see Chap. 2).

Table 4.3 Employment status of the civilian labor force population by sex and immigrant category in the United States, 2007 and 2012

Group	Year	US born citizens	Naturalized citizens born in LA	Immigrants born in LA	Naturalized citizens not born in LA	Immigrants not born in LA
Males						
Employed (thousands)	2007	64,248.7	2,066.3	6,305.1	2,746.7	2,525.7
	2012	61,548.3	2,503.8	5,424.8	3,108.1	2,362.7
Participation rate	2007	71.4	80.1	88.5	73.8	78.1
	2012	68.3	75.8	85.6	72.9	75.7
Unemployment rate	2007	5.3	3.3	6.0	3.1	4.8
	2012	9.2	6.9	10.0	7.3	8.4
Females						
Employed (thousands)	2007	58,823.2	1,862.3	2,937.3	2,452.0	1,911.7
	2012	57,258.7	2,236.8	2,913.3	2,705.7	1,843.3
Participation rate	2007	60.2	59.8	51.4	56.8	54.0
	2012	58.3	60.7	53.7	54.6	52.4
Unemployment rate	2007	4.2	2.6	5.5	2.6	3.8
	2012	7.7	7.7	12.4	6.6	8.5

Source: Current population survey, Bureau of labor statistics and own's calculations

Among Latin American immigrants in United States, the data show that women are less likely to participate in the labor force compared with their male counterpart and with US born women. At the same time, Table 4.3 reveals that Latin American women (both naturalized and immigrants) are the only group to experience slight growth of the participation rate after the recession (between 2007 and 2012), mainly due to the increase of the unemployment. Both, men and women who are immigrants born in Latin America have the highest unemployment rate, especially among women (12.4 in 2012).

Landivar (2012) examines the low participation rate of Latino females and she concludes that it is prevalent even among single-headed female household. This is due to particular cultural barriers to labor market participation – more patriarchal gender orientation; stronger familistic orientations or the difficulty to afford child care (Landivar 2012) – in spite of the evidence of a progressive cultural assimilation between the fertility patterns of Hispanics and non-Hispanics reported by Parrado and Morgan (2008). Besides, research supports the fact that while marriage appears either unrelated or even slightly positively predictive of women's paid employment for non-Hispanic White and for Black women, the effect of marriage is negative among Hispanic women (Flippen 2013) (see Table 4.3).

While the number of employed workers has declined dramatically for immigrants born in Latin America, for their female counterparts the number has reduced only marginally. In the case of men, this is caused by their concentration in agricultural sector and other sectors as construction, maintenance, food preparation and serving, production or transportation. Job opportunities are now scarcer in these sectors and competition from unemployed native-born workers is more intense in United States (OAS 2012). By contrast, Latina women tend to be significantly concentrated in health care and personal services, which have continued to grow despite the current recession (Papademetriou et al. 2010: 34).

The main evidence supporting the effects of the crisis on wages, comes from data on real median weekly earnings of full-time and part-time wage and salary workers by sex and immigrant category (see Table 4.4 and Fig. 4.2). Latin American immigrants in general and naturalized women born in Latin American countries specifically are the groups with the lowest median weekly earnings in 2007 and they maintain their lowest earnings rank during the period. In 2007 the weekly full-time real median earnings for immigrant women born in Latin America was $438 compared to $450 in 2012. As it was the case for Spain and due to their lower earnings, the gender gap among Latin American immigrant is the narrowest.

According to Flippen (2013), one of the most significant effects of the crisis on Latin American immigrant women is their disadvantage associated with their position in the legal system, mainly due to their elevated rate of lack of legal status. Most undocumented immigrants in the U.S. are Latino. Based on the results of her research with Hispanic women in Durham (North Carolina), Flippen (2013) supports the idea that the lack of documentation blocks women's entry into factory and non-niche occupations, where pay is often higher and work more stable, pushing them into childcare. Besides, undocumented women, even net of human capital and other immigration characteristics, and compared with their legal resident

Table 4.4 Real median weekly earnings of salary workers by sex, immigrant category and full or part-time status in the United States, 2007 and 2012[a]

Group		2007				2012			
		Part time		Full time		Part time		Full time	
		Male	Female	Male	Female	Male	Female	Male	Female
US born citizens	Mean	629.55	444.83	1061.16	745.55	590.19	428.83	1084.33	778.11
	Median	363.03	312.76	809.83	595.74	347.38	303.50	835.05	629.63
	SE	14.84	4.57	6.82	4.97	9.97	4.18	8.67	5.99
Naturalized citizens born in LA	Mean	659.62	452.01	873.83	635.78	534.34	468.42	891.96	632.14
	Median	465.42	316.49	651.59	503.03	367.42	317.32	651.34	501.03
	SE	68.19	30.00	35.66	20.90	38.42	43.03	42.19	19.99
Immigrants born in LA	Mean	384.69	275.11	572.32	438.34	419.98	262.80	543.39	449.89
	Median	335.10	223.40	446.80	338.86	283.92	227.49	417.53	347.38
	SE	14.47	8.00	14.73	15.03	35.90	7.09	12.48	13.96
Naturalized citizens not born in LA	Mean	739.72	521.48	1278.70	879.81	666.36	538.74	1138.34	868.77
	Median	474.73	372.34	912.22	651.59	395.81	365.11	835.05	668.04
	SE	63.66	23.35	39.40	36.02	54.40	24.74	34.06	26.85
Immigrants not born in LA	Mean	536.25	476.19	1121.10	766.17	628.05	447.17	1087.40	793.42
	Median	335.10	316.49	819.14	558.50	330.68	267.22	784.95	537.79
	SE	42.83	27.74	36.38	75.77	75.76	33.86	39.07	44.25

Source: Current population survey, Bureau of labor statistics
[a]Data for median weekly earnings has been adjusted for inflation. It is expressed in real dollars for 2006

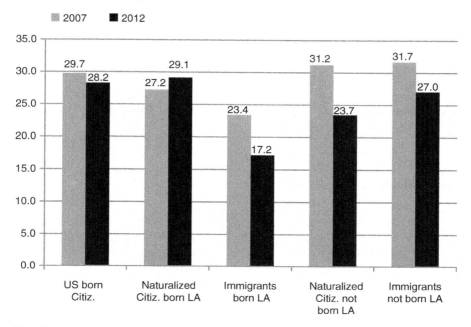

Fig. 4.2 Gender pay gap in United States. Full-time salary workers by immigrant category. 2007 and 2012 (Source: Current population survey, Bureau of labor statistics and own's calculations)

counterparts, tend to work fewer hours per week and to experience greater employment instability.

Contrary to Spanish case, in the United States the crisis has not had the same effect on the voluntary return of migrants as a consequence of unemployment. In the United States, policies and anti-immigrant views have affected undocumented migrants, especially Mexican migrants. The prosecution of illegal entrants has grown exponentially over the past 10 years, together with the number of deportations. In 2002, there were 3,000 prosecutions for illegal entry and 8,000 for illegal reentry; a decade later, in 2012, these prosecutions had increased to 48,000 and 37,000, respectively (Human Rights Watch 2013). Actions to achieve the goal of mass deportation and to create an atmosphere of fear among undocumented migrants have steadily advanced, with the name of 'Attrition Enforcement Policy'. This makes migrants more vulnerable to exploitation and human rights abuses; in *addition* to race, gender, social class and *other* sources of *inequality* (Romero 2008; Montoya and Woo 2011). According to the Human Rights Watch Report (2013), among individuals convicted of immigration offenses in 2012 (illegal entry and reentry), 88 % were Hispanic –most of them Mexican – and the majority of the defendants were men under age 35.

This punitive deportation regime affects far more than just undocumented migrants. It has caused the separation of thousands of migrant families. The separations reveal the human drama of many 'mixed-status families' (Romero

2008) or 'binational families' (Chávez 1992). This term refers to families in which their members have different immigration statuses –some members are US citizens and/or legal residents while others remain undocumented, despite family and marriage ties to the United States. Moreover, the enforcement of immigration laws limits access to work, together with obtaining health care and education services or just to be allowed to walk free on the streets or to drive a car without being arbitrarily detained and deported, regardless of the length of residence in the United States (see Chaps. 6, 8 and 12).

4.4 Conclusion

As previously shown, the effects of the Great Recession differ by gender because employment losses are more prevalent among traditionally male occupations than among female occupations. This pattern is similar for natives and Latino immigrants in both countries. The sinking of employment in construction and related industries has had negative effects on the employment of male immigrants in Spain (Domingo and Recaño 2010) and the US (Engemann and Wall 2010). Accordingly, for both countries, we can call the Great Recession a "man-cession" (Hout et al. 2011). Latin Americans are one of the groups who face lower wages before and during the crisis, both in US and Spain, and for this reason the gender gap for this group tends to be the lowest if compared with natives and immigrants from other regions. In spite of this, it's important to realize that whereas in Spain the *gender gap* in pay has been considerably *reduced for Latin American immigrants, in United States* the gender gap of this group has remained constant between 2007 and 2012.

One conclusion seems unavoidable in terms of gender perspective: gender is intimately bound up with both the impacts of the Great Recession on employment and the job opportunities for migrant women, working in occupations long regarded as paradigmatic "natural" jobs for women (Hondagneu-Sotelo 2011: 805–806). Female migrants are predominantly working in specific service activities – in domestic work and care sectors, as well as in entertainment work – and often under informal employment arrangements. These sectors explain why Latin American immigrant women tend to face non-recognition of credentials, a fact that leads to the devaluation of actual merit and experience, greater chances of being overqualified, lower wages than male migrant workers in similar situations, as well as racial discrimination, and, cultural and systemic barriers to social and legal protection (Ghosh 2009). Moreover, as Ghosh concludes (2009: 25), "irregular immigration status exacerbates the risk of exploitation of women migrant workers who may be more likely to accept very adverse conditions simply for fear of being exposed and possibly deported".

In sum, Latina immigrants experience multiple and interrelated constraints on employment in a highly segregated labor market by gender, ethnicity and nativity (Flippen 2013). The intersectionality theory is useful for understanding Latin

American women's employment patterns. When considering how their particular labor position is constructed, we must focus on intersectional dynamics that interact with preexisting vulnerabilities and with the effects of the Great Recession. First, ethnicity, class, legal status and gender remain closely intertwined and provoke an occupational concentration in the *informal feminized sector*, more vulnerable to exploitation but less affected by the crisis. Secondly, their employment outcomes are also profoundly shaped by family responsibilities and by the type of migratory experience. Thus, according to Flippen (2013), while co-resident children are likely to present demands on Latino women's time, potentially discouraging employment – in a context of strong family values and a traditional division of household labor,[2] non-resident minor children abroad could pose financial demands that encourage women's work. Although neither Spain nor the United States promote work/family conciliation for female workers, Latin American women (primarily from Mexican or Central American communities) in the United States usually migrate after their husbands, and therefore there is a proliferation of Hispanic family households with children born in the United Sates living with two *married* parents. By contrast, Latin American immigration to Spain (mainly from Andean communities) is relatively recent and has occurred in the last decade, with a big outflow of women who have migrated alone as economic migrants, as the result of the labour market's demand for domestic service workers and carers. According to Oso (1998), the existence of this labour niche for female immigrants (essentially live-in) led to the development of feminized migratory flows, and became the principal gateway for female migration to Spain. Since many of these pioneer women in the migratory chain left children in the care of other relatives in their countries of origin, it explains the higher labor market participation of Latin American immigrant females in Spain compared to the United States. Besides, Hispanic immigrant women whose primary language at home is Spanish face language barriers to employment in the US (Tienda and Faith 2006).

Concerning the implications for improving intervention strategies, there are important measures that may be required. First of all, it's necessary to establish legal protection for the rights of women employed in the kind of jobs dominated by women migrant workers – especially for those working in domestic service, regardless of their immigration status (Ghosh 2009). These should be provided with emergency, since these sectors are experiencing worse employment conditions due to economic crisis, also stimulated by the aging of the population in both countries.

Secondly, in the meantime, for the case of Latin American women who have been pioneers in the migratory chain and who left their children in the countries of origin, the destination countries should find ways to consider both ends of the global care chain in order to compensate sending countries for the loss of women's contributions to their families (for instance, when migrant women workers are

---

[2] According to Vega (1995), hispanics are characterized by familism or a strong commitment to family life that is qualitatively distinct from that of non-Hispanic whites.

able to move freely across borders, they can much more easily handle transnational care responsibilities) and to promote permanent residence and family reunification for migrant workers who so wish (Michel 2011). Lastly, for the case of Latin American women with co-resident children, given the growing economic need of their families, the conflict between work and family suggest sustained disadvantage over the course of these women's lives (Flippen 2013). As shown above for the case of United States, childcare is a barrier to work for Latino women with children. With the strong destruction of male employment due to the crisis and the fact that female-headed households are an important target group among the Latino population, the risk of poverty is greater if these women are less likely to work and experience significant family-related labor inactivity.

References

Actis, W. (2009). Inmigrantes de América Latina em Espanha: Uma visao de conjunto. *Revista Migraçoes, 5*, 63–86.

Arango, J., & Jachimovich, M. (2005). *Regularizing immigrant in Spain. A new approach. Migration immigration source.* Washington, DC: Migration Policy Institute. http://www.migrationpolicy.org/article/regularizing-immigrants-spain-new-approach. Accessed 30 Sept 2014.

Arias, P. (2013). El viaje indefinido: la migración femenina en Estados Unidos. In M. J. Sánchez & I. Serra (Eds.), *Ellas se van. Mujeres migrantes en Estados Unidos y España.* México: Instituto de Investigaciones Sociales, UNAM.

Bettio, F., Simonazzi, A., & Villa, P. (2006). Change in care regimes and female migration: The care drain in the Mediterranean. *Journal of European Social Policy, 16*(3), 271–285.

Briones, E., Agudelo, A. A., López, M. J., & Vives, C. (2014). Percepción de las trabajadoras inmigrantes del servicio doméstico sobre los efectos de la regulación del sector en España. *Gaceta sanitaria, 28*, 109–115.

Cachón, L. (2013). Las crisis y su impacto sobre la vulnerabilidad de los inmigrantes en el mercado de trabajo: el caso español. In M. Anguiano & C. Malgesini (Eds.), *Migraciones, crisis internacional y vulnerabilidad social: Perspectivas comparadas* (pp. 73–120). Tijuana (México): El Colegio de la Frontera Norte.

Castañeda, X., & Ruiz, M. (2011). *Caregivers in a binational context: The U.S. – Mexico case. women, migration and the work care in the United States a comparative perspective* (pp. 19–21). Woodrow Wilson Center for International Scholars Press. http://www.wilsoncenter.org/sites/default/files/Women,%20Migration%20and%20the%20Work%20of%20Care.pdf. Accessed 16 Dec 2013.

Castles, S. (2011). Migration, crisis, and the global labour market. *Globalizations, 8*(3), 311–324.

Chávez, L. R. (1992). *Shadowed lives: Undocumented immigrants in American society.* New York: Harcout Brace Jovanovish College Publishers.

Choo, H. Y., & Marx, M. (2010). Practicing intersectionality in sociological research: A critical analysis of inclusions, interactions, and institutions in the study of inequalities. *Sociological Theory, 28*(2), 129–149.

Colectivo, I. O. E. (2012). *Impactos de la crisis sobre la población inmigrante.* Madrid: OIM.

Collins, P. H. (1990). *Black feminist thought: Knowledge, consciousness, and the politics of empowerment.* London: Harper Collins.

Crenshaw, K., et al. (1995). Mapping the margins: Intersectionality, identity polítics and violence against women of color. In K. Crenshaw (Ed.), *Critical race theory. The key writings that formed the movement* (pp. 357–383). New York: The New Press.

Domingo, A., Recaño, J., et al. (2010). La inflexión del ciclo migratorio internacional en España: Impacto y consecuencias demográficas. In E. Aja (Ed.), *La inmigración en tiempos de crisis. Anuario de la Inmigración en España.* Barcelona: Fundació CIDOB.

Encuentro, F. (2011). *Informe España 2011: Una interpretación de su realidad social.* Madrid: Fundación Encuentro.

Engemann, K. M., & Wall, H. J. (2010, January). The effects of recessions across demographic groups. Review, Federal Reserve Bank of St. Louis, 1–26.

Esteban, F. O. (2011). Inmigración extranjera y crisis económica en España. Encrucijadas. *Revista Crítica de Ciencias Sociales, 1*, 51–69.

Expósito, C. (2012). ¿Qué es eso de la interseccionalidad? Aproximación al tratamiento de la diversidad desde la perspectiva de género en España. *Investigaciones Feministas, 3*, 203–222.

Flippen, C. (2013). Intersectionality at work: Determinants of labor supply among immigrant Latinas. *Gender and Society.* doi:10.1177/0891243213504032.

Frank, A. K., & Spehar, A. (2010). *Women's labour migration in the context of globalisation.* Brussels: WIDE. www.wide-network.org. Accessed 16 Dec 2013.

Ghosh, J. (2009). *Migration and gender empowerment: Recent trends and emerging issues* (Vol. 04). Human Development Research Paper (HDRP) Series. http://hdr.undp.org/en/reports/global/hdr2009/papers. Accessed 16 Dec 2013.

Glenn, E. N. (1999). The social construction and institutionalization of gender and race: An integrative framework. In M. M. Ferree et al. (Eds.), *Revisioning gender* (pp. 70–96). New York: Sage.

Grande, R., Del Rey, A., & Fernández, E. (2013). *Movilidad Ocupacional de los Inmigrantes en España: entre la etnoestratificación y la mejora ocupacional.* Communication presented at XI Congreso Español de Sociología, Madrid, 10–12 de Julio de 2013.

Hill-Maher, K. (2004). 'Natural Mothers' for sale: The construction of Latina immigrant identity in domestic service labor markets. In D. Gabbaccia & C. Wayne Leach (Eds.), *Immigrant life in the U.S.: Multi-disciplinary perspectives.* New York: Routledge.

Hondagneu-Sotelo, P. (2011). Más allá de la domesticidad: un análisis de género de los trabajos de los inmigrantes en el sector informal. Papers. *Revista de Sociologia, 96*(3), 805–824.

Hout, M., Levanon, A., & Cumberworth, E. (2011). *Job loss and unemployment in the great recession.* New York: Russell Sage.

Human Rights Watch Report. (2013). *Turning migrants into criminals. The harmful impact of US border prosecutions.* Amsterdam: Human Rights Watch. http://www.hrw.org/sites/default/files/reports/us0513_ForUpload_2.pdf. Accessed 16 Dec 2013.

Juliano, D. (2012). Género y trayectorias migratorias en época de crisis. Papers. *Revista de Sociologia, 97*(3), 523–540.

Kofman, E. (2008). Genre, migrations, reproduction sociale et Welfare state. Un état des discussions. *Les cahiers du CEDREF, 16*, 101–124.

Koser, K. (2009). *The impact of financial crises on international migration: Lessons learned.* IOM Migration Research Series No. 37, Geneva. http://www.iom.ch/jahia/webdav/shared/shared/mainsite/published_docs/serial_publications/mrs_37_en.pdf Accessed 16 Dec 2013.

Kostova, M. (2006). *Una evaluación del último proceso de regularización de trabajadores extranjeros en España (febrero-mayo de 2005). Un año después.* Documento de Trabajo (DT), no. 15. Madrid: Real Instituto Elcano. http://www.realinstitutoelcano.org/documentos/252/252_Kostova_Regularizacion_Extranjeros_Espana.pdf. Accessed 30 Sept 2014.

Landivar, L. C. (2012). *Who opts out? Labor force participation among Asian, Black, Hispanic, and White Mothers in 20 occupations.* Working paper presented at: Work and family researchers network conference. http://workfamily.sas.upenn.edu/wfrn-repo/object/jx41r2x3pa6ok4mo. Accessed 16 Dec 2013.

Leitner, S. (2003). Varieties infamilialism: The caring function of the family in comparative perspective. *European Societies, 5*(4), 353–375.

Levinson, A. (2005a). *The regularisation of unauthorized migrants: Literature survey and country case studies*. Centre on Migration, Policy and Society, University of Oxford. http://www.compas.ox.ac.uk/fileadmin/files/Publications/Reports/Country%20Case%20Spain.pdf. Accessed 28 Feb 2014.

Levinson, A. (2005b). *Why countries continue to consider regularization. Migration information source*. Washington, DC: Migration Policy Institute. http://www.migrationpolicy.org/article/why-countries-continue-consider-regularization. Accessed 28 Feb 2014.

Maguid, A., & Cerrutti, M. (2012). Crisis y migrantes sudamericanos en España. *Voces en el Fénix, 21*, 76–83. http://www.vocesenelfenix.com/sites/default/files/pdf/12_9.pdf. Accessed 28 Feb 2014.

Mahler, S. J., & Pessar, P. (2006). Gender matters: Ethnographers bring gender from the periphery toward the core. *International Migration Review, XL, 1*, 27–63.

McCall, L. (2005). The complexity of intersectionality. *Signs: Journal of Women in Culture and Society, 3*(3), 1771–1800.

Michel, S. (2011). *Introduction. Women, migration and the work of care: The United States in comparative perspective* (pp. 1–5). Woodrow Wilson Center for International Scholars Press. http://www.wilsoncenter.org/sites/default/files/Women,%20Migration%20and%20the%20Work%20of%20Care.pdf. Accessed 16 Dec 2013.

Montoya, E., & Woo, O. (2011). Las familias inmigrantes mexicanas ante las reformas de política migratoria en Arizona. Las percepciones de las leyes antiinmigrantes. *Revista Latinoamericana de Estudios de Familia, 3*, 245–263.

Muñoz Comet, J. (2012). Evolución del empleo y del paro de las mujeres inmigrantes en el mercado de trabajo español. El impacto de la actual crisis económica. *Cuadernos de Relaciones Laborales, 30*(1), 115–137.

OCDE. (2009). *International migration outlook SOPEMI 2009*. París: OCDE.

Oliveira, A. (2012). Social control of immigrant sex workers: Transforming a group recognized as "at risk" into a group viewed as "a risk". *International Journal of Migration, Health and Social Care, 8*(1), 32–41.

Organization of American States (OAS). (2012). *International migration in the Americas*. Second report on the continuous reporting system on international migration in the Americas. http://www.oecd.org/els/mig/G48952_WB_SICREMI_2012_ENGLISH_REPORT_LR.pdf. Accessed 31 Jan 2013.

Oso, L. (1998). *La migración hacia España de mujeres jefas de hogar*. Madrid: Instituto de la Mujer, Ministerio de Trabajo y Asuntos Sociales.

Oso, L., & Parella, S. (2012). Inmigración, género y Mercado de trabajo: Una panorámica de la investigación sobre la inserción Laboral de las mujeres inmigrantes en España. *Cuadernos de Relaciones Laborales, 30*(1), 11–44.

Pajares, M. (2009). *Inmigración y mercado de trabajo. Informe 2009*. Madrid: Observatorio Permanente de la Inmigración /Ministerio de Trabajo e Inmigración.

Papademetriou, D. G., et al. (2010). *Migration and immigrants two years after the financial collapse: Where do we stand? Report for the BBC world service*. Washington, DC: Migration Policy Institute. http://www.migrationpolicy.org/pubs/mpi-bbcreport-2010.pdf. Accessed 31 Jan 2013.

Parella, S., & Petroff, A. (2014). Migración de retorno en España: Salidas de inmigrantes y programas de retorno en un contexto de crisis. In J. Arango et al. (Eds.), *Anuario de la Inmigración en España (edición 2013)*. Bellaterra/Fundació CIDOB: Barcelona.

Parella, S., Petroff, A., & Solé, C. (2013). The upward occupational mobility of immigrant woman in Spain. *Journal of Ethnic and Migration Studies, 39*(9), 1365–1382.

Parrado, E. A., & Morgan, P. (2008). Intergenerational fertility among Hispanic women: New evidence of immigrant assimilation. *Demography, 45*(3), 651–671.

Pascale, C. M. (2007). *Making sense of race, class and gender: Commonsense, power and privilege in the United States*. New York: Routledge.

Pedone, C., Agrela, B., & Gil, S. (2012). Políticas públicas, migración y familia. Una mirada desde el género. Papers. *Revista de Sociologia, 97*(3), 541–568.

Reyneri, E., & Fullin, G. (2011). Labour market penalties of new immigrants in new and old receiving West European countries. *International Migration, 49*(1), 32–57.

Romero, M. (2008). The inclusion of citizenship status in intersectionality: What immigration raids. Tells us about mixed-status families, the state and assimilation. *International Journal of Sociology of Family, 34*(2), 131–152.

Sallé, M. A., Molpeceres, L., & Óngil, M. (2009). *Análisis de la situación laboral de las mujeres inmigrantes: Modalidades de inserción, sectores de ocupación e iniciativas empresariales. Colección Estudios No 110*. Madrid: Instituto de la Mujer.

Sánchez, M., & Serra, I. (2013). *Ellas se van. Mujeres migrantes en Estados Unidos y España*. México: Instituto de Investigaciones Sociales, UNAM.

Sassen, S. (1991). *The global city: New York, London, Tokyo*. Princeton: Princeton University Press.

Solé, C., & Parella, S. (2005). Immigrant women in domestic service. The 'Care Crisis' in the United States and Spain. In H. Henke (Ed.), *Crossing over: Comparing recent migration in Europe and the United States* (pp. 235–256). Cambridge: Lexington.

Terrazas, A. (2011). *Migration and development: Policy perspectives from the United States*. Washington, DC: Migration Policy Institute. http://www.migrationpolicy.org/.../migdevpolicy-2011.pdf. Accessed 31 Jan 2013

Tienda, M., & Faith, M. (Eds.). (2006). *Hispanics and the future of America*. Washington, DC: National Academies.

Tobes Portillo, P. (2011). Inmigración: Crisis económica y protección por desempleo. *Revista del Ministerio de Trabajo y Asuntos Sociales, 91*, 15–28.

Vega, W. A. (1995). The study of Latino families. In R. Zambrana (Ed.), *Understanding Latino families: Scholarship, policy, and practice* (pp. 3–17). Thousand Oaks: Sage.

Vizán Rodríguez, C. (2011). Inmigrantes ante la crisis económica ¿de la precariedad a la exclusión? *Mugak/Centro de Estudios y Documentación sobre el Racismo y la Xenofobia, 54*, 7–13.

Chapter 5
How Are 'the Others' Doing? Highly Skilled Latin American Immigrants and Economic Crisis in the US and Spain

Cristina Bradatan and Neeraja Kolloju

5.1 Introduction

It is generally observed that economic prosperity in a country leads to a large increase in the number of immigrants. Once the standard of life increases, even countries that once used to 'export' labor force, become countries of immigration. This is the case of Southern European countries, for example: Spain, Portugal, and Italy, that used to send large number of emigrants to the United States at the beginning of the twentieth century or to Western Europe in the 1950s. Once their economies started growing significantly in the second half of the twentieth century, they became countries of immigration. Among them, both before and after the latest economic crisis (2008–2012), Spain had the second largest stock of immigrants within European Union (5.2 million in 2008, 5.5 million in 2012; Germany has had the highest stock – 7.2 million in 2008, 7.4 million in 2012) (Eurostat 2009, 2013) and during 2000–2004, Spain also had the highest rate of immigration among European Union countries (Fermin et al. 2005).

It is also logical to believe that an economic crisis would stop people from moving from one country to another and, eventually, make them return. The 'buffer theory,' which became popular in the years after the World War II in Europe, argued for bringing temporary workers precisely using this argument: when economies are working well, immigrants would be helpful in the workforce and they would leave or be sent back whenever an economic downturn would occur (Dobson et al. 2009). Migration during the Great Depression seemed to work in this way as

C. Bradatan
Department of Sociology, Anthropology and Social Work,
Texas Tech University, Lubbock, TX, USA
e-mail: cristina.bradatan@ttu.edu

N. Kolloju (✉)
Department of Sociology, Southern Illinois University, Carbondale, IL, USA
e-mail: kolloju.neeraja@siu.edu

© Springer International Publishing Switzerland 2015   89
M. Aysa-Lastra, L. Cachón (eds.), *Immigrant Vulnerability and Resilience*,
International Perspectives on Migration 11, DOI 10.1007/978-3-319-14797-0_5

immigration to countries such as the USA or Canada decreased significantly (Tilly 2011) (although the changes in the US immigration legislation at the beginning of the century and deportations might have played a role as well). Generally, business cycle affects the rates of employment and wages of all labor force participants, but studies show that immigrants tend to be more affected than the natives (Orrenius and Zavodny 2009; OECD 2009; Raijman and Semyonov 1998) (see Chaps. 1, 2, and 3).

However, as economic crises tend to be global rather than localized nowadays, they do not necessarily lead to a significant decrease in migration rates (Bradatan 2016). The precariousness of economic conditions in the origin country, coupled with a lack of good information about the job market in the receiving country, might keep the migration rates high despite the economic downturn in the receiving country. Also, immigrants do not necessarily leave during an economic crisis as many of them have established their families, added possessions in the new country or lack legal status that makes it challenging to even try to return. Papademetriou and Terrazas (2009), for example, conclude that return migration is strongly related to economic conditions in the *origin* country and ease of circulation between origin and destination, rather than the economic situation in the receiving country. Another point that also needs to be noted is that immigrants are never a homogeneous group. Some immigrants are documented, others are undocumented, some are highly skilled, others low skilled, some migrate for employment, others came as refugees, etc. All these characteristics could make immigrants react differently to an economic downturn either by continuing to emigrate, stay or return from the receiving country.

Due to the heterogeneity of immigrant groups, it might very well be assumed that subgroups with certain characteristics do better or are relatively unaffected during an economic downturn while other groups are in a dire situation. If this is the case and it happens in more than one receiving country (such as Spain and US, for this chapter) it can have significant implications from a conceptual and policy point of view. Conceptually, it would mean that, studying immigrants as one consistent group or as only based on their ethnicity or country of origin is not an acceptable strategy to understand their economic outcomes. If one subgroup (in this case, those highly skilled) is significantly different from the others and more similar to the native born, then the distinction of foreign born/native born is not the best one to use. From a policy point of view, the existence of an economically resilient group would argue for defining specific policies for immigrant subgroups, as is the case in the US with a variety of immigrant visas categories rather than for 'immigrants' as a whole. We would discuss in detail on this in the conclusion.

5.2   Highly Skilled Latin American Migrants in the US and Spain

Immigrants are a growing segment in the US as well as Spain. In the US, the share of foreign born in the job market increased from 10.8 % in 1996 to 16.1 % in 2012 (Mosisa 2013) while the percentage of immigrants in Spanish population went from a mere 1.4 % in 1996 to 11.7 % in 2012. Latin American immigrants represent a significant share in both countries. In 2007, right before the 2008 economic crisis, 43.4 % of all foreign born age 18+ in the US were of Latin American origin, while they represented 47 % of foreign born age 16+ in Spain.

Although both countries witnessed high rates of immigration right before the 2008 economic crisis, their immigration histories are quite different.

In 1986, Spain joined European Economic Community and its economy grew considerably during the following 20 years. Economic prosperity had consequences in terms of migration as well (Reher and Silvestre 2009). While in the 1970s Spain was a country of emigration, the late 1980s and the following decades transformed it into an immigration country (Bradatan and Sandu 2012). This change started with some of the Spanish emigrants returning home. It continued with citizens of rich European countries moving to Spain in search of cheap housing and Mediterranean climate, followed by Latin Americans, Africans and Eastern Europeans looking for better opportunities in a flourishing economic environment. The rate of migration to Spain had thus increased dramatically from 1.6 (per 1,000 population) in 1991, one of the lowest in the European Union (European Economic Community back then), to 9.4 per 1,000 in 2000 and to 17.2 per 1,000 in 2007 (Domingo-Valls and Recaño-Valverde 2007; Fermin et al. 2005; Reher and Requena 2009). Since 2000, and until the 2008 economic crisis, Spain has had the highest rate of immigration among the European Union countries. The stock of immigrants followed suit and their proportion in the population increased from 1.8 % in 1998 to 9.76 % in 2008, reaching 4,473,499 immigrants in 2008 (Ministerio de Trabajo e Inmigración 2009).

In terms of college education, in Spain the differences between the general group of immigrants, Latin American born and natives are significantly smaller than in the US (Table 5.1), with 34.9 % of natives having college education while 22.6 % of Latin American being in this educational group in 2010. However, there are large disparities in education between various groups of foreign born with immigrants from EU15 countries having the highest level of education (44 % college educated in 2010) while only 9.2 % of African immigrants are in this educational group.

Moreover, during the period we can observe two distinct patterns in the data. The percentage of college educated population decreased for all groups between 2006 and 2009, which were the years previous to the negative effects of the Great Recession on employment. But this declining pattern changed, and the percentage of college educated persons increased; first for Latin Americans (2008–2009) and

Table 5.1 Percentage of college educated population ages 25–64 by year, Spain

Group	Percentage with university education, age group 25–64							
	2006	2007	2008	2009	2010	2011	2012	2013
Native born	27.2	28.7	29.1	29.7	31.0	32.9	33.6	34.9
Foreign born	25.2	23.8	23.6	22.9	25.8	23.3	23.8	24.8
Latin Americans	21.2	19.5	18.5	25.2	25.2	22.0	22.1	22.6

Source: Authors' computations, Encuesta de Poblacion Activa, 3rd quarter 2006–2013

afterwards for the natives. However, starting in 2011, the percentage for Latin American dropped again, but continues to grow for natives.

Spanish immigration policies also changed significantly in the past 30 years. Before joining the European Community in 1985, Spain did not have any defined immigration policy as the number of immigrants was negligible. In June 1985, Spain published its first immigration law (The Organic Law on the Rights and Liberties of Foreigners in Spain) introducing the important distinction between immigrants coming from European Community countries (*extranjeros comunitarios*) and immigrants from other countries (*inmigrantes*).[1] The law also included provisions regarding the legalization of the immigrants who were already in the country. In 1991, a second legalization plan was voted and implemented, followed by a third one in 1996. In 1993, the first guest worker program was passed (for workers in agriculture, construction work and other services) (Calavita 2005). In January 2000, the Spanish Parliament approved the *Organic law on the rights and liberties of foreigners in Spain, and their social integration* (*Ley Organica Sobre Derechos y Libertades de los Extranjeros en Espana y su Integracion Social*), which is one of the most liberal immigration laws that exists. The law included not only a new legalization of undocumented immigrants, but also full social rights (public education, participation in the national health system, public housing and social security protection) to all immigrants, *regardless of their legal status*. However, they had to be registered with the local authorities (these authorities are not bound to report the unauthorized immigrants). Some of the provisions of this law were later abolished through the Law No. 8/2000. In 2001, two more migrant legalizations were approved; in 2003 a new law regulated the type of visas and the legal situations of foreigners in Spain (*Ley Organica* 14/2003). After the arrival of the Socialist Party to the government, a new regulation regarding immigration was passed in the late 2004 (Royal Decree 2392/2004). It structured for the first time diverse procedures, for the legal entry in Spanish territory, balancing labor market needs and family reunification rights. It also included provision for the largest immigrant regularization implemented in Spain, which was implemented in 2005 and which benefited about 600,000 immigrants (Cachon 2009). Two years later, in 2007 the Strategic Plan for Citizenship and Integration for the first time explicitly defined specific political principles for immigrants' integration policies. In 2011 a new immigration regulation was passed (Royal Decree 557/2011) which updates the 2004 law according to some European Union norms (Gonzalez 2011). During the Great Recession, there has not been any modification of the main immigration law principles, but the conservative party in power has approved the reduction of social services for immigrants, and particularly for unauthorized immigrants.

The 2008 economic crisis led to an increase in the unemployment rate, to very high levels, especially among immigrants (as described in Chap. 3). The Spanish

---

[1] One of the principles of the European Community (now, European Union) was to facilitate the free circulation of people and goods between the partner countries. Spain had to include in this law special rights for citizens of the European Community.

authorities decided that a good answer to this situation was to persuade immigrants to go back to their countries of origin. The financial incentives were one of the measures designed to persuade the immigrants to go back home. So in 2008, a new law regulated the financial incentives offered to those immigrants who are willing to return to their home countries (Real Decreto-ley 4/2008). The program (*Capitalizacion de prestaciones por desempleo*) allowed migrants to receive their unemployment benefits in their countries of origin only if: they were subject to receive the benefit; they were not naturalized citizens; and if they do not return to Spain in a long period. Due to the incentives of the program the incidence on return migrants has been low (see Chap. 10).

Table 5.2 shows the trend in unemployment rate for native born, foreign born and Latin American born in Spain from 2006 to 2013. Overall, the rate of unemployment for low skilled immigrants (both general group and Latin American ones) saw the highest increase during the economic crisis (from 9.5 % to 31.1 % for foreign born and from 8 % to 29.6 % for Latin Americans). The rate of unemployment also increased significantly for highly skilled Latin Americans (from 3.7 % in 2006 to 20.6 % in 2013) while highly skilled Spanish born saw a more limited increase (from 2.8 % in 2006 to 11.2 % in 2013). The unemployment gap between the high skilled vs. low skilled grew during the recession for all groups, reaching its highest point in 2011 for all groups. However, after 2011 the unemployment gap between the skilled and the unskilled Latin Americans is the narrowest and the unemployment rates are on average 10 points higher than for the natives. This pattern suggests increasing labor vulnerability among high skilled Latin Americans immigrants in Spain. Unlike in the US, the rate of unemployment has deteriorated further since 2010 for all groups, foreign and native born, skilled and unskilled workers.

Data on labor force participation shows that there were very limited changes during the economic crisis, and the differences between native born, foreign born and/or Latin Americans remained relatively unchanged (Table 5.3). Low skilled Spanish born workers continued to have the lowest levels of labor force participation (low 70 %) both before and during the economic crisis while all the other groups (high skilled natives and immigrants and low skilled immigrants) had their rate of labor force participation in the high 80 %–low 90 %.

Unlike Spain, US have a long history of immigration, but the volume and ethnic/racial composition of the foreign born population has changed significantly over time. During the twentieth century the immigration was high until 1920, decreased in the mid-1920s and stayed low until 1965 and started to increase after the 1965 Immigration Act. The 1965 Immigration Act switched from a quota-based legislation, as defined by the 1952 Immigration and Nationality Act, to one favoring family-based immigration. Currently, about 65 % of the US green card holders come to the US based on family connections, while only 22 % (the second largest category) are employment-based (Martin and Midgley 2006). The post-1986 IRCA (Immigration Reform and Control Act) period, when large numbers of immigrants legalized their status, was followed by the decade of the 1990s, when the number of immigrants increased again (three times more than in the 1960s decade). This

Table 5.2 Rate of unemployment, age group 25–64, Spain

Group	2006		2007		2008		2009		2010		2011		2012		2013	
	HS	LS	HS	LS	HS	LS	HS	LS	HS	LS	HS	LS	HS	LS	HS	LS
Native born	2.8	6.1	2.5	6.5	3.2	9.0	5.6	15.3	6.1	17.6	8.4	15.2	10.9	18.8	11.2	19.5
Foreign born	7.0	9.5	9.1	9.5	11.0	15.1	19.0	28.3	18.3	28.3	19.9	26.6	21.3	28.2	19.0	31.1
Latin Americans	3.7	8.0	9.4	8.7	8.7	11.1	20.5	25.4	17.9	27.0	20.8	24.0	24.5	27.2	20.6	29.6

Source: Authors' computations, Encuesta de Poblacion Activa, 3rd quarter 2006–2013

HS highly skilled, *LS* low skilled

Table 5.3 Labor force participation rate, age group 25–64, Spain

Group	2006		2007		2008		2009		2010		2011		2012		2013	
	HS	LS	HS	LS	HS	LS	HS	LS	HS	LS	HS	LS	HS	LS	HS	LS
Native born	90.2	71.3	90.4	71.6	90.3	72.6	90.9	72.8	90.6	74.5	89.8	73.1	90.5	73.9	89.8	74.2
Foreign born (all)	87.0	87.3	87.0	87.6	86.7	87.9	87.4	87.4	86.1	89.4	86.9	83.9	86.4	83.8	85.2	83.5
Latin Americans	91.0	91.0	88.5	91.2	91.0	92.8	92.2	92.1	93.2	92.6	91.1	90.6	88.2	91.5	88.0	89.5

Source: Authors' computations, Encuesta de Poblacion Activa, 3rd quarter 2006–2013
HS highly skilled, *LS* low skilled

Table 5.4 Percentage of college educated population ages 25–64 by year, US

Group	% With University education							
	2006 (%)	2007 (%)	2008 (%)	2009 (%)	2010 (%)	2011 (%)	2012 (%)	2013 (%)
Native born	30.2	31.3	31.90	31.7	32.1	32.8	33.1	33.9
Foreign born (all)	28.5	29.1	29.70	29.8	30.2	29.2	30.2	30.9
Latin Americans (FB)	10.5	10.5	11.00	10.9	11.2	10.8	11.4	11.7

Source: Authors' computations, Current Population Survey, March Supplement, 2006–2013
HS highly skilled, *LS* low skilled, *FB* foreign born

resulted in an increasing share of foreign-born population in the US, from 5 % in the 1970s to the current level of (about) 12.9 % (40 million people) in 2010 (Grieco et al. 2012). While the number of immigrants legally admitted every year is large (around 900,000), the rate of immigration is relatively low (3 per 1,000) in comparison to Spain.

The US immigrants have a lower level of education in comparison to the natives. Among the immigrants, Latin Americans foreign born have significantly lower levels of education than the general group (Table 5.4). In 2013, 33.9 % of the US born aged 25–64 had college education, while only 11.7 % of Latin American born was in this educational group. While some argue that these discrepancies are due to the US immigration policies (West 2010): as a Latin American, and especially as a Mexican, it is difficult to immigrate legally to the US unless one has family connections. Coming as an undocumented worker, on the other hand, might not be an acceptable solution for someone who already invested in his/her education.

The current general immigration law in the US follows the provisions of the 1965 Immigration Reform and Control Act, with most of the immigrants to come to the US based on family connections and only few of them based on work and refugee status. Since 1980, the immigration law has become more and more restrictive in terms of social rights offered to immigrants. In 1981, non-aliens were excluded from Department of Housing and Urban Development (HUD) financial assistance. The aliens' eligibility to access aid for families with dependent children was also restricted. The 1986 Immigration Reform and Control Act was designed to tackle the problem of unauthorized immigration from two directions: (1) by allowing immigrants who lived in the US since 1982 to adjust their status and (2) by introducing sanctions for employers hiring unauthorized immigrants. This act resulted in a significantly large number of immigrants being accepted during the following years (many of them previously living in the US without authorization). During 1988–1991, the immigration regulations changed very little.

In 1988, immigrants who came to the US based on marriage received a conditional immigrant status for the first 2 years of marriage. In 1990, the law allowed an increase in the total immigration under a flexible cap with defined numbers for each category of immigrants. In 1993, NAFTA provisions were introduced for Canadian and Mexican citizens (Mexicans had more restrictions). In 1996, restrictions for legal immigrants seeking public assistance and broader restrictions for illegal immigrants and non-immigrants were implemented. In 1997, the NACARA act was adopted, providing certain rights to certain groups of Central American refugees. Many skilled migrants come in the US either as students (using a F1 or J1 visas) or as temporary workers (H1B or J1 visas). The number of H1B visas was initially caped to 65,000, but, because of a large wave of highly skilled immigrants coming in the 1990s, it got increased in 1998 to 115,000. Most of the beneficiaries of this type of visas come from Asia (India and China). Immediately after September 11th 2001, the immigration laws concentrated on enhancing US security through a more rigorous screening of the visas applicants (L 107–128, 107–173 and the Homeland Security Act of 2002). In 2005–2006, several regulations made the transitions to a permanent resident status easier for immigrant nurses and physicians (L109-423, L 109–477).

Unlike Spain, US did not take any legislative measures to try to repatriate migrants. However, studies show that the rate of immigration for Latin Americans dropped significantly since 2008 (Gandini and Lozano 2016) and in the 2010 the Mexican census for the first time recorded more than a million returned migrants. (INEGI 2011).

As expected, the rate of unemployment increased during the economic crisis for all groups, but much more for the foreign born group and Latin American immigrants (see Chap. 3). Rate of unemployment for highly skilled Latin American immigrants followed suit and increased (from 2.4 % in 2006 to 6.5 % in 2011), but unlike in Spain, it remained lower than that of low skilled native born and it dropped to 5.9 % in 2013. Table 5.5 shows the trend in unemployment rates for native born, foreign born and Latin American born living in the US from 2006 to 2013. The unemployment gap between high and low skilled workers increased during the recession, following and inverse U-shaped pattern for all groups.

Data on labor force participation shows that there were some small changes during the economic crisis: a decrease followed by an increase in the labor force participation. The differences between native born, foreign born and/or Latin Americans remained relatively unchanged (Table 5.6). Low skilled foreign born workers continued to have the lowest levels of labor force participation (high 70 %–low 80 %) both before and during the economic crisis, while highly skilled natives continued to have the highest rate of labor force participation (low to high 80 %). Chapter 4 in this volume gives more details about the differences between genders in labor force participation.

5.3   Conclusion

In this chapter, we compared the unemployment rates and labor force participation rates of high and low skilled immigrants in Spain and US before and during the economic crisis. The literature argues that human capital, context of reception and social capital play an important role in economic integration of immigrants in the

Table 5.5 Rate of unemployment, age group 25–64, US

Group	2006 HS (%)	2006 LS (%)	2007 HS (%)	2007 LS (%)	2008 HS (%)	2008 LS (%)	2009 HS (%)	2009 LS (%)	2010 HS (%)	2010 LS (%)	2011 HS (%)	2011 LS (%)	2012 HS (%)	2012 LS (%)	2013 HS (%)	2013 LS (%)
Native born	2.2	4.9	1.7	4.8	1.9	5.4	4.2	10.0	4.4	11.3	4.0	10.1	3.9	9.2	3.5	8.2
Foreign born (all)	2.8	4.6	2.3	5.1	2.7	6.8	5.8	10.5	6.4	11.2	6.3	10.9	5.1	9.8	5.2	8.3
Latin Americans (FB)	2.4	5.2	2.4	5.5	3.5	7.6	6.8	12.3	6.2	12.3	6.5	11.7	5.7	9.8	5.9	8.3

Source: Authors' computations, Current Population Survey, March Supplement, 2006–2013
HS highly skilled, LS low skilled, FB foreign born

Table 5.6 Labor force participation rate, age group 25–64, US

Group	2006		2007		2008		2009		2010		2011		2012		2013	
	HS	LS	HS	LS	HS	LS	HS	LS	HS	LS	HS	LS	HS	LS	HS	LS
Native born	86.6	75.8	86.5	76.0	86.5	75.9	86.5	75.3	86.3	75.2	85.7	73.6	86.3	73.2	85.7	73.1
Foreign born (all)	82.0	74.8	82.4	75.3	84.1	74.9	82.9	75.0	81.8	75.7	82.7	74.9	81.9	74.9	82.2	74.1
Latin Americans (FB)	80.9	75.3	81.9	75.8	84.7	75.0	82.1	75.6	81.5	75.9	82.3	75.4	82.1	76.0	82.3	74.7

Source: Authors' computations, Current Population Survey, March Supplement, 2006–2013
HS highly skilled, *LS* low skilled, *FB* foreign born

new country. Higher human and social capital and a good context of reception (friendly immigration policies and high rate of economic increase) make it easier for an immigrant to achieve good economic status in the new country. In this research, we looked at what happens when a group of immigrants with high human capital (highly skilled immigrants) are confronted with an economic down-turn (2008 economic crisis).[2] One limitation of this study is the lack of control for the social capital of the subjects included in the analysis, due to the data characteristics.

Unlike low educated immigrants, many of the highly skilled come to the host country using either educational channels (come to study) or in order to get a job. Generally, they have a good knowledge of the host country's language and need less support from the ethnic communities already existing in the host country (Bradatan 2016). Education makes a significant difference in the life of an immi-grant. In the US, for example, a foreign born worker with a bachelor degree or above earned 2.7 times more than one without a high school diploma in 2010 (US Bureau of Labor Statistics 2011). Some studies show that skilled immigrants are less affected than the unskilled ones by the business cycles, but they still suffer more hardship than the native born (Orrenius and Zavodny 2009).

Generally, for skilled immigrants, it is easier to achieve faster economic inte-gration than the unskilled ones due to their high human capital, but the context of reception (business cycle, immigration laws) as well the country of origin/language spoken at home play an important role as well. In Spain, a significant percentage of highly skilled migrants come from Western European countries (UK, France), many of them as expats brought by their home companies to work in Spain. As EU citizens, this group has the right to work in Spain without any problems. Latin American immigrants, on the other hand, have the benefit of speaking the language (with the exception of Brazilians) and, in some cases, qualify to apply for Spanish citizenship after 2 years of legal residency in Spain. In the United States, some skilled migrants get schooled in the US or in another developed country and come with a good knowledge of English. This allows them to get easily inserted in the job market and to get competitive salaries. Those who come with their professional and college degrees from their origin countries find many barriers in using their professional credentials.

While there are significant differences between US and Spain, both countries are characterized by high level of immigration during the past decade and they have a significant Latin American immigrant population. Although in both countries there are regulations aimed to shape the characteristics of the immigrants entering the country (guest-worker programs in Spain, H1B visas in the US), both the US and Spanish immigration legislation is reactive rather than pro-active in terms of immigration. While a significant percentage of immigrants are college educated for both countries, the educational structure of Latin American immigrants differs

---

[2] Due to data limitation, we were unable to include social capital into our analyses.

between Spain and US as only 11.2 % of them[3] in the US had a college degree in 2010 while 25.2 % in Spain had a college degree.

Before 2008, both countries enjoyed a prosperous period. When the 2008 economic crisis started, however, Spain and US adopted different policy positions toward immigrants: Spain preferred to offer financial incentives to those willing to return to their native countries, while in the US it was expected they would leave the country by themselves, or deported by border enforcement authorities (see Chaps. 6, 8 and 13). The Spanish program of facilitating return was not attractive to many immigrants, but the lack of jobs pushed a significant number of foreign born (Latin American included) to return to their origin country (see Chap. 10). This was especially true for those who were able to secure Spanish nationality and, therefore, have the possibility of moving back and forth.

The literature summarized above argues that immigrants are more sensitive than the natives to the effects of business cycles. Within this context, the 2008 economic crisis can be framed as a situation of an extremely unfriendly receiving economic environment (Bradatan 2016). The rates of unemployment for immigrants, generally speaking, should therefore be higher in comparison to natives. While education makes a difference and highly skilled immigrants have better labor force outcomes than low educated ones, studies show that skilled migrants are also sensitive to business cycles.

Our study shows that indeed the rate of unemployment increased significantly for Latin American immigrants both in Spain and US. However, in Spain their situation deteriorated much more significantly than in the US in comparison to their native counterparts. Although generally the economic crisis affected much more significantly the Spanish economy than the US economy, educated native born Spaniards saw only a small increase in their unemployment rates while educated foreigners (and the subgroup Latin American) saw their unemployment rates reaching levels similar to the low skilled Spaniards. One reason for these discrepancies might be due to a high percentage of educated migrants in Spain working in low skilled occupations, something that needs further exploration. Some studies show that generally immigrants in Spain do not follow the same U pattern in terms of occupational achievement (as in the US) and remain in low status occupations even after spending a significant period of time in Spain (Stanek and Veira 2013; Aysa-Lastra and Cachon 2013). Unlike unemployment rates, labor force participation rates were not significantly affected and the differences between highly skilled natives, foreign born in general and Latin American born are generally small. The low labor force participation rate of low skilled Spaniards (low 70 %) is probably due to much more permissive retirement policies.

Overall, the 2008 economic crisis affected in a larger extent the unemployment rates of Latin American born skilled workers relative to the native born from the same educational group in both countries, and its impact was more notable in Spain. Therefore, our study shows that an economic crisis has a stronger effect on the

---

[3] Unless otherwise noted, these figures are reported for the age group 25–64.

unemployment rate of highly skilled Latin American immigrants than on US or Spanish natives. We can conclude that if an economic downturn affects a country, foreign born are the first to lose their jobs, regardless of their level of education. However, possessing high skills serve as a shield to very high unemployment if compared to the unskilled, particularly to unskilled immigrants. This effect is, however, dependent on the characteristics of the receiving country and it can be said that recession led to further marginalization of highly skilled migrants in Spain than in the US. Labor force participation rates of Latin American highly skilled migrants remained high and similar to the ones of the native born in both countries, showing that they continued to look for jobs despite the unfriendly economic environment.

References

Aysa-Lastra, M., & Cachón, L. (2013). Segmented occupational mobility: The case of non-EU immigrants in Spain. *Revista Española de Investigaciones Sociológicas, 144*, 23–47.

Bradatan, C. (2016). Highly skilled migration: Economic crises and other risks. *Population, Space and Place, 22* (forthcoming).

Bradatan, C., & Sandu, D. (2012). Before crisis: Gender and economic outcomes of the two largest immigrant communities in Spain. *International Migration Review, 46*(1), 221–243.

Cachón, L. (2009). *La "España inmigrante": Marco discriminatorio, mercado de trabajo y políticas de integración*. Barcelona: Anthropos.

Calavita, K. (2005). *Immigrants at the margins. Law, race, and exclusion in southern Europe*. Cambridge, UK: Cambridge University Press.

Dobson, J., Lathman, A., & Salt, J. (2009). On the move? Labour migration in times of recession, policy network paper. Retrieved on May 2, 2014, from www.policy-network.net

Domingo-Valls, A., & Recaño-Valverde, J. (2007). Perfil demografico de la población extranjera en España. In E. Aja & J. Arango (Eds.), *La inmigración en España 2006. Anuario de inmigración y políticas de inmigración* (pp. 20–43). Barcelona: Fundación CIDOB.

EUROSTAT. (2009, December 16). Population of foreign citizens in the EU27 in 2008. Eurostat Newsrelease, 184/2009.

EUROSTAT. (2013). Population by citizenship: Foreigners. Retrieved on May 15, 2014, from http://epp.eurostat.ec.europa.edu

Fermin, A., Kjellstrand, S., & Entzinger, H. (2005). *Study on immigration, integration and social cohesion, final report, DG employment and social affairs*. Brussels: European Commission.

Gandini, L., & Lozano, F. (2016). A comparative perspective of the effects of the crisis on occupational segregation and wage differentials of skilled migrants from Latin America and the Caribbean. *Population, Space and Place, 22* (forthcoming).

González, M. (2011). Sobre el nuevo Reglamento de extranjería de 2011. *Revista del Ministerio de Trabajo e Inmigración, 95*, 13–25.

Grieco, E. M., Acosta, Y. D., Patricia de la Cruz, G., Gambino, C., Gryn, T, Larsen, L. J., Trevelyan, E. N., & Walters, N. P. (2012). *The foreign-born population in the United States: 2010*. American Community Survey Reports, US Census Bureau. Retrieved January 26, 2015, from http://www.census.gov/content/dam/Census/library/publications/2012/acs/acs-19.pdf

Instituo National de Estadistica, Geografia e Informatica (INEGI). (2011). Tabulados Basicos. Censo de Poblacion y Vivienda 2010. http://www3.inegi.org.mx. Accessed 14 May 2014.

Iredale, R. (2001). The migration of professionals: Theories and typologies. *International Migration, 39*(5), 7–26.

Martin, P., & Midgley, E. (2006). *Immigration: Shaping and reshaping America*. Washington, DC: Population Reference Bureau.

Ministerio de Trabajo e Inmigracion. (2009, February). Boletín estadístico de extranjería e inmigración, Ministerio de trabajo e inmigración, Gobierno de España, Number 19.

Mosisa, A. (2013). Foreign born workers in the US labor force, Bureau of Labor Statistics. Retrieved on May 04, 2014, from http://www.bls.gov/spotlight/2013/foreign-born/

OECD. (2009). International migration and the economic crisis: Understanding the links and shaping policy responses. In *Chapter 1 in international migration outlook*. Paris: OECD.

Orrenius, P., & Zavodny, M. (2009). Tied to the business cycle: How immigrants fare in good and bad economic times, migration policy institute. Retrieved on May 3, 2009, from www.migrationpolicy.org

Papademetriou, D. G., & Terrazas, A. (2009). *Immigrants and the current economic crisis*. Washington, DC: Migration Policy Institute.

Raijman, R., & Semyonov, M. (1998). Best of times, worst of times of occupational mobility: The case of Russian immigrants in Israel. *International Migration, 36*, 291–312.

Reher, D. S., & Requena, M. (2009). The national immigrant survey of Spain. A new data source for migration studies in Europe. *Demographic Research, 20*, 253–278.

Reher, D. S., & Silvestre, J. (2009). Internal migration patterns of foreign-born immigrants in a country of recent mass immigration: Evidence from new micro data for Spain. *International Migration Review, 43*(4), 815–849.

Stanek, M., & Veira-Ramos, A. (2013). Occupational mobility at migration – Evidence from Spain. *Sociological Research Online, 18*(4). Retrieved January 26, 2015, http://www.socresonline.org.uk/18/4/16.html

Tilly, C. (2011). The impact of the economic crisis on international migration: A review. *Work, Employment and Society, 25*(4), 675–688.

US Bureau of Labor Statistics. (2011). Labor force characteristics of foreign born summary. Retrieved on March 10, 2012, from http://www.bls.gov/news.release/forbrn.nr0.htm

West, D. (2010). *Brain gain: Rethinking U.S. Immigration policy*. Washington, DC: Brookings Institute Press.

Chapter 6
Confluence of the Economic Recession and Immigration Laws in the Lives of Latino Immigrant Workers in the United States

Cecilia Menjívar and María E. Enchautegui

6.1 Introduction

The Great Recession is now recognized as the most serious economic crisis since the Great Depression (Grusky et al. 2011), with profound implications for many aspects of workers' lives (Scott and Leymon 2013; Treas 2010) (see Chap. 1). Concurrent with this economic decline, immigration law enforcement escalated, and undocumented immigrant labor increasingly became criminalized (Chacon 2009; Dowling and Inda 2013; Meissner et al. 2013). In this chapter we argue that this climate of increased enforcement has to be brought into the analysis for a fuller examination of the economic experiences of Latino immigrants during the Great Recession.

Various studies have traced immigration and immigrant outcomes during the Great Recession. In an examination of immigration trends to the United States as they intersected with the Great Recession, Massey (2012) found that even though legal immigration from Mexico leveled off in the midst of the economic crisis, not all forms of immigration responded in the same way, with temporary worker migration (e.g., H-visa holders) increasing between 2009 and 2010. However, these changes in migratory flows point to the increased vulnerability of this population, Massey notes. Furthermore, net undocumented immigration became near zero during the Great Recession. The Great Recession also provoked a geographical redistribution of immigrants (Ellis et al. 2014; FitzGerald et al. 2011; Singer and Wilson 2010). Latino immigrants in particular exhibited high mobility out of areas most impacted by the recession, many of which were also

C. Menjívar (✉)
Sanford School of Social & Family Dynamics, Arizona State University, Tempe, AZ, USA
e-mail: menjivar@asu.edu

M.E. Enchautegui
The Urban Institute, Washington, DC, USA
e-mail: MEnchaut@urban.org

© Springer International Publishing Switzerland 2015   105
M. Aysa-Lastra, L. Cachón (eds.), *Immigrant Vulnerability and Resilience*,
International Perspectives on Migration 11, DOI 10.1007/978-3-319-14797-0_6

areas of traditional immigration settlement (Cadena and Kovak 2013). With respect to employment outcomes, Latino immigrants, who were more likely to hold union membership, lost union jobs at higher rates during the Great Recession than comparable native-born workers, after controlling for various other factors (Catron 2013). Importantly, although immigrants lost more employment during the Great Recession they gained more employment during the recovery, even as the quality of the jobs gained might had declined (Enchautegui 2012).

Missing from these accounts is how the immigration enforcement climate prevalent *during* the Great Recession shaped immigrants' outcomes and work experiences during this period of constrained economic opportunities. Immigration enforcement in all its manifestations intensified after 2002 (Meissner et al. 2013). At the Southern Border there was fencing, vehicle barriers, apprehensions, and technology to detect illegal crossers; at ports of entry, technologies to track visitors improved; and in the interior, worksite enforcement, arrests, document tracking and authentication and deportations became more common (Meissner et al 2013). After the passage of the 1986 Immigration Reform and Control Act federal funding allocated to core immigration enforcement agencies grew exponentially, but it grew even more rapidly after 2002 (Meissner et al 2013). And while the economy was experiencing its deepest economic downturn between 2008 and 2009 and a slow recovery heading in to 2010, the enforcement machine did not subside. Between fiscal years 2008 and 2010, during the Great Recession, 2.7 million individuals were apprehended, over 1.1 million were removed from the United States, 1.8 were returned and 676,000 were declared inadmissible (Department of Homeland Security 2012). Laws that were passed in 1996 and after 9/11, such as the Illegal Immigration Reform and Immigrant Responsibility Act (IIRIRA) of 1996, the Antiterrorism and Effective Death Penalty Act (AEDPA) of 1996 and the USA PATRIOT Act of 2001 expanded the categories of noncitizens who can be deported, restricted the ability to appeal deportations, and weakened judicial review in deportation cases (Hagan et al. 2011; Menjívar and Kanstroom 2014). These enforcement actions have resulted in the management of immigration through the criminal justice system and the concomitant criminalization of undocumented workers (Chacon 2009; Dowling and Inda 2013).

In addition to being the target of enforcement, undocumented immigrants are located at the crux of the confluence of enforcement of immigration laws and the reduction in economic opportunities during the Great Recession. Undocumented immigrants cannot rely on the government-provided safety net when left without jobs because they are ineligible for these programs. These immigrants are excluded from the Supplemental Nutritional Assistance Program, Temporary Assistance for Needy Family, Medicaid and now also from health care subsidies under the Affordable Health Care Act exchanges. Further, since unauthorized immigrants are not legally employed they are effectively excluded from unemployment insurance, the principal income stabilizing program of the Great Recession (Vroman 2010). Going back to their home countries to return later, or to engage in circular migration, has become almost impossible given stricter border enforcement strategies we see today. Unable to count on the government-provided safety net undocumented workers will try to find work anyway they can. In fact, Enchautegui (2012) and Kochhar (2010) find that immigrants did better in terms of employment gains than native workers during the recovery (see Chap. 2). Stronger enforcement in the way of deportations, document certification, and stricter penalties for fraudulent documents, coupled with the need to work, means that a larger number of unauthorized immigrants will seek refuge in jobs that are further underground in order to avoid been detected.[1] Moreover, since stricter enforcement started well before the onset of the Great Recession (Meissner et al. 2013) undergroundness (and immigrant workers' vulnerability) may have intensified during the Great Recession, but likely started before and has continued after the recovery.

Research shows that enforcement affects the labor market outcomes of immigrants (see Chauvin et al. 2013). Wages and occupational returns declined for undocumented immigrants with the increase in enforcement after the passage of the 1986 Immigration Reform and Control Act–IRCA and after 1996 with the passing of IIRIRA and AEDPA (Donato and Massey 1993; Gentsch and Massey 2011). Labor market outcomes weakened after 9/11 with the passage of the USA Patriot Act (Orrenius and Zavodny 2009). Stricter immigration laws targeting undocumented immigrants in local areas affect the locational choices of immigrants and have pushed undocumented immigrants to informality (Leerkes et al. 2012; Parrado 2012; Lofstrom et al. 2011). But, the recessionary economic context of the Great Recession also plays a key role as immigrant's strategies to handle stricter enforcement may be more constrained in periods of scarcity.

In this chapter we examine the effects of the Great Recession as it intersects with immigration enforcement and the concomitant criminalization of immigrant workers (see Dowling and Inda 2013). We contend that the labor market outcomes and experiences of Latino immigrants during the Great Recession and recovery have to be examined through the double lens of declining economic opportunity and rising enforcement with its corollary criminalization of immigrant workers, a trend that needs to be traced to the years prior to the Great Recession. We discuss the legal context which we argue leads more undocumented immigrants further underground, and we focus on Arizona to demonstrate how these trends come together in immigrants' lives, using data from an ongoing qualitative study of immigrants in the area of Phoenix. We then turn to nationally representative data from the American Community Survey (ACS) and Current Population Survey (CPS), and construct indicators of undergroundness to examine trends before, during and after the Great Recession. This mixed-methods examination allows us to explore in depth nuances in immigrant vulnerability resulting from the deterioration of the labor market in the midst of increased immigration enforcement and the criminalization of immigrant workers.

---

[1] Fussell (2011) identified a "deportation threat dynamic," a social mechanism through which physical appearance, language use, and labor practices are associated with undocumented status and which in turn permits unscrupulous employers to use deportation as a threat.

6.2 Legal Context

The legal context that immigrants face today is multi-pronged, composed of at least two government levels—the federal and the state/local—a system that dates back to well before the onset of the Great Recession. At the federal level, the Illegal Immigration Reform and Immigrant Responsibility Act (IIRIRA) of 1996 (H.R. 3610; Pub. L. 104–208; 110 Stat. 3009–546, 104th Congress, September 30th, 1996), a complex piece of legislation signed into law by President Clinton, has deeply affected the lives of immigrants in multiple ways, as it contained legislation directly impacting immigrants but also specific directives for those who enforce the law. A direct result of the implementation of this law has been the historic high number of deportations and detentions, family separations, and increased criminalization of immigrant workers and their practices. In this chapter we will focus narrowly on presenting certain aspects of the law that more directly impact on the lives of immigrants as workers.

Under title IV of IIRIRA, the U.S. Attorney General was charged with creating three pilot programs to verify employment eligibility. The then INS was required to conduct a pilot project to test one of these. This pilot was launched in 1997 through a coordinated effort between the INS and the Social Security Administration. The Basic Pilot Program grew substantially from 2001 on, and an Act of Congress required its expansion to all 50 states by December 1, 2004. The program, now internet-based with expanded high tech features like photo matching and interface software, was renamed E-verify in 2007. It compares information from an I-9 employment form to data from the Department of Homeland Security and the Social Security Administration to confirm employment eligibility. An automatic flagging system prompts employers to double-check cases that result in a mismatch. Immigration and Customs Enforcement (ICE) and United States Citizenship and Immigration Services (USCIS) coordinate and manage the program, and upgrades now allow for naturalization data checks, as well as real-time border inspection arrival and departure for non-citizens to be checked against E-verify. In 2011, the program introduced self-check so that workers could verify their own employment eligibility and in 2013 E-verify released a database that allows the public to find employers enrolled in E-verify. As the USCIS website (http://www.uscis.gov/e-verify/what-e-verify) notes, "E-Verify's most impressive features are its speed and accuracy." Importantly, although the program has grown substantially, the federal government does not make it mandatory (http://www.uscis.gov/e-verify/what-e-verify). Yet, according to the National Council of State Legislatures (http://www.ncsl.org/research/immigration/everify-faq.aspx), by the end of 2012, 20 states required E-Verify for some or all of their employers. Federal contractors are required to use E-Verify.

E-verify allows for what has been called "silent raids" of businesses that hire out-of-status immigrant workers. Thus, rather than the media spectacles of the raids when ICE agents would descend on businesses to arrest undocumented employees, these "silent raids" allow ICE agents to more efficiently spot undocumented immigrants through audits of employers' records. These "silent raids" are believed to be more effective because with the more visible workplace raids only those workers who were present on the day of a raid would be detained, whereas these audits allow ICE agents to identify all employees, present or not on the day the agents show up, who are working without proper documentation (through mismatches in the database). They are also believed to be cost-efficient because instead of needing to deploy hundreds of agents to arrest a few immigrants, one ICE agent can go through many records. In a later section we detail how this federal law works in conjunction with new state-level laws to facilitate the signature strategies of immigration enforcement today—detection, detention and deportation (the "3 Ds" of enforcement).

Furthermore, under IIRIRA the definition of a crime for which immigrants—even those holding permanent legal residence—can be deported was expanded, and the category of "aggravated felony" now includes a broad category of (redefined) criminal offenses that carry the most severe penalty—deportation. In 2009, the U.S. Supreme Court ruled that the use of false documents constituted "aggravated identity theft," that carries a mandatory 2-year prison sentence, if the person *knowingly* uses, without lawful authority, a means of identification belonging to another person. This federal statute has been used to charge with "aggravated identity theft" the undocumented immigrant workers who use someone else's documents to work even if they do not know the owner of the documents, as in the case of the (mostly) Guatemalan workers in Postville, Iowa (Camayd-Freixas 2009). Even though the U.S. Supreme Court later ruled that using someone else's document to procure employment does not constitute identity theft, some law enforcement agencies have continued to investigate immigrant workers in the name of "identity theft investigations" (e.g., the Maricopa County Sheriff's Office). Thus, the civil violation of using someone else's social security to work can today be elevated to a felonious crime with grave consequences for undocumented immigrant workers charged with this violation. In some cases, however, as the case of Arizona below will show, cases of identity theft fall under crimes of moral turpitude and constitute felonies under federal statute.

At the state level, beginning in the mid-2000s a flurry of immigration-related legislation and ordinances were passed in various states (see Table 6.1 for the quantity and chronology of this legislative activity), often predating the onset of the Great Recession. This heightened legislative activity itself was predated by other similar proposals, most famously Proposition 187 in California. And although historically there have been similar proposals that reflect nativist sentiment and xenophobia, today such legislative efforts are further bound up in fears of terrorism, crime and economic insecurity.

Specifically, beginning in 2005 these new forms of internal border control have become more prevalent (Leerkes et al. 2012). With increases in immigration to all states resulting from a surge in border enforcement that has prevented the circular migration patterns common in the past (see Massey et al. 2002), the internal mobility of immigrants (Cadena and Kovak 2013), and the supposed inaction on the part of the federal government to contain undocumented immigration, many

Table 6.1 State legislation related to immigrants, 2005–2011

Year	Introduced	Passed legislatures	Vetoed	Enacted	Resolutions	Total laws & resolutions
2005	300	45	6	39	0	39
2006	570	90	6	84	12	96
2007	1,562	252	12	240	50	290
2008	1,305	209	3	206	64	270
2009	1,500[a]	373	20	222	131	353
2010	1,400[a]	356	10	208	138	346
2011[b]	**1,607**	**318**	**15**	**197**	**109**	**306**

Source: National Conference of State Legislatures, http://www.ncsl.org/research/immigration/
state-immigration-legislation-report-dec-2011.aspx
[a]2009–2010 estimates
[b]As of Dec. 7, 2011

states "have taken matters in their own hands" and passed many pieces of legislation.[2] However, not all state-level laws and ordinances are the same; some have
sought to integrate immigrants (e.g., "sanctuary policies") while others have
focused on disrupting life for immigrants and creating conditions so hostile that
immigrants will "self deport." Some scholars (see Mitnik and Halpern-Finnerty
2010) argue that there has been too much emphasis on state-level laws that are
negative, anti-immigrant or that cause harm to the immigrants, when in fact states
have passed laws with an inclusionary objective as well. Indeed, this is the case, but
with some important patterns: (a) the more inclusionary laws were passed earlier, in
the 1980s, 1990s, and early 2000s, whereas a substantial portion of the legislative
activity in recent years has focused on exclusionary legislation; (b) localities that
have experienced rapid growth of their foreign-born population and with a high
percentage of owner-occupied housing are more likely to introduce exclusionary
policies (Walker and Leitner 2011); and (c) exclusionary laws have tended to be
passed in new destinations, particularly in the south (Leerkes et al. 2012).[3]
Although in recent years there was a decline in state-level legislation, this activity
grew again in 2013, with an increase of 64 % over 2012 levels (NCSL 2014). Thus,
the fact remains that there are a number of state-level laws, of various magnitudes,
directions and objectives, in place around the country today (Ellis et al. 2013;

---

[2] Importantly, whereas immigrants have moved to the so-called "new destinations," they have
continued to settle disproportionally in a few traditional "gateway" destinations, such as New
York, Los Angeles, Miami, and Chicago (Singer 2004); indeed, many of these new destinations
"have not experienced a significant foreign-born presence for at least a century, if ever" (Ellis et al.
2013: 3). What these new destinations have seen is a *relative* increase in the Latino population,
sometimes multiplying its size, as the initial numbers were very low to begin with.

[3] This legislative activity may in some ways be related to the observation above. New destinations,
with very small populations of Latino immigrants that then increased to several times their size
(though remaining relatively small in comparison to the size of these populations in traditional
gateway points) have tended to react more strongly to these demographic changes by proposing
more anti-immigrant legislation.

FitzGerald et al. 2011; Parrado 2012), with potentially detrimental effects for the lives of immigrants.

Another layer of enforcement that links the federal and state levels took place through 287(g) programs, and now through Secure Communities and other programs under the broad umbrella of ICE's Agreements of Cooperation in Communities to Enhance Safety and Security (ACCESS) (Menjívar and Kanstroom 2014). The 287(g) program allowed state and local law enforcement entities to enter into a partnership with the federal enforcement agency (ICE) under Memoranda of Agreement (MOA) to set the conditions for the expanded enforcement at the local level we see today, with possible increased limitations on immigrant workers. An analysis of 287(g) found that this program did not only target individuals who had committed serious crimes, was unevenly applied in the different jurisdictions, and that it was mainly a "jail model" (Capps et al. 2011). Importantly, by increasing the likelihood that immigrants will come into contact with law enforcement, these programs have significantly increased the policing of immigrant in the interior of the country (Kanstroom 2007).

These "enforcement-only" state-level laws, ordinances, and new forms of collaboration with federal immigration authorities have direct impact on immigrant workers. The most popular types of these exclusionary pieces of legislation seek to target employment and to enhance enforcement. These laws include making it a crime to hire day laborers (or for day laborers to solicit work by a sidewalk), making E-verify mandatory for all businesses, and making it a crime to enter into business transactions with undocumented immigrants (IPC 2012). The social costs of these enforcement policies are far-reaching, overpassing the undocumented immigrants themselves, since most undocumented co-reside with natives and U.S.-born children (Enchautegui 2013a).

Significantly, rather than exerting their effect independently of the federal government's strategies, state laws do not contradict or supersede federal authorities in their effects on the lives of immigrants. Nor do they simply "mirror" federal law (see IPC 2012). Rather, laws at the various bureaucratic scales work to reinforce one another, effecting a "force multiplier," as advocates for the increased participation of states in these matters have labeled this multipronged approach (Waslin 2010). Federal laws control who comes in and who is expelled, and policies at the state and local levels shape how immigrants live once they are in the country, in effect, complementing each other. Indeed, a key feature of the U.S. immigration regime today is its multilayered character, composed of federal, state, and local legislation with each layer magnifying the power and control of the other layers.

Importantly, even as state legislatures propose and pass "enforcement-only" laws, the business community in several of these states has been critical of this approach, as these laws tend to hinder economic growth, further exacerbating the effects of the Great Recession and jeopardizing recovery. One study that estimated the effects of HB 56 in Alabama showed that this law could lead to a reduction in the state's GDP by up to $10.8 billion due to losses in earnings, state income taxes, and sale tax collections (Addy 2012). Another study that examined the costs of local-level enforcement (Martinez 2011) found that these measures lead to significant losses in state revenue in part due to the national-level backlash they trigger, which translates into a setback to the tourism and convention industries, as the case of Arizona shows (Fitz and Kelley 2010). Thus, unsurprisingly, the Arizona Employers for Immigration Reform has actively opposed this type of legislation, opposition that seems to be having an effect in the state legislature.

6.3   A Focus on Arizona

In the midst of the explosion of state-level laws and ordinances, Arizona quickly began to take the lead and set itself apart, setting trends for anti-immigrant policies that other states would follow. For these reasons we find it instructive to examine this case in depth. Although it may be dismissed as exceptional or deviant given that this state has carved out a category of its own when it comes to immigration enforcement, this case exemplifies how immigration enforcement and the Great Recession have coalesced in the lives of Latino immigrant workers and, thus, it is relevant for the broader discussion in this volume.

Perhaps Arizona has attracted the most attention for passing SB 1070 in 2010, the state's immigration law that sought to criminalize the presence of undocumented immigrants in the state, required law-enforcement officers to check the legal status of people stopped during an investigation of possible crimes, and made it a crime for undocumented immigrants to solicit work. The 9th Circuit Court determined that two sections of SB 1070 (one which prohibited day laborers from congregating to seek employment because the practice obstructed traffic, and another that made it a crime to transport or harbor undocumented immigrants— both directed at a common labor practice among Latino immigrant workers) were either unconstitutional or preempted by federal law. And in June 2012 the U.S. Supreme Court determined that most of what was contained in SB 1070 is unconstitutional. However, it upheld Section 2B, which requires police officers to ask for an individual's identification in the course of a crime investigation and, thus, Section 2B is law in Arizona today.

Significantly, Arizona's SB 1070 is only one piece of legislation (though it has claimed the most media attention) among a tapestry of harsh immigration laws that Arizona legislators have passed since 2005, with direct implications for immigrant workers. Arizona was the first state to restrict undocumented immigrants' access to jobs (Leerkes et al. 2012) and one of the first to gain notoriety for aggressively implementing a memorandum of agreement with ICE through 287(g) in order to coordinate state and federal law enforcement efforts. It is also the first state to make E-verify an all-employer, statewide program and to pass the most comprehensive and restrictive legislation affecting immigrant workers (Lofstrom et al. 2011) in the form of the Legal Arizona Workers Act (LAWA) of 2007 (effective January 1, 2008). Under LAWA employers are prohibited from knowingly or intentionally hiring unauthorized workers after December 31, 2007, just as the Great Recession got under way. Employers who do not comply could have their business licenses suspended for ten days and the employer needs to submit a sworn affidavit within three business days and be put on probation; a second violation will permanently revoke their business license. The County Attorney offices across Arizona's 15 counties enforce the law, which also requires Arizona employers to use E-verify to validate Social Security numbers and employees' immigration status. Although LAWA can be seen as redundant because already federal law dictates that it is against the law to "knowingly" or "intentionally" hire undocumented immigrants, the state version goes further in its punitive consequences than its federal counterpart. LAWA has been challenged by several groups, including the business community, but in 2009 the U.S. Supreme Court upheld it and therefore it is the law in Arizona.

Although the presumed intent of LAWA was to reduce the number of undocumented immigrant workers in the state, it had the unintended consequence, as Lofstrom et al. (2011) note, of pushing these workers further underground and into informal work arrangements. These researchers found that LAWA reduced employment opportunities in the wage and salary sector for undocumented immigrants, leading them to shift to self-employment.

Complementing LAWA, in 2007 the state of Arizona reaffirmed legislation that allows the state to charge undocumented workers with a Class 4 Felony[4] if they use fake or legitimate social security cards belonging to someone else for the purposes of employment, redefining what used to be a civil offence into a felonious crime. The Maricopa County Sheriff's Office (MCSO) created a Criminal Employment Squad to arrest individuals found to be using borrowed or fake Social Security numbers to secure employment. Indeed, the raids that the MCSO has been conducting in businesses across the county (75 as of this writing) are framed as identity theft investigations. Arizona's identify theft law (in contrast to the federal statute) does not contain the "*knowing*" element and thus a person does not have to know that an identity card actually belongs to someone else, a situation that permits the prosecution of a much larger group of individuals caught working with a false ID. The Maricopa County Attorney's Office Special Crimes Bureau then charges and prosecutes individuals (arrested during a workplace raid) under Arizona law, since state law does not require the higher proof of "*knowing*" that the false ID belongs to an existing person, and can also charge the workers with the felonious crime of moral turpitude for identity theft or forgery. These charges carry multiple serious consequences, including jail without bail (because Arizona passed a law in 2006 denying bail to undocumented immigrants charged with a felony). Most significantly, under federal law, individuals convicted of a crime of moral turpitude,

---

[4] Class 4 felonies have a presumptive of 2 years and 6 months in prison and an aggravated term of 3 years and 9 months (Ariz. Rev. Stat. § 13–701). For example, theft of property worth between $3,000 and $4,000 is a "class 4 felony." Source: http://www.criminaldefenselawyer.com/resources/criminal-defense/felony-offense/arizona-felony-class.htm (Accessed March 4, 2014).

which includes felony charges of identity theft, are ineligible for relief from deportation and also inadmissible in the future.

This legal context is juxtaposed with the economic crisis of the Great Recession, which hit Arizona particularly hard, given the state's economy's reliance on one of the worst hit sectors—housing. Arizona, along with Florida, Michigan, California and Nevada, was hit the hardest during the Great Recession, with the collapse of the housing market (and the subsequent slowdown in the construction sector). Homes lost more than half of their value, leaving many with huge mortgages and consequently short sales and foreclosures went up rapidly. According to the U.S. Department of Labor, Arizona lost 271,400 jobs during the recession (Beard 2010)—one of the highest in the nation—and has experienced one of the worst post-recession recovery (Arizona Business Journal n.d.). This state experienced the second-worst job loss percentagewise (after Nevada) from December 2007 through 2013; the state lost one in every nine jobs, unemployment increased from 3.5 % before the recession started to 9 %, and personal income in current dollars declined (Vest 2010). According to forecasters, Arizona fell near the bottom (or to the bottom in some cases) on practically every economic measure (Vest 2010).

6.3.1 Immigrants' Experiences on the Ground

Against this political-economic backdrop, immigrant workers in Arizona have experienced the confluence of the Great Recession and immigration laws in particularly harsh fashion. The threat of workplace raids has created a climate of insecurity and fear for undocumented immigrant workers but also for anyone who either works alongside them or has relatives in this legal predicament. The omnipresent threat of raids, which are portrayed by the MCSO as efforts to combat crime and identity theft, has direct effects on immigrant workers, who become more susceptible to exploitation in the form of unpaid hours, increased workloads, no breaks during work hours, and indiscriminate firings (Menjívar 2013).

Furthermore, fearful employers began to fire workers who could not produce proof of work eligibility even before LAWA officially went into effect on January 1, 2008. In her research in Phoenix, Menjívar heard of several cases in which employers would preventively fire immigrant workers for fear of the new law. In one case, a Guatemalan woman who came to Phoenix to work in order to support her two children and mother in Guatemala explained that she had been working at a factory making musical instruments but was fired as LAWA came into effect: "When I came here I worked, I started working 2 months after I came. I was working at a musical instrument factory. I was doing well. But then *la ley del empleador* (LAWA) came and the owner of the factory fired all of us because she wanted only people with good papers. Since then it's been worse and worse. No one wants to hire, everyone is scared of the law." In another case, a woman explained that at the car wash where she worked the managers had always hired immigrants to work and about half of the workers came from Guatemala, most from the same hometown. But after a workplace raid in a business next door, the managers grew worried that the same could happen to them; thus, "just in case," they decided to fire all workers, even those with "good papers."

Therefore, although LAWA's objective was to reduce the number of undocumented workers in the state, it has mainly exacerbated the vulnerability of those workers already living in the state (see also Lofstrom et al. 2011). In the case of the Guatemalan woman mentioned above, after she was fired from the factory, she started cleaning houses with a Mexican woman who was her neighbor. However, she was working as an assistant and the main cleaner would only pay her a fraction of what she charged per house because employment was unstable as their employers would cancel cleaning jobs regularly. The main cleaner explained to her that too many people canceled cleaning jobs on them and work had become too unstable, so she could not afford paying her more. The Guatemalan woman attributed the situation to the recession, as people needed to cancel the cleaning of their homes, but also to the restrictions that LAWA placed on immigrant workers as it dramatically reduced their employment options and created conditions for exploitation among the workers. In another case, each member of a Salvadoran family whom Menjívar has followed for years mentioned that they knew someone who had been cheated out of their wages (see also Fussell 2011; Milkman et al. 2010); the mother of the family explained: "These days you hear about employers owing their employees thousands and they don't pay, and what will the workers do? What? Go to the police? Of course, there is nothing one can do." Thus, many of these workers lost their jobs and their economic insecurity increased, particularly in light of the economic downturn. Consequently, employment options for undocumented immigrants decreased during the recession and though they seem to have improved post-crisis, these jobs have become more precarious and informal, a trend exacerbated as the impacts of the economic recession started to be felt.

6.4 Broader Patterns

In this section we move to a general analysis to show other aspects of the confluence between immigration enforcement and the economic crisis that complement the case we examined in Arizona. We analyze data from the ACS from 2001 to 2012 and March CPS from 2001 to 2013 to examine whether there is evidence that the confluence of stronger enforcement and declining economic opportunities during the Great Recession pushed immigrants further underground. To this end, we concentrate on the outcomes of not-incorporated self-employment, participation in undocumented occupational niches, and employment in small businesses. Since undocumented immigrants cannot be identified in these data, we present data for noncitizens, Latino noncitizens and Latinos with up to a high school diploma (no post-secondary education) as proxies for what could be the patterns for the unauthorized population. More than two thirds of all undocumented immigrants are Latinos and about 70 % do not have college education (Enchautegui 2013b; Passel and Cohn 2009). All figures presented are based on employed persons.

To measure undergroundness in national data we focus on three indicators: the share of not-incorporated self-employed workers, the share working in undocumented niche occupations and the share employed in small businesses. We focus on not-incorporated self-employment because it is more informal since it does not require registration or formal creation of a business. Self-employment has been used as an indicator of informality (Bohn and Lofstrom 2012), and stricter enforcement may lead employers to hire undocumented workers as contractors rather than employees, increasing self-employment (Bohn and Lofstrom 2012). On the part of the workers, self-employment could be a way to avoid detection by not having to be checked through E-Verify or Social Security identification requirements and avoid being part of the tax system. We also analyze employment in what we call "unauthorized immigrant niche occupations." These are "back of the shop" occupations, requiring no licensing, little contact with the public, where it is easier for undocumented immigrants to go undetected in an era of enhanced enforcement. The following occupations were tabulated in this group: housekeepers, maids, private household workers, cooks, kitchen workers, miscellaneous food preparation workers, janitors and farm workers. We also look at employment in businesses with less than 10 employees. We speculate that it is easier for undocumented immigrants to go undetected in small businesses. Larger employers are more visible, may be more tuned into using E-Verify, have more resources to sort out undocumented workers, may be under more scrutiny by immigration authorities, and may invest more in keeping their reputation. All this suggests that working for a small business could be an indicator of undergroundness. We also present data on hourly wages, although the expected pattern in wages in today's climate of enforcement and constrained employment opportunities is unclear. Fluctuations in aggregate demand tend to be reflected in employment, not on wages, and wage changes were small during the Great Recession in comparison to prior recessions (Bewley 1999; McDonald and Solow 1985; Elsby et al. 2013). In addition, the wages of undocumented immigrants may already be quite low leaving little room for further cuts. That said, we trace hourly wages for hourly workers before, during, and after the Great Recession.

Figure 6.1 shows not-incorporated self-employment rates for natives, naturalized citizens, noncitizens and Latino noncitizens. Self-employment rates *declined* during the Great Recession for native and naturalized workers but *increased* for noncitizens, especially noncitizen Latinos. The rising not-incorporated self-employment agrees with the findings of Bohn and Lofstrom (2012) in their analysis of increased enforcement in Arizona. Among Latino noncitizens, not incorporated self-employment started at 6.4 % in 2001, with sharper increases after 2004, and went up to 9.5 by 2012.

Figure 6.2 plots not-incorporated self-employment for Latino workers with up to a high school diploma. Here again noncitizens exhibit the highest increase in self-employment, growing steadily since 2002 and overpassing naturalized citizens in 2009. The self-employment rate of Latino natives with up to a high diploma

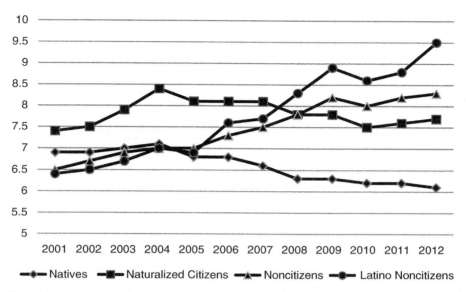

Fig. 6.1 Percentage self-employed not incorporated by nativity and citizenship, 2001–2012 (Source: Tabulations based on American Community Survey 2001–2012 from IPUMS: Steven Ruggles, J. Trent Alexander, Katie Genadek, Ronald Goeken, Matthew B. Schroeder, and Matthew Sobek. *Integrated Public Use Microdata Series: Version 5.0* [Machine-readable database]. Minneapolis: University of Minnesota, 2010)

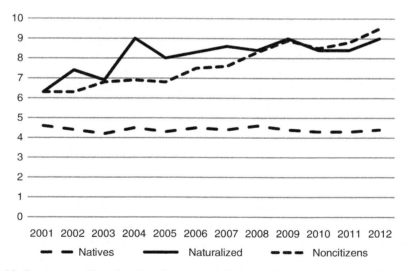

Fig. 6.2 Percentage self-employed not incorporated: Latinos with up to a high school diploma by nativity and citizenship, 2001–2012 (Source: Tabulations based on American Community Survey 2001–2012 from IPUMS: Steven Ruggles, J. Trent Alexander, Katie Genadek, Ronald Goeken, Matthew B. Schroeder, and Matthew Sobek. *Integrated Public Use Microdata Series: Version 5.0* [Machine-readable database]. Minneapolis: University of Minnesota, 2010)

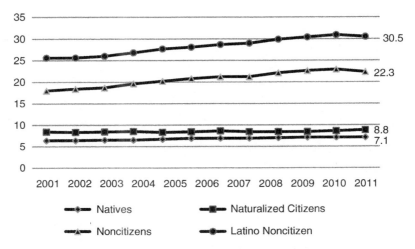

Fig. 6.3 Percentage in undocumented niche occupations by nativity and citizenship (including construction): 2001–2012. Note: Occupations are classified according to 1990 categories in IPUMS. Undocumented niche occupations are housekeepers, maids, private household workers, cooks, kitchen workers, miscellaneous food preparation workers, janitors. farm workers, construction helpers and laborers (Source: Tabulations based on American Community Survey 2001–2012 from IPUMS: Steven Ruggles, J. Trent Alexander, Katie Genadek, Ronald Goeken, Matthew B. Schroeder, and Matthew Sobek. *Integrated Public Use Microdata Series: Version 5.0* [Machine-readable database]. Minneapolis: University of Minnesota, 2010)

remained virtually unchanged and that of naturalized Latinos stabilized after 2005. Noncitizen Latinos with up to a high school diploma show the sharpest increase in not incorporated self-employment rates.

Another indicator we trace is employment in undocumented niche occupations. We argue that during this period of heightened enforcement and criminalization of undocumented labor, unauthorized immigrants seek refuge in occupations where detection by authorities is more difficult. These occupations require little interaction with customers, are "back of the shop" jobs and no licensing is required. Since construction was the industry whose employment was most affected during the Great Recession, we provide figures including and excluding construction helpers and laborers. This information is presented in Figs. 6.3, 6.4, and 6.5.

The share of noncitizens and Latino noncitizens in undocumented niche occupations grew, especially after 2004, and accelerated during the Great Recession. It was 25 % in 2001 and 30 % in 2013 among Latino noncitizens (Fig. 6.3). This growth is observed when construction occupations are included or when they are excluded and it is more evident among Latino noncitizens with low levels of education. The percentage of lower educated Latino noncitizens in niche occupations excluding construction (Fig. 6.5) grew from 23 % in the early 2000s to 27 in 2013.

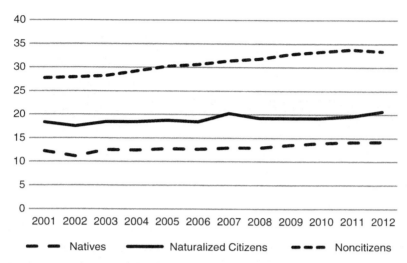

Fig. 6.4 Percentage in undocumented niche occupations: Latinos with up to high school diploma by nativity and citizenship (including construction), 2001–2012. Note: Occupations are classified according to 1990 categories in IPUMS. Undocumented niche occupations are housekeepers, maids, private household workers, cooks, kitchen workers, miscellaneous food preparation workers, janitors and farm workers, construction helpers and laborers (Source: Tabulations based on American Community Survey 2001–2012 from IPUMS: Steven Ruggles, J. Trent Alexander, Katie Genadek, Ronald Goeken, Matthew B. Schroeder, and Matthew Sobek. *Integrated Public Use Microdata Series: Version 5.0* [Machine-readable database]. Minneapolis: University of Minnesota, 2010)

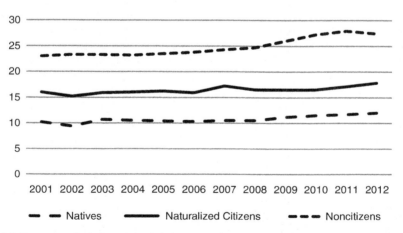

Fig. 6.5 Percentage in undocumented niche occupations: Latinos with up to high school diploma by nativity and citizenship (excluding construction), 2001–2012. Note: Occupations are classified according to 1990 categories in IPUMS. Undocumented niche occupations are housekeepers, maids, private household workers, cooks, kitchen workers, miscellaneous food preparation workers, janitors and farm workers (Source: Tabulations based on American Community Survey 2001–2012 from IPUMS: Steven Ruggles, J. Trent Alexander, Katie Genadek, Ronald Goeken, Matthew B. Schroeder, and Matthew Sobek. *Integrated Public Use Microdata Series: Version 5.0* [Machine-readable database]. Minneapolis: University of Minnesota, 2010)

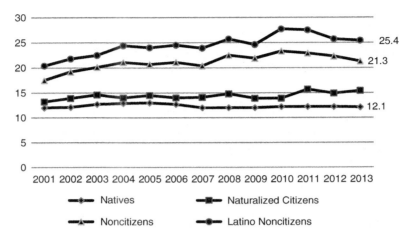

Fig. 6.6 Percentage working in small businesses by nativity and citizenship: 2001–2013. Note: Small business is defined as having from one to nine employees. Self-employed workers are excluded (Source: Tabulations based on March Current Population Surveys from IPUMS:. Miriam King, Steven Ruggles, J. Trent Alexander, Sarah Flood, Katie Genadek, Matthew B. Schroeder, Brandon Trampe, and Rebecca Vick. *Integrated Public Use Microdata Series, Current Population Survey: Version 3.0.* [Machine-readable database]. Minneapolis: University of Minnesota, 2010)

We next investigate changes in the characteristics of the employers who hire noncitizen immigrants. Based on the Annual Social and Economic Supplement of the CPS (March) from 2001 to the most current available, March 2013, we use information about the size of the employer. We tabulated the percentage who worked for small employers, defined as those with 1–9 employees. Self-employed workers are excluded in this analysis. In 2013 only 12 % of native workers were employed in small businesses, about the same percentage as in the early 2000s (Fig. 6.6). The percentage of noncitizens and Latino noncitizens in small businesses was much higher, 21 % and 25 %, respectively. Only noncitizens and Latino noncitizens show an upward trend in the percentage working in small businesses during the period examined. In 2001, 20.4 % of all Latino noncitizens worked in small businesses; it grew to 25.4 % by 2013. Figure 6.7 focuses on Latinos with up to a high school diploma. Differences in the percentage of low educated Latinos working in small businesses among natives, naturalized citizens and noncitizens was very small in the early 2000s but then started to grow primarily because of the increase in the rates for noncitizens.

Lastly, we turn to real hourly wages (in 2013 prices, for hourly paid workers) with CPS data from 2001 to 2013 for all workers by nativity and citizenship and for Latinos with up to a high school diploma (Fig. 6.8). In the count of real wages no downward tendency is evident for any of the groups. Rather, there is wage stagnation. Other research has discussed the "lost decade in wages," pointing to the stagnation in growth rates of real wages since the early 2000s, especially at the bottom of the wage distribution (Mishel and Schierholz 2013). But overall,

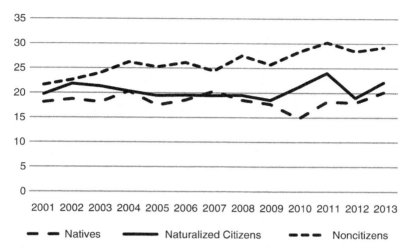

Fig. 6.7 Percentage working in small businesses: Latinos with up to a high school diploma, by nativity and citizenship, 2001–2013. Note: Small business is defined as having from one to nine employees. Self-employed workers are excluded (Source: Tabulations based on March Current Population Surveys from IPUMS:. Miriam King, Steven Ruggles, J. Trent Alexander, Sarah Flood, Katie Genadek, Matthew B. Schroeder, Brandon Trampe, and Rebecca Vick. *Integrated Public Use Microdata Series, Current Population Survey: Version 3.0.* [Machine-readable database]. Minneapolis: University of Minnesota, 2010)

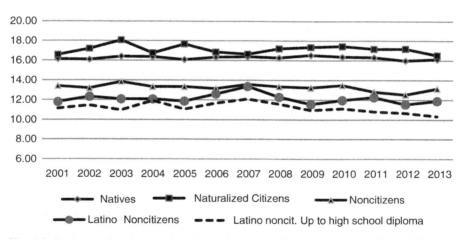

Fig. 6.8 Real mean hourly wage by citizenship and nativity, and education, Hourly Workers: 2001–2013. Note: Series adjusted for inflation using the Bureau of Labor Statistics deflator calculator, 2013 prices Tabulations of hourly wages, weighted by earnings weights (Source: Tabulations based on March Current Population Surveys from IPUMS:. Miriam King, Steven Ruggles, J. Trent Alexander, Sarah Flood, Katie Genadek, Matthew B. Schroeder, Brandon Trampe, and Rebecca Vick. *Integrated Public Use Microdata Series, Current Population Survey: Version 3.0.* [Machine-readable database]. Minneapolis: University of Minnesota, 2010)

the trends in Fig. 6.8 corroborate prior work that argues that wages tend to hold during recessions and that the main adjustment takes place through employment (Bewley 1999; Elsby et al. 2013; McDonald and Solow 1985). With respect to the wages of the undocumented, deportations and reduced undocumented immigration due to border enforcement at the Southern border, the Great Recession, and structural changes and shifts in demographic trends in Mexico (see Passel et al. 2013), may have stabilized the supply of undocumented workers, possibly preventing further declines in wages. Furthermore, many of these workers are earning quite low wages already, with little room for further declines.

6.5 Conclusion

The working premise of this chapter is that the climate of heightened enforcement at both the federal and local levels and the concomitant criminalization of undocumented immigrant workers coupled with limited economic opportunities during the Great Recession drove undocumented immigrants further underground. We argued that the double lens of punitive immigration laws and limited economic opportunity provides a fuller approach for understanding the economic experience of immigrants during the crisis. Our national data do not allow for identification of undocumented immigrants, the population at the crux of the confluence of enforcement and economic scarcity. To get closer to this population we tabulated outcomes for noncitizens and for lower educated Latinos by citizenship status and complemented this analysis with results from an ongoing qualitative study of immigrants in Phoenix, Arizona.

Our review of current laws and enforcement practices, many of which rest on the criminalization of immigrants as workers, showed the potential for these laws to influence immigrants' lives and their economic outcomes. Information from our interviews with immigrants in Phoenix speaks about "undergroundness" under the confluence of stricter enforcement and limited economic opportunity: factory employers laying off workers preemptively, workers looking for employment in private households, and wage theft and other working conditions violations. The national data examined also suggest that the confluence of the law and limited economic chances drove immigrants into informality, niche occupations and smaller, more difficult to detect employers. However, also consistent with the climate of rising enforcement, our data show that these changes did not start with the Great Recession but instead surfaced earlier, from 2003 to 2005, lending credence to our argument that stronger immigration law enforcement and the criminalization of undocumented immigrants on which these new strategies for enforcement rest are behind these trends. These trends, already under way, together with the economic downturn contributed to exacerbate the vulnerability of immigrants by worsening conditions in the labor market. A vicious cycle that Chauvin, Garcés-Mascareñas and Kraler (2013) identified in several European cases seems to be occurring in the United States as well, in which employment precariousness becomes the source and the consequence of legal marginality for immigrants. Comparisons to Latino noncitizens with low levels of education provide another vantage point to disentangle economic trends from immigration law enforcement trends. The trends associated with further undergroundness are revealed with more poignancy among lower educated Latino noncitizens, the group where undocumented labor is concentrated.

We did not find, however, wage trends unique to noncitizens nor to lower educated Latino noncitizens. This is consistent with prior work that has identified little decline in real wages during economic recessions (Bewley 1999; McDonald and Solow 1985; Elsby et al. 2013). With respect to the unauthorized population it could be that their wages are already quite low as to stand further decline and that the supply of undocumented workers subsided during the years of the Great Recession. In the end, our work demonstrates the increased vulnerability of Latino immigrant workers under conditions that make it increasingly difficult to assert their rights, especially when much of what they do is criminalized. Although undocumented Latino immigrants may be able to find employment during or after an economic crisis, the kind of jobs they secure under the current immigration regime contribute to their undergroundness and may diminish their rights as workers.

Acknowledgments We would like to thank Evelyn Cruz for her help in deciphering the details of Arizona immigration laws. All errors remaining are, of course, ours.

References

Addy, S. (2012). A cost-benefit analysis of the new Alabama immigration law. Center for Business and Economic Research, Culverhouse College of Commerce and Business Administration. University of Alabama. http://cber.cba.ua.edu/New%20AL%20Immigration%20Law%20-%20Costs%20and%20Benefits.pdf. Accessed 3 Feb 2014.

Arizona Business Journal. (n.d.). Arizona job recovery among nation's worst post-recession.http://www.bizjournals.com/phoenix/print-edition/2013/08/30/arizona-job-recovery-among-nations.html. Accessed 5 Feb 2014.

Beard, B. (2010). Arizona recession is finally over, economists say. The Arizona Republic. http://www.azcentral.com/business/articles/2010/09/21/20100921arizona-recession-officially-over.html. Accessed 11 Feb 2014.

Bohn, S., & Lofstrom, M. (2012). Employment effects of state legislation against the hiring of unauthorized immigrant workers (No. 6598). Discussion paper series, Forschungsinstitut zur Zukunft der Arbeit.

Bewley, T. F. (1999). *Why wages do not fall in the recession?* Cambridge, MA: Harvard University Press.

Cadena, B. C., & Kovak, B. K. (2013). *Immigrants equilibrate local labor markets: Evidence from the great recession (No. w19272).* Cambridge, MA: National Bureau of Economic Research.

Camayd-Freixas, E. (2009). *Postville: La criminalización de los Migrantes.* Guatemala: F&G Editores.

Capps, R., Rosenblum, M. R., Rodriguez, C., & Chishti, M. (2011). *Delegation and divergence: A study of 287(g) state and local immigration enforcement.* Washington, DC: Migration Policy Institute.

Catron, P. (2013). Immigrant unionization through the great recession. *American Sociological Review, 78*(2), 315–332.

Chacon, J. M. (2009). Managing immigration through crime. *Columbia Law Review, 109*, 135–148.

Chauvin, S., Garcés-Mascareñas, B., & Kraler, A. (2013). Working for legality: Employment and migrant regularization in Europe. *International Migration, 51*, 118–131.

Department of Homeland Security. (2012). Immigration year book 2012. http://www.dhs.gov/yearbook-immigration-statistics-2012-enforcement-actions. Accessed 12 Feb 2014.

Donato, K. M., & Massey, D. S. (1993). Effect of the immigration reform and control act on the wages of Mexican migrants. *Social Science Quarterly, 74*(3), 523–541.

Dowling, J., & Inda, J. X. (Eds.). (2013). *Governing immigration through crime: A reader.* Palo Alto: Stanford University Press.

Ellis, M., Wright, R., & Townley, M. (2013). The allure of new immigrant destinations and the great recession in the United States. *International Migration Review.* doi:10.1111/imre.12058.

Ellis, M., Wright, R., Townley, M., & Copeland, K. (2014). *The migration response to the Legal Arizona workers act. Political Geography,* 42: 46–56.

Elsby, M. W., Shin, D., & Solon, G. (2013). *Wage adjustment in the great recession* (Working paper 19478). Cambridge, MA: National Bureau of Economic Research.

Enchautegui, M. E. (2012). *Hit hard but bouncing back: The employment of immigrants during the great recession and recovery.* Washington, DC: Urban Institute.

Enchautegui, M. E. (2013a). *More than 11 million: Unauthorized immigrants and their families.* Washington, DC: Urban Institute.

Enchautegui, M. E. (2013b). *A comparison of today's unauthorized immigrants and the IRCA legalized: Implications for immigration reform.* Washington, DC: Urban Institute.

Fitz, M., & Kelley, A. (2010). *Stop the conference: The economic and fiscal consequences of conference cancellations due to Arizona's SB 1070.* Washington, DC: Center for American Progress. http://www.americanprogress.org/wp-content/uploads/issues/2010/11/pdf/az_tourism.pdf. Accessed 10 Feb 2014.

FitzGerald, D., Alarcón, R., & Muse-Orlinoff, L. (Eds.). (2011). *Recession without borders: Mexican migrants confront the economic downturn.* San Diego: Center for Comparative Immigration Studies, University of California.

Fussell, E. (2011). The deportation threat dynamic and victimization of Latino migrants: Wage theft and robbery. *Sociological Quarterly, 52*(4), 593–615.

Gentsch, K., & Massey, D. S. (2011). Labor market outcomes for legal Mexican immigrants under the new regime of immigration enforcement. *Social Science Quarterly, 92*(3), 875–893.

Grusky, D. B., Western, B., & Wimer, C. (2011). *The great recession.* New York: Russell Sage.

Hagan, J. M., Rodriguez, N., & Castro, B. (2011). Social effects of mass deportations by the United States government, 2000–10. *Ethnic and Racial Studies, 34*(8), 1374–1391.

IPC (Immigration Policy Center). (2012). Q&A guide to state immigration laws: What you need to know if your state is considering anti-immigrant legislation. http://www.immigrationpolicy.org/sites/default/files/docs/State_Guide_to_Immigration_Laws_Updated_021612.pdf. Accessed 2 Feb 2014.

Kanstroom, D. (2007). *Deportation nation: Outsiders in American history.* Cambridge, MA: Harvard University Press.

Kochhar, R. (2010). *After the great recession: Foreign born gain jobs; native born lose jobs.* Washington, DC: Pew Research Center.

Leerkes, A., Leach, M., & Bachmeier, J. (2012). Borders behind the border: Exploration of state-level differences in migration control and their effects on US migration patterns. *Journal of Ethnic and Migration Studies, 38*(1), 111–129.

Lofstrom, M., Bohn, S., & Raphael, S. (2011). *Lessons from the 2007 legal Arizona workers act.* Public Policy Institute of California. http://www.ppic.org/content/pubs/report/R_311MLR.pdf. Accessed 4 Feb 2014.

Martinez, G. (2011). *Unconstitutional and costly: The high price of local immigration enforcement.* Washington, DC: Center for American Progress. http://www.americanprogress.org/wp-content/uploads/issues/2011/01/pdf/cost_of_enforcement.pdf. Accessed 10 Feb 2014.

Massey, D. S. (2012). Immigration and the great recession (A great recession brief). The Russell Sage Foundation and the Stanford Center on Poverty and Inequality.

Massey, D. S., Durand, J., & Malone, N. (2002). *Beyond smoke and mirrors: Mexican immigration in an Era of economic integration.* New York: Russell Sage.

McDonald, I. M., & Solow, R. M. (1985). Wages and employment in a segmented labor market. *The Quarterly Journal of Economics, 100*(4), 1115–1141.

Meissner, D., Kerwin, D. M., Chishti, M., & Bergeron, C. (2013). *Immigration enforcement in the United States: The rise of a formidable machinery.* Washington, DC: Migration Policy Institute.

Menjívar, C. (2013). Central American immigrant workers and legal violence in Phoenix, Arizona. *Latino Studies, 11*(2), 228–252.

Menjívar, C., & Kanstroom, D. (Eds.). (2014). *Constructing immigrant "Illegality": Critiques, experiences, and responses.* New York: Cambridge University Press.

Milkman, R., González, A. L., & Narro, V. (2010). *Wage theft and workplace violations in Los Angeles: The failure of employment and labor law for low-wage workers.* Los Angeles: UCLA Institute for Research on Labor and Employment.

Mishel, L., & Shierholz, H. (2013). *A decade of lost wages: The key barriers to shared prosperity and a rising middle class.* Washington, DC: Economic Policy Institute. http://www.epi.org/publication/a-decade-of-flat-wages-the-key-barrier-to-shared-prosperity-and-a-rising-middle-class/. Accessed 9 Feb 2014.

Mitnik, P. A., & Halpern-Finnerty, J. (2010). Immigration and local governments: Inclusionary local policies in the Era of state rescaling. In M. W. Varsanyi (Ed.), *Taking local control: Immigration policy activism in U.S. Cities and states* (pp. 51–72). Stanford: Stanford University Press.

NCSL (National Council of State Legislatures). (2014). 2013 Immigration report (overview). http://www.ncsl.org/research/immigration/2013-immigration-report.aspx. Accessed 4 Feb 2014.

Orrenius, P. M., & Zavodny, M. (2009). The effects of tougher enforcement on the job prospects of recent Latin American immigrants. *Journal of Policy Analysis and Management, 28*(2), 239–257.

Parrado, E. A. (2012). Immigration enforcement policies, the economic recession, and the size of local Mexican immigrant populations. *Annals of the American Academy of Political and Social Science, 641*(1), 16–37.

Passel, J. S., & Cohn, D. (2009). *A portrait of unauthorized immigrants in the United States.* Washington, DC: Pew Hispanic Research Project.

Passel, J. S., Cohn, D., & Gonzalez-Barrera, A. (2013). *Population decline of unauthorized immigrants stalls, may have reversed.* Washington, DC: Pew Research Center's Hispanic Trends Project.

Scott, E. K., & Leymon, A. S. (2013). Making ends meet during the great recession: How child care subsidies matter to low-wage workers. *Journal of Poverty, 17*(1), 63–85.

Singer, A. (2004). *The rise of new immigrant gateways.* Washington, DC: Brookings Institution.

Singer, A., & Wilson, J. H. (2010). *The impact of the great recession on metropolitan immigration trends.* Washington, DC: Metropolitan Policy Program, Brookings Institution.

Treas, J. (2010). The great American recession: Sociological insights on blame and pain. *Sociological Perspectives, 53*(1), 3–17.

Vest, M. J. (2010). *Recession is over: Let recovery begin!* Tucson: University of Arizona's Economy, Economic and Business Research Center, Eller College of Management.

Vroman, W. (2010). The role of unemployment insurance as an automatic stabilizer during a recession. Impaq International: Report submitted to the Department of Labor. Retrieved from http://wdr.doleta.gov/research/FullText_Documents/ETAOP2010-10.pdf. Accessed 7 May 2014.

Walker, K. E., & Leitner, H. (2011). The variegated landscape of local immigration policies in the United States. *Urban Geography, 32*(2), 156–178.

Waslin, M. (2010). Immigration enforcement by state and local police: The impact of the enforcers and their communities. In M. W. Varsanyi (Ed.), *Taking local control: Immigration policy activism in U.S. cities and states* (pp. 97–114). Stanford: Stanford University Press.

Part II
Understanding Immigrant Adaptation in Difficult Times

Chapter 7
Changes in the Perception of Latin American Immigrants in Host Countries During the Great Recession

María Ángeles Cea D'Ancona and Miguel S. Valles Martínez

7.1 Natives' Perceptions of Immigrants and Economic Momentum

Is it only in times of economic crisis when host countries' perceptions of immigration turn negative? Moreover, do motives related to *material interests* solely explain opposition to immigration (or a proportion of it) during times of economic turmoil? Based on population studies with different emphases, the literature reviewed offers a variety of responses. Some authors have underlined that competition for scarce resources triggers ethnic prejudice (Allport 1954; Blumer 1958; Quillian 1995); that it magnifies the imagined or estimated number of immigrants; or that it may lead to appeals to restrict their entry – or even that immigrants should be expelled from the country (Castles and Kosack 1973; Walker and Pettigrew 1984; Coenders and Scheepers 1998; Bommes and Geddes 2000). More recently, it has been concluded that competition for scarce resources is the main cause of social conflict in disadvantaged neighborhoods, extending to the second and third generation immigrant population (Kleiner-Liebau 2011). Also, while stable economic conditions help reduce perceptions of threat and prejudice, negative economic expectations for the future reduce tolerance toward immigrants and minorities (Sari 2007). In the same vein, it has been stated that low wage laborers and economically vulnerable groups express greater anti-immigrant feelings than those who are well-off (Scheve and Slaughter 2001; Pettigrew et al. 2007; Clark and Legge 2009), including immigrants themselves. The Eurobarometer 53 collected in 2000 (SORA 2001) highlighted negative attitudes towards those belonging to ethnic minorities in the European Union. In the U.S., the study of Telles and Ortiz (2009) showed that Mexican-Americans with lower education showed the greatest

M.Á.C. D'Ancona (✉) • M.S. Valles Martínez
Departamento de Sociología IV, Facultad de Ciencias Políticas y Sociología,
Universidad Complutense de Madrid, Madrid, Spain
e-mail: maceada@ucm.es; msvalles@ucm.es

© Springer International Publishing Switzerland 2015
M. Aysa-Lastra, L. Cachón (eds.), *Immigrant Vulnerability and Resilience*,
International Perspectives on Migration 11, DOI 10.1007/978-3-319-14797-0_7

rejection towards immigration. On the contrary, more educated respondents exhibit lower levels of ethnocentrism; place more emphasis on cultural diversity, and are also more optimistic about the economic impacts of immigration (Bobo and Licari 1989; Citrin et al. 1997; Chandler and Tsai 2001; Hainmueller and Hiscox 2010; Cea D'Ancona and Valles 2014).

Nevertheless, these are neither the only factors nor are they universal results. Citrin et al. (1997) also found that an increase in optimism about the economy coincided with an increase in opposition to immigration. Burns and Gimpel (2000) state that personal and national economic outlook play only a small role in predicting whites' attitudes toward immigration. In Spain, the greatest increase in opposition towards immigration also coincided with a period of economic growth and a greater demographic presence of immigrants (Cea D'Ancona 2004; Cea D'Ancona and Valles 2008, 2014). As noted by Portes and Rumbaut (2006), periods of intensive immigration are always marked by stiff resistance from the host population, who see the waves of newcomers as a threat to the integrity of the national culture. Brücker et al. (2002) connect racial attitudes in Europe with the defense of cultural homogeneity; Cachón (2005) does so with nationalism.

The economic threat (immigrants take jobs from natives, end up on welfare and increase the tax burden) is an important factor explaining the rejection of immigration, but there is also a cultural threat. People who wish to reduce the flow of immigrants into their country often see the newcomers as a menace to cherished cultural traditions (Simon 1993; Espenshade and Hempstead 1996). Using data from the 1994 General Social Survey (GSS) in the U.S., Chandler and Tsai (2001) also found that college education and perceived cultural threats (especially to the English language) have the most impact upon views on immigration. Other variables are political ideology, economic outlook, age, and gender. Race, income, and fear of crime appear to have negligible effects.

It is also important to take an ethnocultural view of national identity. Analyzing the 1996 GSS and focus groups, Schildkraut (2005) shows that Americans who take an ethnocultural view of national identity (that is, to be American is to be born in the U.S., to live in the U.S. and to be Christian) are more supportive of restricting immigration. Wong (2010) uses the 1996 and 2004 GSS to show that those who define the American community in exclusive terms are more restrictionists, more opposed to birthright citizenship, and to extending citizenship rights to legal permanent residents. Also, *ideology* has higher impact upon attitudes to immigration than other factors (political conservatives hold more negative attitudes toward current immigration than are political liberals). One exception is when immigration is framed as a national threat to security (Lahav and Courtemanche 2012).

7.1.1 Relevance and Feasibility of a Comparative Perspective: United States and Spain

The relevance of Latin American immigration in the U.S. and Spain, as well as its different degrees of integration in both countries, explains the interest in the comparative analysis of perceptions and attitudes towards these immigrant group. The rejection of immigration depends not only on the economic and material position of the native population (Brader et al. 2009; Valentino et al. 2013) but also on the characteristics of the immigrants (their ethnicity, their economic and job status, cultural and religious distinctiveness, and population size). The latter is evident in Europe, where the fear of loss of national identity is prominent in explaining xenophobia. This is manifested primarily in the greater rejection of immigrants who are perceived as different and less able to integrate into Western societies, i.e. Muslims (Schnapper 1994; Sartori 2001; Strabac and Listhung 2008). By contrast, Latin American immigrants are perceived as closer and more able to integrate in Spain (Cea D'Ancona et al. 2013); but not in US where "Latino immigrants are the «new Blacks», having been stereotyped and stigmatized as the perennial and inassimilable underclass" (Davies 2009: 378). The problem lies in the lack, in both countries, of fully comparable surveys on Latin American immigration and attitudes toward immigration in general. As Muste (2013: 398) states, in his article about the dynamics of opinion on immigration in the United States, 1992– 2012, "Public opinion about immigration has undergone substantial change over time but inconsistent coverage of immigration in public opinion surveys has limited our understanding of opinion change". Other authors (Lapinski et al. 1997; Segovia and DeFever 2010) share the criticism (referring also to academic survey organizations such as American National Election Studies (ANES) and the General Social Survey (GSS)) that few questions have been asked about immigration and that those questions have not been preserved in the time series.

In the U.S. most survey organizations began assessing opinion on immigration when the issue became nationally prominent in the late 1980s and early 1990s. In Spain, a country of emigration till the late 1970s, it was not until 1990 when various series of specific surveys on attitudes towards immigration began to be collected. These surveys were conducted by an independent organization, ASEP (Análisis Sociológicos, Económicos y Políticos), and a public center, CIS (Centro de Investigaciones Sociológicas). From 2007 the Spanish Observatory on Racism and Xenophobia (OBERAXE) has been funding annual opinion polls on attitudes to immigration in order to follow the evolution of racism and xenophobia. These survey data is collected through face-to-face interviews carried out by the CIS from 2007 to 2012 (The analytical reports, by Cea D'Ancona and Valles, are published by OBERAXE and the surveys can be accessed in the CIS database). Although the data available does not allow for a detailed analysis of changes in opinion regarding specific immigrant groups, it does for views and attitudes towards immigration in general, before and during the current crisis. This is why we begin by providing an overview of attitudes towards immigration in general, and then move to Latin American immigration in particular.

7.2   Changes in Attitudes Towards Immigration on Both Sides of the Atlantic: Surveys in the U.S., Europe and Spain

7.2.1   Transatlantic Surveys

Transatlantic Trends: Immigration (TTI) survey (a telephone poll) has been conducted yearly from 2008 to 2011 to sound out U.S. and European public opinion on a range of immigration and integration issues. Spain is one of the European countries included in the last three surveys but it was not polled in 2008 (the countries included this year were the United States, the United Kingdom, France, Germany and Italy). The more general *2013 Transatlantic Trends* survey is the twelfth in that series (beginning in 2002) where, for the first time, immigration questions were preceded by questions about foreign, security and economic policy. Drawing from these data sets for the period 2009–2013, the following key findings are highlighted to provide context to the comparisons in this chapter.

The first contextual data related to the perception of the crisis on both sides of the Atlantic is available in TT Topline Data 2013, thanks to question Q21 whose wording was "And regarding the extent to which you or your family has been personally affected by the current economic crisis, would you say that your family's financial situation has been. . . (greatly affected, somewhat, not really, not affected at all)". Whereas in the U.S., in the first three years of the crisis (2009–2011), two-thirds or more of respondents declared they felt affected by it, in Spain this feeling gradually increased, to reach a peak in 2013. The average European figures show that Spain is part of the group of countries most affected by the crisis. However, there is also another group (northern European countries) whose populations have been less affected by the Great Recession (Fig. 7.1).

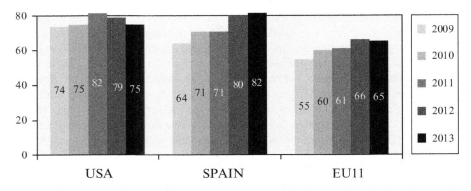

Fig. 7.1 Personally affected by the Economic Crisis 2009–2013 (US, Spain, EU11)
Results for EU11 are based on eleven European Union member states: France, Germany, Italy, the Netherlands, Poland, Portugal, Slovakia, Spain, United Kingdom, Romania and Sweden

The *Transatlantic Trends Key Findings 2013 Report* also points out that this economic crisis drove negative attitudes toward issues like immigration. "A majority (64 %) of those who felt personally affected by the economic crisis also considered immigration to be a problem (only 16 % saw it as an opportunity). Of those not affected by the economic crisis, 47 % considered immigration to be a problem while 26 % perceived it as an opportunity". In the U.S., perceptions of immigration as a problem have changed less than in the case of Spain: 54 % of Americans in 2009 and 47 % in 2013, compared to 58 % of Spaniards in 2009 and 44 % in 2013. The strongest pessimism was registered in the United Kingdom (66 % in 2009, 64 % in 2013). At the same time, the optimistic attitude ("immigration is more of an opportunity") has seen an upward trend among both Americans (39 % in 2009, 46 % in 2013) and Spaniards (36 % in 2009, 44 % in 2013); and above all in Germany (48 % in 2009, 62 % in 2013). Lower percentages of optimism are found among British respondents (27 % in 2009, 29 % in 2013) or Italians (32 % in 2009 and 2013); although the weakest optimism was recorded in other European countries, such as Turkey (18 % in 2013) and Slovakia (16 % in 2013).

When asked about whether "immigrants take jobs away" (from native-born citizens), growing agreement was recorded among respondents in the United States from 2009 (52 %) to 2011 (57 %), followed by a downward trend in 2013 (50 %). In the case of Spain, agreement has followed a downward trend every year from the start of the crisis (43 % in 2009, 33 % in 2013). Except in the United Kingdom, Europeans polled repeatedly over those years (in France, Germany, Italy, the Netherlands and Spain) expressed disagreement rather than agreement with the statement that immigrants, in general, take jobs away from native workers in those countries.

When the question refers to the statement: "immigrants are a burden on social services", respondents in the U.S. and U.K. were the most worried in 2011. In both countries 63 % of their polled populations were in agreement; but in 2013 a downward trend of 6 and 7 % points respectively was recorded. Respondents in Spain were less worried in 2013 (41 %) than in 2011 (55 %). But other European countries maintain a similar degree of agreement at both dates. That is the case of France (55–57 %), Germany (46–49 %) and Italy (51–52 %). Spain, relative to other countries, has registered more positive opinions towards immigration, even relative to the U.S.

On the issue of integration (over the most recent years of the current crisis), majorities on both sides of the Atlantic maintained or increased their optimism about the success of immigrant integration in general. The evolution of this opinion in the United Sates was as follows: 59 % (2010), 56 % (2011) and 61 % (2013). Similar figures were recorded in Spain: 54 %, 62 % and 63 %. Italian respondents jumped from 37 % in 2010 to 59 % (2011) and 60 % (2013). But public opinion in France, Germany or the U.K. was more evenly split, with almost every figure fewer than 50 %. On the other hand, when the focus is on the integration of "children of immigrants who were born in [COUNTRY]", both Europeans and Americans respondents elevated their positive percentage of answers. That is, the children of immigrants were considered to be "well" or "very well" integrated into the society to where their parents had emigrated. But the trend followed from 2010 to 2013 is downwards in the cases of the U.S. (79 %, 74 % and 68 %), Spain (78 %, 72 % and 73 %), the U.K. (68 %, 66 % and 55 %) and France (54 %, 59 % and 43 %). Only Germany's positive responses grow (50 %, 54 % and 59 %), and the opinion in Italy fluctuates (65 %, 77 % and 66 %).

Certainly, when other more specific groups of immigrants are evaluated, greater variations appear. That is the case of Muslim immigrants, seen as less well integrated than immigrants in general, both in Europe and in America. In the U.S. 45 % in 2010 and 50 % in 2011 viewed this group well or very well integrated (Hispanic immigrants: 65 % in 2010 and 59 % in 2011). Similar figures for Muslim immigrants were collected in France. Spain recorded the minimum percentage in 2010 (21 %) and 2011 (29 %). Data in the rest of the European countries polled fell in between. On the other hand, another interesting variation appears when populations in these host societies are asked about legal and illegal immigrants. The former only cause worries to 1 (or fewer) out of 4 respondents, no matter the side of the Atlantic or the year. But the latter are viewed negatively by 6 out of 10 in the U.S., and by 7 or 8 out of 10 in the European countries polled.

A final key finding selected from the TTI data sets refers to government management of illegal immigration from the point of view of public opinion. Among the Europeans respondents included in the TTI (2008–2011), majorities of Italians (around 55 %) and British (*circa* two-thirds) stated that illegal immigrants should be required to return home. This is also the option with greatest backing among Spaniards in 2011 (57 %), however only 48 % and 49 % chose this option in 2009 and 2010 respectively. Nine percentage points was also the increase recorded in France, from 2009 (35 %) to 2011 (44 %), while in Germany 52 % in 2009 (and 50 % in 2010 and 2011) preferred legalization. Americans appear more evenly divided: 49 % opted for legalization in 2008 and 2011 (44–45 % in 2009–2010); compared to 43 % and 47 % supporting return in 2008 and 2011 respectively, (48–47 % in 2009–2010).

7.2.2 Spanish Immigration Surveys

In Spain it is possible to analyze changing attitudes towards immigration before and during the Great Recession, due to specific annual surveys that have maintained the same sample base (not panel design) and questionnaire design: the "face-to-face" OBERAXE-CIS surveys, which enable the same indicators to be tracked longitudinally until 2012 in the Spanish population aged 18 years and over. Applying three multivariate analytical techniques (factor, cluster and discriminant) to the set of indicators in each survey gives us a typology of attitudes towards immigration, whose changes are described in Cea D'Ancona (2004, 2007) and in the series of annual reports on the evolution of racism and xenophobia conducted by the authors of this chapter from 2008 to 2013. Figure 7.2 shows the drop in explicit rejection of immigration from 1993 to 1996. From 2000 rejection rose again, with noticeable increases in 2001, 2002, 2007 and 2011. In 2011 this amounted to 40 % of the sample. But unlike the 2009 and 2010 surveys, in 2011 the profile of those classified as having ambivalent attitudes towards immigrants was closer to tolerance than rejection; in particular it highlights their greater acceptance of living with immigrants; the approval of immigrants being granted rights, and the fact that those with ambivalent attitudes are also the least resistant to a multicultural society (Cea D'Ancona and Valles 2013). The change in this ambivalent profile coincides with increasing education and income; respondents' position left of center on the political ideology scale; a greater confidence in people; and less recent experience of unemployment. These variables led to a more open attitude to immigration. The higher average figures define tolerant individuals, while the lower ones define those adverse or resistant to immigration (more elderly people; the less educated; those in less qualified jobs and with lower income; those ideologically on the right; firm religious believers; those distrustful of and without personal experience of emigration).

Figure 7.2 also shows that rejection of immigration increases as does the perception of an excess number of immigrants; and the view of immigration laws as being "too tolerant", while the opinion of "unrestricted acceptance of political refugees" decreases (in surveys which include these indicators). Moreover, the view of facilitating the entry of immigrants "only with a contract" increased.[1]

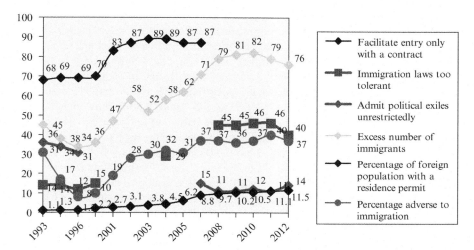

Fig. 7.2 Indicators for acceptance of immigration in Spain related to immigration policy and other topics. CIS (1993–2005) and OBERAXE-CIS (2007–2012) surveys (total percentage of respondents)

---

[1] In the Special Eurobarometer 380 (TNS 2012a), Spain stood as the third most favorable to labor immigration (51 %), behind the Finns (56 %) and the Swedes (60 %). As for political asylum, the most favorable countries were Sweden (95 %), Denmark (92 %) and the Netherlands (91 %). Spain stood in eleventh position (85 %).

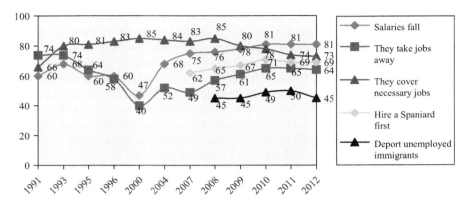

Fig. 7.3 Changes in agreement over the effects of immigration on the labor market. CIS (1991–2005) and OBERAXE-CIS (2007–2012) surveys (percentage of total respondents)

In 2011 the perception of an excess number of immigrants dropped slightly, at the same time as their actual presence in Spain starting falling. However, the desire for a tougher immigration policy remained stable. Not so in 2012, when the perception of the presence of immigrants continued to wane, contributing to less rejection (a three point decrease). This is in consonance with the news provided by the social media (Cea D'Ancona and Valles 2014).

In Spain the consideration of immigration as a problem and threat is also crucial in explaining xenophobia. This takes on special significance in four key areas: employment, access to basic social rights, preserving one's culture, and the fear of increased crime. Times of economic crisis, and the decline in economic resources and employment, tend to activate stereotypes that have traditionally encouraged xenophobic discourse: "immigrants take away jobs" and "immigrants contribute to lower wages". This is evidenced by survey data collected in Spain.

Figure 7.3 shows the upward trend in both beliefs, and the drop in recognition that "immigrants cover necessary jobs" (which the Spanish do not do). In turn, there has been an increase in opinion favorable to the expulsion of immigrants in long-term unemployment (29 % in 2005 to 50 % in 2011) and the discourse on preference in the workplace: "when hiring someone, people prefer to hire a Spaniard before an immigrant" (62 % in 2007, 69 % in 2011). Both items are included in the OBERAXE-CIS surveys and their trends are associated with the increase in unemployment in both the native and immigrant population (unemployment rates stood at 11.3 % in 2008, rising to 21.5 % in 2011 when the surveys were run) (see Chap. 3).

7.2.3 North American Immigration Surveys

In his analysis of public opinion on immigration in US, integrating trends from ANES, GSS, Gallup, Pew, and media surveys from 1992 to 2012, Muste (2013) reveals a pattern of rapid, sharp increases in anti-immigrant sentiment in response to events such as the 1994 election (Bush vs. Clinton) and 9/11 (the terrorist attacks), followed by declines over several years that stabilize at lower levels. Concerns about competition for jobs and border enforcement rank high, whereas fears about other immigration impacts have declined or stabilized, and support for deporting illegal immigrants is already low in the United States. The analysis begins with questions about respondents' preferred levels of immigration before moving to perceptions of the impacts of immigrants on the economy and society.

In all surveys, majorities support reducing immigration levels. According to the *General Social Survey* (GSS): biennial surveys of face-to-face interviews, 34 % (in 2008) and 35 % (in 2010) were in agreement with the existing level of immigration. Proponents of reducing the number of immigrants dropped from 53 % to 49 % (2008–2010), although earlier, in 2000, the figure was only 42 % of respondents. In the *Gallup Poll* (telephone surveys) since 2002, support for reducing immigration has ranged from 39 % to 51 %, with high points during the 2005 congressional debate over immigration and in 2009 following the onset of the recession, then a decline to just 35 % in 2012.

Regarding the impacts of immigration and immigrants on the U.S. economy, culture, and in general, the surveys analyzed by Muste (2013) indicate ambivalence over the impact of immigrants. Growing beliefs in immigrants' positive impacts coexist with steady concerns about employment and crime. Since 2001, between 52 % and 67 % have said that immigration is a "good" rather than a bad thing (Gallup), with positive opinion dipping slightly following 9/11 (10 % points) and the 2008 economic crisis (6 % points). From 2001 to 2007 beliefs that immigrants would worsen the economy rose from 32 % to 46 % (Gallup).

The greatest consistency and negativity in public opinion on immigrants' impacts concerns jobs. In 2004 and 2008 about 45 % of respondents agreed or strongly agreed that it was "extremely" or "very" likely that immigrants would take away jobs (ANES: *American National Election Studies*). From 2001 to 2007, about one-half of respondents believed immigrants would not have "much effect" on job opportunities (Gallup), but some one-third of respondents thought immigrants would make opportunities "worse".

And when asked about illegal immigrants, public opinion on policy is also ambivalent, and responses influenced by references to immigrants' location and job status. From 2006 to 2012, solid (but somewhat unstable) majorities favored allowing currently illegal immigrants to continue working in the U.S. and not be deported (Gallup). In contrast, opinion toward potential illegal immigrants outside U.S. borders is overwhelmingly negative: between 50 % (in 2008) viewed that spending on border security should be increased (ANES) and 58 % said that "controlling and reducing illegal immigration" was a "very important" "foreign policy goal" in 2004 and 2008 (ANES). There is also strong support for states acting in the area of immigration policy, with about 60 % approving the Arizona immigration law's citizenship verification component over the 3 year period since its passage in 2010 (Pew: telephone interviews).

In this review of survey trends, economic problems in 1991–1992, 2001, and 2008–2010 did not increase opposition to immigration. By contrast, opposition increased in the wake of bitter debates over immigration policy in 1994–1996 and 2006–2007, and the events of 9/11. Muste (2013: 400–402) states that "opinion about immigration levels is clearly sensitive to events directly relevant to immigration, such as the 1994 election and California's Proposition 187, and to national security (9/11) concerns. Economic downturns, such as that beginning in 2008, appear to foster moderate restrictionism at most".

7.3 The Specificity of Latin American Immigration on Each Side of the Atlantic

7.3.1 The Dual Perception of Latin American Immigration in Spain

The fact that Latin American immigrants are the second most numerous in Spain (27.1 % in 2012, 29.8 % in 2008) after Europeans is an important factor to consider when analyzing attitudes towards immigrants and their integration. Also, it is about this group that Spaniards think when discussing immigration. Figure 7.4 shows that, when asked, "When talking about foreign immigrants living in Spain, who do you immediately think about?" (a question not included in the 2012 survey), the mention of Latin Americas has been increasing, halving the previously dominant response: "Moroccans (North Africans)". In the case of the Latin American population, this development is in line with their greater presence in the statistics of foreigners with residence permits; however, this is not the case of Morocco, whose mention in excess during the 1990s contributed to the news of illegal immigrants in dinghies arriving on Spanish beaches (Cea D'Ancona 2004). As regards specific mentions of Latin American immigrants in the CIS-OBERAXE surveys, the two most frequent references in 2011 are to Ecuador and Colombia (6 % and 3 %). These were the two most numerous Latin American nationalities in Spain from 2006 to 2012. The highest figure was reached in 2006: Ecuadorians: 12.5 % and Colombians: 7.5 %. These two are followed by Peruvians (3 %) and Argentinians (2.9 % of the 3,021,808 foreigners with residence permit in Spain in that year).

The importance of Romanian immigration from 2007 on (after their inclusion to the EU) meant Latin America lost its relative weight, falling to slightly lower figures in 2012 (7.2 % Ecuadorians and 5 % Colombians, closer now to Bolivians and Peruvians, with 2.9 % and 2.6 % respectively of a total of 5,411,923 foreign residents). In the nineties the Argentinians were the most numerous Latin American nationality in Spain (representing 3.4 % of the 538,984 foreigners in 1996) and the image of the Latin American immigrant which was most widespread (arousing a higher percentage of sympathy). However, at that time Peruvians and Dominicans also had a similar weight (3.3 % each) (see Chap. 1).

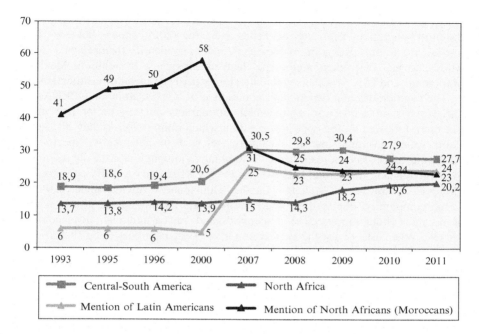

Fig. 7.4 Growth in foreigners (Central-South America and North Africa) living in Spain, plus mentions of Latin American and North African (Moroccan) immigrants in the CIS 1993–2000 surveys and the OBERAXE CIS 2007–2011 (percentages)

On the mention of immigrants, it should be noted that an eminently economic connotation (racial classism or class racism) is prevalent. However, even within the group of those considered by the native Spanish population to be economic migrants, there are distinctions; nuances that are better captured in qualitative cross-sectional analysis. The following reflection made by an Iranian immigrant in one of the discussion groups for the MEXEES II (2010–2011) project may serve as an example: "many Spaniards, when people talk to them about immigrants, think about Arabs, Muslims, Africans: those are the immigrants. A person from Latin America is perhaps not as much an immigrant as a Moroccan".

When mentioning specific immigrants, ethnic distinctiveness intervenes, as this is the first thing to be noticed. Skin color acts as a first barrier that prevents the acceptance and integration of immigrants. In turn, a specific culture: Chinese, Japanese, Muslim, Native American is associated with a stigma which is attached to the person, even if it does not fit reality. This is the mark of an "irreducible difference" (Wieviorka 2009: 100), which can lead to distance and racism. Its effect is more harmful amongst those who have Spanish nationality, either from having been born in the country or having arrived at an early age (with their parents or through international adoptions). The "you never stop being an immigrant" argument – even though you feel Spanish – is also corroborated with regard to North American society, in opposition to Alba and Nee's Assimilation Theory (2003), which advocates the gradual loss of ethnic identification over time, which ends at the third generation. The study by Telles and Ortiz (2009) shows, however, that most of the fourth generation of Mexican-Americans identify themselves as non-white and feel that others stereotype them as Mexicans. In addition, Mexican immigrants and U.S. Mexicans with dark skin experience racial discrimination.

The mention of Latin American immigrants is also reflected in the OBERAXE-CIS surveys, in a question about which immigrants do they prefer (are more likeable), followed by the opposite question: which immigrants do they like least. Latin Americans are first in likeability (referred to generically; specific to "Argentineans", "Ecuadoreans" and "Colombians", although in 2012 the reference to "Argentineans" lost ground, as it did in the MEXEES surveys). By contrast, the "Moors" or "Moroccans", along with the "Romanians" (often associated to the Roma community, due to their large number), are the immigrant groups which arouse most phobias or rejection in Spaniards, and are at a significant distance from the rest. When asked why, the most common response continues to be "because of their relationship with crime" (20 % in 2012); "they are bad people" (10 %); "they don't integrate, they form ghettos" (10 %); "because of their customs and ways of life" (9 %); and, "they're violent, aggressive and cause problems" (8 %).

Qualitative research from the MEXEES projects (Cea D'Ancona and Valles 2010; Cea D'Ancona et al. 2013) goes further, recording that, in contrast to Latin Americans, the fact that they do not adapt to customs or ways of life is particularly highlighted. More specifically, it is stated that they invade public areas; and that they do not respect minimum rules of community living ("they don't know how to behave"). Mention is made of specific nationalities, such as Ecuadorians, recorded before the crisis: "it is very rare to see Ecuadorians with Spaniards". In favor of Latin Americans, both before and during the crisis, testimonials have been gathered (repeated among both natives and other immigrants) which stress that this group is very respectful (details such as giving up their seat to an elderly person on public transport, or simply beginning any request with "please").

The discourse on integration[2] ("you have to integrate and adapt, and learn Spanish, if necessary, and do whatever it takes to integrate") has led in Spain to a preference for Latin American immigrants because of a shared language; a determining factor in integration, according to Portes and Rumbaut (2006), but also religion and customs. Referring to Latin American immigrants, one hears: "proximity", "similarity", "you can talk to them"; "at least they understand you"; "a past that unites us"; "half of them have Spanish blood"; "they have names like ours"; "they have our culture". Cultural proximity is also argued when justifying the preference for Europeans: "we share the same culture"; "the same values".

---

[2] When OBERAXE-CIS surveys pose hypothetical assumptions in order to allow the entry of immigrants or not, the cultural criterion (translated by the indicator "adaptation to the lifestyle of the country") continues to be the main one, slightly ahead of the economic and employment criterion (e.g. "they should have a job qualification that Spain needs"), both before and during the economic crisis, with an average score of 7.8 in 2008 and 7.95 in 2012 (for the economic and employment criterion, mean percentages are 7.2 in 2008 and 7.4 in 2012).

It is precisely the cultural proximity attributed to them which enables both groups of foreigners (European and Latin American) to be perceived as more easily integrated into Spanish society, particularly if they have a high level of education and professional qualifications (Cea D'Ancona et al. 2013: 218–254). At the opposite extreme are the Muslims, commonly perceived as more distant and less able to integrate within European societies (Sartori 2001; Strabac and Listhung 2008; Kleiner-Liebau 2011).

7.3.2 The New Perception of Latin American Immigrants in the U.S.

According to Brader et al. (2009) negative Hispanic stereotypes have been gaining relevance in the U.S. They state that 1996 can be considered the turnaround date, when "the impact of negative black stereotypes on attitudes toward immigration faded, while the impact of negative Hispanic stereotypes increased dramatically". They explain this change by measuring the effects of *affect* (of the native majority towards Asians, Africans and Hispanics); the so-called dimension of ethnocentrism, following Kinder and Kam (2009), and comparing these with the effects of socio-economic variables, or fear of difficult economic times (the so-called dimension of *material interests*). Although the fieldwork coincided with times of "great economic anxiety" (just before the 2008 election campaign), the cited authors' "*racial animus*" has proved to be a more powerful predictor than factors related to "*economic threat*", when forecasting opinion on the effects of immigration on the American economy and culture.

Moreover, these authors state that (beyond "*general ethnocentrism*") it is the attitudes of white Americans toward Hispanics which reveal the greatest effects on each dependent variable examined. That is, the negative perceptions of immigrants regarding employment; the opinions opposing toughening migration policy measures; or those in favor of granting social benefits to immigrants. The results of this study tally with those reported by other researchers (Segovia 2009; Pérez 2008; Burns and Gimpel 2000), which also show that Americans increasingly think more about Hispanics when discussing immigration, and that these thoughts are mostly negative.

In a recent contribution, Valentino et al. (2013) complement the previous analysis, using their 2008 internet survey and ANES surveys (to replicate their findings with data from 1992, 1994, 1996, 2000, 2004 and 2008). They also adopt, as a new focus of attention, the presence in the press of news reports on groups of immigrants from 1985 up to the present. They note that in the case of *Latinos*, greater media attention (since 1994) tallies with the growing demographic weight of this group, as well as certain legislative milestones or other such events (such as the 1994 adoption of Proposition 187 in California, aimed at curtailing many of the social benefits received by "illegal immigrants"). In other words, they attempt to compensate for the lack of perspective or historic demographic contextualization in previous studies, together with including the role of the media in shaping attitudes towards immigration during specific periods in the past.

Again they argue that this is a "*group-specific affect*" (and not general *ethnocentrism*) on the type of attitudes with greatest predictive power of opinion on immigration policy in contemporary American society. They recognize that this "*group-specific model*" or "*context-dependent theory of opinion on immigration*" is not as satisfying as a theoretical framework based on a general ethnocentrism that would predict opposition to immigration in any social system. They express their self-criticism noting that observing how exo-groups become the focus of attention at specific times in history cannot be translated straight into the proposition: majorities oppose all policies that benefit any exo-group. They insist that their theoretical model "requires more information about the social and historical context and debates about particular policy domains before one can fully explain opinion shifts or variation across society at any point in time" (Valentino et al. 2013: 164).

Similarly, another school of thought contends that contemporary anti-immigrant hostility is grounded in stereotypes of particular immigrant groups and their portrayal by parties and the mass media. For example, Branton et al. (2011) also uses the 2000 and 2004 ANES survey to demonstrate that correlates of non-Hispanic whites' attitudes to immigration changed in the aftermath of the September 11th, 2001 terrorist attacks. Specifically, media exposure of *Latinos* became a significant predictor of attitudes towards immigration only after September 11th, suggesting that portrayals of immigration shifted after the attacks.

As put forward at the start of this chapter, Latin American immigrants are the "new Blacks", having been stereotyped and stigmatized as the perennial and inassimilable underclass (Davies 2009: 378). The essay "The Hispanic Challenge" by Huntington (2004a) is an example of the discourse that demonizes *Latino* newcomers: Latin American immigration emerges as the great threat to national identity, previously anchored and secure in white, Anglo-Saxon Protestantism. This is an argument embedded within his wider construct of "the clash of civilizations" (Huntington 2004b) and retreats into old stereotypes of *Latinos'* lack of initiative, self-reliance, and ambition; their laziness; mistrust of those outside the family; and devaluation of education. A very controversial set of works, those of Huntington, where the "use of data is highly tendentious and misleading" (Etzioni 2005: 485); his hypotheses do not resist the test "with data from the U.S. Census and national and Los Angeles opinion surveys" (Citrin et al. 2007: 31); or Huntington's picture of Mexicans does not resist "evidence that Mexican Americans are in fact assimilating culturally" (Telles 2006: 7).

7.4 Final Observations

The comparison between Spain and the U.S. shows similarities and differences in perceptions of Latin American immigrants. Unlike the U.S., their acceptance in Spain is greater, since they are seen as closer to and better integrated into Spanish society, sharing a common language, religion and culture, as well as historical ties. Along with Spain's more remote past of American colonization, we can link the more recent Spanish emigration to Latin American countries for economic and political reasons. But not all Latin American immigrants are equally accepted. More favored are the *Latinos* rather than the Indigenous American immigrants, as well as those who are better-off. Ethnic discrimination is still present in both countries, as in the whole of the European Union, as revealed by the Special Eurobarometer 393 (TNS Opinion and Social 2012b).

Ethnic discrimination, then, is combined with economic discrimination or class-based racism ("everything depends on your wallet"; better if you are also white). Skin color identifies a country; a particular socioeconomic strata. Those who do normal jobs look better than those who do jobs that natives do not want to do, as this work is socially discredited: observations that show that the famous 'vicious circle' still exists, underlined by Gunnar Myrdal in his famous work, *An American Dilemma: the Negro Problem and the Modern Democracy* (1944). It is the lower social status of blacks which explained the prejudice against them from the white majority and other ethnic groups. Attitudes became more negative, the more their social status deteriorated.

The crisis itself has not affected the specific perception of Latin Americans in Spain, although it has of immigrants in general. They are blamed more, for instance, for the deterioration in the labor market and social benefits. There is an increased desire for their expulsion and a discourse on preference (of natives vs. immigrants regarding access to work or social benefits). This is so to a greater extent among people with less education,[3] in a worse economic and employment situation (exposed to greater competition against the immigrant population), more conservative, and advocates of national identity. However, recent survey data gathered in Spain in 2012 shows that the rejection of immigration in general has declined three points since the most critical point recorded in 2011, despite the worsening economic crisis. This has also contributed to a lower perception of the presence of immigrants and the fact that the media is talking more about the return of immigrants and the emigration of Spaniards than immigrants entering the country.

So, as in the U.S., economic threat is a key factor in explaining xenophobia, but so is the cultural threat. The latter works in favor of Latin American immigration in Spain but not in the U.S. And in both countries rejection increases, the more threatening the immigrant population is perceived, due to their group size, ethnic features, or economic, religious or cultural situation. The more time spent living in Spain, the more the mutual acceptance between natives and foreigners, but also the decline in their numbers and the increased presence of immigrants who are seen as more easily "integrated". Nor should we forget the waning presence of immigrants

---

[3] In the light of the evidence on stereotyping and ethnocentrism, the education effect is more likely to highlight differences in tolerance, ethnocentrism, sociotropic assessments, or political correctness than is exposure to competition from immigrants (Citrin et al. 1997; Card et al. 2012; Hainmueller and Hopkins 2013).

in political discourses and the media in 2012, compared to 2010 and 2011, coinciding with local and national elections. As Sari (2007) also maintains, the perception of immigration as a threat increases when presented as a "problem" by politicians and the media.

References

Alba, R., & Nee, V. (2003). *Remaking the American mainstream*. Cambridge, MA: Harvard University Press.

Allport, F. H. (1954). *The nature of prejudice*. Cambridge, MA: Addison-Wesley.

Blumer, H. (1958). Race prejudice as a sense of group position. *Pacific Sociological Review, 1*, 3–7.

Bobo, L., & Licari, F. C. (1989). Education and political tolerance. *Public Opinion Quarterly, 53*, 285–307.

Bommes, M., & Geddes, A. (2000). *Immigration and welfare*. London: Routledge.

Brader, T., Valentino, N., Jardina, A. (2009). *Immigration opinion in a time of economic crisis: material interests versus group attitudes*. Resource document. Center for Political Studies. University of Michigan. http://papers.ssrn.com/sol3/papers.cfm?abstract_id=1449415. pdf. Accessed 16 Oct 2013.

Branton, R., Cassese, E. C., Jones, B. S., & Westerland, C. (2011). All along the watchtower. *Journal of Politics, 73*, 664–679.

Brücker, H., Epstein, G. S., McCormick, B., Saint-Paul, G., Venturi, A., & Zimmermanne, K. (2002). Managing migration in the European Welfare State. In T. Boeri, G. Hanson, & B. McCormick (Eds.), *Immigration policy and the welfare system* (pp. 1–167). New York: Oxford University Press.

Burns, P., & Gimpel, J. G. (2000). Economic insecurity, prejudicial stereotypes, and public opinion in immigration policy. *Political Science Quarterly, 115*(2), 201–225.

Cachón, L. (2005). *Bases sociales de los sucesos de Elche de septiembre de 2004*. Madrid: Ministerio de Trabajo y Asuntos Sociales.

Castles, S., & Kosack, G. (1973). *Immigrant workers and class structure in Western Europe*. Oxford: Oxford University Press.

Card, D., Dustmann, C., & Preston, I. (2012). Immigration, wages and compositional amenities. *Journal of the European Economic Association, 10*, 78–119.

Cea D'Ancona, Mª Á. (2004). *La activación de la xenofobia en España*. Madrid: CIS/Siglo XXI (Monografía no 210).

Cea D'Ancona, Mª Á. (2007). *Inmigración, racismo y xenofobia en la España del nuevo contexto europeo*. Madrid: Ministerio de Trabajo y Asuntos Sociales. OBERAXE.

Cea D'Ancona, Mª Á., & Valles Martínez, M. S. (2008). *Evolución del racismo y la xenofobia en España [Informe 2008]*. Madrid: OBERAXE. Ministerio de Trabajo e Inmigración.

Cea D'Ancona, Mª Á., & Valles Martínez, M. S. (2010) *Xenofobias y xenofilias en clave biográfica: relatos entrelazados de autóctonos y foráneos*. Madrid: Siglo XXI.

Cea D'Ancona, Mª Á., & Valles Martínez, M. S. (2013). *Evolución del racismo y la xenofobia en España [Informe 2012]*. Madrid: OBERAXE. Ministerio de Empleo y Seguridad Social.

Cea D'Ancona, Mª Á., & Valles Martínez, M. S. (2014). *Evolución del racismo y la xenofobia en España [Informe 2013]*. Madrid: OBERAXE. Ministerio de Empleo y Seguridad Social.

Chandler, C. R., & Tsai, Y. M. (2001). Social factor influencing immigration attitudes. *The Social Science Journal, 38*, 177–188.

Citrin, J., Green, D., Muste, C., & Wong, C. (1997). Public opinion toward immigration reform. *Journal of Politics, 59*(3), 858–881.

Citrin, J., Lerman, A., Murakami, M., & Pearson, K. (2007). Testing Huntington: Is hispanic immigration a threat to American identity? *Perspectives on Politics, 5*(1), 31–48.

Clark, J. A., & Legge, J. S. (2009). Economics, racism, and attitudes toward immigration in the New Germany. *Political Research Quarterly, 50*(4), 901–917.

Coenders, M., & Scheepers, P. (1998). Support for ethnic discrimination in The Netherlands, 1979–1993. *European Sociological Review, 14*(4), 405–422.

Davies, I. (2009). Latino immigration and social change in the United States. *Policy Journal of Business Ethics, 88*, 377–391.

Espenshade, T. J., & Hempstead, K. (1996). Contemporary American attitudes toward U.S. immigration. *International Migration Review, 30*, 535–570.

Etzioni, A. (2005). The real threat: An essay on Samuel Huntington. *Contemporary Sociology, 34*(5), 477–485.

Hainmueller, J., & Hiscox, M. J. (2010). Attitudes toward highly skilled and low-skilled immigration. *American Political Science Review, 104*, 61–84.

Hainmueller, J., & Hopkins, D. J. (2013). *Public attitudes towards immigration.* Centre for Research and Analysis of Migration. London: University College. Discussion Paper Series CPD 15/13.

Huntington, S. (2004a). The Hispanic challenge. *Foreign Policy, 141*, 30–45.

Huntington, S. (2004b). *Who are we? The challenges to America's national identity.* New York: Simon & Shuster.

Kinder, D. R., & Kam, C. D. (2009). *US against them.* Chicago, IL: University of Chicago Press.

Kleiner-Liebau, D. (2011). Aprender del dilema alemán. In L. Cachón (Ed.), *Inmigración y conflictos en Europa* (pp. 151–198). Barcelona: Hacer Editorial.

Lahav, G., & Courtemanche, M. (2012). The ideological effects of framing threat on immigration and civil liberties. *Political Behavior, 34*, 477–505.

Lapinski, J., Peltola, P., Shaw, G., & Yang, A. (1997). Trends: Immigrants and immigration. *Public Opinion Quarterly, 61*, 356–383.

Muste, C. P. (2013). The polls-trends. The dynamics of immigration opinion in the United States 1992–2012. *Public Opinion Quarterly, 77*(1), 398–416.

Pérez, E.O. (2008). *Juan for All?* Paper presented at the annual meeting of the Midwest Political Science Association, Chicago.

Pettigrew, T. F., Wagner, U., & Christ, O. (2007). Who opposes immigration? *Du Bois Review, 4*(1), 19–39.

Portes, A., & Rumbaut, R. G. (2006). *Immigrant America.* California: The University of California Press.

Quillian, L. (1995). Prejudice as a response to perceived group threat. *American Sociological Review, 60*, 586–611.

Sari, O. L. (2007). Perceptions of threat and expressions of prejudice toward the new minorities of Western Europe. *Journal of International Migration and Integration, 8*, 289–306.

Sartori, G. (2001). *La sociedad multiétnica.* Madrid: Taurus.

Scheve, K. F., & Slaughter, M. J. (2001). Labor market competition and individual preferences over immigration policy. *The Review of Economics and Statistics, 83*, 133–145.

Schildkraut, D. J. (2005). *Press one for english.* Princeton: Princeton University Press.

Schnapper, D. (1994). The debate on immigration and the crisis of national identity. In M. Baldwin-Edwards & M. A. Schain (Eds.), *The politics of immigration in Western Europe* (pp. 127–139). London: Frank Cass.

Segovia, F. (2009). *Social factors influencing the immigration policy preferences of European Americans.* Dissertation thesis, University of Michigan.

Segovia, F., & DeFever, R. (2010). The polls-trends: American public opinion on immigrants and immigration policy. *Public Opinion Quarterly, 74*, 375–394.

Simon, R. (1993). Old Minorities, New Immigrants. In P. I. Rose (Ed.), *Interminority affairs in the U.S.* (Annals of the American Academy of political and social science, Vol. 530, pp. 61–73). Thousand Oak: Sage.

SORA. (2001). *Attitudes towards minority groups in the European Union*. Vienna: European Monitoring Centre on Racism and Xenophobia.

Strabac, Z., & Listhung, O. (2008). Anti-Muslim prejudice in Europe. *Social Science Research, 37*, 268–286.

Telles, E. E. (2006). Mexican Americans and the American Nation. A response to Professor Huntington. *Aztlán: A Journal of Chicano Studies, 31*(2), 7–23.

Telles, E. E., & Ortiz, V. (2009). *Generations of exclusion: Mexican Americans, assimilation, and race*. New York: Russell Sage Foundation Publications.

TNS Opinion and Social. (2012a). *Special Eurobarometer 380/Wave EB 76.4. Awareness of home affairs*. European Commission. Directorate-General Home Affairs and co-ordinated by Directorate-General for Communication.

TNS Opinion and Social. (2012b). *Special Eurobarometer 393 / Wave EB 77.4. Discrimination in the EU in 2012*. European Commission. Directorate-General Justice and co-ordinated by Directorate-General for Communication.

Valentino, N. A., Brader, T., & Jardina, A. E. (2013). Immigration opposition among U.S. Whites: General ethnocentrism or media priming of attitudes about Latinos? *Political Psychology, 34*(2), 149–166. doi:10.1111/j.1467-9221.2012.00928.x.

Walker, I., & Pettigrew, T. F. (1984). Relative privation theory. *British Journal of Social Psychology, 23*, 301–310.

Wieviorka, M. (2009). *El racismo*. Madrid: Gedisa.

Wong, C. J. (2010). *Boundaries of obligation in American politics*. New York: Cambridge University Press.

Chapter 8
In Times of Uncertainty: The Great Recession, Immigration Enforcement, and Latino Immigrants in Alabama

Meghan Conley

8.1 The Great Recession in the Lives of Latinos and Latino Immigrants

From a purely economic perspective, the Great Recession has disproportionately impacted minorities, including Latinos. Across measures of unemployment, income, poverty, and wealth, Latinos have consistently fared worse than whites, and the recession has exacerbated these prevailing disparities. Between 2007 and 2009, the national unemployment rate more than doubled from 4.6 % to 9.3 % (Bureau of Labor Statistics 2008, 2010). However, the aggregate data mask differences in rates of unemployment across race, as white unemployment has traditionally peaked at much lower rates than that of blacks and Latinos. Thus, whereas the white unemployment rate stood at 8.5 % in 2009 (an increase from 4.1 % in 2007), the Latino unemployment rate soared to 12.1 % (an increase from 5.6 % in 2007).

Unemployment has had predictable consequences for the income, debt, and poverty of Latino households. Between 2007 and 2009, the median household income of Latinos decreased by 5 %, and their median household debt increased by 42 % (Taylor et al. 2011a). By 2010, approximately 13.2 million Latinos, or 26.6 % of the resident Latino population of the United States, lived below the federal poverty line, compared to just 9.9 % of whites (DeNavas-Walt et al. 2011).

Latino households, on average, have significantly less wealth than their white counterparts, and their wealth has only declined since the onset of the economic downturn. During the Great Recession, the net worth of Latino households decreased from $18,539 in 2005 to just $6,325 in 2009, a decline of 66 %—more than all other racial and ethnic groups. In comparison, the net worth of whites decreased by just 16 % during the same time period, from $134,992 to $113,149

M. Conley (✉)
University of Mary Washington, Fredericksburg, VA, USA
e-mail: mconley@umw.edu

© Springer International Publishing Switzerland 2015
M. Aysa-Lastra, L. Cachón (eds.), *Immigrant Vulnerability and Resilience*,
International Perspectives on Migration 11, DOI 10.1007/978-3-319-14797-0_8

(Taylor et al. 2011a). Much of the decline in household wealth among Latinos can be attributed to the housing market collapse, since home equity is a primary source of wealth in minority households, and since Latinos disproportionately reside in the five states hit hardest by the housing crisis—Arizona, California, Florida, Michigan, and Nevada.

Among Latinos, those who are immigrants are disproportionately likely to live in precarious financial situations, meaning that they are particularly vulnerable during times of economic instability and among those most susceptible to economic hardship (Orrenius and Zavodny 2009; Papademetriou and Terrazas 2009). Latino immigrants tend to have lower educational attainment than the overall foreign-born population, and they are overrepresented in temporary labor market industries, such as construction and hospitality (Passel 2006). As a consequence, Latino immigrants have been hit especially hard by the recent economic slowdown and the contraction of the housing market (Kochar 2008).

Still, the impact of the Great Recession on Latinos and Latino immigrants extends far beyond its disparate effects on employment, income, and wealth. As the recession has worn on, the United States has experienced a surge in anti-immigrant rhetoric and immigration enforcement, much of which has been directed at those of Latin American ancestry and origin. US policymakers have also used the recession as a rhetorical tool to advance comprehensive state-level restrictionist legislation throughout the nation. The escalation of immigration enforcement and the steady devolution of immigration enforcement authority to state and local police officers, combined with a tendency to conflate Latinos with unauthorized status, has rendered Latino immigrants increasingly vulnerable to the ongoing social consequences of the Great Recession.

8.2 The Role of Economic Downturns in the Scapegoating of Immigrants

The US population evinces a deep ambivalence toward immigrants and immigration, simultaneously embracing the nation's immigrant origins while remaining wary of successive waves of immigrant newcomers. This ambivalence is influenced in part by economic conditions, as periods of economic insecurity correspond to higher levels of xenophobia and anti-immigrant sentiment (Higham 1985; Olzak 1992). Citizens fear the labor market impacts of immigrants, particularly on the wages and employment opportunities of the US-born (Espenshade and Hempstead 1996; Espenshade and Belanger 1998), even though little evidence indicates that immigrants negatively influence the overall wages or unemployment rate of the population (Friedberg and Hunt 1995). Still, support for restrictionist policies corresponds to the belief that immigrants harm the economy as a whole (Citrin et al. 1997).

Not surprisingly, then, proposals to restrict immigrants and immigration, as well as demands for increased immigration enforcement, are often tied to the perceived economic well-being of a society. As such, in 2009, at the height of the economic downturn in the United States, a national public opinion survey found increased support for the deportation of unauthorized immigrants, and decreased support for a variety of legalization measures, suggesting that expanding support for enforcement may be one effect of the downturn (Cosby et al. 2013).

8.2.1 The Devolution of Immigration Enforcement and Proliferation of State Immigration Laws

Immigrant scapegoating is predictable during periods of economic insecurity. Yet, few could have foreseen the extent to which restrictionist legislation proliferated throughout the United States in the wake of the Great Recession, as conservative policymakers and pundits emerged to decry the federal government's inability to secure the nation's borders and deport the more than 11 million unauthorized immigrants residing within the interior. In 2010, Arizona passed sweeping anti-immigrant legislation, signifying a fundamental shift toward the attempted criminalization of unauthorized immigrants by individual states (Fan 2012). Shortly thereafter, representatives in more than half of the state legislatures in the nation introduced similar bills. By the following year, Utah, Indiana, Georgia, South Carolina, and Alabama had passed Arizona copycat laws.

Arizona's controversial legislation, "The Support Our Law Enforcement and Safe Neighborhoods Act," which was known more prominently as SB 1070, was broadly supported by state residents (Morrison Institute for Public Policy 2010). Although the law's rhetoric centered on the portrayal of unauthorized immigrants as a criminal presence and, hence, a threat to the security of the state's authorized residents, the role of the economic downturn in Arizonans' approval of the bill should not be underestimated. Even before the passage of SB 1070, Arizonans were concerned about the impact of unauthorized workers on the employment prospects of authorized residents, as evidenced by the 2007 Legal Arizona Workers Act (LAWA), which required employers to verify the work eligibility of all employees and allowed the state to penalize employers who knowingly hired unauthorized workers. This concern deepened following announcements of the national recession. Thus, a survey of Arizona residents conducted annually from 2006 through 2009 indicates a strong shift in negative attitudes toward immigrants after 2008. Anti-immigrant sentiment increased again in 2009, following the collapse of the Arizona housing market and rising state unemployment rates (Diaz et al. 2011). These findings suggest that underlying anxieties about the economy, no less than fears of the unauthorized as a "criminal element," may have played a considerable role in support for Arizona's law.

Among other provisions, SB 1070 required law enforcement officers to make a "reasonable attempt" to determine the citizenship or immigration status of an individual who was stopped during the course of the officer's regular duties—such as during traffic stops or arrests—or whenever the officer had a "reasonable suspicion" that the individual was unlawfully present in the United States. Although this "show me your papers" provision of Arizona's law seemed quite groundbreaking at the time, it actually mirrored the steady devolution of immigration enforcement powers from federal to state and local authorities that has occurred over the last decade. Following the 9/11 attacks on the World Trade Center in New York, the federal government spearheaded the institutionalization of cooperative partnerships across federal, state, and local law enforcement agencies. In matters related to immigration enforcement, cross-agency cooperation has meant that state and local law enforcement agencies are used as "force multipliers" to implement federal immigration law (Conley 2013a). These cooperative mechanisms transpire in various ways, including delegation of immigration authority and the routine and institutionalized sharing of biometric data across local, state and federal law enforcement agencies, through programs like 287(g) and Secure Communities. Thus, state level restrictionist legislation like SB 1070 follows on the heels of more than a decade of increased enforcement against immigrants in the United States.

Of course, increased restrictions on immigration and heightened enforcement procedures do not target all immigrants equally. In the United States, contemporary portrayals of unauthorized migration focus heavily on the "Latino threat" (Chavez 2008; Lugo-Lugo and Bloodsworth-Lugo2010; see, for example, Huntington 2004, 2005). Equally, Latino migration is often portrayed through visual imagery reminiscent of floodwaters and invasion, and discourse surrounding the US-Mexico border suggests crisis and anarchy (Chavez 2001). In policing the borders of belongingness, Latinos are depicted as unmistakably other. Unauthorized immigrants, in turn, are racialized as non-white—and, more specifically, as Latino and Mexican. As Ngai (2004: 58) elaborates,

> Europeans and Canadians tended to be disassociated from the real and imagined category of illegal alien, which facilitated their national and racial assimilation as white American citizens. In contrast, Mexicans emerged as iconic illegal aliens. Illegal status became constitutive of a racialized Mexican identity and of Mexicans' exclusion from the national community and polity.

Latinos continue to be associated with unauthorized status in contemporary mainstream society. In point of fact, more than half of all respondents in a 2012 national poll of non-Latinos overestimated the percentage of Latinos in the United States who were unauthorized, while a full third of respondents estimated that the *majority* of Latinos in the United States were unauthorized (Barreto et al. 2012).

The conflation of race and legal status means that Latinos are often the targets of immigration enforcement. During the Great Depression, for example, the US government forcibly deported and repatriated hundreds of thousands of Mexicans and Mexican Americans, despite the fact that many were either US citizens or long-term residents of the United States (Ngai 2004). More recently, investigations by the federal government, scholars, and civil rights organizations have discovered patterns of biased policing against Latinos in the state and local enforcement of immigration law (Coleman and Kocher 2011; Department of Justice 2011, 2012; Kee 2012; Shahshahani 2009, 2010).

The perception that "Latino" is synonymous with "unauthorized immigrant" also helps to explain why Latino immigrants are disproportionately likely to be apprehended by immigration dragnets and deported. Thus, although immigrants from Latin America constituted only 77 % of the estimated 11.1 million unauthorized immigrants residing in the United States in 2011, they accounted for 93 % of those apprehended and identified for deportation through the Secure Communities program (Kohli et al. 2011) and for nearly 96 % of all deportations (US Department of Homeland Security 2012).

The simultaneous escalation and devolution in immigration enforcement powers, combined with the tendency to interpret Latino as other, has contributed to a sense of vulnerability and uncertainty among Latinos and Latino immigrants in the United States. The involvement of state and local law enforcement agencies has made immigration enforcement ubiquitous in everyday life, at traffic safety stops, churches, flea markets, schools, neighborhoods, day laborer pickup sites, worksites, courts of law, and jails (see, for example: Bauer 2009; Coleman and Kocher 2011; Menjívar and Abrego 2012; Weissman and Headen 2009). This omnipresence of enforcement—which I have elsewhere referred to as the immigration enforcement lottery (Conley 2014)—relentlessly threatens unauthorized immigrants with the consequences of detection, discretion, detention, and deportation. In this lottery system, once an unauthorized immigrant is detected by a police officer who is empowered to enforce immigration law, that immigrant is potentially subject to a seemingly endless variety of discretionary enforcement policies, which further determine a series of discretionary consequences, including detention and deportation. Thus, any interaction with a member of law enforcement could reasonably—though not necessarily—result in the eventual removal of an unauthorized immigrant (De Genova 2002).

The potentially harsh consequences of the enforcement lottery inspire constant feelings of apprehension among immigrants. Amid periods of uncertainty and escalated enforcement, unauthorized immigrants often report tension and anxiety, emotions that relate to a host of concerns—of being discovered, detained, deported, and separated from family (Dreby 2012; Marquardt et al. 2011). Responses to these fears often manifest in constant vigilance—as unauthorized immigrants are perpetually watchful of law enforcement—and defensive maneuvers—as unauthorized immigrants attempt to avoid interactions with law enforcement, immigration agents, or others perceived to have the authority to enforce immigration law.

Of course, it is not just the lives of the unauthorized that are touched by the escalation in harsh enforcement policies. More than half of all Latinos in the United States—including those who are US born—worry about the possibility of deportation for themselves, a family member, or a friend (Clark et al. 2007). This speaks to the fact that unauthorized immigrants, especially those from Latin America, often live in mixed status families, or families whose members have different immigration statuses (Taylor et al. 2011b). In such families, at least one member is unauthorized, while others are either US citizens or authorized immigrants.

Given the uncertainty that characterizes the enforcement lottery, Latinos are understandably wary of police. Thus, a poll of Latinos living in Chicago, Houston, Los Angeles, and Phoenix found that the increasing involvement of state and local law enforcement in immigration matters has had chilling effects on the willingness of both foreign-born and US-born Latinos to report crime (Theodore 2013). Of those surveyed, 44 % reported that they were less likely to contact law enforcement if they were the victim of a crime, and 45 % were less likely to volunteer information about a crime that they had witnessed, because they worried that police would ask about their immigration status or the status of people they knew.

The effects of this devolution in immigration enforcement on wariness of police interaction are heightened for unauthorized Latino immigrants. Thus, of those surveyed who were unauthorized, 70 % reported that they were less likely to contact police to report a crime (ibid). The fear that any encounter with the police could result in immigration consequences is not entirely unfounded. In fact, the American Immigration Lawyer's Association (AILA), a national organization of more than 11,000 attorneys and law professors who practice and teach immigration law, document that "any contact with the police, no matter how innocent or trivial, can result in immigration enforcement and removal." (Alonso et al. 2011: 3). Accordingly, many unauthorized immigrants fear law enforcement and feel as though they cannot rely on the legal system to protect their civil rights (Abrego 2011), even though unauthorized immigrants are entitled to civil rights protections by law. Practically speaking, this translates into the fact that unauthorized Latino immigrants and their families live in a perpetual state of vulnerability, rendered so by the ubiquity of immigration enforcement in everyday life, the conflation of Latino and unauthorized status, and the real or perceived lack of recourse for unauthorized immigrants who are victimized.

8.3 Latino Immigrant Vulnerability in Everyday Life: The Case of Alabama HB 56

The state of Alabama offers a telling example of Latino immigrant vulnerability in the aftermath of the Great Recession and its backlash against unauthorized immigrants. In this southern state, immigrant scapegoating took the form of the "Beason-Hammon Alabama Taxpayer and Citizen Protection Act," an Arizona-copycat bill known in shorthand as HB 56. When this legislation passed in 2011, the Alabama economy, like much of the United States, was still reeling from the effects of the recession. The state's unemployment rate stood at 9.9 % (Alabama Department of Industrial Relations 2011), slightly higher than the national unemployment average of 9.1 %. Accordingly, concerns over the state's economy occupied a substantial role in legislative support for the bill. HB 56 was portrayed as a "jobs bill" (Beason 2012) that aimed to increase employment opportunities for US citizens by making life so difficult for the unauthorized residents of the state that they would spontaneously "self deport."[1]

Scapegoating is immediately apparent in the rhetoric used by Alabama policymakers to legitimate HB 56. Senator Beason, the bill's co-sponsor, argued, "We have a problem with an illegal [sic] workforce that displaces Alabama workers. We need to put those people back to work. That's the number one priority" (White 2011). Representative Brooks, a staunch ally of the bill, went so far as to claim, "As your congressman on the House floor, I will do anything short of shooting them [unauthorized immigrants]... Anything that is lawful, it needs to be done because illegal aliens [sic] need to quit taking jobs from American citizens" (Camia 2011). At the time, unauthorized immigrants—who comprised just 2.5 % of the state population—accounted for roughly 4.2 % of the state's labor force (Passel and Cohn 2011).

Alabama's law quickly became known as the harshest and most comprehensive state immigration law that the United States had ever seen. Much like Arizona SB 1070, HB 56 empowered state and local law enforcement officers to engage in immigration enforcement duties, including checking immigration status during the course of a lawful stop and requiring officers to check the immigration status of those who were booked, jailed, or convicted of a crime. HB 56 also criminalized those who "harbor" or transport unauthorized immigrants, immigrants who fail to carry their immigration documents, and unauthorized immigrants who solicit or perform work. Additionally, the Alabama law mandated that employers use the federal E-Verify program, an electronic employment eligibility verification system intended to determine the legal status of newly hired employees.

The Arizona copycat provisions of HB 56 have undoubtedly contributed to a heightened sense of vigilance among the unauthorized residents of Alabama and their family members, who must be ever watchful of law enforcement officers, even as they go about their everyday lives. One US-born citizen married to an unauthorized immigrant from Latin America explained this fear in the face of perpetual uncertainty as follows:

---

[1] "Self-deportation," also known as "attrition through enforcement," is an extremist strategy whose explicit intention is to so greatly complicate the lives of unauthorized residents that they will voluntarily return to their countries of origin. According to this reasoning, unauthorized immigrants will pack their belongings and return to their countries of origin once the perceived costs of living in the United States (such as expectations of increased enforcement, including lengthy detention stays and eventual removal) outweigh the perceived benefits (such as future wage earnings). The terminology was popularized during the 2012 presidential debates, when Republican candidate Mitt Romney declared his support for "self deportation." However, the strategy has been promoted by restrictionist organizations for much longer. See, for example: Vaughn (2006), *Attrition through Enforcement: A Cost Effective Strategy to Shrink the Illegal Population*; Krikorian (2005), *Downsizing Illegal Immigration: A Strategy of Attrition through Enforcement*; Numbers USA, "How Attrition through Enforcement Works"; Federation for American Immigration Reform (2008), "Attrition of Illegal Immigrants through Enforcement."

It scares me a lot because [my spouse] has to drive an hour [to work] and an hour back. . . It was always, "When you're leaving your workplace, call me. When you get home, call me. If you're halfway, call me. When you get there, call me." I won't see [my spouse] until 5:30, because I'm working, but [my spouse] sends me a text: "OK, I've left work." [My spouse] sends me another text: "I'm here." [My spouse] sends me another text: "I'm at home," because [my spouse] has to pass by the school to pick up the kids.

The fear of police interaction is not solely confined to those who could be stopped while driving. HB 56 has also had a chilling effect on the willingness of immigrants to report instances of victimization. In one example, the unauthorized parents of a teenager who had been sexually assaulted refused to report the assault because they were concerned that Alabama police would interrogate the family about their immigration status (Conley 2013b). This fear was grounded in stories that had been told in immigrant communities throughout the state, especially in Alabama's rural towns. In such communities, immigrants reported that police had begun knocking on doors in their neighborhoods looking for unauthorized immigrants with outstanding warrants. If someone who was not under investigation happened to answer the door, the police would nonetheless question that unlucky individual about his or her own immigration status. Sometimes, a police officer would wait outside, hidden, if no one answered the door; once the resident finally emerged from the house to drive to work or the grocery store, the officer would follow and stop the individual for driving without a license (ibid). Thus, it seemed that unauthorized residents had great reason to fear police interaction in the wake of HB 56.

Still, Alabama's law went much further than the comprehensive legislation enacted in Arizona or other copycat states, and the law did not stop at expanding the immigration enforcement powers of state and local police officers. HB 56 also broadened the roles and responsibilities of public and private sector employees in determining the citizenship and immigration status of Alabama residents. In so doing, Alabama legislators created bureaucratic enforcement mechanisms to target the routine aspects of living and working in Alabama. According to Representative Hammon, the bill's co-sponsor, HB 56 was designed to "attack every aspect of an illegal alien's [sic] life" (Chandler 2011). Thus, the law required that residents provide proof of citizenship or lawful immigration status prior to entering into a "business transaction" with the state of Alabama, and it rendered unenforceable any existing or future public and private sector contracts with unauthorized immigrants. HB 56 also mandated that school administrators determine the citizenship or immigration status of newly enrolling students. These provisions, on top of the expanded role for police officers in immigration enforcement, intended to make everyday life exceedingly difficult for the unauthorized residents of Alabama.

How successful was the law in accomplishing this task? According to Mary Bauer, the Legal Director of the Southern Poverty Law Center, a civil rights organization based in Alabama,

HB 56 has devastated the immigrant community in Alabama. It would be hard for me to overstate the human tragedy that has been unleashed upon Alabama by HB 56. Under the provisions of this law that are currently in effect, undocumented persons are unable to interact with the government—in any way and for any purpose. It has turned a significant class of people, effectively, into legal non-persons, subjecting them to a kind of legal exile. It has destroyed lives, ripped apart families, devastated communities, and left our economy in shatters.[2]

Bauer's testimony that unauthorized immigrants were unable to "interact with the government in any way and for any purpose" after the passage of HB 56 is hardly an exaggeration. Since HB 56 compelled government employees to determine the citizenship status of anyone who applied for public services and prohibited the government from entering into a "business transaction" with unauthorized immigrants, but did not specify the scope of these provisions, public sector employees often erred on the side of caution by denying routine services. Accordingly, in Blount County, Alabama, an area with a larger than average population of both Latino and foreign-born residents compared to the rest of the state, the Allgood Alabama Water Works Company displayed the following notice:

Attention **ALL** water customers: to be compliant with new laws concerning immigration you must have an Alabama driver's license or an Alabama picture ID card on file at this office... or you may lose water service [emphasis in original].

In the months following the implementation of HB 56, Alabama residents who could not prove lawful residence to the satisfaction of untrained public sector employees were denied access to public utilities (including water and electricity), child welfare assistance (even for US-born children), library cards, public school-sponsored after-school programs, and business licenses (Fleischauer 2011; Kennedy 2011; Southern Poverty Law Center 2012).

HB 56 also prohibited Alabama courts from enforcing existing contracts between unauthorized immigrants and private entities, but, again, the law failed to specify how this provision should be applied in practice. The resulting ambiguity left attorneys and immigration rights advocates wondering if child support payments, work contracts, and loan and rental agreements for cars, trailers, and houses would be enforceable under the law. Unscrupulous employers invoked this provision to prey upon unauthorized workers, often refusing to pay for services rendered by day laborers and other contract employees, and threatening to call police or immigration authorities if the workers asserted their rights to compensation or safe working conditions. Private business owners, too, took advantage of HB 56. In one example, a used car dealership in Northern Alabama repossessed a car—even though the owners were current on their loan and had made more than $3,000 in payments; the manager of the dealership explained that "He could no longer sell to 'illegals' [sic] because he might lose his business license" (Southern Poverty Law Center 2012: 27–28).

Finally, since HB 56 required public schools to collect data on the immigration status of newly enrolling children, many feared that school employees would report unauthorized immigrant children and their parents to immigration officials. One

---

[2] Testimony presented at the Congressional Ad Hoc Delegation to Alabama, November 21, 2011.

resident of Alabama testified about the impact of this fear on the days immediately following implementation of this portion of the law:

The [school] bus was empty, none of the kids want to go to school, because they were scared that their parents won't—when they come back, their parents won't be there. I saw this twelve-year-old running to the bus because she got a test that day. And the mother went running after her, crying, saying, "You cannot go to school." She was scared. And I was at the window looking at this—this scene. And I couldn't—They start crying. [The girl] said, "I want to go to school, Mom," and [the mom] said, "No, you can't… They can take you." And they start crying, and I start crying too. And at that point I was like, this cannot be happening. People with good hearts, with sense of justice could see that this is not right.[3]

In actuality, HB 56 did not authorize public schools or their employees to directly enforce immigration law, and school officials, including superintendents and principals, reached out to local communities after the law's implementation to assure them that school employees would not report unauthorized immigrant children and parents to Immigration and Customs Enforcement. Yet, this did little to calm the fears of nervous parents, who pointed to the well-publicized examples of discrimination against Latino children in Alabama's schools. In one such example, a teacher asked a previously enrolled fourth-grader about her immigration status and the status of her parents, despite the fact that schools can only ask about the immigration status of newly enrolled students (Lyman 2011); in another case, a mother was barred from attending a book fair at her daughter's school because she could not provide proof of authorized residency. In the aftermath of the law, Latino children, including those born in the United States, were told to "go back to Mexico." At one school in Northern Alabama, the principal separated schoolchildren based on perceptions of their immigration status, which, in turn, were based on ethnicity. Following the implementation of HB 56, the superintendent of Birmingham noted that the city's schools experienced a higher than usual rate of student absentees, and newspaper articles indicated that an estimated 2,000 Latino children across the state of Alabama stayed home from school (Gomez 2011; Robertson 2011).

8.3.1 Racializing the Unauthorized: Immigration Enforcement and Latinos in Alabama

As Mary Bauer stated, the impacts of HB 56 on the everyday lives and vulnerabilities of Alabama's unauthorized residents cannot be overstated. However, the law's effects were felt especially hard in Alabama's Latino communities. Since there is no way to identify an unauthorized immigrant by sight alone, members of our communities—teachers, legislators, doctors, neighbors, and law enforcement

---

[3] Testimony presented at the United States Commission on Civil Rights Field Briefing in Alabama, August 17, 2012.

officers—make assumptions about a person's immigration and citizenship status based on a variety of biases about what it means to be or look "American." At the same time, Latinos are often mistaken as both foreign and unauthorized, even if they are US-born citizens or authorized residents of the United States (Bohon and Macpherson Parrot 2011). This is particularly true in places with little history of Latino settlement, such as much of the Southeastern United States (Singer 2004). In a region that has long been characterized by a color line drawn along a white and black binary (Marrow 2009), Latinos complicate racialized understandings of belongingness, and their visible racial and ethnic markers signal their conspicuousness as distinct others.

In Alabama, Latinos cannot avoid the prying eyes and questions of those who perceive them as not fully American. Two experiences in particular highlight the constructed otherness of Latinos in Alabama. In one example, a Texas-born Latino resident of Alabama was told that he needed to show "American ID" (Southern Poverty Law Center 2012: 19) to purchase alcohol at a large retail chain. Yet, an African American woman who made a similar purchase immediately afterward was only asked for her driver's license, because, according to the cashier, it was apparent that "she's American" (ibid: 19). In another story, a Latina was told that she could not use her Puerto Rican birth certificate to renew the registration on her car. Despite the fact that Puerto Rico is, of course, a territory of the United States, and that Puerto Ricans are US citizens, the woman was told that she needed to provide a US birth certificate (ibid). In both of these examples, it was not the immigration status of these Latinos that encouraged others to question their belongingness—after all, both were US-citizens by birth. Rather, visible markers of their ethnic heritage, including skin color, prompted others to demand proof, not just of identification, but of their status as Americans. HB 56 has thus empowered ordinary citizens to enforce the boundaries of belongingness.

Given that US citizen Latinos have been harassed by Alabamans who were intent on enforcing the real or imagined provisions of HB 56, there is little wonder that the unauthorized Latino residents of the state have felt hypervisible. Certainly, at least part of this hypervisibility was by design. For example, since the Alabama law prevented unauthorized immigrants from entering into business transactions with the state, those who lived in mobile homes could not pay the annual fee required to renew their home's registration; thus, unauthorized residents could not update the decal on their home, which was visible to any passersby. As a result, many Latino immigrants who lived in mobile homes felt that they were easy targets, and many mobile home communities across the state were abandoned en masse after HB 56 was enacted (Conley 2013b).

Initially, it seemed as though HB 56 had succeeded in making everyday life completely unmanageable for unauthorized Latino residents, so unsustainable that many gave up and left the state. Anecdotes from teachers, clergy, business owners, and community members suggested that many unauthorized immigrants—their students, congregants, employees, and neighbors—had deserted the state, fleeing the law and its punitive effects. One Sunday school teacher in the northwestern Alabama town of Russellville testified to this before a Congressional Ad-hoc

Delegation: "When HB 56 came into effect, my classrooms became empty," she explained. "The students were crying. My nieces received goodbye letters from their friends saying they had to leave." Isabel Rubio, director of the Hispanic Interest Coalition of Alabama (HICA), a nonprofit organization dedicated to the social, civic, and economic integration of Latino families in the state, confirmed the widespread fear that Latinos felt in the wake of the law:

> There's really been this huge terror in the Latino community, people who have been afraid to go to school, go to church, go to work, just because they're afraid that they'll get stopped for "driving while Latino."

8.4 Resisting Vulnerability in Times of Uncertainty

In Alabama, Latino immigrants have been rendered increasingly vulnerable by the ubiquity of immigration enforcement in the aftermath of the Great Recession. The specter of the enforcement lottery, which has been made possible by the devolution of immigration enforcement powers to state and local police officers, and the bureaucratic enforcement policies of HB 56, have forced immigrants to confront the very real possibility of immigration enforcement consequences in everyday life. From a heightened wariness of police interaction to anxieties over mundane behaviors, such as driving to work, sending children to school, and paying property taxes and utility bills, HB 56 has shaped and constrained the ways that Latino immigrants interact with the world around them.

Yet, it would be mistaken to assume that the unauthorized residents of Alabama have quietly accepted the uncertainties of immigration enforcement. Even as Latino immigrants have been rendered vulnerable by HB 56 and the enforcement lottery, so too have they resisted the policies and practices that structure their vulnerability. Over time, the ubiquity of immigration enforcement has made everyday life so precarious for Alabama's unauthorized residents that they have been forced to choose between leaving the state and struggling in opposition. And while some have given up and left, many more have stayed behind, tied to the state by jobs, children, homes, communities, and the memories of years or even decades lived in Alabama. The vast majority of unauthorized immigrants and their families continue living in Alabama in spite of the state's draconian law. Rather than inspiring unauthorized residents to "self-deport," HB 56 has actually galvanized the Latino immigrant community to organize in resistance to the policies and practices that render them vulnerable (Conley 2013b). As Rubio recalls:

> The weird twist is that we have really gotten people engaged, just realizing that [they] might be undocumented, but [their] kids were born here, and so they have a right to be here, and [they] have a stake in this fight, so [they] have to stay and fight.

Since the passage of HB 56, immigrants in Alabama have engaged in acts of resistance ranging from massive protests and marches at the state Capitol to civil disobedience at immigrant detention centers. They have organized "know your rights" trainings across the state and knocked on doors in immigrant neighborhoods to raise awareness of the law. Immigrants have also formed grassroots *comités populares*—popular (or people's) committees—to empower themselves and others who are directly impacted by anti-immigrant laws with the tools and structures needed to fight back against the uncertainties and vulnerabilities of heightened enforcement practices. They have "come out of the shadows"—as undocumented, unafraid, unashamed, and unapologetic—and encouraged others to do the same.

Alabama's immigrants and their advocates have also demanded an end to HB 56 and to the policies and practices that criminalize unauthorized immigrants. In many ways, those who champion the rights of immigrants—and, by extension, the civil liberties of all residents—are winning. Some of the most devastating portions of the Alabama law—including the provision requiring school officials to ask students about their immigration status—were permanently enjoined by the 11th Circuit Court of Appeals. It is true that other portions of the law are still in effect, and that the uncertainties posed by the enforcement lottery continue to manifest through cross-agency cooperation programs like 287(g)[4] and Secure Communities. In a deeper sense, however, Alabama's immigrants have prevailed in that they have refused to accept the practices that threaten to disrupt their lives and families.

As a case study, Alabama provides an extreme example of the escalation of immigration enforcement in the United States and its consequences for the uncertainty that immigrants feel in everyday life. HB 56 also provides a cautionary tale of the ways that periods of economic crisis can facilitate the scapegoating of immigrants, intensifying the vulnerability of Latino immigrants in particular. That Alabama's immigrants have not quietly accepted the vulnerabilities of these harsh enforcement practices is a testament to their creativity and resilience. In these uncertain times, Alabama's Latino immigrants have insisted on the right to a sense of security.

References

Abrego, L. J. (2011). Legal consciousness of undocumented Latinos: Fear and stigma as barriers to claims-making for first and 1.5-generation immigrants. *Law and Society Review, 45*(2), 337–370.

Alabama Department of Industrial Relations. (2011, August 19). *Alabama's July unemployment rate is 10%*. Press Release. Alabama Department of Labor.

Alonso, A., Macleod-Ball, K., Chen, G., & Kim, S. (2011). *Immigration enforcement off target: Minor offenses with major consequences. Research report*. Washington, DC: American Immigration Lawyer's Association.

---

[4] Although many 287(g) programs have been phased out across the nation, parts of Alabama continue to operate under the 287(g) jail enforcement model, which authorizes designated officers in Alabama's jails to verify the immigration status or legal presence of those who have been arrested and booked.

Barreto, M. A., Manzano, S., & Segura, G. (2012). *The impact of media stereotypes on opinions and attitudes towards Latinos. Research report*. Pasadena, CA: National Hispanic Media Coalition.

Bauer, M. (2009). *Under siege: Life for low-income Latinos in the south. Report*. Montgomery, AL: Southern Poverty Law Center.

Beason, S. (2012, January 26). *Beason statement on the impact of HB 56 on Alabama unemployment rate. Press Release*. Gardendale, AL: Beason for Congress.

Bohon, S. A., & MacPherson Parrot, H. (2011). The myth of millions: Socially constructing 'illegal immigration'. In C. D. Lippard & C. A. Gallagher (Eds.), *Being brown in Dixie: Race, ethnicity, and Latino immigration in the new South* (pp. 99–113). Boulder: First Forum Press.

Bureau of Labor Statistics. (2008, September). *Labor force characteristics by race and ethnicity, 2007*. Report 1005. Office of Employment and Unemployment Statistics, Division of Labor Force Statistics. Washington, DC: US Department of Labor.

Bureau of Labor Statistics. (2010, August). *Labor force characteristics by race and ethnicity, 2009*. Report 1026. Office of Employment and Unemployment Statistics, Division of Labor Force Statistics. Washington, DC: US Department of Labor.

Camia, C. (2011, July 13). GOP lawmaker blasted for 'shooting' immigrants rant. *USA Today*.

Chandler, K. (2011, April 5). Alabama House passes Arizona-style immigration law. *The Birmingham News*.

Chavez, L. (2001). *Covering immigration: popular images and the politics of the nation*. Oakland, CA: University of California Press.

Chavez, L. (2008). *The Latino threat: Constructing immigrants, citizens, and the nation*. Stanford, CA: Stanford University Press.

Citrin, J., Green, D. P., Muste, C., & Wong, C. (1997). Public opinion toward immigration reform: the role of economic motivations. *The Journal of Politics, 59*(3), 858–881.

Clark, A., Cohn, D., Fry, R., Funk, C., Gonzales, F., Kochar, R., Livingston, G., Passel, J., Taylor, P. (2007, December 13). *2007 National survey of Latinos: As illegal immigration issue heats up, Hispanics feel a chill. Research Report*. Washington, DC: Pew Hispanic Center.

Coleman, M., & Kocher, A. (2011). Detention, deportation, devolution and immigrant incapacitation in the US, post 9/11. *The Geographic Journal, 177*(3), 228–237.

Conley, M. (2013a). I now pronounce you polimigra: Narrative resistance to police-ICE interoperability. *Societies Without Borders, 8*(3), 373–383.

Conley, M. (2013b). *Immigrant rights in the nuevo South: Enforcement and resistance at the borderlands of illegality*. Unpublished dissertation, The University of Tennessee, Knoxville.

Conley, M. (2014). *Multiplying forces in the homeland security state: The immigration enforcement lottery and everyday illegality*. Presented at the American Sociological Association Annual Meeting.

Cosby, A., Aanstoos, K., Matta, M., Porter, J., & James, W. (2013). Public support for Hispanic deportation in the United States: The effects of ethnic prejudice and perceptions of economic competition in a period of economic distress. *Journal of Population Research, 30*, 87–96.

De Genova, N. P. (2002). Migrant 'illegality' and deportability in everyday life. *American Review of Anthropology, 31*, 419–447.

DeNavas-Walt, C., Proctor, B., Smith, J.C. (2011, September). *Income, poverty, and health insurance coverage in the United States: 2009*. Report P60-239. Washington, DC: US Census Bureau.

Department of Justice. (2011, December 15). *Department of Justice releases investigative findings on the Maricopa County Sheriff's Office: findings show pattern or practice of wide-ranging discrimination against Latinos and retaliatory actions against individuals who criticized MCSO activities*. Press Release. Washington, DC: Department of Justice.

Department of Justice. (2012, September 18). *Justice Department releases investigative findings on the Alamance County, N.C., Sheriff's Office: Findings show pattern or practice of discriminatory policing against Latinos*. Press Release. Washington, DC: Department of Justice.

Diaz, P., Saenz, D. S., & Kwan, V. S. Y. (2011). Economic dynamics and changes in attitudes toward undocumented Mexican immigrants in Arizona. *Analyses of Social Issues and Public Policy, 11*(1), 300–313.

Dreby, J. (2012). The burden of deportation on children in Mexican immigrant families. *Journal of Marriage and Family, 74*, 829–845.

Espenshade, T. J., & Belanger, M. (1998). Immigration and public opinion. In M. M. Suarez-Orozco (Ed.), *Crossings: Mexican immigration in interdisciplinary perspectives* (pp. 365–403). Cambridge, MA: Harvard University Press.

Espenshade, T. J., & Hempstead, K. (1996). Contemporary American attitudes toward US immigration. *International Migration Review, 30*(2), 535–570.

Fan, M. D. (2012). Rebellious state crimmigration enforcement and the foreign affairs power. *Washington University Law Review, 89*, 1269–1308.

Fleischauer, E. (2011, November 6). Decatur utilities: No water or power for illegal immigrants. *Decatur Daily*.

Friedberg, R. M., & Hunt, J. (1995). The impact of immigrants on host country wages, employment and growth. *The Journal of Economic Perspectives, 9*(2), 23–44.

Gomez, A. (2011, October 4). Alabama immigration law marked by Hispanic school absences. *USA Today*.

Higham, J. (1985). *Strangers in the land: Patterns of American nativism, 1860–1925*. New Brunswick, NJ: Rutgers University Press.

Huntington, S. P. (2004). The Hispanic challenge. *Foreign Policy, 141*(2), 30–45.

Huntington, S. P. (2005). *Who are we? The challenges to America's national identity*. New York: Simon & Schuster.

Kee, L. (2012). *Consequences & costs: Lessons learned from Davidson County, Tennessee's jail model 287(g) program. Report*. Nashville, TN: The ACLU of Tennessee.

Kennedy, V. (2011, October 24). Library card requires proof of citizenship at North Shelby. *The Birmingham News*.

Kochar, R. (2008). *Latino labor report, 2008: Construction reverses job growth for Latinos. Research report*. Washington, DC: Pew Hispanic Center.

Kohli, A., Markowitz, P. L., & Chavez, L. (2011). *Secure communities by the numbers: An analysis of demographics and due process. Research report*. Berkeley, CA: The Chief Justice Earl Warren Institute on Law and Social Policy.

Krikorian, M. (2005). *Downsizing illegal immigration: A strategy of attrition through enforcement*. Washington, DC: Center for Immigration Studies.

Lugo-Lugo, C. R., & Bloodsworth-Lugo, M. K. (2010). 475° from September 11: Citizenship, immigration, same-sex marriage, and the browning of terror. *Cultural Studies, 24*(2), 234–255.

Lyman, B. (2011, October 4). MPS parent says child asked for immigration status. *Montgomery Advertiser*.

Marquardt, M. F., Steigenga, T. J., Williams, P. J., & Vasquez, M. A. (2011). *Living illegal: The human face of unauthorized immigration*. New York: The New Press.

Marrow, H. (2009). New destinations and the American colour line. *Ethnic and Racial Studies, 32*(6), 1037–1057.

Menjívar, C., & Abrego, L. (2012). Legal violence: Immigration law and the lives of Central American immigrants. *American Journal of Sociology, 117*(5), 1380–1421.

Morrison Institute for Public Policy. (2010, September 1). *New poll results: majority of Arizonans favor provisions within SB 1070. Press Release*. Phoenix, AZ: Morrison Institute for Public Policy.

Ngai, M. M. (2004). *Impossible subjects: Illegal aliens and the making of modern America*. Princeton: Princeton University Press.

Olzak, S. (1992). *The dynamics of ethnic competition and conflict*. Stanford: Stanford University Press.

Orrenius, P. M., & Zavodny, M. (2009). *Tied to the business cycle: How immigrants fare in good and bad economic times*. Washington, DC: Migration Policy Institute.

Papademetriou, D. G., & Terrazas, A. (2009). *Immigrants and the current economic crisis: research evidence, policy challenges, and implications.* Washington, DC: Migration Policy Institute.

Passel, J. (2006). *The size and characteristics of the unauthorized migrant population in the U.S.: Estimates based on the March 2005 current population survey. Research report.* Washington, DC: Pew Hispanic Center.

Passel, J., & Cohn, D. (2011). *Unauthorized immigrant population: National and state trends, 2010.* Report. Washington, DC: Pew Hispanic Center.

Robertson, C. (2011, October 3). After ruling, Hispanics flee an Alabama town. *New York Times.*

Shahshahani, A. (2009). *Terror and isolation in Cobb: How unchecked police power under 287(g) has torn families apart and threatened public safety. Report.* Atlanta, GA: The ACLU of Georgia.

Shahshahani, A. (2010). *The persistence of racial profiling in Gwinnett: Time for accountability, transparency, and an end to 287(g). Report.* Atlanta, GA: The ACLU of Georgia.

Singer, A. (2004). *The rise of new immigrant gateways.* Washington, DC: Brookings Institution.

Southern Poverty Law Center. (2012). *Alabama's shame: HB 56 and the war on immigrants. Report.* Montgomery, AL: Southern Poverty Law Center.

Taylor, P., Kochhar, R., Fry, R., Velasco, G., & Motel, S. (2011a). *Wealth gaps rise to record highs between whites, blacks and Hispanics. Research report, Pew Social and Demographic Trends.* Washington, DC: Pew Research Center.

Taylor, P., Lopez, M. H., Passel, J., & Motel, S. (2011b). *Unauthorized immigrants: Length of residency, patterns of parenthood. Research report.* Washington, DC: Pew Hispanic Center.

Theodore, N. (2013). *Insecure communities: Latino perceptions of police involvement in immigration enforcement. Research report.* Oakland, CA: Policy Link.

US Department of Homeland Security. (2012). *2011 yearbook of immigration statistics.* Washington, DC: Office of Immigration Statistics.

Vaughn, J. (2006). *Attrition through enforcement: A cost effective strategy to shrink the illegal population.* Washington, DC: Center for Immigration Studies.

Weissman, D. M., & Headen, R. C. (2009). *The policies and politics of local immigration enforcement laws: 287(g) program in North Carolina. Report.* Raleigh, NC: American Civil Liberties Union of North Carolina and Immigration & Human Rights Policy Clinic.

White, D. (2011, June 2). Alabama legislature passes Arizona-style immigration bill. *The Birmingham News.*

Chapter 9
Transnational Latin American Immigrant Associations in Spain During the Economic Recession: A Top-Down Model of Integration and Transnationalism at Stake?

Héctor Cebolla-Boado and Ana López-Sala

9.1 Introduction

The profound and long-lasting economic crisis that Spain is suffering since 2008 has imposed dramatic changes in its economic, social and institutional dynamics, as well as in the realm of migration and its political management. These changes have not only reduced the strength of arrival flows, but have also reinvigorated outmigration, which was simply unthinkable only a few years ago (Arango 2013). As a result, migrants in Spain have adopted different strategies to face increasing challenges, including high levels of unemployment, an ever expanding segmentation of the labor market as well as significant restrictions in the access to social services due to budgetary constraints (see Chaps. 2, 3 and 5).

In this chapter we seek to study a rather unexplored form of vulnerability in the resilience strategies adopted by Latin American migrants living in Spain (see Chap. 1). We look at the impact that the economic crisis had on the survival and activity of transnational migrant associations and, more specifically, the impact that the recession is having on what we previously defined a "top-down model of integration and transnationalism" (Cebolla-Boado and López-Sala 2015). To do so, we updated a survey conducted in the context of the Comparative Immigrant Organizations Project (CIOP) developed between 2010 and 2012 by the Center for Migration and Development (University of Princeton) and coordinated by

H. Cebolla-Boado (✉)
In Spanish: Departamento de Sociología II, Universidad Nacional de Educación a Distancia (UNED), Madrid, Spain
e-mail: hector.cebolla@gmail.com

A. López-Sala
In Spanish: Instituto de Economía, Geografía y Demografía, Consejo Superior de Investigaciones Científicas (CSIC), Madrid, Spain
e-mail: ana.lsala@cchs.csic.es

© Springer International Publishing Switzerland 2015
M. Aysa-Lastra, L. Cachón (eds.), *Immigrant Vulnerability and Resilience*,
International Perspectives on Migration 11, DOI 10.1007/978-3-319-14797-0_9

prof. Alejandro Portes.[1] Our driving hypothesis here is that after several years of economic crisis and drastic cuts in public spending (particularly since 2011, with a new and conservative government in office), this model of immigrant integration and transnationalism with a strong participation of transnational immigrant organizations financed by the State was in danger of undergoing a drastic transformation.

The CIOP unveiled important differences in the European and U.S. approach to migrant organizations, which were highlighted by Portes and Fernández-Kelly (2015). Regardless of its internal heterogeneity, the European strategy appear to promote a systematic exchange between officials and leaders of migrant organizations, who are unofficially appointed as informal representatives of communities and migrants as a whole. Among new immigration countries, such as Spain, a number of associations have gained a leading role in the definition and implementation of immigrant integration policies. Public funds have been granted in priority to senior organizations with stronger connections to officials in origin and destination countries. In other words, this model is severely subsidized by elected officials seeking representative stakeholders to legitimize their policies. We defined this approach as a top-down model of integration and transnationalism (Cebolla-Boado and López-Sala 2012, 2015). By contrast, the U.S. took a *laissez faire* approach towards immigrant organizations and their activities, and has seldom intervened in an active manner. Instead, the influence of immigrant associations in the U.S. public sphere has been less subsidized and articulated through civic engagement and lobbying.

We expect that the crisis should "Americanize" the top-down model that was developed in Spain. In this article we develop this argument and contrast its empirical grounds by using pre and recession data for the Spanish case.[2]

The chapter is divided in two parts. First, we describe the origins and development of the literature on migrant organizations in Spain. We also describe the emergence of the top-down model to integration and transnationalism, created to accommodate incorporation and co-development policies and to legitimize them among the native population, the new immigrants and long-term foreign residents. Second, we describe the effect of the crisis in the survival strategies of transnational Latin American immigrant organizations. We also explain the results of the survey conducted in 2013 to contrast the hypothesis of the "Americanization" of the Spanish approach to ITAs.

---

[1] The project benefited from the funding provided by the Russell-Sage Foundation and the Fundación Carolina.

[2] The first round of this survey was collected in 2010, when the impact of the crisis was already visible although the economic hardship suffered by organizations had not reached the level we are witnessing in 2104.

9.2 Spanish Research on Latin American Immigrant Associations

The initial literature on Latin American migrant associations in Spain originated in the early 1990s as the first migration flows in Spain settled. The aim of most of this first wave of studies was merely descriptive. Some sought to differentiate the objective and strategies of pro-immigrant associations and migrant associations (Casey 1997). Other contributions analyzed the social participation of specific migrant communities, mostly Peruvians and Dominicans (the most populous groups at the time), as well as Argentineans distinguishing between Spanish organizations and newly created ethnic-national organizations formed by newcomers (Veredas 1998; Pérez 2000; Gallardo and Paredes 1994; del Olmo 1990). Research on Latin American migrant associations gained momentum in the first years of the last decade stimulated by the intensification of Ecuadorian and Colombian immigration, followed by unprecedented Bolivian flows.

Despite of its lack of tradition, the Spanish research on immigrant organizations has evolved along the lines of the mainstream international research agenda. To start with, some have adopted the structure of opportunities perspective (Tarrow 1994; Ibarra 2007; Ireland 1994; Koopmans and Statham 2000), which examines the influence of host country institutions in the organizations' potential and the intensity of their mobilization. This approach was adopted by Veredas (2003, 2004) who analyzed the links between migrant associations and Spanish political institutions, the determinants of ethnic mobilization and the incentives that migrants had for participating in associations.

In the mid-1990s, research on Latin American immigrant organizations refocused to the field of participation among groups and individuals that are excluded from the political community (Martín 2004; Escrivá et al. 2009; Morales and González 2006). At the same time, the influential transnational perspective shaped the Spanish research agenda and gave impetus to the analysis of economic, social, and political dimensions of transnational activities of migrants. In this sense, the study of the role of migrant associations in granting political transnationalism was inspired by the preexisting European and American literature (Portes et al. 1999; Portes 2003; Østergaard-Nielsen 2003; Cortés and Sanmartín 2009, 2010). The collective dimension of transnationalism through forms of economic, social, and political actions of immigrant associations has been a cornerstone in this research with organizations fitting together their role in integration policies in Spain with development initiatives in countries of origin.

More recently, the literature diversified and gained complexity by incorporating different objectives including the study of leadership and the views that migrants had about their host societies through the prism of associations (Verdugo and Gómez 2006) or the impact of political and civic participation in the institutionalization of the associational fabric (Morales et al. 2009). Lastly, some other studies also adopted a comparative perspective (Aparicio and Tornos 2010). Few scholars have worked on the role that associations had in policy making (Bruquetas et al. 2008).

A final remark: most of the past research on Latin American migrant organizations has been fostered and stimulated by public funds. The academic literature on immigration and integration in Spain was developed mainly due to the strong and continuous demand from public administrations who wanted to develop novel interventions and sought in academic research guidelines to face the challenge of incorporating immigrants. Therefore, most Spanish academic research on immigration is strictly empirical and informed by policy-oriented considerations. As we shall see, in Spain, the scientific research has developed parallel to political practice and the interest of administrations to understanding how migrant associations work to inspire integration policies. In the coming section we explain the role that these organizations have had in the definition and management of these policies and, more recently, in the domain of international cooperation.

9.3   The Role of Immigrant Associations in the Design and Implementation of Spanish Immigrant and Cooperation Policies: Forging a Top-down Model of Integration and Transnationalism

The transformation of Spain from an emigration to an immigration country was an unprecedentedly fast and intense process. In 10 years, Spain went from having slightly positive migration rates, to becoming one of the main destinations for migrants both in the Europe and globally. The scarce experience in managing migration explains the reactive approach and ambivalence of its policy during a number of years. Three other facts added complexity to the construction of the Spanish immigration policy. First, the idea that Spain had to converge to European Union standards in setting the basis of its own immigration policy. Second, the inherent difficulties in policy making in the context of a decentralized institutional environment. And third, the extraordinary economic conditions that benefited the country over the last decade and the intense demand for foreign workers in productive areas which were intensive in labor.

Despite of this complexity, Spain managed to create formal and informal mechanisms of coordination between the administration and public institutions as well as NGOs, trade unions and migrant associations. Accordingly, the Spanish migration policy became highly concerted, with social organizations having a significant symbolic and consultative role. These sought to increase the legitimacy of policy making, to improve the access to migrants and migrant communities from the part of the administration and to improve the levels of efficacy (López-Sala 2005; Bruquetas et al. 2008). Specifically speaking about migrant association, their active role in the definition of policies spread the idea that participation and mediation was a pre-requisite for social integration, and that associations were the only valid stakeholder that could represent the entire migrant populations.

Ibarra (2007) puts it in clear terms when he described the system as "participation by invitation" more than "participation by incursion".

How did the link between Spanish institutions and migrant associations evolved over time? The evolution of integration policy in Spain can be summarized in three periods. During the early 1990s integration was not an explicit concern of immigration officials. Towards the end of 1994 and promoted by the Socialist government another phase in Spanish immigration policy began. During this period integration was actively promoted for the first time and immigration was perceived, as a permanent phenomenon which must be addressed from the point of view of settlement. The measures taken were conservative and attempted to resolve specific challenges caused by the presence of immigrants in certain social spheres and geographical areas. These concerns were echoed in public opinion and media outlets. In sum, this policy change was the result of political will and social demands. Nevertheless, during these years it is more appropriate to speak of integration procedures rather than integration policy in its strictest sense (López-Sala 2005). Up to that point, integration had been an area where non-official actors such as trade unions and NGOs deployed innovative but uncoordinated practices (Cachón 1998). In the mid-1990s groups such as trade unions, religious organizations and immigrant associations implemented integration procedures, with resources mainly provided by the government. Later, local authorities also became involved, particularly municipal and regional governments. Therefore, we may refer to a creative process which transferred integration policy novel practices and recommendations from civil society to government. This "innovative role of the periphery" to use the terminology of Zincone (1998), allows us to conclude that during this period immigrant integration policy was constructed "from the ground up", with the financial support of the state. As several authors have mentioned "this entrustment changed the position of these partners, vis-à-vis administrative and political authorities and, to a certain extent, may have altered their very nature [...] In many cases such organizations have become very financially dependent on public administration funds and this dependence has marked their agenda" (Bruquetas et al. 2008). This statement fully applies to those immigrant associations that indirectly started to center their activity to act as part of the administration in the aim of fostering social integration and became severely dependent of public subsidies.

Since 2004 integration became a key issue in the Spanish immigration policy. The Socialist government that came into office in 2004 established a Spanish integration model based on triennial programs, the first of which was presented in 2007 and the second in 2011. Three basic principles inspire the Spanish model of integration: equality and non-discrimination; the recognition of full social, economic, cultural and political citizenship for immigrants; and 'interculturalism' (promoting interaction between people from different origins and cultures, and respecting cultural diversity). The recommendations these programs proposed are essential to understanding the role of immigrant association and their activities in the formulation of immigrant policies. Among the objectives of these programs, participation is of utmost importance. These programs also viewed immigrant participation as a prerequisite for an intercultural society and concentrated on immigrant associations as the most straightforward and efficient channel to achieve this goal. Among its objectives, the programs prioritized the consolidation of the immigrant association movement and promoted the creation of such organizations, devoting a significant part of the budget to this aim. In brief, these programs reinforced a trend that was inherent in the Spanish approach to integration, prioritizing the inclusion of non-official agents in the formulation of integration policies, increasing the role of immigrant associations and the incentives immigrants had to organize themselves in associations that were supposed to have priority access to public funding for the deployment of their interventions (Cachón 2009).

From 2005 onwards, changes in the political landscape and its aims strongly affected the previously described model. The traditional focus on social integration shifted to a new general objective, that of international aid and cooperation with migrant sending countries. As soon as the administrations started to be interested in these two objectives and facilitated access to public funds accordingly, migrant associations started to develop these lines of actions, by strengthening their transnational activities (Cebolla-Boado and López-Sala 2012). Immigration has been a part of the vocabulary of development aid and cooperation in Spain since 2007. In that year, the Annual Cooperation Program (Ministry of Foreign Affairs) detailed specific actions on migration and development, which for the first time were centered on two main purposes: to promote new initiatives that increase the impact of remittances on the development of communities of origin; and, to view migration as a mutually beneficial phenomenon. For that year, the Annual Cooperation Programs mentioned that participation, promotion and leadership of immigrant organizations were considered crucial to achieving several objectives in this area of the Spanish Policy (Østergaard-Nielsen 2011). This expansion of the agenda of immigrant organizations let us to identify a pre-crisis top-down model of integration and transnationalism since integration practices and transnational activism have been boosted in a top-down manner by official policies. In sum, immigrant associations in Spain have assumed a semi-official role on the design and implementation of integration and development public policies. Consequently, immigrant organizations are often co-opted by public administrations, through funding and access to lobbying, as a way to institutionalize the representation of the growing stock of migrants in the country and enhance efficiency.

9.4 Latin American Immigrant Associations in Times of Economic Crisis: Limited Resources and Changing Realities

The impact that this pre-crisis model had on the development and consolidation of transnational activities were already analyzed in previous stages of this research (Cebolla-Boado and López-Sala 2015). The link between administrations and migrant associations was formalized through interventions directed at providing social and legal assistance to the migrants, as well as some political lobbying for social and economic rights. In this first stage, the well-being of immigrants was the priority of the organizations' actions, and they focused on the destination country. The most frequent pattern of institutional change for transnational immigrant associations in Madrid was the evolution from a strict civic focus to a development focus. Three reasons explained this renovated interest among civic migrant associations in the field of development: the emergence of co-development during the central years of the last decade as an important issue in the official Spanish agenda, as mentioned previously; a relative maturation of migration inflows that lessened the importance of activities oriented toward newcomers during the economic boom period; and the ambition of organization leaders whose careers pushed them toward politics in their countries of origin. The involvement of civic organizations on development in their countries of origin resulted from the explicit requirements of funding institutions in Spain with whom they were already connected. Their interest in development was not completely exogenous, but the timing of their involvement was highly determined by their access to public resources.

During the first stage of this research we conducted a survey that allowed us to understand how the existing resources were distributed across migrant organizations and how access to these funds affected their profiles. In principle, the pattern was the following: associations had a high degree of formality in 2010 (inscription in the official registers was a requisite for applying to public funds), organizations were on average 10 years old and had a broad type of contacts with administrations at different levels (local, regional and national). Regarding their level of participation in the system of cooptation from the part of the public administrations, a significant degree of segmentation emerged. Fifty percent of the organizations had very limited access to public resources and, also, small budgets (less than 500 euros/month). By contrast, 17 % of them had large budgets (over 10,000 euros/month). The latter group reported to have an easy access to officials and public resources, which they acknowledged, represented the largest share of their own budgets (80–100 %). Our data indicates that the seniority of the organization is a significant determinant of having contacts with officials and therefore of access to public resources. The objective of updating our previous research could be now clearer. The intense economic crisis that Spain is suffering has imposed severe budget cuts in different areas of social spending; making access to public resources not only more challenging, but also more demanding in terms of requisites. Has this reduction in public resources affected the top-down model that prevailed during the period of economic expansion and became a cornerstone of the Spanish integration system? And, has the crisis also affected the transnational activity of migrant associations, which was strongly subsidized?

The current economic recession has not reduced the presence of migrant organizations in those areas where integration policies were defined and their implementation agreed. Yet, the logic of austerity has impacted in a radical manner the public approach to integration and transnational cooperation. As a consequence, organizations have been increasingly unable to access the resources that they received to provide services for immigrants or their co-nationals in origin. For instance, the budget of the National Social Integration Fund was drastically reduced in 2010 and 2011 and cancelled in 2012. The National Social Integration Fund was established in 2004 by the Socialist Government to promote social cohesion and to support the reception, integration and educational development of immigrants. It financed training, employment creation and intercultural mediation programs carried out by non- governmental organizations, immigrant associations, regional governments and municipal councils. According to the *Plan de Ciudadanía e Inmigración* (PECI), one of the explicit aims of this public fund was to provide tools and specific instruments to migrant organizations in their role as promoters of immigrant integration. The PECI also contributed to stabilize the framework that favored the dialogue between officials, firms, trade unions and NGOs in the definition of the appropriate immigration policy. In 2009 the fund received 200 million Euros. However, during the economic recession, the Ministry of Labor and Social Security eliminated the fund's entire resource allocation in the 2012 general budget. This suppression has been seen as one of the hardest cuts delivered to public policies for immigrant integration in recent years.

Between 2011 and 2013 the general national budget for immigration and integration was reduced in 58 %. Austerity has also decreased dramatically in other funds aiming at social integration across regions. Cuts in spending have been more intense in those regions where migrants are over-represented such as Madrid, Catalonia or Valencia. International aid and cooperation is also one of the most affected areas by cuts in public spending across different levels of the administration. Between 2010 and 2013 this budget was reduced by 70 %. Accordingly, we developed the expectation that the transnational activities of migrant organizations were undergoing and intense transformation if not suppressed. We also expected mortality among associations to peak as a consequence of the economic crisis.

The economic crisis has also importantly changed the priorities among organizations. In the first quarter of 2014 unemployment reached 36 % among foreigners, 10 % point above the corresponding rate for natives. Logically, the living conditions of many migrant households significantly deteriorated. Migrant organizations reacted to this changing context by becoming providers of welfare and easing return or outmigration for those who had chosen to do so. In fact, the most important Latin American immigrant associations in Spain have coordinated with the Spanish administrations in charge of developing programs for foster the return of migrants to their countries of origin. The list includes Ecuadorian, Colombian or Bolivian organizations such as Rumiñaui, AESCO or ACOBE that were key stakeholders in the first public plans promoting return (López-Sala 2013). Assistance to returnees became not only a new strategic area of intervention for migrant organizations but also, and maybe more importantly, a renewed source of public funds.

9.5 Data and Methods

Data used in this paper come from an update of the study on organizations which were initially surveyed in 2010. The study collected information from immigrant associations of diverse origins in the Municipality of Madrid. In that survey the selection of immigrant groups was based on three dimensions: size, comparability, and internal diversity. Among Latin Americans, groups selected included Colombia, Ecuador, Peru and the Dominican Republic, which offer diverse histories, migratory sequences and profiles. The selection of association from these four origin countries allowed us to incorporate the study of immigrant communities with long standing presence (Peru and Dominican Republic), but also incorporate the largest and more recent immigrant communities in Spain (Ecuador and Colombia).

The survey sought to sample organizations using a preliminary inventory of national immigrant associations. Various registers were used to build this inventory. First, we examined the association registries provided by the embassies in Spain, the umbrella confederations and the centers for participation and integration of immigrants of the regional government of Madrid (CEPIs). This information was compared with three other formal registers: the National Register of Associations of the Ministry of Home Affairs, the Register of Religious Associations of the Ministry of Justice, and the Non-governmental Organizations Dedicated to Development Register of the Ministry of Foreign Affairs and Cooperation. A breakdown of the associations that had received financing to carry out development projects in their countries of origin was solicited from the local government of the Municipality of Madrid, the regional government of the Community of Madrid, and the Spanish Agency of Cooperation and Development (AECID) of the Ministry of Foreign Affairs.

A questionnaire was distributed in 2010 to a sample of the associations included in this inventory. The survey conducted in Madrid included 85 associations with significant transnational activities (out of 700 existing). A simple follow up of the survey (Transnational Immigrant Associations Survey [TIAS] 2013) was conducted at the end of 2013 to check whether the organizations existed or continue to have significant activity (of either transnational or local scope), and if they had received any public funds. The follow up was done using an online survey which only 15 % of the initial sample responded. Non-responses were recuperated using alternative means such as direct contacts using emails, telephone and, when available, the organization website. Out of all the initial organizations included in the survey in 2010, Moroccans were excluded from our follow up (7) and 10 organizations, all without websites or Facebook profiles, where unreachable; so attrition in the follow up phase amounted to 15 % of the Latin American organizations.

9.6   Results of the Transnational Immigrant Associations 2013 Follow-Up

The aim of the follow-up phase of the survey (TIAS 2013) was to explore survival rates after 3 years of an intense economic crisis with significant cuts in public spending. Before exploring this idea, it is necessary to provide a conceptual clarification of what we mean by associations' survival. Our understanding of survival in this analysis is not strictly speaking coming from having or not received a direct confirmation by the organization leaders of the existence of the association in 2013. The enormous difficulties to get valid answers from the organizations forced us to adopt a more flexible strategy, which transformed our dependent variable into a proxy of significant activity. By significant activity we understand that the organization responded to our contact or, if not, a confirmation of its activity was obtained from announcements of publicly or privately funded projects, their websites or alternative sites on the Internet (including Facebook and Twitter) confirming the existence of meetings, projects or organizational gatherings hold in 2013. In those cases, a dependent variable was constructed taking the value of 1 if activity was observed and 0 when the organizations did not respond to our contact and we did not confirm any activity in 2013. A second dependent variable was further elaborated to distinguish among the valid observations, which measures the organizations access to public funds (1/0). A summary of our descriptive findings is provided in the first Figure (Fig. 9.1). Two thirds (66.3 %) of the surveyed organizations in 2010 had significant activity 3 years after. Out of them, 29.4 % had benefitted from any type of access to public funds.

In our follow-up we could also confirm that among the organizations that received public funds in 2010, 54.5 % continued to receive them in 2013, which suggests the cuts in public spending faced in the period under study. By contrast, 80.5 % of those who did not receive public support at the start of the observation period, remained in the same situation in 2013.

A number of hypotheses were formulated to understand organizations' survival strategies in the context of the top-down model of integration and transnational engagement through immigrant organization as described and contrasted in our previous research (Cebolla-Boado and López-Sala 2015). Specifically, the empirical analysis we present in this chapter corresponds to the fact that after several years of economic crisis and drastic cuts in public spending the Spanish model of immigrant organizations might have transformed. Our analysis of this transformation of immigrants' organizations in Spain is structured along four hypotheses that are inspired by the path dependence of the top-down model.

- Resources: more resourceful associations are more likely to survive in 2013. The resources include both private and public funds, but the distinction is relevant since our argument is that the economic context of immigrant organizations created during the economic expansion of Spain in the 2000s fostered dependence from public funds among a large and representative number of

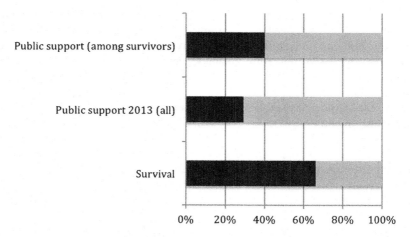

Fig. 9.1 Presence of transnational immigrant associations in the 2013 survey follow-up (Source: TIAS (2013))

associations that could be considered insiders to the Spanish policy of migrant integration. In other words, we expect that access to public funds in the past could increase the likelihood of maintaining a significant activity in 2013.

- Seniority: in our previous description of the top-down model we detected that seniority was a key element for organizations to have access to public funds. We interpreted this pattern as suggesting that the administration selected more stable counterparts among migrant organizations at the start of the development of the integration policies to legitimize or implement them. As a consequence we expect seniority to increase the likelihood of survival.
- Contacts at the highest level in origin and destination: having reported access to contacts at the highest level of the Spanish administration (national level) could be a sign of granted temporal stability. By contrast, we expect that contact with the National level administration in origin could have a different effect. Since the purpose of the Spanish administrations was to make use of transnational organizations not only to implement integration policies but also to channel co-development initiatives; and the share of the public budget aimed at International Aid and Development has been one of the most affected chapters by the cuts in public spending, we expect this variable to be an irrelevant predictor of survival.
- Size: we expect that the larger the organization, the higher probability of survival. Therefore, size of the organization should be a significant predictor of its chances of survival over time. In a context of decreasing funds allocated for migrant organizations and a more intense competition for it, immigrant associations could diversify their funding strategies and evolve towards a more grassroots model of financing their activities. In this case, larger organizations (both by its population of members and/or participants in their activities) could have an easier transition and access to alternative sources of funding.

To test these hypotheses we use Linear Probability Models (LPM, with robust standard errors) for both dependent variables: survival and access to public funds. LPMs were chosen against its most straightforward alternative (logistic regression) because they are easier to interpret. Note, however, that the results we present and discuss hereafter are stable if using the appropriate models for dichotomous dependent variables.

The results of our analyses on the determinants of survival as shown in Table 9.1, only confirm hypothesis 1 (resources). Indeed, although the budget size does not seem to matter significantly, having had access to public funds in 2010 and the share out of the total budget that these funds represented are significant and important determinants of survival 3 years after. In other words, it is not the amount of resources in general that an organization enjoyed in the past that determines its survival, but whether these were public or private funds, which we take as an indication of the status of being an insider organization.

Surprisingly, organization's seniority is non-significant. We could interpret this as a sign of how in a context of more competition for scarce resources, the know-how on gaining access to public funds becomes more important than having a brand or a traditional position in the field we analyze. Note however, the sign of the estimate here is negative (something that confirms that older organizations were also more likely to remain active in 2013).

Having contacts at origin or destination is also non significant in our analysis. In our understanding this suggests an important transformation of the top-down model as a consequence of the economic recession. Our assumption was that organizations having had contacts in the past with the national-level administration (above and beyond contacts with the local and regional governments) were more institutionalized and more likely to benefit from the insider status in this top-bottom model. Note again that the sign of both effects is the predicted one (positive).

Finally, it should be remarked that the number of members in the organization or the average number of participants in its events are not significantly associated with survival in 2013 so there are no statistical bases to affirm that organizations adapted to their strategies to a more grass-roots based model.

Since estimates shown in Table 9.1 are not comparable (given their measurement in different units), Fig. 9.2 summarizes the standardized magnitude of their effects. This is also important since the criterion of statistical significance is not very informative in analysis conducted with small samples. The comparison of the effects yields no doubt that access to public funds is the key organizational asset to survival.

A rather similar scenario could be described by looking at access to public funds in 2013 (see Table 9.2). Access to resources in 2010 became a key predictor in an even clearer way than in the model on survival. Seniority or contacts behave empirically as in the previous model. Note, however the number of members and participants in the organizational events is not significantly associated with access to public funds, which could reveal that the scarce funds available are being directed to more strategically efficient associations and not necessarily to traditional ones.

Table 9.1 Coefficients of linear probability models on organizations' survival from 2010 to 2013

		M1	M2	M3	M4	M5	M6	M7	M8
Resources	Budget size	0.033							
		0.03							
	Public funds 2010		0.310***						
			0.11						
	% Budget public			0.004***					
				0.00					
Year register					−0.007				
					0.01				
Contacts	Spain					0.009			
						0.04			
	Country of origin						0.068		
							0.12		
Size	N. members							−0.000	
								0.00	
	N. participants								0.000
									0.00
Constant		0.562***	0.537***	0.568***	15.641	0.633***	0.628***	0.649***	0.626***
		0.11	0.08	0.07	21.62	0.12	0.07	0.06	0.07
Goodness of fit	N	66	67	68	62	68	66	64	62
	F	1.453	8.397	6.612	0.478	0.070	0.304	0.335	0.541
	R^2	0.019	0.101	0.085	0.009	0.001	0.005	0.006	0.008

$p < .1$; **$p < .05$; ***$p < .01$

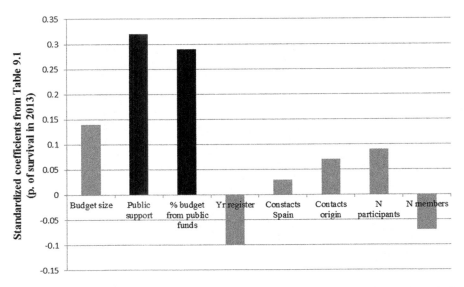

Fig. 9.2 Summary of standardized predictors on the probability of organizations' survival (Source: TIAS (2013))

The summary of these effects using standardized coefficients shows the relative strength of predictors where a strong path dependence from previous access to public funds seems to be the privileged explanation (see Fig. 9.3).

9.7 Concluding Remarks

Austerity and the subsequent cuts in public spending in Spain have dramatically transformed the landscape of immigrant transnationalism, international cooperation and humanitarian aid. These trends in public spending and changes in policy priorities during the current economic crisis negatively impacted the activity of Latin American immigrant associations. The update of our 2010 survey in 2013 (TIAS 2013) (after a number of years of enduring economic recession), allowed us to estimate that 1/3 of these organizations disappeared or has no current activity. We therefore conclude that the rate of mortality reached 30 %; out of them, 29.4 % benefitted in 2010 from access to public funds. We can also confirm that among the organizations that received public funds in 2010, 54.5 % continued to receive them in 2013, which indicates the impact of the cuts in public spending faced in the period 2010–2013. These figures allow describing the context in which Latin American organizations survive and are currently operating in Spain.

The empirical evidence provided suggests that access to public funds, which before the crisis allowed to develop a thick fabric of active transnational organizations, is associated to the pattern of associational mortality in 2013. Better-funded

Table 9.2 Coefficients of linear probability models on organizations' access to public funds in 2013

		M1	M2	M3	M4	M5	M6	M7	M8
Resources	Budget size	0.084**							
		0.03							
	Public funds 2010		0.273*						
			0.15						
	% Budget public 2010			0.005**					
				0.00					
Yr. register					−0.007				
					0.01				
Contacts	Spain					0.025			
						0.05			
	origin						0.104		
							0.16		
Size	N. members							0.000***	
								0.00	
	N. participate								0.000*
									0.00
Constant		0.104	0.273***	0.247***	15.077	0.324*	0.333***	0.373***	0.352***
		0.13	0.10	0.09	28.52	0.16	0.09	0.08	0.09
Model info.	N	44	44	45	43	45	43	41	40
	F	6.255	3.500	6.711	0.264	0.283	0.438	57.998	3.410
	R²	0.127	0.077	0.134	0.007	0.007	0.011	0.039	0.039

* p < .1; ** p < .05; *** p < .01

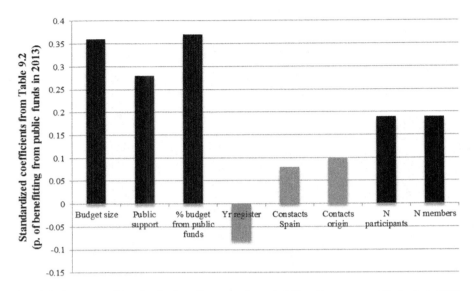

Fig. 9.3 Summary of standardized predictors on the probability of access to public funds in 2013 (Source: TIAS (2013))

organizations, with more privileged connections to the administrations have more favorable survival rates during the economic crisis. In other words, only those organizations that are considered essential by the administrations have positive prospects in the short run. Organizations with contacts with the administration are precisely the ones that are still represented in the consultative institutions in which immigrant organizations have traditionally participated. As a positive indirect consequence of this complex context and the increasing constraints that organizations face, the level of professionalization and expertise imposed by a more demanding system of access to public funds, will improve the efficacy and efficiency of immigrant transnational organizations in Spain. Of course this will impose a strong centralization of the existing resources, increasing the already existing inequality among organizations. Segmentation of the organizations market is probably increasing and will do so even more in the near future.

At the moment, there are no statistical bases to affirm that organizations adapted their strategies to a more grass-root based model, as in the case of the United States. Access to private funds coming directly from the grassroots of organizations is unlikely to develop in the current scenario. Distinguished organizational leaders report that even though their initial strategy was to shift towards this type of resources, immigrant households, as one the groups that are more severely affected by the economic downturn are currently unable to contribute significantly to their preferred organizational strategies. Further research is needed to unveil if, as soon as the economy stabilizes, immigrants would start to contribute to their organizations, pushing toward the 'Americanization' of the traditional 'top-down' model of transnational organizations in Spain.

References

Aparicio, R., & Tornos, A. (2010). *Las asociaciones de inmigrantes en España. Una visión de conjunto*. Madrid: Observatorio Permanente de la Inmigración. Ministerio de Trabajo e Inmigración.

Arango, J. (2013). *Exceptional in Europe? Spain's experience with migration and integration*. Washington: Migration Policy Institute.

Bruquetas, M., Garcés, B., Morén, R., Penninx, R., & Vieytez, E. (2008). Immigration and Integration policy making in Spain. IMISCOE working paper, 21. Amsterdam: University of Amsterdam.

Cachón, L. (1998). Los Sindicatos Españoles y La Inmigración. *Migraciones, 4*, 71–109.

Cachón, L. (2009). *La España inmigrante: marco discriminatorio, mercado de trabajo y políticas de integración*. Barcelona: Anthropos.

Casey, J. (1997). Les associacions i la integració d'immigrants estrangers. *Revista Catalana de Sociología, 6*, 9–22.

Cebolla-Boado, H., & López-Sala, A. (2012). A top-down model of transnational immigrant associationism: Migrant organizations in the definition of development and integration policies in Spain. Princeton: Center for Migration and Development. Working papers, n. 12-04b.

Cebolla-Boado, H., & López-Sala, A. (2015). Transnational Immigrant organizations in Spain: Their role in development and integration. In A. Portes & P. Fernández-Kelly (Eds.), *The state and the grassroots: Immigrant transnational organizations in four continents* (pp. 382–419). New York: Berghahn Books.

Cortés, I., & Sanmartín, A. (2009). Las practicas transnacionales de los inmigrantes vinculadas al desarrollo. Un estudio a partir del contexto español. *Revista del Ministerio de Trabajo y Asuntos Sociales, 80*, 191–210.

Cortés, I., & Sanmartín, A. (2010). Transnacionalismo político: políticas migratorias de vinculación de los estados de origen y de las asociaciones de inmigrantes en España. Los casos ecuatoriano y colombiano. XV Encuentro de Latinoamericanistas españoles, pp. 1146–1164.

Del Olmo, M. (1990). *La construcción cultural de la identidad. Inmigrantes argentinos en España*. Madrid: Universidad Complutense de Madrid.

Escrivá, A., Bermúdez, N., & Moraes, N. (Eds.). (2009). *Migración y participación política. Estados, organizaciones y migrantes latinoamericanos en perspectiva local-transnacional*. Madrid: Consejo Superior de Investigaciones Científicas.

Gallardo, G., & Paredes, M. (1994). *Mujer inmigrante y asociacionismo desde la perspectiva de la experiencia de la Asociación de Mujeres dominicanas en España*. Madrid: II Jornadas sobre Mujer e Inmigración. Consejería de Bienestar Social.

Ibarra, P. (2007). Participación y poder: de la legitimación al conflicto. In I. Ahedo & P. Ibarra (Eds.), *Democracia participativa y desarrollo humano* (pp. 37–56). Madrid: Dykinson.

Ireland, P. (1994). *The policy challenge of ethnic diversity: Immigrant politics in France and Switzerland*. Cambridge: Harvard University Press.

Koopmans, R., & Statham, P. (2000). Migration and ethnic relations as a field of political contention: An opportunity structure approach. In R. Koopmans & P. Statham (Eds.), *Challenging immigration and ethnic relations politics. Comparative European perspectives* (pp. 13–56). Oxford: Oxford University Press.

López-Sala, A. (2005). Matters of state? Migration policy-making in Spain as a new political domain? *Migration, 43*, 35–49.

López-Sala, A. (2013). Managing uncertainty: Immigration policies in Spain during economic recession (2008–2011). *Migraciones Internacionales, 7*, 39–69.

Martín, A. (2004). Las asociaciones de inmigrantes en el debate sobre las nuevas formas de participación política y ciudadanía: reflexiones sobre algunas experiencias. *Migraciones, 15*, 113–143.

Morales, L., & González, A. (2006). Las Asociaciones de Inmigrantes en Madrid: una nota de investigación sobre su grado de integración política. *Revista española del tercer sector, 4,* 129–174.

Morales, L., González, A., & Jorba, L. (2009). Políticas de incorporación y la gestión del asociacionismo de la población de origen inmigrante a nivel local. In R. Zapata (Ed.), *Políticas y gobernabilidad de la inmigración en España* (pp. 113–138). Barcelona: Ariel.

Østergaard-Nielsen, E. (2003). The politics of migrants' transnational political practices. *International Migration Review, 37,* 760–786.

Østergaard-Nielsen, E. (2011). Codevelopment and citizenship: the nexus between policies on local migrant incorporation and migrant transnational practices in Spain. *Ethnic and Racial Studies, 34,* 20–39.

Pérez, G. (2000). Redes comunitarias de los inmigrantes peruanos en Madrid. *Ofrim, 6,* 201–215.

Portes, A. (2003). Theoretical convergencies and empirical evidence in the study of immigrant transnationalism. *International Migration Review, 37,* 874–892.

Portes, A., & Fernández-Kelly, P. (Eds.). (2015). *The state and the grassroots: Immigrant transnational organizations in four continents.* New York: Berghahn Books.

Portes, A., Guarnizo, L., & Landolt, P. (1999). The study of transnationalism: pitfalls and promise of an emergent research field. *Ethnic and Racial Studies, 22,* 217–237.

Tarrow, S. (1994). *Power in movement. Social movements and contentious politics.* Cambridge: Cambridge University Press.

Verdugo, R., & Gómez, A. (2006). Narraciones políticas y procesos de enmarcamiento del discurso de las asociaciones del Foro para la Integración Social de los Inmigrantes de España. *Papers, 81,* 149–169.

Veredas, S. (1998). *Las asociaciones de inmigrantes marroquíes y peruanos en la Comunidad de Madrid.* Madrid: Universidad Complutense de Madrid. Facultad de Ciencias Políticas y Sociología.

Veredas, S. (2003). Las asociaciones de inmigrantes en España. Práctica clientelar y cooptación política. *Revista Internacional de Sociología, 36,* 207–225.

Veredas, S. (2004). Factores condicionantes de la movilización étnica entre la población inmigrante extracomunitaria, Papers, 72, 87–111.

Zincone, G. (1998). Illegality, enlightenment and ambiguity. A hot Italian recipe. *South European Society and Politics, 3,* 43–81.

Part III
Linking the Effects of the Great Recession in Destination and Origin Countries

Chapter 10
International Migration and Employment in Latin America: Uncertain Times and Changing Conditions

Jorge Durand and María Aysa-Lastra

10.1 Introduction

The relationship between migration and employment in Latin America is a complex phenomenon with a variety of dimensions that change over time. At a first glance, a general and logical argument to explain any migration flow might be that those employed do not usually migrate to another country, although this is not always the case. However, neither it is the opposite case, those unemployed do not always emigrate, and less so in current times, when substantial financial resources are required to cross a national border.

Although employment is a key factor in the study of migration, what frequently defines individuals' migration itineraries is the main feature of employment: wages. Wage differentials in a regional and international context are one of the key components of emigration, which is consistent with neoclassical theories (Stark 1991) and the so called "rational choice" approaches (for a critique see Hechter and Kanazawa 1997). Nonetheless, wage differentials are not a sufficient condition. In addition, there must a substantial demand for labor that motivates workers to migrate.

Moreover, even if wage differential could prompt workers to migrate, it does not determine the place of destination. Migrants do not only go to those places where they can earn the highest wages. Certainly, they are looking for better wages, but there are myriad of factors at the personal, family and social levels that determine the migration to a specific location rather than another (Massey et al.1987; Flores-Yeffal 2013).

J. Durand (✉)
Universidad de Guadalajara CUCSH – CIDE, México
e-mail: j.durand.mmp@gmail.com

M. Aysa-Lastra
Department of Sociology and Anthropology, Winthrop University, Rock Hill, SC, USA
e-mail: aysalastram@winthrop.edu

© Springer International Publishing Switzerland 2015   183
M. Aysa-Lastra, L. Cachón (eds.), *Immigrant Vulnerability and Resilience*,
International Perspectives on Migration 11, DOI 10.1007/978-3-319-14797-0_10

Even a flip of a coin can define whether to stay of leave. For many migrants, and certainly for young migrants, it is considered a rite of passage (Hondagneu-Sotelo 1994). But, the place of destination is not left to luck to decide. Here, there is no room for adventure or improvisation. In general, migrants go where they have relations, friendships, contacts and cultural and linguistic affinities (Massey and Aysa-Lastra 2011).

There are not fixed rules and uniform employment and migration patterns in Latin America. Each country's paths and pace towards development as well as the effects of economic junctures are different. Today (in 2014), Brazil and Chile are solid, stable and growing economies, while Argentina might be at the verge of a new economic crisis. In the last decade the economies of Panama, Peru and Colombia have consistently registered high growth rates, while the Mexican economy has only grown moderately. Bolivia and Guatemala, with a high presence of indigenous populations, have not found the strategies that take large proportions of the population out of poverty and marginalization. Still trapped in the past, Honduras and Paraguay follow the outdated landowner model and have been unable to develop and implement an agrarian reform.

The recipes implemented in each country to face economic downturns in the 1990s were different. Even today, the aftermaths of those policies are still felt in many social sectors. For example, Ecuador and El Salvador adopted the dollar as their official currency; in Argentina, parity with the dollar was imposed to later on change it again for the Argentinian peso. In Peru, soles and dollars are simultaneously exchanged in daily transactions and Mexico, as well as in other countries, implemented a free market exchange rate, or a floating exchange rate, that usually goes upwards.

Development levels in Latin America are, as expected, diverse (Table 10.1). There are regions in which extreme poverty and marginalization are still very high. Latin America, as a whole, has not been able to solve the vicious inherited discrimination practices from colonial times, particularly towards black and indigenous populations, whom continue to be the most disadvantaged group on the continent. According to the rankings of the Human Development Index listed in Table 10.1 (Malik 2013), only two countries, Chile and Argentina are ranked within the group of countries with very high development (as is the case of the US and Spain, the main destination countries for Latin American migrants); in the next level, high development countries, we found 12 in the region. The leading countries in this group are Uruguay, Panama, Cuba, Mexico and Costa Rica. Among the countries with medium development, we identify 10 countries. Among the lowest ranked countries in this level we found Honduras, Nicaragua and Guatemala, countries that have been devastated by long periods of political unrest and instability and natural disasters. There is only one country with low level of development, Haiti, with scores similar to Yemen and Uganda.

Despite the disparities and heterogeneity among Latin American countries, it is possible to establish tendencies and define indicators that allow for an analysis of

Table 10.1 Human development index by level and rank for selected countries, 2013

Country	HID level	HID rank	% of population aged 60 and over	Population aging rank
Destination countries				
United States	Very high	3	19.5	23
Spain	Very high	23	22.9	25
Origin countries				
Central and South America				
Chile	Very high	40	14.0	65
Argentina	Very high	45	14.9	62
Uruguay	High	51	18.4	47
Panama	High	59	10.2	85
Mexico	High	61	9.3	94
Costa Rica	High	62	10.3	84
Venezuela	High	71	9.3	96
Peru	High	77	9.2	97
Brazil	High	85	11.0	79
Ecuador	High	89	9.3	95
Colombia	High	91	9.3	93
Belize	Medium	96	5.7	142
Suriname	Medium	105	9.5	91
El Salvador	Medium	107	9.5	90
Bolivia	Medium	108	7.2	117
Paraguay	Medium	111	8.0	106
Guyana	Medium	118	5.3	147
Honduras	Medium	120	6.4	130
Nicaragua	Medium	129	6.7	124
Guatemala	Medium	133	6.5	127
Caribbean				
Cuba	High	59	18.3	48
Dominican Republic	Medium	96	9.0	98
Haiti	Low	161	6.7	125

Source: United Nations Development Programme (2013), United Nations, Department of Economic and Social Affairs, Population Division (2013).

migration and employment within the region. In order to understand migration from Latin American countries, it is not enough to look at the flows to US, Canada and Europe, but there is also a need to incorporate human mobility within the region. This chapter is divided in three sections. The first section centers on the demographic factor, which is the key component for migration and employment. Second, we focus on employment, wages, substandard employment, professional employment, and gender disparities in the labor market. Once we have established the main elements in our analysis, demographic structure and employment, then we study migration trends and its contemporary equivalent, return migration to the region.

10.2   The Demographic Factor

Migration and employment patterns are inextricably linked to the population structure. However, the interpretation of the demographic elements must include other indicators. For example, a key feature of low developed countries is that generally they have large contingents of workers but little and scarce capital. The inability of a country to generate employment, among other things, is related to an excess of labor supply from younger (and larger) cohorts that move into the working age groups year after year. Therefore, the excess of labor supply and its pressures on the resources available generate the conditions for emigration of young workers. Nonetheless, these processes are neither mechanical, nor automatic; each case presents its own features and should be analyzed independently.

In this sense, the Brazilian case is unique. Brazil is a country with 197 million inhabitants, a controlled fertility rate of 1.8 children per women (lower than the rate for Chile), a high level of internal migration, very low international migration and a net migration rate of zero (PRB 2014). It is also a country with a vast territory, and although rich in natural resources, we also observe high levels of poverty, which have declined since 2003. Still in 2010, 6 % of the population lived with less than $1.25 dollars a day, and 35 % lived with less than $5.00 dollars a day (World Bank 2014). The consolidation of Brazilian social institutions and the development of its industrial capacity have resulted in economic growth, higher levels of employment and increasing real wages.

On the other hand, in 2010, Mexico had 112 million inhabitants and about 10 % of its population has emigrated to other countries, with 89.4 % of this migrant population living in the United States (INEGI 2014). Mexico and Brazil have similar conditions, vast territories, controlled and low fertility (2.2 children per women in Mexico), and high poverty levels (in 2012, 0.7 % of the Mexican population lived with under $1.25 dollars, and as Brazil, 35 % percent of the population lived with less than $5.00 dollars a day). However, Mexico and the United States not only shared one of the largest international borders (2,000 miles), but one with the highest traffic of goods and persons, and a history of territorial and migratory agreements (and disagreements) that play a determinant role in the dynamics of the northbound Mexican migration (Delano 2011).

From our comparison between Brazil and Mexico, we can argue that although the demographic factor is key to maintain migration dynamics; it does not stimulate it. In Mexico, the very high population growth during the 1950s contributed to maintain the contemporary migration flow, which was initiated during WWII.

The population explosion in most Latin American countries created a deficit in the generation of employment. There were more workers coming into the labor force each year than new jobs available for these incoming members of the labor force. For example, in Mexico in the 1970s, the cohorts ages 10–19 accounted for 11.4 million children, which were equivalent to 23.6 % of the population. Twenty years later, in the 1990s the demographic growth of the population was increasing, the cohorts ages 10–19 accounted for 20 million, equivalent to 24.6 % of the population (INEGI 2014). These figures indicate that on average, the Mexican economy needed to generate a million new jobs each year. According to Escobar (2001) there are three marked periods with different patterns of job growth in Mexico in the recent decades. First, a period of market instability and no job generation between 1982 and 1987. Second, a period of slow job growth from 1988 to 1994 which was followed by a major crisis in 1995. And then, a third period of rapid growth from 1996 to 2000. Therefore, in the 1980s and 1990s, the Mexican economy did not increase the demand for labor that would have employed its youth population. Consequently, the emigration of near one million Mexicans in working ages allowed certain equilibrium.

The structural conditions behind the emigration of millions of Mexicans to the US are changing. The total fertility rate for Mexico declined between 1960 and 2013 from 7.3 to 2.2 children per women (Passel et al. 2012; CONAPO 2014). According to Hanson and McIntosh (2009) the Mexican-US migration flow will decline from its peak in 1990, and by 2030 it will only be a third of the level in 2000. Moreover, exogenous shocks are also promoting this decline. In 2007, when the signs of the foreseen crisis started to emerge, the Mexican labor migration to the US declined, and it is estimated than in 2012 only about 150,000 workers traveled north (MMP 2014).

In the United States, Mexicans and Latino immigrants are increasingly discriminated against, racialized, and subjected to restrictive and punitive legislation and deportations, and although conservative positions dominate the immigration discourse in Europe in some institutions, there is a debate about the benefits of immigration. The European Commissioner for Internal Affairs Cecilia Malnström argues that immigration is not a threat but rather, it is an opportunity. Her argument is based on the fact that in the next decades, those in the working age groups will have diminished as a proportion of the total European population. One case in point is Spain. According to the population projections of the Spanish Bureau of Statistics (INE 2012), in 2051 34 % of the population will be older than age 65 and the dependency ratio, which currently is 50 %, will double to 100 %. Latin American populations are currently younger, while in 2013 it is observed that the old age support ratio for Europe is 4, for Latin America this figure is 9, indicating that the number of people of working age to the population over age 60 is double in Latin America. But this panorama will change as in 2050, when the old age support ratio for Europe is expected to be 2 and drastically reduced to 3 for Latin America (UN 2014). During the last 30 years, Latin America experienced a fast paced demographic transition and it is time for its population structure to gray.

Table 10.1 shows the proportion of population 60 years and over for all countries in the region. The rank goes from Japan (1) with 32 % of its population over 60 to the United Arab Emirates (201) with less than 1 % of elderly in its population. If we divide the rank of all countries in 4 tiers: very high, high, medium and low, we observe that most countries in Latin America already are among the group of countries with high or medium proportions of elderly population (UN 2014).

10.3 Employment and Minimum Wage in Latin America

During the so called lost decade of the 1980s, the adjustments of the public debt in the region triggered the implementation of the Washington Consensus policies which created a decline in the level of job growth and the quality of jobs available in the 1990s. Moreover, the region did not escape the effects of multiple financial crises originating in Mexico (the tequila effect in 1995), the Asian crisis in 1997, and just afterwards, the financial crises in Russia and Japan. The Asian crisis had large impacts in Brazil's economy. Furthermore, El Niño, and hurricanes George and Mitch had devastating effects in multiple Central American countries. In 1998, the region registered slow growth (2.4 %) and high unemployment (above 9 %). It can be said the 1990s is a decade without significant job growth in Latin America and a period of the deterioration of labor conditions with the implementation of labor reforms that in the name of "competitiveness" which led to the growth of temporary contracts, the informalization of labor, and a decline in social security coverage (ILO 2013). Labor statistics for this transitional period also indicate growth of discouraged workers in the region.

It is not a coincidence that while large cohorts of young workers were entering the labor force in a regional economy that was recovering from the debt negotiations of the 1980s, was going through the implementation of neoliberal policies, and was hit by various exogenous financial crisis and natural disasters, the United States registered the largest growth of labor immigrants from the region and the emigration to a blossoming Southern Europe started to emerge.

The first decade of the twentieth first century is marked by the 9/11 attacks in New York, Washington, Madrid and London, which created an scenario of uncertainty and insecurity that has led to the increasing border enforcement and policing of immigrants. The labor markets in Latin America were responsive to the economic effects triggered by the terrorist attacks in the centers of the developed world. Still in 2003, Latin America registered slow economic growth and no progress in employment.

The year 2004 marks a turning point for labor markets in the region. Figure 10.1 shows labor force participation rates, unemployment rates and the employment to population ratio for the population ages 15 and older. The trends in the figure indicate that starting in 2004 unemployment rates began a steady decline which, although partially interrupted during the Great Recession (2008–2010), has continued its upward trend afterwards. The period between 2004 and 2008 is the first sustained period of declining unemployment in the region after two decades of structural adjustments and financial crises.

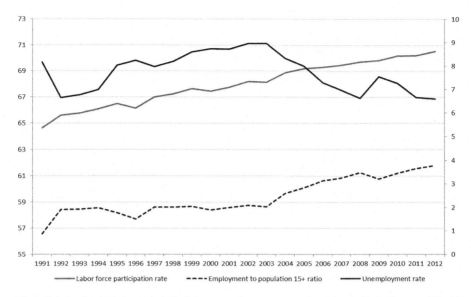

Fig. 10.1 Latin American and Caribbean employment indicators 1991–2012 (Source: World Development Indicators downloaded through the World Bank Data. Indicators used are modeled ILO estimates)

10.3.1   Minimum Wage

Although employment trends are relevant, in our initial argument, we stated that wage differential is the key to explain the migration trends within and from the region. Therefore, in the next paragraphs we examine the minimum wage to establish comparison at the regional and international levels (see Table 10.2). Minimum wage is the minimum sum payable to a worker for work performed or services rendered within a given period. It is guarantee by law according to the country's economic and social conditions and it may not be reduced either by individual or collective agreement. Minimum wages are not indicators of median wages at the country level, and unfortunately there are not available statistics to know the number of persons earning minimum wage. Nonetheless, it is a homogenous indicator that allows us to compare across countries in the region.

In 2012, the minimum legal wage in Chile was 333 US dollars a month, equivalent to 5,701 real dollars a year (OECD 2014). There are workers in small manufacturing jobs that might earn this wage, but those are few. The majority of blue collar workers earn higher salaries, therefore, we can consider the Chilean working class as well remunerated.

In Mexico, the current minimum wage is 65.58 pesos a day equivalent to 5 dollars (Secretaria del Trabajo y Prevision Social 2014). In Mexico, as well as in other countries, the minimum wage is used as a measure to estimate fees, fines and scholarships, among others. Minimum wage is adjusted for inflation, so it increases

Table 10.2 Monthly minimum wage for selected countries, 2010

Country	Minimum wage (US $)	Minimum wage (international $)[a]	Ratio of US to country wage	Ratio of Spain to country wage
Destination countries				
United States	$1,242.58	1,242.58	1.00	0.84
Spain	$1,043.96	1,043.96	1.19	1.00
Origin countries				
Argentina	$456.85	$695.50	1.79	1.50
Bolivia	$110.23	$275.50	4.51	3.79
Brazil	$299.65	$332.89	3.73	3.14
Colombia	$260.76	$678.69	1.83	1.54
Costa Rica	$387.66	$434.67	2.86	2.40
Chile	$332.56[b]	$475.08[b]	2.62	2.20
Ecuador	$253.55	$507.20	2.45	2.06
El Salvador	$80.79	$161.60	7.69	6.46
Guatemala	$185.54	$371.00	3.35	2.81
Haiti	$125.65	$251.20	4.95	4.16
Honduras	$279.26	$558.60	2.22	1.87
Mexico	$121.56	$202.67	6.13	5.15
Nicaragua	$132.83	$332.00	3.74	3.14
Panama	$370.56	$741.20	1.68	1.41
Paraguay	$191.87	$333.83	3.72	3.13
Peru	$200.30	$383.80	3.24	2.72
Uruguay	$294.13	$367.63	3.38	2.84
Venezuela	$303.49	$505.83	2.46	2.06

Source: Jobs database from the World DataBank (http://www.worldbank.org/), World Bank
[a]Adjusted by the ratio of purchasing power parity conversion factor to US dollar market exchange rate (World DataBank Development Indicators 2014)
[b]OECD (2014) statistics

about 4 % or 5 % each year. Table 10.2 lists legal minimum wage by country. Although there are variations across the region, minimum wage in Latin America is about 3,180 dollars a year or 265 dollars a month (World Bank 2014).

However, although there are differences at the regional level the reference point for the purposes of this chapter is the minimum wage in the United States or Spain, the two main destination countries for Latin American migrants. Minimum wage in the US for 2012 was 7.25 dollars per hour as established under the Fair Labor Standard Act 1938–2009 (US Department of Labor 2014), or 1,160 dollars a month. The minimum wage in Spain (Ministerio de Empleo y Seguridad Social 2013) in 2012 was of 641.4 euros a month or about 855 dollars. The minimum wage in Spain has increased from 570.6 monthly euros in 2007 to 633.3 euros in 2010 and after this period its increases have been marginal. The second and third columns in Table 10.2 show the ratio of wages in US and Spain to wages in the region. On average, US wages are 4.5 times the wages in Latin America. Mexico and El

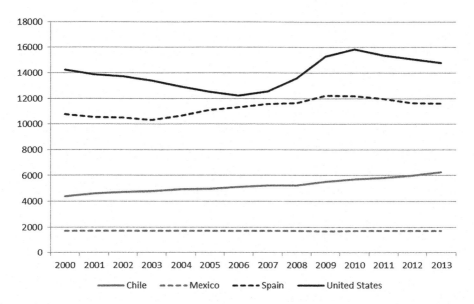

Fig. 10.2 Real annual minimum wages by country, 2000–2013 (Source: Figure elaborated from OECD (2014) data on real annual minimum wages)

Salvador are the countries with the largest wage differentials. The Spanish minimum wage is 4 times those in Latin America including Colombia and Ecuador, but it is 9.5 times the minimum wage in Bolivia.

Although wage differentials are substantial, they change over time. Figure 10.2 shows time trends for real annual minimum wages in the US, Spain, Chile and Mexico. In the case of Chile, minimum wages have increased resulting in a reduced wage gap over time. In 2013, the gap was smaller than before the Great Recession. In Mexico, minimum wages have stagnated, and the wide gap with the US minimum wage reached its highest level in 2010. To assess the magnitude of the gap, we compare the annual real minimum wage in Mexico in 2012, which was 1,713 dollars with that of the Spain (11,633 dollars) and in the US (15,080 dollars) (OECD 2014).

The association between wage gaps and migration is even more relevant in recent times given the increasing costs of migration, particularly high for unauthorized immigrants. Unauthorized immigrants who cross the border with a "coyote" pay differential rates according their country of origin. The minimum cost of crossing the border with a coyote for Mexicans is 5,000 dollars, for Central Americans is 8,000 dollars, for Ecuadorians or Peruvians is 12,000 dollars (LAMP 2014). Therefore, the cost of crossing the border is equivalent to about 2 years of earnings for workers at the lower end of the labor structure, which is where most of the immigrants are concentrated.

In the case of the migration to Europe, and particularly to Southern Europe, everything depends on having a visa. If a visa is available, then the cost of the trip is about $1,500 euros. The difference in cost and risk of migration to the US versus Europe might explain why large numbers of migrants from Andean countries (Ecuador, Colombia, Peru and Bolivia) diversified their destinations towards Europe in the late 1990s, where the demand for low skilled workers was raising and visas were not required.

One of the objectives of this chapter is to give context to the Latin-American migration, not only as a South-north migration (including transit migration or the migration of persons in transit to other countries), but as an intra-regional migration. Migrations within the region were primarily developed during the 1970s and 1980s, mainly due to population growth, recurring economic crisis and political instability. These initial intra-regional migrations partially (with the exception of the Mexican case) established routes and social networks that facilitated the large South-north flow of the 1990s.

As shown in Tables 10.1 and 10.2, there are differentials in levels of development and wages within the region that partially explain migratory flows from Guatemala to Mexico, Nicaragua to Costa Rica, and Bolivia and Paraguay to Argentina, and most recently from neighboring countries to Chile and Brazil.

Guatemalans have migrated to Mexico for more than a century to participate in agricultural activities in Chiapas and as domestic workers, where they have ethnic and linguistic affinity with the indigenous Mayan populations in the border region. There is an on-going regularization program for the annual flow of about a million workers, who are joined by their families (Secretaria de Relaciones Exteriores 2011).

In South America, the 1970s and 1980s the Venezuelan oil boom and the political instability in Colombia triggered a large migration between these two countries, with concentration in the agricultural activities in the regions of Zulia and Andes. During these decades and still today, there is agricultural migration from Bolivia and Paraguay to Argentina, with increasing concentrations of migrations in the neighborhoods of Buenos Aires.

10.3.2 Vulnerable Employment

The Latin American labor market, as any other labor market in an industrialized society, is stratified. We find the "good jobs" or the professional jobs, where wages are not directly contingent on output, have defined paths for promotion, job stability and fringe benefits. And there are the "bad jobs," those with low wages, temporary jobs and without access to fringe benefits or promotions (Kalleberg 2011). The International Labor Organization (ILO) (2014) has defined vulnerable employment as "the sum of work by unpaid family workers and the self-employed or workers who, working on their own account or with one or more partners, hold jobs for which remuneration is directly dependent upon the profits derived from the goods and services produced, and have not engaged on a continuous basis any employees to work for them" (UN 2014). In 2012, 48 % of workers held vulnerable

Table 10.3 Employed population by status in employment by area of residence for selected Latin American Countries (2012)

Country	Wage worker	Employer	Own account worker	Auxiliary family worker	Domestic service worker	Vulnerable employment
Bolivia	37.5	4.8	33.4	21.6	2.6	54.9
Urban	51.0	5.3	31.1	8.7	3.8	39.8
Rural	15.8	4.1	37.1	42.2	0.6	79.3
Brazil	61.8	3.8	24.6	3.0	6.8	27.7
Urban	66.6	4.1	20.6	1.4	7.2	22.1
Rural	35.6	1.8	46.3	11.7	4.5	58.0
Colombia	42.7	4.8	43.1	5.6	3.7	48.6
Urban	46.3	4.9	40.9	3.9	4.1	44.7
Rural	30.7	4.7	50.7	11.4	2.4	62.1
Costa Rica	69.1	3.7	18.8	1.4	6.9	20.2
Urban	71.1	3.9	17.1	0.9	7.1	17.9
Rural	65.4	3.3	22.2	2.4	6.7	24.6
Ecuador	51.2	3.7	32.8	9.9	2.4	42.7
Urban	56.3	4.2	31.0	5.6	2.8	36.6
Rural	41.0	2.9	36.3	18.2	1.6	54.5
Guatemala	49.3	2.8	30.8	13.7	3.5	44.5
Urban	54.7	3.5	27.7	10.2	4.0	37.9
Rural	43.6	2.1	34.0	17.3	2.9	51.3
Mexico	61.7	4.7	22.7	6.4	4.5	29.2
Urban	69.3	4.8	17.9	3.5	4.5	21.4
Rural	53.9	4.6	27.6	9.5	4.4	37.1
Nicaragua	40.2	6.9	30.0	17.7	5.2	47.7
Urban	47.1	5.5	30.1	11.5	5.8	41.6
Rural	30.4	8.9	30.0	26.4	4.3	56.4
Paraguay	45.0	5.5	34.8	8.4	6.3	43.2
Urban	57.5	7.0	24.0	3.8	7.8	27.7
Rural	26.5	3.3	50.9	15.2	4.0	66.1
Peru	45.6	5.4	34.8	11.6	2.6	46.3
Urban	53.3	5.7	31.7	6.2	3.2	37.9
Rural	23.5	4.6	43.7	27.2	1.0	70.9

Source: Table elaborated from indicators published by ILO (2013)

employment. While this figure was 10.1 % for developed economies and the European Union, it was 31.7 % for Latin America (Malik 2013).

Table 10.3 shows the different distribution of vulnerable employment for rural and urban areas. In 2012, vulnerable employment among all workers in Costa Rica, Brazil and Mexico, which are recipient countries for Latin American migration, is below 30 %. However, the differences between the rural and the urban areas are large, particularly for Brazil, which has 22 % of urban vulnerable employment but 58 % of rural vulnerable unemployment. Fifteen percent of the Brazilian population is employed in agriculture, and in rural areas the percentage of agricultural workers among all workers is 66.6 % indicating that a substantial number of agricultural workers have vulnerable employment. For all other sending countries including Colombia, the percentage of vulnerable employment is above 40 %; the extreme case is Bolivia, where vulnerable employment is 54.9 %.

The percentage of agricultural and mining workers in many sending countries of intra-regional migrants is above the average for the region. For example, 33 % of the employed population in Bolivia is employed in agriculture and mining, 28.3 % in Ecuador, 32.3 % in Guatemala and Nicaragua, 27.2 % in Paraguay and 26 % in Peru (ILO 2014). Therefore, there is a concentration of vulnerable employment in the traditional employment sectors in rural areas.

In this scenario, it is easy to understand that intra-regional migration has served as a way to improve living conditions. Even if migration flows are dynamic and responsive to economic cycles and the policies of the countries of destination, one certain and constant feature in the lives of many generations of Latin American intra-regional and international migrants is that the quality of life and the working conditions in the rural areas of many countries in the region are still below acceptable international standards.

Agricultural day laborers or *jornaleros*, are workers who work for a wage paid daily and according to their productivity during the planting and harvesting seasons. In Latin America, this type of work was a seasonal option for many peasants. However, over time it became the main activity for landless peasants. *Jornaleros* are itinerant, follow the picking seasons and usually live in camps where living and working conditions are precarious. Wages for day laborers are similar to the minimum wages previously described. *Jornaleros* and day laborers are considered vulnerable workers.

The production of agricultural commodities at the global level depends to a large extent on agricultural day laborers. New techniques and the production in greenhouses are labor intensive. Therefore, there is a growing demand for agricultural workers, particularly at the peak of the harvesting season or in specific dates (e.g. Strawberry harvesting season in Huelva, Spain; Valentine's Day for flower growers in Colombia). The agricultural work in these new environments is physically demanding and requires manual dexterity and skills. Therefore, there is a demand for young and experienced agricultural workers. The qualities required in workers for jobs in the production of agricultural commodities in large scale operations are increasingly difficult to find in the developed countries. Therefore, it is needed to "import" labor from other regions or countries. In Latin America, as mentioned before, there are multiple examples of the migration of agricultural day workers.

Although domestic work is not considered vulnerable employment according to the ILO standards, it is certainly within the "bad jobs" category because it shares all the characteristics of jobs in the last tier of the labor market. In 2012, 5.1 % of workers in the region were employed as domestic workers (ILO 2014). In Table 10.3, we find the distribution by country and it ranges from 7.8 % in Paraguay to 2.5 % in Ecuador (only considering urban areas). The supply of domestic workers is the product of a large young population in working ages, low educational levels, geographical concentration of black and indigenous populations in certain areas, rural/urban and international wage differentials, and the demand for elderly care and housekeeping services.

In the last decade, the population of Latin America experienced a population momentum, or the period of time in which the population in the working age groups will be the largest in relation to the population younger than 15 and older than 65, which marks the beginning of the effects of the structural process of population aging in the region (Palloni 2002). In the coming decades, the region will generate a demand for domestic workers, given the aging population and the unequal distribution of household chores and elderly care among men and women. In the area of elderly care, domestic workers are better remunerated and training in nursing is valued. One important difference in the future for the global demand for elderly care is the available institutional infrastructure in each country. At the moment in Latin American countries elderly care is already becoming a burden for families, given the slow development of social security systems and infrastructure to provide the services needed.

These workers are attracted by differentials in wages at the regional and international levels; exchange rates; and differentials in the cost of living across regions. Rich countries demand domestic services and elderly care, and the upper and middle classes have the resources to finance it. Domestic work is a gender and ethnic specific labor niche which can result in discrimination and overexploitation of an already vulnerable population.

In Europe, Latin American immigrant women found a fast growing and durable labor niche. There are three factors that generated the global demand for domestic work and elderly care. First, the massive incorporation of women to the labor market. Second, the sustained economic growth that allowed the expansion and raised incomes of the middle class in developed countries; and third, increases in life expectancy. These changes ensure a sustained demand for female workers in which has been called the global care chains.

During the Great Recession women employed in this sector fared better than their male counterparts employed in construction (see Chap. 4).

International day laborers and domestic workers supply the increasing demand of low paid jobs in key occupations given the globalization of agricultural commodities and the increasing and unequally distributed proportions of elderly populations worldwide. Although the demand for domestic employment has increased the proportion of non-agricultural informal employment in Latin America has declined for males and females and more rapidly for young workers (see Fig. 10.3), which suggests as we describe in the next section changes in the patterns of incorporation of new generations of Latin Americans in the labor market.

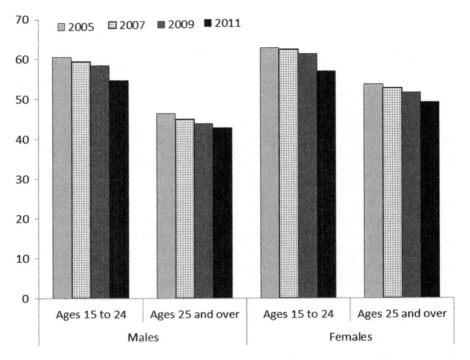

Fig. 10.3 Average percentage of non-agricultural informal employment by sex and age, in selected Latin American countries, 2005–2011 (Source: Graph elaborated from data published by ILO (2013))

10.3.3 Professional Employment and the Gender Gap

In the last decades, the supply of higher education in Latin America has increased and diversified. This is a radical change in the region and opens options to increase the human capital of the countries and therefore the productivity of their labor force. In Mexico, Brazil, Argentina and Chile, offer multiple options to pursue graduate education (masters and doctoral degrees). In Chile, higher education was privatized during the Pinochet years and it has become unaffordable for a population that demands and claims access to higher education subsidized by the state, or at least with a payment system linked to family income, as it was before Pinochet.

In Brazil, the problem is the differential access to higher education by race. The White population has higher access to the public and private systems. For this reason, Brazil has implemented a system similar to the American affirmative action, to reduce the effects of racial discrimination in access to higher education. The program "University for All" (*Universidad para Todos*), created by the Ministry of Education, provides total or partial (50 % and 25 %) scholarships to study in private institutions of higher education (whether for profit or non-profit). Scholarships are offered to Brazilian nationals with a family income lower than 3 minimum salaries. Other requirements are: having completed high school in a public school or as scholarship recipients in a private school, experiencing a learning disability, or committing to be a teacher in the public education system. A percentage of the scholarships are reserved for those who self-identify as indigenous, black or *mulatos* (mixed races).

Mexico offers a wide array of scholarships for tuition and board, to study masters or doctoral degrees, for Mexicans nationals and foreigners. The only condition is that students must apply and be accepted in an institution listed in the catalogue of Universities belonging to the list that CONACYT (National Council for Science and Technology) has compiled. In Mexico, foreigners must pay modest fee for a college degree and they also have access to scholarships for graduate education. In addition, there are a variety of new centers of higher education located in medium and small urban areas. These centers offer technical education and provide the opportunity to obtain a degree to many potential migrants, who after finishing their studies might not see migrating to the US as a valuable alternative.

In Argentina, public universities are for the most part tuition free, for nationals and foreigners. Their circulation of college students and college graduates in the region also allows for the integration of the young educated population in different labor markers. Access to residence permits and formal immigration processes for this population are nowadays more rapid and easy to process than in the past.

In South America, the circulation of persons is considered a fundamental feature for the development of the region. This notion has notably eased intraregional human mobility. In addition, there is an agreement to facilitate the immigration of nationals from members of MERCOSUR and the Andean Community, Including the possibility of working in any country in the region.

There is also a radical change in access to higher education by gender. For example, in Mexico, between 1980 and 2001, the number of enrolled college students increased more than double, but the number of women in higher education tripled. This increase is partially explained by the demographic structure, but it is mainly a product of the incorporation of women in productive activities outside of the family realm and into the labor market. There are even some areas in which women have higher grades and graduation rates than males (Bustos 2003). However, this trend in women's increasing access to higher education has not translated in equal pay, as in the US and Spain. In Latin America, males earn 17 % more than women controlling for age and educational level (Ñopo and Winder 2009).

To summarize the trends in this section, Fig. 10.4 shows declining trends in youth labor force participation rates by educational level and sex between 2005 and 2011. The data indicates a decrease in labor force participation rates for those between 15 and 24 years without primary education and secondary education and no changes for those in higher education. This trend points to the fact that Latin American youth are spending more years in the school system, increasing their human capital to access the labor market with a higher productivity.

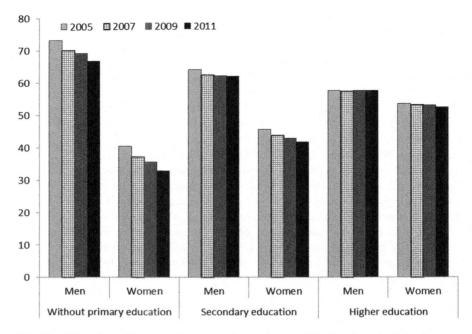

Fig. 10.4 Youth labor force participation rates by educational level and sex in Latin America (2005–2011) (Source: Malik 2013)

10.4 Origins and Development of International Migration in Latin America and the Caribbean

10.4.1 International Migration from Latin America

The element that triggers Latin American migration in the twentieth century is the recruitment of the labor force needed by the US during and after of WWII. In 1942 the Bracero Program was implemented to recruit temporary agricultural workers. This program lasted for long 22 years sowing the seeds for the large presence of Mexicans immigrants and their descendants in the US. After WWII, there is labor recruitment from Puerto Rico for the harvest of sugar cane in Florida, and afterwards labor was also recruited from Jamaica and Haiti. The results were that the US east coast agricultural labor was supplied for several decades by immigrants from the Caribbean and the West Coast by Mexican immigrants.

In the 1960s, political conflicts in the region, the effects of the Cold War and the Castro revolution, generated at least three waves of Cuban immigrants, which thanks to their welcoming in the 1970s in South Florida have developed enough political clout to pass in 1996 The Cuban Adjustment Act, a law that provides permanent residence and other integration benefits to Cuban immigrants who arrive to US soil, but not to those who are captured by the US Coast Guard at sea.

Thereafter, in 1965, United States invaded the Dominican Republic, as a preventive measure to block the Cuban influence, particularly among young students who had suffered and fought against the Trujillo dictatorship and that at the time were affiliated with the leftist parties. In addition to the provision of guns and soldiers, the United States implemented on the island a generous visa program for Dominicans who wanted to go to America, and in this way it successfully disarticulates the revolutionary movement, and begins the migration flow from the island.

In the 1970s the main suppliers of a cheap labor force to the US were Mexico, Puerto Rico, Cuba and the Dominican Republic; immigrants from these four countries still account for the majority of the Hispanic-Latino population in the US. Among the Hispanic population in 2010, Mexicans accounted for 63 %, Puerto Ricans 9.2 %, Cubans 3.5 % and Dominicans 2.8 %. In total these four groups account for 78.5 % of the Hispanic population in the US (Ennis et al. 2011).

The South American migration, specifically those from the Andean region (Colombia, Ecuador, Peru and Bolivia) started to travel to the US in the 1960s, when the US did not require a visa for countries of the Western Hemisphere and migrants could easily apply for residency. In 1965, the Immigration and Nationality Act was passed and the implementation of the quota system reinforced this process. In the last two decades, when the number of applications exceeded the visas available for South Americans, immigrants started to look for alternative routes (through Mexico) to cross the US border or the Atlantic Ocean. In 2010, the South American origin population accounted for 5.5 % of Hispanics in the US (Ennis et al. 2011).

In the 1980s and 1990s, the remnants of the Cold War reached Central America. Once again the Cold War was a catalyst for the migration process in the region. In Nicaragua, people from the upper and middle classes who were linked to the Somoza dictatorship migrated to South Florida. The war in the region continued with the "contras" operating from Honduras and generated a political, economic and social crisis that triggered the migration of the middle and lower sectors of society. People from the middle classes went to the US, while the poor migrated to Costa Rica. In Costa Rica, Nicaraguans account for 85 % of the foreign born in the country. According to the 2000 census (Barquero 2005), 29 % of Nicaraguan men were employed in agriculture while 49 % of women were domestic workers.

Central America at the time was an unstable area, particularly El Salvador, where the civil war incited the massive migration of middle and lower sectors to the US and Canada. Many political figures escaped to Mexico and afterwards to the US. The group that follows is Guatemalans, who were also affected by a low intensity war which had long lasting effects among indigenous communities who were persecuted and disproportionately affected during the conflict. Guatemalans went first to Mexico as refugees, and later they continued their way to the US. Lastly in 1999, Hondurans are incorporated in larger numbers to the Central American migration flow, when the US authorized temporal protection status to the victims of Hurricane Mitch and a number of visas were granted to "environmental" migrants. In 2010, Central Americans accounted for 7.9 % of the Hispanic origin population living in the US (Ennis et al. 2011).

During the decades of political, economic and social turmoil in Latin America, people considered migration as a strategy to maintain if not to improve their living standards as limited options were offered to a growing population. During the 1980s, well known as the lost decade, military dictatorships in Argentina, Chile, Uruguay, Bolivia and Brazil expelled intellectuals and migrants from the middle classes who found refuge in Mexico, Canada, France, England and Sweden among other countries.

However, periods of significant migration growth have coincided with the end of dictatorships in many countries. The long road to reinstitute democratic systems and develop democratic institutions, as well as external indebtedness and a change in the economic model resulted in the largest emigration flow. Perceptions about the future were elusive and discouraging and solutions to the problems neither were clear nor foreseeable. Urban economies and particularly the urban economies of large cities were no longer providing jobs to large contingents of newly arrived workers. The US, which was the traditional destination for Latin American migrants, had closed its doors after passing the Immigration Reform and Control Act (IRCA) of 1986 and migrants already in the US started to compete in a saturated and stratified labor market in which the new Central American migrants were arriving in large numbers. In Peru and Brazil, children of earlier Japanese immigrants embraced the open door policy from the Japanese government and many traveled to Asia.

Spain, a traditionally migrant sending country, became a preferred destination for Latin American immigrants during the 2000s. Spanish refugees arrived to Latin America during the Civil War and Franco's dictatorship. Also, after WWII, two million Spanish workers migrated temporarily to central and northern European countries. The 1970s crisis marks a period of settlement of migration in Europe. As in the case of the US, restrictive policies and barriers to circulation resulted in the permanent settlement of migrants in their destination countries. At the end of the 1980s, with their incorporation into the European Union, southern European countries became immigrant countries. First, they served as waiting rooms for migrants in their itineraries to traditional destinations. However, at the same time Greece, Italy, Portugal and Spain, were undergoing a rapid period of economic growth. Their labor markers demanded migrants, whom arrived in large numbers in the next two decades. Cachon (2002) divides the contemporary migration to Spain in three stages: before 1985, from 1985 to 2000 and after 2000. At this writing (2014) we might anticipate that there is already a fourth stage that started in 2009 as a result of the Great Recession, a the subsequent jobless recovery (see Chaps. 2 and 3). This stage is characterized by substantial return migration to Latin America or migration to third countries (see Chap. 11).

The first migrants to arrive to Spain at the end of the 1980s were Dominicans, followed by Colombians escaping from a period of political armed conflict, urban terrorism and a deep economic decline. In 1990, with the banking crisis, Ecuadorians rapidly integrated to the South American migration flow. In the 2000s, there is the arrival of Bolivians although not in large numbers. Nationals from Colombia, Ecuador and Bolivia did not require a visa to travel to Spain.

However, Peruvians did require a visa to migrate, which imposed barriers for them. Many Peruvians went instead to Argentina and Chile. Argentinians also had opportunities to enter in Europe and many of them legalized their residence through their Italian or Spanish ancestry. Immigrants from Paraguay, Venezuela and Cuba also arrived to Spain. Latin American migration to Spain expanded at a rapid pace in 1999 and peaked in 2007, then in 2008 with the Great Recession (see Chap. 1) it slowed down, and by 2014 the data shows net negative migration flows (Cachon 2014).

10.4.2 Intra-regional Migration

After describing the contemporary patterns of Latin American migration to the US and Spain, we focus on intra-regional migration. Several Latin American countries collected recent census data that allows for the estimation of return migration trends within the 5 year window before the date of the census. In Mexico, a long form questionnaire was collected in one of every ten households. According to INEGI (2014), there were about 1,100,000 Mexican residents who decided to return from the United States between 2005 and 2010 and about 25 % of them were children and youth, which indicate the return of entire family units.

According to the last Argentinian census 1.8 million persons (out of 40 million inhabitants) were foreign born, which represent 4.5 % of the population, a lower percentage than at the beginning of the twentieth century, when one of every three inhabitants was a European immigrant. Results from the census shows that 77 % of immigrants were from neighboring countries, particularly Paraguay, followed by Bolivia, Chile, Peru, Uruguay and Brazil (INDEC 2014).

In Chile, there is a notable increase of intraregional migration, which is sustained by its continuous economic growth. In 1980, official statistics reported that there were about 85,000 foreigners and in 2011 this population reached 352,000 of whom 37.1 % were Peruvians, 17.2 % Argentinians and 6.7 % Bolivians (Organization of American States 2012).

Nevertheless, to describe intraregional migration patterns it is necessary to look at uniform data collected for all countries by the World Bank (2014) in 2011. Based on the international migration statistics we estimated an index of immigration intensity, which is the ratio between the resident population and emigrants, or those who left the country. We recognize that the data on population is a reliable statistic, while the accuracy on the estimation of emigrants might vary.

El Salvador is the Latin American country with the highest migratory intensity index, in a tier that we characterized as explosive. One in every five Salvadorans lives abroad. El Salvador is a small but densely populated country, with an ethnically homogeneous population of mestizos and scarce indigenous populations. El Salvador is ranked 107 and categorized at a medium human development. Salvadoran migrants started to move north in the 1980s fleeing from a bloody and cruel civil war within the context of the Cold War. Nonetheless, in 2014, it is a

Table 10.4 Index of migration intensity by country

Categories according to the index of migration intensity	Ratio of population by emigration (%)	Countries (%)
Explosive	20–40	Surinam (39), El Salvador, (20.5)
Massive	10–20	Belize (16.1), Cuba (10.9), Dominican Rep. (10.1), Mexico (10.7), Nicaragua (12.5), Uruguay (10.5)
High	5–10	Bolivia (6.8), Ecuador (8.7), Guatemala (6.1), Haiti (9.9), Honduras (7.5), Paraguay (7.9)
Medium	3–5	Chile (3.7), Panamá (4.0), Peru (3.7), Colombia (4.6)
Low	0–3	Argentina (2.4), Brazil (0.7), Costa Rica (2.7), Venezuela (1.8)

Source: Own elaboration with data from the World Bank (2014)

country with a positive and stable growth and a dollarized economy. It ranks in third place within the Central American context after Panama and Costa Rica. In general, the migration from El Salvador, as well as the migration from Central America, can be considered a unidirectional migration flow to the US.

In the next level on Table 10.4, we find Cuba and the Dominican Republic in the Caribbean and Mexico, Nicaragua and Uruguay in continental Latin America. Although as described previously the flows of Cubans and Dominicans are particularly salient for the composition of the US migrant flow from Latin America, we believe that Mexico is the country the better represents what we categorize as massive migration. The volume of emigrants from Mexico is exceptional and it is ranked first place in the World Bank database on international migration with 11.8 million migrants, even above China and India (World Bank 2014). The Mexican migration to the United States can be characterized as centennial and unidirectional. Ninety percent of Mexican emigrants travel to the US (INEGI 2014). This migration stream is particular because both countries shared an international border, solid historical, diplomatic and trade relations and high power asymmetry in international spheres.

Among the four countries with the largest flows of emigrants to the US, only the Dominican Republic, and in a lesser extent Cuba, have interrupted the unidirectional migration pattern to the US. The pattern is different for South American countries, which have diversified their destinations. Peru is the country with the most dispersed emigration. Peruvians migrate to the US, Japan, Italy, Chile, Argentina, Ecuador and Australia. Ecuadoreans migrate mostly to Southern European countries, with Spain as its main destination. Colombians, although concentrated in the US and Spain, have diversified destinations and they also have an important presence in the United Kingdom. Both the Ecuadorean and Colombian governments have played active roles in connecting, communicating and engaging with their communities abroad.

Although there are at least three structural trends that have eased the need to emigrate from the region: less demographic pressure, economic stability and growth, as well as important investments in the provision of human capital, the Great Recession and its effects on employment (see Chaps. 2 and 3) have resulted in a decline in unauthorized and authorized migration to the US and Spain as well as return migration to the region. The out migration flows from the region reached their highest level in 2007, and starting in 2008 the volume has receded as the demand for immigrant labor decreased as a result of a decline in the activity of the economy. Migration has declined and for many migrants return is seen as a viable option.

The temporal decline in immigrant employment has been powerful enough to slow immigration. If we look back to the patterns of migration to large cities in Latin America, we observe the same pattern in the 1980s. Contemporary migration is a labor market phenomenon; if there are no jobs, the immigrant labor supply declines. However, the Great Recession in the US did not generate a massive return of migrants, but in the Spanish case, where the crisis has not only been deep but very long, substantial return migration to Latin America or a subsequent migration to a third country has been observed in the data. The National Institute of Statistics in Spain (INE) (2012) projected that for the period 2012–2021 the net migration flow in −1,305,300 persons. Spain for the first time in 2013 lost population due to low fertility and emigration of some Spaniards, but more importantly due to return migration.

The long term structural changes on immigration issues, whose effects were accentuated during the Great Recession, have resulted in development and discussion of migration related legislation in many countries in Latin America. Since 2008, there are three types of voluntary return programs implemented by some countries in the region. The first one is the assisted voluntary return (*retorno voluntario de atención social*) with financial assistance for travel expenses and a cash supplement and which required a commitment from the migrant to promise not to return to the destination country for 3 years. Second, productive voluntary return (*retorno voluntario productivo*) which is inscribed within the "Migration and Development" agenda and aims to support entrepreneurs who have business projects in their countries of origin. The third type is the payment of unemployment insurance and other accumulated benefits to the migrants who want to return to their countries of origin and guarantee that will not return to the host country for at least the next 3 years. This third program is implemented within the framework of bilateral agreements (e.g. between Ecuador and Spain, and Colombia and Spain), but due to its characteristics, its adoption has not been significant among migrants.

For some migrants who have returned under these provisions, the 3 year window has already expired. However, the recovery period after the crisis in the US has been a jobless recovery and in Spain the unemployment is still at historically high levels. For the moment, there are no incentives for the returnees to migrate again. Nonetheless, when the economy recovers and the demand for immigrant employment increases, the experience of these migrants, the established networks and the institutional framework developed during the immigration boom will serve to facilitate once again the flow of needed workers.

10.5   Conclusions

Latin America faced the near collapse of their economies in the 1980s due to a lack of re-payment capacity and high levels of foreign indebtedness. Paradoxically, at this writing Latin America has fared in better conditions the aftermath of the Great Recession than the US and especially, Europe.

The conditions in the region today are certainly better than they have been in the last three decades, at the time when many of the current migrants were born. Given the growth and economic stability in the region, it is not a bad time to return. The real average minimum wage has increased in the region from a base of 100 in 1990 to 160 in 2012 (ILO 2013); the youth unemployment is declining in the region, while it is increasing in highly developed countries; and, growth in employment are concentrated in the developed and developing middle classes (16 % and 12 % for 2008–2013 respectively) (ILO 2014).

Although the economic picture is an inviting one, the levels of drug trafficking related crime and urban violence have increased significantly. For many migrants, the communities they left have changed due to persistent insecurity. That is the case of Mexico and many countries in Central America, which are involved in a spiral of violence similar to the period of violence in Colombia in the 1980s and 1990s. In addition, the democratization process of the majority of the countries in the region guarantees the continuing construction of strong and stable social institutions (as it is the case in Brazil, Chile and Mexico).

The status of international migration in the region is complex. Most countries experience multiple and simultaneous processes: emigration, immigration, transit and return. However, governments have recognized the importance of these processes and there are multiple legislative initiatives on migration issues. Most countries are reforming their population laws and adopting principles based on migrants' human rights. Furthermore, UNASUR is considering intraregional migration as a fundamental factor for the development of the region. This position has already been crystallized in regularization process such as *Patria Grande* in Argentina and other similar processes in Brazil, Mexico, Uruguay and Chile.

There is also progress in trials for free movement zones for migrants in the Andean Community, MERCOSUR, CA4 in Central America and CARICOM. In many of these examples, governments have transitioned from free trade zones to free travel zones. The South American Migration Conference has advanced the idea of opening national labor markets, as in the case of the Schengen zone in Europe (but without language barriers), and even consider the possibility of creating a South American citizenship.

There is no doubt that in 2014, when the traditional destinations for Latin Americans are experiencing their own economic crises and generating hostile environments for migrants, Latin America is in a better position to receive their nationals and benefit from their experiences and skills. It is too soon to evaluate the results, but contrary to what is happening in the "north," in Latin America there is the political will to advance in the resolution of concerns related to extraregional and intraregional migration processes.

References

Barquero, J. A. (2005). La migración internacional en Costa Rica: estado actual y consecuencias. Paper presented at the civic education workshop. University of Costa Rica. http://ccp.ucr.ac.cr/bvp/ppt/CharlaMig2005.pdf. Accessed 14 May 2014.

Bustos, O. (2003). *Mujer y educación superior. Recuperación de la matrícula universitaria a favor de las mujeres. Repercusiones educativas, económicas y sociales.* Mexico: ANUIES.

Cachon, L. (2002). La formación de la "España Inmigrante": Mercado y Ciudadanía. *Revista Española de Investigaciones Sociológicas, 97*(02), 95–126.

Cachon, L. (2014). La inmigración en España tras el fin de "El Dorado". In G. Moreno (Coord.), Anuario de la Inmigración en el País Vasco 2013. Bilbao: Universidad del País Vasco.

Consejo Nacional de Poblacion. (2014). Proyecciones de la Poblacion 2010–2050. Secretaria de Gobernacion. http://www.conapo.gob.mx. Accessed 4 Oct 2014.

Instituo National de Estadistica, Geografia e Informatica (INEGI). (2014). Tabulados Basicos. Censo de Poblacion y Vivienda 2010. http://www3.inegi.org.mx. Accessed 14 May 2014.

Delano, A. (2011). *Mexico and its diaspora in the United States: Policies of emigration since 1848.* New York: Cambridge University Press.

Department of Labor. (2014). Minimum wage chart. http://www.dol.gov/whd/minwage/chart.pdf. Accessed 14 May 2014.

Ennis, S. R., Rios-Cargas, M., & Albert, N. G. (2011). *The Hispanic population: 2010. 2010 census briefs C2010BR-04.* Washington, DC: US Department of Commerce.

Escobar, A. (2001). Employment trends in Mexico: Reversing a 15-year loss? Paper presented at University of California, Davis. https://migration.ucdavis.edu/rs/printfriendly.php?id = 35_0_3_0. Accessed 14 May 2014.

Flores-Yeffal, N. Y. (2013). *Migration-trust networks: Social cohesion in Mexican US-bound emigration.* College Station: Texas A&M University Press.

Hanson, G. H., & McIntosh, C. (2009). The demography of Mexican migration to the United States. *American Economic Review: Papers and Proceedings, 99*(2), 22–27.

Hechter, M., & Kanazawa, S. (1997). Sociological rational choice theory. *Annual Review of Sociology, 23*, 191–214.

Hondagneu-Sotelo, P. (1994). *Gendered transitions: Mexican experiences of immigration.* Berkeley: University of California Press.

Instituto Nacional de Estadística (INE). (2012). Proyecciones de población a largo plazo. http://www.ine.es. Accessed 14 May 2014.

Instituo Nacional de Estadística y Censos (INEC). (2014). Tabulados básicos de Población. http://www.indec.mecon.ar/. Accessed 14 May 2014.

International Labor Organization (ILO). (2014). *Global employment trends 2014: Risk of a jobless recovery?* Geneva: International Labour Office.

International Labour Organization (ILO), Regional Office for Latin America and the Caribbean. (2013). *Labour overview. Latin America and the Caribbean.* Lima: International Labour Organization.

Kalleberg, A. L. (2011). *Goob jobs, bad jobs. The rise of polarized and precarious employment systems in the United States, 1970s to 2000s.* New York: Russell Sage Foundation.

Latin American Migration Project. (2014). Selected results. http://lamp.opr.princeton.edu/. Accessed 14 May 2014.

Malik, K. (2013). *The rise of the South: Human progress in a diverse world.* Geneva: International Labor Organization.

Massey, D. S., & Aysa-Lastra, M. (2011). Social capital and international migration from Latin America. *International Journal of Population Research, 2011*, Article ID 834145.

Massey, D. S., Alarcon, R., Gonzalez, H., & Durand, J. (1987). *Return to Aztlan: The social process of international migration from Western Mexico.* Berkeley: University of California Press.

Mexican Migration Project. (2014). Selected results. http://mmp.opr.princeton.edu/. Accessed 14 May 2014.

Ministerio de Empleo y Seguridad Social. (2013). Evolución del Salario Mínimo Interprofessional. http://www.empleo.gob.es/es/informacion/smi/contenidos/evolucion.htm. Accessed 14 May 2014.

Ñopo, J. P., & Winder, A. N. (2009). *New century, old disparities: Gender and ethic wage gaps in Latin America*. Washington, DC: BID.

Organization for Economic Co-operation and Development (OECD). (2014). OECD StatExtracts. Real minimum wages. http://stats.oecd.org/Index.aspx?DataSetCode = RMW. Accessed 14 May 2014.

Organization of American States. (2012). *International migration in the Americas: Second report of the continuous reporting system on international migration in the Americas*. Washington, DC: Organization of American States.

Palloni, A. (2002). Demographic and health conditions of ageing in Latin America and the Caribbean. *International Journal of Epidemiology, 31,* 762–771.

Passel, J., Cohn, D., & Gonzalez-Barrera, A. (2012). Net migration from Mexico falls to zero— and perhaps less. Pew Hispanic Center. http://www.pewhispanic.org. Accessed 4 Oct 2014.

Population Reference Bureau. (2014). Population data sheet. http://www.prb.org/pdf13/2013-population-data-sheet_eng.pdf. Accessed 14 May 2014.

Secretaria de Relaciones Exteriores (SRE), Gobierno de la Republica, Estados Unidos Mexicanos. (2011). Lanzamiento del Programa de Regularización en México a favor de nacionales guatemaltecos. Press Release. http://embamex.sre.gob.mx/. Accessed 14 May 2014.

Secretaria del Trabajo y Previsión Social (STPS), Gobierno de la Republica, Estados Unidos Mexicanos. (2014). Tabulado del Salario Mínimo General Promedio http://www.conasami.gob.mx/pdf/salario_minimo/sal_min_gral_prom.pdf. Accessed 14 May 2014.

Stark, O. (1991). *The migration of labor*. Cambridge: Blackwell.

United Nations Development Programme. (2013). *Human development report 2013*. New York: United Nations.

United Nations, Department of Economic and Social Affairs, Population Division. (2013). *World population ageing 2013. ST/ESA/SER.A/348*. New York: United Nations.

United Nations, Department of Economic and Social Affairs, Statistics Division. (2014). Millennium development goals indicators: Definition of vulnerable employment. http://unstats.un.org/unsd/mdg/Metadata.aspx?IndicatorId=0&SeriesId=772. Accessed 14 May 2014.

World Bank. (2014). World DataBank. http://databank.worldbank.org/data/home.aspx. Accessed 14 May 2014.

Chapter 11
Economic Status and Remittance Behavior Among Latin American and Caribbean Migrants in the Post-recession Period

Manuel Orozco

11.1 Introduction

Remittances constitute a key form of migrant transnational engagement. In 2012, remittances to Latin America and the Caribbean reached over US$61 billion, representing a major source of income for many families, communities, and countries in the region (Orozco 2014). Migrant remittances can serve an important role in reducing poverty and enabling development. Moreover, remittances often supplement other sources of income, allowing recipients to make greater investments in their health, education, housing and/or businesses.

Prior to the recession Latino immigrants were already an economically vulnerable group. Although only 4 % were unemployed, 48 % had earnings under US$25,000, 20 % already lived on poverty, and on average their financial strength was weak (American Community Survey (ACS) 2008). A survey carried out in 2007 (Orozco and Castillo 2009) showed that only 39 % of immigrants own a bank account, arguing that not having legal status was the main reason they did not own an account. Moreover, even though 60 % held savings in amounts of US$4,000, the majority did so informally due to lack of financial access or awareness of available, affordable and accessible financial institutions that they could use to mobilize their savings into checking accounts. These migrants kept these savings mostly as a mitigating mechanism in case of illness (60 %), an approach that reflected the reality that a minority of immigrants (8 %) owned medical insurance.

It is essential to note that remittances are the product of a great deal of hard work and sacrifice on the part of migrants. When migrants are economically vulnerable, so is their ability to remit. Figure 11.1 shows how remittances to Latin America and

M. Orozco (✉)
International Fund for Agricultural Development and Inter-American Dialogue,
Washington, DC, USA
e-mail: morozco@thedialogue.org

© Springer International Publishing Switzerland 2015   207
M. Aysa-Lastra, L. Cachón (eds.), *Immigrant Vulnerability and Resilience*,
International Perspectives on Migration 11, DOI 10.1007/978-3-319-14797-0_11

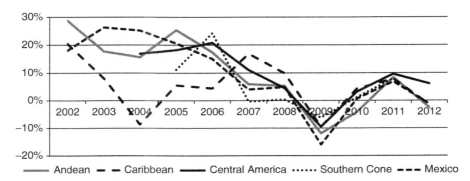

Fig. 11.1 Growth rate of migrant remittances to Latin America and the Caribbean (%), 2001–2012. Note: These data include all remittance flows into the region, including remittances from Europe and intra-regional transfers (Source: Tabulations based on "Remittances to Latin America and the Caribbean," Inter-American Development Bank. Accessed February 26, 2014, http://remittances.fomin.org)

the Caribbean dropped during the 2008–2009 U.S. recession, when migrants faced greater difficulties in the labor market as described in the Part I of this volume.

As the U.S. economy has shown signs of recovery, Latin American and Caribbean migrants have generally been able to regain employment (Table 11.1). Dominicans, Haitians, and Jamaicans have shown slight increases in unemployment, however. This may be due to an influx of Caribbean migrants to the labor markets of the regions surveyed. According to ACS 1-Year Estimates, the working-age Haitian population in Florida grew 16 % from 2009 to 2012, as a result of existing social networks and the 2010 earthquake that devastated large urban centers. The working-age Dominican population in New York grew 14 % during that same period, and the working-age Jamaican population in New York grew 11 %. This is compared to only 1 % population of growth of the working-age Mexican and Salvadorian populations in California during the same period, and a 3 % decline of the working-age Honduran population in Florida.

Employment alone does not provide a complete picture of Latin American and Caribbean migrants' current economic situation. This survey considers a wide range of factors, including savings, debt levels, and risk mitigation strategies to provide a nuanced portrait of economic resilience and vulnerability among migrants.

The economic conditions of Latin American and Caribbean migrants have improved only modestly since 2009. Despite some signs of recovery, migrants remain in a vulnerable position in terms of their income, savings, and debt levels. In many cases, their vulnerability can also be understood as a product of their legal status.

Key findings of this chapter include:

- Latin American and Caribbean migrants have been able to modestly increase their earnings and savings since the 2008–2009 recession;

Table 11.1 Unemployment rate for Latin American and Caribbean migrants in United States, by country of origin

Country of origin	Population in U.S., 2012	Unemployment rate 2009 (%)	Unemployment rate 2012 (%)	Changes in employment by industry in the U.S. 2009 to 2013
Colombia	677,000	6.6	6.0	+10 % education, health care, and social services; −6 % professional, scientific and management
Dominican Republic	957,000	8.1	8.6	No significant, nationwide changes by industry
Guatemala	859,000	8.5	7.5	−3.5 % construction; +2 % in arts, entertainment, recreation, accommodation and food services
Haiti	606,000	9.2	10.6	No significant, nationwide changes by industry
Honduras	522,000	10.7	7.9	−1.5 % construction; +2 % educational services, and health care and social assistance
Jamaica	681,000	8.4	8.9	No significant, nationwide changes by industry
Mexico	11,563,000	7.5	6.3	−2 % construction; small increases in other sectors
El Salvador	1,272,000	8.4	6.4	No significant, nationwide changes by industry
U.S. (native born)	273,000,000	6.4	6.0	No significant, nationwide changes by industry

Source: Tabulations based on American Community Survey (ACS), Population profile in the United States, 2012 and 2009, 1 year estimates. Unemployment rate is measured for non-institutionalized population 16 years of age and older

- Remittances have also recovered, with flows increasing 12 % from 2009 to 2013 to the countries included in this analysis;
- Of the 2,000 migrants surveyed, 60 % have bank accounts in the U.S.; bank account ownership is correlated with gender, education, length of time in the United States, and immigration status;
- Over 70 % of respondents save money in some way, but only 26 % of those who save reported doing so formally with a savings account in the past 12 months;
- Debt is relatively low, with 46 % respondents reporting no debt at all, and an additional 33 % owing less than US$2,000;
- Only 20 % of respondents feel "confident" that they could obtain US$2,000 for an unexpected expense;
- Taking migrants' debt ratios, risk levels, incomes, and savings into consideration, one in three migrants can be classified as economically vulnerable;

- Transnational family structures and the gender of the migrant may impact remittance-sending practices and family finances;
- Most migrants prefer sending remittances through remittance agencies, but a growing number are interested in switching to other methods of remitting, such as online transfers.[1]

In light of this research, migrants are in a slightly better economic position than they were in 2009, but remain vulnerable in a number of ways. To ensure the economic well-being of migrants – and the families back home who rely on their economic contributions – steps must be taken to enhance financial access, economic opportunities and mobility patterns, so people can keep developing productive transnational projects and lives. These positive and beneficial practices, which took decades to develop, are currently declining (see Chap. 12).

The chapter is organized in three parts. First it explores the extent to which migrants from Latin America and the Caribbean recovered economically from the recession. The following section looks in more detail into the financial position of migrants by exploring how critical financial indicators, like debt, savings, risk mitigation and income fare among them. The third section analyzes remitting behavior, particularly as to whether immigrants are shifting their transfers from conventional cash-to-cash. The last section offers some recommendations that can help enhance migrants' economic capabilities.

11.2   Survey Methodology

The following analysis is based on a 2013 survey of 2,000 Latin American and Caribbean migrants living in five major metropolitan areas: New York, Chicago, Miami, Los Angeles, and Washington, D.C. These cities have some of the largest Latin American and Caribbean migrant populations in the United States, both in terms of the number of inhabitants as well as in terms of the share of the overall population (Motel and Patten 2012). Within these five cities, particular migrant groups were selected based on their population size. Table 11.2 shows the survey breakdown by diaspora group and location.[2]

Survey teams were stationed in migrant neighborhoods with heavy foot traffic, and often stood outside remittance agencies. They greeted potential respondents

---

[1] Surveys were conducted outside of remittance agencies, which may affect the results. However, the preference for remittance agencies over other forms of remitting has been documented in a number of other surveys (see Orozco and Castillo 2008).

[2] The national origin groups selected are not representative of all Latin American and Caribbean migrants in the U.S. (for information on the largest national origin groups, see Lopez et al. 2013). The locations selected represent some of the largest population centers for the national origin groups in question. The survey sample does not include the sizable number of migrants living in semi-urban and rural areas.

Table 11.2 2013 survey by country of origin and interview location

	Haiti	Mexico	Honduras	Dominican Republic	El Salvador	Guatemala	Jamaica	Colombia
New York	0	200	0	100	0	0	100	100
Chicago	0	300	0	0	0	50	0	0
Washington, DC	0	0	0	0	100	0	0	0
Miami	100	0	100	0	0	0	0	100
Los Angeles	0	500	0	0	100	150	0	0
Total	100	1,000	100	100	200	200	100	200

and explained that the objective of the survey was to understand how they sent remittances. If the respondent did not report sending remittances, the survey was discontinued. Likewise, if respondents had not been born in one of the specified countries, the survey was discontinued. This survey includes the views of foreign-born migrants, and not the views of second or third generation migrants. Surveys were conducted in Spanish for all Spanish-speaking migrants. For Jamaican and Haitian migrants, surveys were conducted in English.

In order to evaluate whether the financial position of migrants has changed since the 2008–2009 U.S. recession, 2013 survey data were compared with earlier surveys from 2009 to 2010. The 2009 survey, which was very similar in methodology and was carried out by the same survey teams, included the views of 1,150 respondents in six U.S. cities. The cities selected in 2009 were the same as in the 2013 survey, with the addition of Boston. The 2009 survey included Mexicans, Dominicans, Salvadorans, Guatemalans, Bolivians, Ecuadorians, and Colombians. Survey questions focused on migrants' remitting habits, their financial position, and the ways in which they were experiencing the recession. Tables 11.3 and 11.4 show the survey breakdown by migrant group and U.S. city.

The 2010 survey included 2,000 migrants in five U.S. cities: New York, Chicago, Miami, Los Angeles, and Washington, D.C. It drew from the same migrant groups and cities as the 2013 survey. Survey questions focused on remitting habits, migrants' ownership of financial products, and their use of technology.

Despite slight differences in composition, the three surveys are methodologically similar and allow for interesting comparisons of the economic position of Latin American and Caribbean migrants. One major difference is that the 2013 survey delves more into the political realm, asking migrants how a potential immigration reform act might impact their economic position.

11.3 Recovery from the Recession

The 2008–2009 recession had a severe impact on the economic well-being of migrants. By 2013, however, there were some signs of recovery in the U.S. In general, Latin American and Caribbean migrants have been able to increase their earnings, savings and capacity to remit to their families.[3] Comparing 2013 and 2009 survey data, there have been improvements in earnings, and, to a lesser extent, in employment indicators. Over this period, the number of people earning less than

---

[3] Results of non-parametric significance tests for ordinal dependent variables (Kruskal Wallis) indicate statistically significant differences at the 1 % level between 2013 and 2009 samples in terms of annual personal income categories below US$20,000 (see Table 11.5). Significance tests for two samples with unequal variances (t-tests) indicated that share of savings between the 2009 and 2013 samples were statistically significantly different at the 1 % level (also shown in Table 11.5). The 2013 sample was ranked higher for annual personal income and share of sample that reported saving.

Table 11.3 2009 survey of migrants by country of origin and interview location

	Mexico	Dominican Republic	El Salvador	Guatemala	Bolivia	Ecuador	Colombia
New York	0	100	0	0	0	100	0
Washington, DC	0	0	100	0	100	0	0
Los Angeles	200	0	100	100	0	0	0
Boston	0	100	50	0	0	0	0
Miami	0	0	0	0	0	0	100
Chicago	100	0	0	0	0	0	0
Total	300	200	250	100	100	100	100

Table 11.4 2010 survey of migrants by country of origin and interview location

	Haiti	Mexico	Honduras	Dominican Republic	El Salvador	Guatemala	Jamaica	Colombia
New York	0	200	0	100	0	0	100	100
Chicago	0	300	0	0	0	50	0	0
Washington, DC	0	0	0	0	100	0	0	0
Miami	100	0	100	0	0	0	0	100
Los Angeles	0	500	0	0	100	150	0	0
Total	100	1,000	100	100	200	200	100	200

Table 11.5 Income and employment, 2009 and 2013

Income and employment Indicators		2009 (%)	2013 (%)
Income	Avg. annual income less than US$20,000	52	46**
	Avg. annual income between US$20,000 and 25,000	21	26*
	Avg. annual income over US$25,000	27	28
Employment	Migrants with full time work	80	82
Savings	Percent of migrants saving	42	70**

Note: (a) $^*=p<0.05$; $^{**}=p<0.01$ for t-test of the difference between the means from 2009 to 2013 samples. (b) For employment and savings n = 2,000 for 2013 sample; for income n = 1,825 for 2013 sample. For 2009 n = 1,313 for employment; n = 1,282 for savings, and n = 1,183 for income

US$20,000 annually decreased by six percentage points and those earning over US$25,000 increased by one percentage point. More than two thirds of migrants continued to have full-time jobs: in 2009, 80 % reported having full-time jobs, and in 2013, 82 % reported having full-time employment (see Table 11.5).

Savings rates also show signs of recovery. In 2007, 57 % of migrants reported some form of savings. In the survey migrants were asked whether they save, formally or informally, regardless of the method used to set money aside. Savings are understood as money that is left after all expenses have been met or taken out from a household's disposable income. This figure dropped to 42 % in 2009 (Orozco 2009), but in 2013 had risen back up to 70 %. The results also show that those migrant savers have been able to regain their capacity to significantly increase their stock of savings, as national trends among non-immigrant populations show (IMF 2012). Moreover, migrants who save were able to nearly double their stock of savings from 2009 to 2013 among most nationalities surveyed. Savings and bank account ownership are discussed in further detail in the next section.

In addition to allowing for larger amounts of savings, the improvements in earnings also appear to have translated into an increase in the frequency of remittance sending and stability in the amount sent per transfer (around $208.00). Frequency increased from 12 to 13 transfers annually or by an additional remittance transaction in each year, thus raising remittance flows by 12 %.[4] It is worth noting that the increase in the number of transfers per year is observed more among women. Remitting behaviors and methods will be further analyzed in Sect. 12.7.

As the previous tables have demonstrated, migrants' economic position has improved modestly between 2009 and 2013, particularly with regard to their earnings, savings and capacity to remit. The following sections analyze migrants' current financial position and remitting behavior in greater depth.

---

[4] Significance tests for two samples with unequal variances (t-tests) were conducted for both number of transfers each year, and amount sent for each transfer by year. The 2013 sample mean was statistically significantly higher than the 2009 sample mean for number of transfers each year at the 1 % level. There was not a statistically significant difference between the means for 2009 and 2013 in dollar amount per transfer at conventional levels.

11.4   Latin American and Caribbean Migrants' Financial Position

This section focuses on migrants' financial position as it relates to bank account ownership, savings practices, debt, and other financial elements, which are important to assess how financial literacy, access to banking and savings practices have evolved during the recovery period.

11.4.1   Financial Product Ownership in the United States

As shown in Fig. 11.2 about than 60 % of migrants hold bank accounts in the United States. Bank account ownership is highest among Colombians, Guatemalans, and Jamaicans (over 70 %). However, only 54 % of Mexicans and 26 % of Hondurans have bank accounts. About 56 % of migrants hold a checking account and 46 % hold a savings account. In order to assess the access to banking among migrants it is important to consider patterns for others groups. According to post recession data (FDIC 2012), there are 8.2 % unbanked households in the U.S. Among foreign born households this figure increases to 13.5 %, and among Hispanics, is even higher, there are about one in every five households without bank accounts.

In most cases, there have been improvements in bank account ownership between 2005 and 2013. Some of the greatest increases can be seen among Mexicans (29–54 %), Guatemalans (31–78 %), and Colombians (62–82 %).

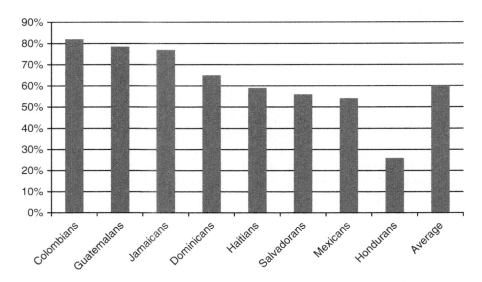

Fig. 11.2 Migrants with U.S. Bank accounts, 2013 (Source: Survey data)

Table 11.6 Characteristics of bank account ownership in the United States, 2013

| Variables | Categories | Ownership of bank accounts (%) | |
		No	Yes
Financial institution type	Bank	0	99
	Credit union	0	1
Gender	Female	43	42
	Male	57	58
Education	College graduate	0	7
	Some college	3	14
	High school	26	40
	Elementary	48	30
	Did not complete elementary	23	10
Annual personal income	Less than US$10,000	10	2
	Between US$10,001 and 15,000	30	8
	Between US$15,001 and 20,000	28	22
	Between US$20,001 and 25,000	21	29
	Between US$25,001 and 30,000	8	17
	Between US$30,001 and 35,000	2	11
	More than US$35,000	0	12
Legal status	Undocumented	85	31
	Temporary protected status	3	7
	Legal resident	8	35
	US citizen	4	27
Number of years living abroad		6 years	11 years

Prevalence of bank account ownership has not changed notably among Salvadorans, Dominicans and Ecuadorians, for this last group might have even declined (Orozco et al. 2010b).

In addition to variation across nationality, demographic factors play a role in bank account ownership. Table 11.6 shows some of the characteristics of bank account holders. Length of stay in the US, legal status and citizenship as well as education are statistically significant determinants of bank account ownership among Latino immigrants.

Migrants were also asked about the range of financial products they own, shedding light on how they use the formal financial system. After bank accounts, the most commonly owned products are credit cards, with 50 % of the respondents answering positively. Products such as life insurance or personal loans were relatively uncommon among migrants.

Those who did not hold bank accounts cited a variety of reasons. Nearly half of migrants without accounts said that their legal status was the main reason. It is important to note that there are in fact ways for undocumented migrants to access accounts in the US. However, many people are not aware of this. The Mexican government was the first to promote and provide a *matricular consular* or an official form of identification for unauthorized immigrants through its consular offices

Table 11.7 Reasons why migrant does not hold a bank account, 2013 (percentage of all choice responses)

Reason	HAI	MEX	HON	DOM	SAL	GUA	JAM	COL	ALL
Lack of identification documents	13	51	74	5	59	34	17	53	48
I don't need an account	26	23	16	50	24	36	44	15	25
I don't trust banks	15	13	1	23	10	13	4	18	12
I don't have enough money to open an account	31	6	7	23	1	0	13	5	7
I don't know how to open an account	5	4	3	0	3	2	0	3	3
A credit or overdraft problem	8	2	0	0	2	6	13	5	2
Very high fees and minimum balance requirements	0	2	0	0	1	6	9	0	2
Other reasons	3	0	0	0	0	2	0	3	0

(Delano 2011). This program was then followed and implemented by governments of other countries. Since this is an official document, for identification purposes only, it was accepted for a brief period of time by financial institutions and unauthorized migrants could open bank accounts. The implementation of additional immigration and security measures in the US and the fear of persecution among immigrants (see Chaps. 6, 8, 12 and 13 in this volume) might prevent immigrants from approaching banking institutions. In addition, multiple considerations about this particular form of identification and its acceptability in by banking institutions were discussed in the floor of the U.S. Congress and led to H.R. 815 which prohibits the use of consular cards as a form of identification to open accounts in financial institutions (Bruno and Storrs 2005). A quarter of migrants responded in our sample, "I don't need an account." This response is commonly heard among low-income groups and can often be traced back to poor financial education, fear of approaching a banking institution, and living in a cash-based environment, which is particularly risky as rates of wage theft among unauthorized immigrants have increased (Fussell 2011). Finally, not trusting financial institutions factored into some migrants' responses when asked why they did not own a bank account (see Table 11.7).

The reasons for not holding a bank account vary by nationality. Haitians most frequently cites lack of money to open a bank account, while Dominicans, Guatemalans and Jamaicans responded that they did not need an account. Among Mexicans, Hondurans, Salvadorans and Colombians, the lack of identification prevented their access to the US banking system.

11.4.2 Financial Product Ownership in Home Country

Because many migrants maintain transnational ties with their home countries (including investments back home), having access to financial products and services in their homelands is critical to maintain and develop their cross-border activities. The survey investigated respondents' financial product ownership in their home country. The results show that only 11 % respondents have bank accounts in their home country.

Among those with bank accounts in their home country, the most common financial products used in respondents' home countries were checking and savings accounts. A smaller share of migrants in the sample had medical insurance, personal loans and credit card accounts in their home country. However, if we compare the use of financial services in their home countries and in the US (Table 11.8), there are not large differences but in the use of checking accounts among those banked, medical insurance, due to the structure of the health care system in the US and credit cards. The higher prevalence in the use of credit among banked immigrants might be related to limited access to loans and credit in their home countries.

Among the people included in this group are those migrants who tend to send more money per remittance transfer (US$260 per transfer on average compared to US$212 in the overall sample), transfer money more frequently (14 times a year compared to 13), and over the course of more years. These migrants also tend to have lived longer in the US and are predominantly males. Interestingly, however, the percentage of people with account ownership back home does not differ across legal status. As in the US, those with higher income are also more likely to have bank accounts in their home country (see Table 11.9).

Table 11.8 Migrant bank account and financial products in home country and the US, 2013

Product ownership	Home country (%)	US (%)
Checking account	28	56
Savings account	51	46
Certificate of deposit (CD)	5	7
Personal loan	17	12
Medical insurance	17	37
Life insurance	9	12
Credit card	17	50
Debit card	13	–

Note: Total percentages will be greater than 100 because respondents could choose more than one option

Table 11.9 Characteristics of those owning accounts in their home country, 2013

Demographic characteristics		(%)
Marital status	Single	20
	Married or living with partner	72
	Other (widowed, divorced, etc.)	9
Gender	Female	25
	Male	75
Education	College graduate	9
	Some college	20
	High school graduate	41
	Completed elementary school	19
	Some elementary school	11
Occupation	Professional or business person, entrepreneur	27
Legal status in the US	Undocumented	29
	Temporary protected status	7
	Legal resident	32
	U.S. citizen	32
Personal income	Less than US$10,000	4
	Between US$10,001 and US$15,000	8
	Between US$15,001 and US$20,000	9
	Between US$20,001 and US$25,000	8
	Between US$25,001 and US$30,000	13
	Between US$30,001 and US$35,000	20
	More than US$35,000	29

11.5 Savings, Debt, and Risk Mitigation

Beyond current income and employment status, certain aspects of migrants' financial profile are likely to help (or hinder) their sustained economic well-being. Savings, debt, and risk mitigation play an important role in determining the stability of migrants' financial position, and thus can offer clues about attaining long-term financial independence. In this context, financial independence should be understood as financial resources and skills that enable people to comfortably meet their basic needs. Financial independence relies on four endowments: a stable income above the cost of living, a solid stock of assets, financial access, and money management skills (Orozco et al. 2012). Practically speaking, two migrants with the same income will be in categorically different positions, depending on whether they save, the amount of their stock of savings, their levels of debt, and methods to deal with emergencies or unexpected problems. Migrants' asset cumulative strategies not only have implications for their financial stability, but also are key factors for their social integration, and intergenerational patrimony transmission which is likely to result in improved chances of social mobility.

Roughly 70 % of respondents reported having some sort of savings and 61 % were actively saving. Including those who reported not saving, the average savings among all migrants surveyed was US$3,447.[5] Among the 70 % of migrants who save, the total average savings is US$5,954. The amount of savings ranged widely. Nevertheless, half of the respondents had US$4,500 or more in savings.

When asked how they have saved within a 12 month period, responses were varied. Nearly one in three was not actively saving; the rest used a mix of practices, with 41 % putting their savings in a bank account (15 % checking and 26 % savings). There are differences in the use of bank accounts for immigrants' savings across countries. Immigrants from Mexico, Honduras and Jamaica were more likely to save in cash at home or in their wallets than migrants from the Dominican Republic, Haiti, El Salvador, Guatemala or Colombia. Mexicans and Hondurans were also more likely to give their money to another family to save (12 % and 25 %, respectively). A considerable proportion of Mexican and some Central American immigrants use informal savings systems which are likely to be based on trust among close social networks with strong bonds.

Respondents saved for more than one motive, but a significant share saved for sudden illness (68 %) and/or higher education (42 %), which indicates their willingness to sustain and invest in their human capital. Investments in education among migrants are particularly important since a substantial proportion of the young Americans are second generation Hispanic immigrants (Ennis et al. 2010). Other forms of asset accumulation were home improvements, and car acquisition (47 % of respondents mentioned at least one of these items). Less than one-fifth of all respondents were saving to invest in small businesses, either in the U.S. or in their home country and only one in ten respondents were actively saving for retirement (see Table 11.10).

In analyzing migrants' financial position, although savings is an extremely important indicator of stability, debt is another indicator that must be considered. Respondents were asked whether they held any debt (credit card, education loans, or any other type). Forty-six percent responded that they did not owe money, while 33 % owed amounts under US$2,000. Moreover, their debt to income ratio is low, at 15 %, and their average net worth (factoring only liquid savings and debt) is US$2,000. Debt to income ratio is a metric typically used by mortgage lenders to assess how much a person can afford to borrow. The typical threshold is 33/38, 33 % for housing and 38 % for all forms of debt. A 15 % ratio is regarded as quite low and subject to lending. The loan amount, however, will depend on the person's gross income, not on the ratio itself. Because the average migrant's income is relatively low, their borrowing capacity is relatively limited.

Table 11.11 shows that indebtedness varies by nationality. Migrants from Honduras and Haiti are less likely to report debt, and migrants from the Dominican Republic reported debt with more frequently. Dominican migrants are certainly one of the more established migrants groups in the US. While migrants from Honduras

---

[5] This estimate includes those who reported zero savings; it does not include those who refused to answer. The total number of migrants in the sample that reported savings (zero and greater) is 1,427.

Table 11.10 Reasons for saving, and saving method, 2013

Reason for saving (N = 3,125)	Percentage mentioning[a]	Percentage of all reasons for saving[b]
Emergency: Illness	68	27
Asset: higher education (for self or children)	42	17
Remittances	36	14
Asset: home improvement	26	10
Retirement	22	9
Emergency: death in the family	16	6
Asset: buy used or new car	13	5
Investment: small business in home country	12	5
Asset: purchase appliances or furniture	8	3
Celebrate a special occasion (nonreligious)	6	2
Investment: small business in the United States	4	2
Celebrate a religious occasion	1	0

Note: [a]Total percentages will be greater than 100 because respondents could choose more than one option
[b]Percentage is obtained from all responses

have on average a shorter length of stay and might also have limited social networks. Migrants from Haiti, although a well-established community in South Florida, might still have limited access to credit.

The analysis of debt by annual income level among migrants indicates that 46 % of migrants have no debt and among this group the average savings were $5,439. For the remaining 54 % percent of migrants who reported debt, a third of them owed less than $2,000 and had savings that range on average between $4,487 and $6,375 dollars. Only 11 % of the migrants interviewed owed more than $5,000 dollars and among those the average savings were at least $6,227 dollars.

In addition to considering savings and debt, the survey looked at whether migrants were able to cover an unexpected expense. The ability to deal with unexpected costs like a medical bill or car repair is an important indicator of economic strength and stability, and as mentioned before is considered by some migrants as motivations to save.

Table 11.12 indicates variations on migrant's capacity to mitigate risk. Migrants were asked whether they felt confident that they could obtain US$2,000 to cover an unexpected expense. Less than 20 % felt confident that they could obtain US$2,000, and another 32 % believed they could probably do so. Respondents that were more confident in their ability to access the resources for an unexpected expense were among those who held substantial amounts of savings. The analysis by gender and nationality indicates that on average male migrants are more confident than females and that Hondurans, Guatemalans and Colombians are among the groups with the

Table 11.11 Total debt percentage distribution by nationality, 2013 (%)

Country	No debt (%)	Less than US $0.5 (%)	US$0.5–$ 0.999 (%)	US$1–$ 1.999 (%)	US$2–$ 4.999 (%)	US$5–$ 9.999 (%)	US10–$ 19.999 (%)	US$20–$ 49.999 (%)	US$50 or more (%)
(Units in thousands of dollars)									
Haiti	64	6	6	12	5	3	2	1	1
Mexico	44	17	14	11	7	2	4	1	1
Honduras	69	15	4	7	1	3	0	0	0
Dominican R.	23	12	6	21	19	16	3	0	0
El Salvador	40	6	9	9	19	14	5	0	1
Guatemala	53	10	8	6	5	7	7	1	4
Jamaica	44	9	13	17	6	6	2	2	1
Colombia	46	5	3	6	13	11	9	8	1
Average	46	13	10	10	9	6	4	1	1

Table 11.12 Capacity to mitigate risk: ability to get US$2,000 for unexpected expense, by gender and nationality (2013)

Variable	Category	Confident (%)	Probable (%)	Unlikely (%)	Unable (%)	Did not know (%)
Gender	Female (n = 851)	17	36	23	8	16
	Male (n = 1,149)	20	33	18	9	20
Nationality	Haiti (n = 100)	18	33	22	3	24
	Mexico (n = 1,000)	16	34	18	11	20
	Honduras (n = 100)	27	26	26	16	5
	Dom. Republic (n = 100)	7	28	4	3	58
	El Salvador (n = 200)	14	44	36	7	1
	Guatemala (n = 200)	21	36	31	8	5
	Jamaica (n = 100)	15	20	9	8	48
	Colombia (n = 200)	40	36	13	2	10
Financial practice	Does not save (n = 601)	8	37	21	11	23
	Saves (n = 826)	27	35	17	6	14
Average amount saved (US$)		8,172	2,874	2,213	1,146	1,817

strongest levels of confidence in their capacity to mitigate the effects of an event that requires an unexpected expense, while migrants from the Dominican Republic and Jamaica show the lowest levels of certainty.

11.6 A Vulnerable Community?

In order to make sense of how migrants fared financially, four variables were computed to examine the extent of vulnerability among the migrants sampled. These figures are typically used in the literature to assess a person's financial position and combine elements associated with financial capability: savings, income, debt and risk mitigation resources (Brobeck 2008; Lusardi et al. 2011). The following variables were used to develop a Vulnerability Index:

1. Debt ratio: Debt to income ratio. Coded 0 (having debt ratio over 0.25), 1 (having debt ratio below 0.25).
2. Risk: Confidence in obtaining US$2,000 in the event of an unexpected expense. Coded from 0 (unable) to (1) confident that could obtain the money.

Table 11.13 Financial position of migrants, 2013

Variable	Category	Vulnerable (%)	Middle (%)	Stable (%)
Debt ratio	Has ratio over 0.25	43	57	0
	Has ratio under 0.25	31	41	28
Risk	Could not obtain US$2,000	64	36	0
	Could obtain US$2,000	6	50	44
Income	Income below US$20,000	60	40	0
	Income above US$20,000	14	46	40
Savings	Does not have US$2,000 saved	78	22	0
	Has over US$2,000 in savings	27	47	27
Extent of vulnerability		33	44	23

3. Income: Having annual income above or below US$20,000. Coded 0 (earning under US$20,000), 1 (earning over US$20,000).
4. Savings: Whether the respondent has US$2,000 in savings or not. Coded 0 (not saving over US$2,000), 1 (saving over US$2,000).

Respondents were classified as "Vulnerable" if they were coded as "0" on three or four of the variables (i.e. had debt ratio above .25, earnings under US$20,000, savings under US$2,000, or were unable to find funds for unexpected expenses). Those in the middle were people who were coded as "1" for two of those four components, and those considered financially stable were coded as "1" for three or more variables. One in three migrants were considered vulnerable, and one quarter as stable, and 44 % were in the middle. The variable that has the most important impact on immigrant vulnerability is savings capacity, as 78 % of immigrants did not have at least $2,000 in savings (see Table 11.13).

Table 11.14 compares some variables based on migrants' financial positions. Those who are more vulnerable, for example, appear to be among those who have been in the United States for fewer years, don't have children, are women, have less than high school education, or are unauthorized immigrants.

To further understand which of these characteristics may influence migrants' financial vulnerability; a logistic model was estimated to identify its determinants (see Eq. 11.1). The dependent variable indicates whether the respondent is vulnerable in at least three of the items previously considered:

$$\begin{aligned} \mathrm{L}\left(\mathrm{P}(Vulnerability)/(1-\mathrm{P}\left(Vulnerability\right)\right) = b_0 + b_1 Age + \\ + b_2 Being\ single + b_3 Gender + b_4 Lower\ Education + \\ + b_5 Professional\ Occupation + b_6 Years\ Living\ in\ the\ U.S. + \\ + b_7 Legal\ Status + b_8 Owning\ an\ account\ in\ home\ country \end{aligned} \quad (11.1)$$

The regression results shown in Table 11.15 indicate that migrants with documented status had a statistically significantly lower probability of being in a

Table 11.14 Characteristics of migrants' financial position, 2013

Variable	Category	Vulnerable	Middle	Stable
Remittances	Average amount remitted	US$180	US$219	US$245
	Number of times sending money in a year	12	13	13
	Years sending money	6	8	8
	Age	34	37	38
	Years in the U.S.	8	10	11
Marital status	Single	40 %	39 %	21 %
	Married or living with partner	29 %	46 %	25 %
	Other (widow, divorced, etc.)	34 %	46 %	20 %
Children	My children live with me in the United States	26 %	45 %	29 %
	My children live in my home country	34 %	43 %	24 %
	Children are in both countries	29 %	44 %	27 %
	I don't have children	44 %	41 %	15 %
Gender	Female	37 %	44 %	20 %
	Male	31 %	43 %	26 %
Education	Completed university	11 %	48 %	41 %
	Some university	19 %	46 %	35 %
	Completed high school	26 %	45 %	29 %
	Completed elementary school	43 %	41 %	16 %
	Did not finish elementary school	44 %	38 %	18 %
Occupation	Professional	15 %	43 %	42 %
	Business person, entrepreneur	9 %	47 %	45 %
Legal status	Undocumented	45 %	41 %	14 %
	Temporary protected status	23 %	43 %	34 %
	Legal resident	25 %	45 %	30 %
	U.S. citizen	17 %	47 %	37 %
Owning a bank account in home country	Does not own an account	34 %	44 %	22 %
	Owns an account	26 %	40 %	34 %

Table 11.15 Estimated coefficients of logistic regression on vulnerability, 2013

Independent variables	B	S.E.	Exp(B)
Legal status	−.283**	.062	.753
Years abroad	−.018	.013	.982
Primary education	.200**	.066	1.222
Age	−.008	.008	.992
Gender	−.215	.115	.806
Professional and business	−.800**	.267	.449
Single	.155	.120	1.168
Constant	−.540	.342	.583
Owns an account back home	−.547	.342	.579
Pseudo R^2 (Cox & Snell) = .192			
Pseudo R^2 (Nagelkerke) = .282			

Note: ** = $p < 0.01$

vulnerable financial position compared to undocumented migrants. Likewise, migrants whose highest educational attainment level was elementary education had a greater likelihood of being in a vulnerable financial position than those with higher educational attainment. Once occupation is included in the model, length of stay in the US is no longer a significant predictor of financial vulnerability.

11.7   Remittance-Sending Behavior

Because sending money home is one of the most important financial activities that migrants perform, understanding their remitting behavior is crucial, particularly in reference to changes after the recession. Remittance behavior is studied with a focus on sender characteristics, sending practices, and the extent of the sender's involvement in family finances.

11.7.1   Characterizing Remittance Sending: Amounts and Beneficiaries

As the economy has improved, so has migrants' ability to remit, however slightly. When these data is disaggregated by gender, it shows that women are responsible for much of the increase, a pattern that is consistent with the performance of Latino immigrants in the US labor market during this period (see Chaps. 1, 2, 3 and 4). Whereas male migrants are sending remittances of nearly the same amount and frequency in 2013 as they did in 2009, female respondents reported sending more money, and more frequently. On average, female migrants who remit send money home 13 times a year, as opposed to 11 times a year in 2009 (see Table 11.16).[6]

When compared by nationality, the increases also vary. Guatemalan migrants, who have tended to send less money and to do so less frequently, showed large increases in both amount and frequency over the 2009–2013 period. This low figure may be due to the fact that Guatemalans have been sending remittances for fewer years than other groups included in the survey, especially if compared them with Mexicans.

As shown in Table 11.17 gender may impact to whom migrants send money. Of those respondents who sent money to a spouse, 86 % were male while only 14 % were female. More men (60 %) sent money to a non-immediate family member than female respondents (40 %). In contrast, slightly more women sent money to a son or daughter in their home country than men (57–43 %). The feminization of

---

[6] Per means comparison tests (t-tests) of two samples with unequal variances, the mean number of times female migrants sent remittances between 2009 and 2013 was statistically significantly different at the 5 % level.

Table 11.16 Average amount sent and number of annual transfers by country, 2009 and 2013

	Average amount sent (US$)		Average number of transfers per year	
Variables	2009	2013	2009	2013
All respondents	222	212	12	13
Gender				
Males	232	229	12	12
Females	189	207	11	13
Country				
Colombia	179	213	14	16
Dominican Republic	174	196	12	10
El Salvador	209	237	11	14
Guatemala	167	212	7	12
Mexico	227	234	12	13

Table 11.17 Gender and nationality of remitters, by relationship to recipient (%), 2013

Variables	Categories	Parent(s)	Spouse	Son/ daughter	Sibling(s)	Grand-parent(s)	Other family members
Gender	Female	50	14	57	42	51	40
	Male	50	86	43	58	49	60
Nationality	Haiti	24	3	2	38	13	20
	Mexico	47	20	10	12	5	6
	Honduras	39	41	9	8	0	2
	Dominican Republic	31	18	9	18	1	23
	El Salvador	52	20	14	8	5	1
	Guatemala	44	16	13	14	7	7
	Jamaica	47	3	11	18	4	17
	Colombia	36	9	24	15	3	15

migration is a phenomenon that emerged in the 1990s along with increasing and more diversified migration from Latin America. The participation of women in migration processes and in global labor markets has had multiple implications for child rearing practices, investments in education and health for the children left behind, and for the potential migration experiences of these children.

Some patterns emerge in the distribution of remittance recipients across nationalities (see Table 11.17). The largest number of respondents reported sending money to their parents, with the fewest respondents sending money to grandparents—with the exception of Haitians (13 %). A spouse was the second beneficiary, with Honduras having the highest percent (41 %) of beneficiaries being a spouse.

In terms of transnational family ties, men constituted a larger share of respondents with children living in either the home country only, or in both their home

Table 11.18 Gender and nationality of respondents, by children's country of residence, 2013

Variable		Children in US (%) (n = 687)	Children in home country (%) (n = 558)	Children in both countries (%) (n = 182)	No children (%) (n = 542)
Gender	Female	48	34	40	46
	Male	52	67	60	54
Nationality	Haiti	59	4	8	29
	Mexico	35	30	9	26
	Honduras	27	47	4	22
	Dominican Republic	51	15	19	15
	El Salvador	29	32	16	24
	Guatemala	35	29	3	33
	Jamaica	26	18	9	47
	Colombia	27	31	10	32

country and the United States (see Table 11.18). Of those respondents with children living in just their home country, two-thirds were men. As traditionally in male dominant migration flows, more men than women had children living in both the United States and their home countries. Although more women are migrating internationally with life trajectories of their own as opposed to be tied migrants, still a larger percentage of male respondents reported children left behind in their countries of origin. In contrast, the share of men and women with children living with them in the U.S. was more even.

The combination of the lower share of women sending money to spouses and the slightly higher share sending money directly to sons and daughters, alongside the male dominated gender distribution of respondents with children only living in their home countries, may highlight differences in family structures between male and female migrants.

11.7.2 Income Dependence on Remittances

According to migrants, remittances were not the single source of income for roughly two-thirds of the remittance recipient households (see Table 11.19). Of the recipient households that rely on other sources of income in addition to remittances, about one-quarter earn wages. Although the amount earned from rent or business ownership was the highest on average, only 9 % of remittance recipient households generate income from rent or businesses. The largest share of recipient households with multiple income sources generates funds from other sources that are less profitable on average than formal employment, businesses, or rentals. These results are also consistent with work performed in Latin America and the

Table 11.19 Income dependence on remittances, 2013

Variable		Respondents (%)	Average monthly income from other sources (US$)
Only income remittance (n =2,000)		30	
Type of income of those with other sources of income besides remittances[a] N = 1,404	Work	24	296.95
	Rent or business	9	378.95
	Other	34	130.33

[a]Total percentages will be greater than 100 because respondents could choose more than one option. The average income amounts were taken from fewer observations than the percentages, as some respondents did not provide amounts for other sources of income. N: Work = 192; Business = 76; Other = 226

Caribbean, where income dependence on remittances is found to be no more than 60 % of all income (Orozco et al. 2010b).

Finally, there appears to be a relationship between bank account ownership and the amount, frequency, and duration of the remittances. Migrants who send to relatives with bank accounts send more money on average ($201 vs $234, on average respectively). They also send money more frequently (7 vs 8 times, respectively) and for a longer duration of time (12 vs 13 years, respectively) (Orozco et al. 2005).

11.7.3 Disposition to Change in Remitting Methods

Most respondents' preferred method for sending remittances in both 2009 and 2013 was through a remittance agency. Moreover, remittance agencies have gained in popularity over less formal means of remitting: only 5 % of migrants sampled in 2013 indicated travelers (courier or someone they know who is traveling back to their home country, commonly known as a "viajero") or others as their preferred method, compared to 12 % in 2010.

A higher percentage of respondents in 2013 were open to switching remittance methods (58 %) than in 2010 (47 %), particularly through online services or mobile banking. This is consistent with a larger share of respondents that checked their bank accounts online in 2013 compared to 2010. Interestingly, however, a smaller share of migrants in 2013 than in 2010 expected to switch from their current methods, which are largely cash-based, to direct deposit. In 2010, just 7 % of migrants who were willing to switch sending methods said they were most likely to consider online sending. By 2013, this had grown to 18 %, as Table 11.20 shows.

Table 11.20 Disposition to change in remittance methods, 2010 and 2013[a]

		2010	2013
Variable		Yes (%)	Yes (%)
Willing to change method for sending money (2010: n = 1,000) (2013: n = 1,970)		47	58
Method most likely to switch to (2010: n = 470) (2013: n = 1,145)	Remittance card[b]	9	29
	Direct deposit in a bank account	75	41
	Internet	7	18
	Cell phone mobile transfer	4	12
	Other	5	0

[a]Preferences for sending remittances by their means, 2009 and 2013 are ranked in the same order. However, there are statistically significant differences in the means for remitting via banks and viajeros from 2009 to 2013. The average for remitting via banks was statistically significantly higher in 2009 than 2013 (at 1 % level). The average for remitting using viajeros was statistically significantly higher in 2009 than 2013 (at 1 % level)

[b]A remittance card allows the recipient to receive their remittance on a plastic card, much like a debit card. They can then use the card to withdraw the funds from an ATM or to make purchases

11.8 Exploring Opportunities for Financial Inclusion of Migrants in the U.S.

The economic recovery in the United States has enabled migrants to send money in a slightly increased manner. However, such recovery has not contributed significantly to improving the economic and financial positions of most migrants. Although financial vulnerability among migrants is complicated by a number of factors (such as legal status), there are strategies that can help ameliorate these vulnerabilities, such as leveraging increasing access to financial products and services.

In addition, survey responses about the marketplace for money transfers point to shifting issues: migrants are interested in switching to more technology-driven methods of remitting, while increasing numbers of migrants hold bank accounts.

Financial vulnerability among Latin American and Caribbean migrants in the U.S. can be mitigated through savings mobilization and increased access to financial products. Strategies to expand this access include:

1. *Increasing access to financial products and services among migrants in the United States.*
   Banks and other financial institutions should offer products and services oriented towards migrants, including products with lower fee structures such as low-cost checking accounts with debit cards, and Internet and mobile money transfer services. Because many migrants have savings, their assets can be mobilized into US financial institutions if they open new bank accounts or use alternative financial products such as prepaid debit cards. These efforts need to be culturally

sensitive and take into account the effect that criminalization of immigrants is having in their confidence to approach financial institutions.

2. *Improving financial literacy among migrants and remittance recipients.*
   Some existing financial education models have yielded important results in achieving the economic independence of remittance clients (Orozco et al. 2010a). Financial education can be delivered in many ways, such as through partnerships between nonprofit organizations and financial institutions, or by incorporating educational elements into a financial institution's business and marketing strategies.

3. *Promoting transnational savings products.*
   An enabling regulatory environment should be in place to allow migrants to open bank accounts in their home country while living abroad. The relatively low percentage of migrants with bank accounts in their home country (11 % of respondents) represents an opportunity for innovation and product development. Once these accounts exist they can be leveraged to extend financial services to this population.

4. *Offering banking products to remittance recipients.*
   The low percentage of migrants who own bank accounts (60 % in the US and only 11 % in their home country) presents a key opportunity for the supply of affordable savings accounts accompanied with other financial products. Bank account ownership among recipients, in turn, has a double effect in increasing the volume of remittances and revenue for payout institutions: migrants tend to send more remittances to those recipients who have bank accounts in their home country.

5. *Developing Internet-based money transfers.*
   As the number of migrants using the Internet to manage their bank accounts has grown, so has migrants' interest in using online money transfer services. Several companies are now capturing an important market share for money transfers relying on account-to-cash and account-to-account payments via the Internet. Money transfer operators should be encouraged to innovate and assimilate new payment technologies and offer migrants the option to use the Internet or mobile phone applications for their transfers. These instruments may become central to future remittance flows.

It is important to consider the effects of the current shifting political landscape. If the United States Congress were to pass an immigration reform act that regularized the status of undocumented migrants, how would this impact the financial positions and behaviors of migrants? Undocumented migrants would likely have access to a wider range of opportunities – better paying jobs, better access to social and financial services – that would help them improve their financial position. This, in turn, would enable them to remit more, as the evidence presented in this chapter suggests.

Survey results shed light on the effects of a potential immigration reform. Regardless of nationality, more than half of non- US citizen respondents thought they would be able to send more money home if an immigration reform bill were to pass. A slightly larger share of women estimated they would send more, whereas a larger share of men expected their remittance frequency and amount would stay largely unchanged. Slight differences emerged by country of origin as well. The share of Haitians, Guatemalans and Mexicans that expected their remittance frequency and amount to stay mostly the same was 59 %, 34 % and 33 %, respectively. Migrants from these three nationalities had the highest share of respondents that indicated no change in their remittance behavior if immigration reform were to pass. Jamaicans and Salvadorans had the highest share of migrants that estimated their remittances would increase as a result of reform.

Over three-fourths of respondents, regardless of their immigration status, believed that their access to financial services would improve with reform. Of those migrants that specified their immigration status, mostly undocumented migrants and migrants with temporary protected status responded to the question of whether immigration reform would improve their access to financial and banking services. Most considered that a potential reform would improve their access to credit and medical insurance. Less than 20 % of those who said they would be eligible to formalize their status say would open a bank account.

11.9 Conclusion

This chapter provides insights into the financial position of migrants in the aftermath of the 2008–2009 U.S. economic crisis. Comparing 2013 survey data with earlier surveys conducted in 2009 and 2010, the report considers a wide range of factors – including savings, income, debt levels, and financial access – to provide a nuanced analysis of migrants' economic situation.

As the survey data suggests, migrants' recovery from the 2008–2009 crisis has been modest. In general, Latin American and Caribbean migrants have been able to slightly increase their earnings, savings, and capacity to remit from 2009. However, they remain in a vulnerable position. Assessing migrants' savings, income, debt, and risk mitigation resources, the data analyzed in this chapter indicate that one in three migrants is in an economically vulnerable position. Women, recent arrivals, and those with low levels of education or without paperwork are among those who are most economically vulnerable.

It is important for financial institutions, development organizations, and political and community leaders to take note of these results. Financial vulnerability among Latin American and Caribbean migrants in the US can be mitigated through savings mobilization and increased access to financial products and services. This report is intended to serve as a point of departure for a much-needed discussion on financial inclusion strategies for migrants and other economically vulnerable populations.

References

American Community Survey. (2008). *2007 Selected characteristics of the foreign-born population by region of birth: Latin America*. American fact finder: 2007 American Community survey 1-year estimates. US Census Bureau: Washington, DC.

Brobeck, S. (2008). *Understanding the emergency savings needs of low- and moderate-income households: A survey-based analysis of impacts, causes, and remedies*. Washington, DC: Consumer Federation of America.

Bruno, A., & Storrs, K. L. (2005). *Consular identification cards: Domestic and foreign policy implications, the Mexican case and related legislation* (Report for congress no. RL32094). Washington, DC: Congressional Research Service.

Delano, A. (2011). *Mexico and its diaspora in the United States: Policies of emigration since 1848*. New York: Cambridge University Press.

Ennis, S. R., Ríos-Vargas, M., & Albert, N. G. (2010). *The Hispanic population* (2010 census briefs C2010BR-04). Washington, DC: U.S. Department of Commerce.

Federal Deposit Insurance Corporation (FDIC). (2012). *2011 FDIC national survey of unbanked and underbanked households*. Washington, DC: Federal Deposit Insurance Corporation.

Fussell, E. (2011). The deportation threat dynamic and victimization of Latino migrants: Wage theft and robbery. *Sociological Quarterly, 52*(4), 593–615.

International Monetary Fund (IMF). (2012). *United States: Selected issues* (Country report no. 12–214). Washington, DC: International Monetary Fund.

Lopez, M., Gonzalez-Barrera, A., & Cuddington, D. (2013). *Diverse origins: The nation's 14 largest Hispanic-origin groups*. Washington, DC: Pew Hispanic Center.

Lusardi, A., Schneider, D., & Tufano, P. (2011). *Financially fragile households: Evidence and implications* (Working paper no. 17072). Washington, DC: National Bureau of Economic Research.

Motel, S., & Patten, E. (2012). *Characteristics of the 60 largest metropolitan areas by Hispanic population*. Washington, DC: Pew Hispanic Center.

Orozco, M. (2009). *Understanding the continuing effect of the economic crisis on remittances*. Washington, DC: Inter-American Development Bank.

Orozco, M. (2014). *Trends and patterns in remittances to Latin America and the Caribbean*. Remittance Industry Observatory, no. 1. Washington, DC: IAD.

Orozco, M., & Castillo, N. (2008). *Latino migrants: Remittances, finances, and health*. Washington, DC: The Inter-American Dialogue.

Orozco, M., & Castillo, N. (2009). *Latino migrants: A profile on remittances, finances, and health*. Washington, DC: IAD.

Orozco, M., Lowell, L., Bump, M., & Fedewa, R. (2005). *Transnational engagement, remittances and their relationship to development in Latin America and the Caribbean*. Washington, DC: Institute for the Study of International Migration, Georgetown University.

Orozco, M., Burgess, E., & Ascoli, N. (2010a). *Is there a match among migrants, remittances, and technology?* Washington, DC: The Inter-American Dialogue.

Orozco, M., Castillo, N., & Romei, L. (2010b). *Toward financial independence: Financial literacy for remittance senders and recipients*. Washington, DC: The Inter-American Dialogue.

Orozco, M., Burgess, E., Castillo, N., & Romei, L. (2012). *Financial independence: A toolkit for financial education*. Washington, DC: The Inter-American Dialogue.

Chapter 12
Great Recession, Migration Management and the Effect of Deportations to Latin America

Ninna Nyberg Sørensen

12.1 Introduction

International migration systems are subject to constant directional and numeric shifts. Just within the last 100 years, Latin America has shifted from being a heavily immigrated region[1] to in the second half of the twentieth century become a region of emigration, to today once again attracting population. To account for such shifts and direct our attention to the expansion of global capitalism and globalization (Robertson 2003, 2008), related de- and re-territorialized forms of survival and resilience that migrant communities divided by state borders have been able to maintain by developing 'multi-stranded social relations' (Basch et al. 1994), a transnationalist perspective has gained force in migration studies.

Much has happened to transnational theorizing since its early and somewhat optimistic inception 20 years ago (Basch et al 1992, 1994; Rouse 1992; Smith 1994; Kearney 1995). Its use (and misuse) has caused critical refinements (e.g. Guarnizo and Smith 1998; Portes et al. 1999; Smith 2000; Levitt and Glick Schiller 2004; Glick Schiller and Faist 2009) and led to new research emphasizing transnational governmentality (e.g. Baker Cristales 2008; Pecoud 2013) and the growing economy and market-based governance structures arising in the enactment and as a result of state efforts to manage migration flows (Hernández-León 2008; Sørensen and Gammeltoft-Hansen 2013). Transnational migration theory has also slipped into migration policy debates, in particular those paying attention to the intersection between migration and development (Sørensen et al 2002; Orozco 2005; Castles and Delgado Weiss 2008; Phillips 2009; Sørensen 2011). Attention to power

---

[1] In 1914 half of Buenos Aries' population was for example foreign born. See 'The Tragedy of Argentina', The Economist, February 15, 2014, p. 18.

N.N. Sørensen (✉)
Danish Institute for International Studies, Copenhagen, Denmark
e-mail: nns@diis.dk

© Springer International Publishing Switzerland 2015   235
M. Aysa-Lastra, L. Cachón (eds.), *Immigrant Vulnerability and Resilience*,
International Perspectives on Migration 11, DOI 10.1007/978-3-319-14797-0_12

asymmetries and the fact that transnational incorporation may be the privilege of those migrants who manage to exchange residence for citizenship while others are able to transnationalize little more than their working force (Brotherton and Barrios 2011: 297), have led a new generation of transnational scholarship to question whether transnational spaces are what they once were or have lost terrain to global capitalist economic forces and increasing unequal neoliberal globalization. In the following I situate my discussion in this theoretical 'aftermath', paying attention to the effects the Great Recession and related increase in return migration (both 'voluntary' and forced) on migrant-sending communities and societies in Latin America.

The following review of Latin American migration and its effect on origin countries is not based on having studied the same national migrant group(s) in the same localities over time, but rather on having followed different geographies of migration to/from the Caribbean in the early 1990s, to/from the United States, to/from Europe, to/from South America during the 2000s, to lately focusing mainly on movements occurring to/from Central America. Each migration flow has had its own particular historical path and has been circumscribed by specific social, economic and geo-political developments. However, to understand how the dual effect of economic recession and stricter migration control regimes affects sending communities in Latin America quite differently, it is useful to draw on migration experiences that not only are different in composition, but also differs in terms of context and timing of their take off. In this way broader generalizations can be avoided.

The chapter is organized in the following way. It begins by retrieving some of the Latin American migration trajectories directed towards the United States and Europe I have studied over the years. It then examines the somewhat taken-for-granted relation between migration and development in much current policy discourse. Following the logic of this discourse the chapter turns to volume: of migrants and of remittances. Directing our attention to the Great Recession and the effects of stricter border regimes and deportations of primarily undocumented migrants to Latin America it is suggested that what "unsettles" the link between migration and development cannot be reduced to cross-country or cross-economy variations. Nor can it be solely attributed to the ways in which toughened migration control regimes and deportations are related to the economic recession. While this obviously is the case, a more interesting question is how historical mobility patterns converge with more recent transformations in the neoliberal political economy and shapes the social organization of Latin American migration as it currently unfolds on the ground.

12.2   Departure

When I in the early 1990s began to study international migration, my first encounter was with Dominican migrants in New York. Few had sought refuge during the Trujillo dictatorship (1930–1961), more had followed in the turmoil following his overthrow, and the great majority had come in search of work and better living standards during the 1980s and continued to arrive during the 1990s. By then up to one million Dominicans contributed to the *latinization* of the United States and the transnationalization of Dominican economic, social, political and cultural relations. A few professionals had managed to find occupations according to their skills; others had worked their way up from the garment industry and other factory jobs. Walking the streets of Washington Heights and Dominican neighborhoods in South Bronx, one found hundreds of small and medium sized enterprises, including *bodegas* or small grocery stores, restaurants, travel agencies (often located next to stores selling over-size suitcases), cab and limousine operations, beauty parlors, *botánicas* (shops selling religious artifacts and alternative health products), small factories, and financial agencies that were founded and operated by Dominican migrants (Sørensen 1994). These businesses matured during the following decades (Krohn-Hansen 2013).

Like other Latin American migrants of that epoch, Dominicans travelled back and forth with relative ease between New York City and the island. One key mechanism of establishing a transnational community linking New York City to various local communities in the Dominican Republic was the periodic trips small entrepreneurs made to encourage new potential migrant investors and expand their markets. During such journeys, small business owners filled their empty suitcases with inputs needed for business such as garment designs, fabrics, and parts (Portes and Guarnizo 1991). Although on a minor scale, the suitcases of migrant entrepreneurs' wives and independently traveling women were often filled with fashion clothes, cosmetics, and household appliances that later would form the basis of informal 'backdoor' businesses in the Dominican Republic. Income earned through these activities became invested in formalizing the businesses, in financing the migration of other family members, and in transnationalising lives and livelihoods (Sørensen 1998). Newcomers often arrived on tourist visas that subsequently were overstayed. Many managed to legalize an undocumented stay over a 3–5 year period; others to live, study and work without legal documentation. Going from New York to Santo Domingo I once found myself sitting next to a Dominican passenger, travelling on somebody else's passport, who while click-clacking her rosary and mumbling *Santa Marias* and *Virgin de Altagracias'* to the rattle of the accelerating engines turned to me and said : "I usually fly American Airlines. Contrary to Continental they know that Dominicans travel with many suitcases. We are travelers".

Migration to the United States was based on social networks. Lack of access to such transnational circuits proved decisive for the migration options at hand. When I later during the 1990s began studying the migration trajectories of Latin American women in Spain, I found that the migration of in particular domestic workers stemming from rural, poorer and 'darker' or indigenous social strata of the population was determined by their lack of access to US-bound transnational networks (Sørensen and Stepputat 2001). However, due to Spanish women's recent entrance on the labor market, labor contracts in domestic service were easy to obtain, and if not readily available before migrating, entrance as tourist and later formalization of migrant status was a possible, if not always easy, way to start new migration projects. Income, whether earned in New York's thriving business sector or at the bottom of the European labor market – together with other forms of social, cultural and political remittances – appeared to have a tremendous developmental effect on local sending communities (Sørensen 2004).

Intrigued by the knowledge, skills, strategies and tactics that Dominican migrants were mobilizing in order to overcome obstacles put on their border-spanning existence by (relatively relaxed) migration policies in the United States and in Europe, and inspired by emerging transnational deconstructions of prevailing assimilationist approaches, I began referring to them as "natives to transnational space" (Sørensen 1998), and later, with Karen Fog Olwig, coined the term "mobile livelihoods" in an attempt to analytically normalize the behavior of people so adept at migrating that the crossing of a state border not always constituted the most important life experience or context upon which to evaluate their mobility (Olwig and Sørensen 2002). Borders mattered, of course, not least to a new group of returnees increasingly found in countries of origin: the young 'misbehavers' who often against their will were sent back by their parents to be re-socialized into traditional Latin American norms for good conduct. Contrary to the small but growing number of young marginalized Dominican men who began to be deported on charges of dealing drugs on the streets of New York – and the young women charged with selling sex in different European cities (at times as victims of human trafficking) – their forced return took place within family networks.

Continuing research travels between Copenhagen, Madrid, Santo Domingo and Lima towards the end of the 1990s, I began noticing Latin American passengers being escorted onboard commercial flights by migration authorities. Migrants were being deported, but in small numbers and with little fuzz. In 1998, traveling towards Peru, two passengers boarded the Madrid- Bogota-Lima flight with police escort. As soon as the police had shown the travelers to their ordinary passenger seats in the back of the aircraft, the officers left. While sharing a few cigarettes (!) in the rear end bar midway over the Atlantic, I learned that they were deported upon an unsuccessful attempt to enter Spain. They had arrived in a group of 12, who all had paid a 'travel organizer' around USD 2,500 for the entire arrangement includ-ing tickets and paperwork. The remainder of the group passed migration and most likely took up jobs in Madrid's care and service sector few days upon arrival. The two deportees disembarked in Bogota.

While carrying out a comparative study on Dominican and Colombian migrants in Europe,[2] Luís E. Guarnizo and I found that many of the Dominican migrants I had interviewed in Spain a decade earlier were still struggling to make ends meet through dead-end jobs in the domestic sector. Many recently arrived Colombians,

---

[2] The collective project entitled 'New Landscapes of Migration: A comparative study of mobility and transnational practices between Latin America and Europe' involved Colombian and Domin-ican migrants in Spain, Italy, the United Kingdom and Denmark. Field work and quantitative survey data collection was generously funded by the Danish Council for Social Science Research.

on the other hand, through their relatively better educational levels, had managed to leave the domestic and other service sectors after 2–3 years. Dominican businesses in Madrid were fewer and smaller in scale than those found in New York, Dominican associations less influential in Dominican and Spanish politics. Colombians, on the other hand, already had established restaurants and other businesses. During interviews Dominicans, to a larger extent than Colombians, maintained that the main purpose of their migration was to build a house in the Dominican Republic, save enough money to start a small business, and then return. And many new houses – either finished ones or still under construction – could be found throughout the Dominican Republic (Sørensen and Guarnizo 2007).[3] Others were contemplating buying real estate in Spain, not necessarily because they wished to settle for good, but because the booming Spanish economy apparently presented a better investment opportunity. When the bubble burst in 2008, they – like many Bolivian, Ecuadorian and Peruvian migrants – lost years of hard work and sacrifice and were left with debts way beyond the loans originally financing their migration. Faced with a severe Spanish unemployment rates, many saw no other choice than to return empty-handed to Latin America.

Moving to Central America in late 2005 offered an opportunity to observe patterns of international migration from El Salvador, Guatemala and Honduras when the Great Recession sat in. My pre-recession arrival coincided with the presentation of the first Human Development Report – *Una Mirada al Nuevo Nosotros: El Impacto de las Migraciones* – that acknowledged the importance of remittances and the emergence of a complex set of social and economic activities that migration contributed to the development of El Salvador (UNDP 2005). The report departed from the new migration-development policy parlor taken up by the World Bank and various International Organizations and argued that the most important resource for development was the country's mobile population. The analytical lens applied was transnational, state action to make migration work for development was recommended.

Ironically, local efforts to institutionalize transnational governance structures through policies taking the migration-development policy recommendations on board occurred in tandem with growing government unease over rising deportation statistics. Deported migrants no longer disembarked from commercial passenger flights, but arrived – on a daily basis – with their hands plastic flexi handcuffed in planes chartered by US Immigration and Customs Enforcement (ICE). Their arrival remained hidden from the electronic monitors announcing the landing of other passengers in the arrival halls. They carried little if any luggage and – stripped of their remittance potential – were allowed entrance through the back doors only to, hours later, be dumped directly on the street as prime examples of what Bauman as

---

[3] Similar migration-related housing booms occurred throughout Latin America, see e.g. Guarnizo and Días (1999) for Colombia, Kyle (2000) and Mata-Codesal (2013) for Ecuador, Paerregaard (2008) for Peru, Camus (2008) and Sørensen (2011) for Guatemala.

an antidote to celebrated remittance superheroes has termed disposable human waste or rather wasted humans (Bauman 2004).

This rather lengthy retrospective narrative of Latin American migration makes evident that just as migration processes are reversible (Durand and Massey 2010), also social progress obtained through migration can be reversed. The Great Recession increased migrant vulnerability abroad as well as back 'home'. How, then, are we to make some kind of meaningful sense out of complex, changing, and reversible migration experiences? If the relationship between migration and development is complex and multi-dimensional, how do we (re-)organize the premises on which migration-development policy debates build?

12.3   Interlude: Considering the Volume of Flows

According to the latest United Nations' population figures, migrants born in Latin America and the Caribbean represent the second largest regional diaspora group in the world, with 26 million living in North America, 5.4 million living in another Latin American country than that of their birth, and 4.5 million living in Europe (United Nations 2013). Many Latin American migrants remain undocumented. It is commonly estimated that more than 40 % of for example the Central American population living in the US lack legal immigration status whereas another 10 % reside under Temporary Protection Status (Sørensen 2014). Undocumented migration to Europe is far smaller in scale than that to the United States, estimated at 1.9–3.8 million migrants in 2008, compared to over 11 million in the United States at the same time (Morehouse and Blomfield 2011).

Since the 1980s, emigration has been a powerful factor in Latin America's economic growth, leading some countries to establish policies attempting to reincorporate nationals abroad into the national polity and in other ways leverage migration for development. Mexico with its state remittance supply programs remains the example most often referred to (although problematic to generalize from); another prime example is El Salvador that through a combination of pleas for Temporary Protection Status (TPS) for its citizens in the United States and promotion of migration-development programs has attempted to include migrants in the national polity (Baker-Cristales 2008). Recent shifts from US-bound to cross-Atlantic flows would explain initial increases in remittances to Ecuador; Spanish co-development policies have been decisive for developing migration-development policies. Other states, for example The Dominican Republic, Guatemala and Honduras, have been more reactive, approaching migration-development issues in only limited and diffuse manners (Orozco and Yansura 2013), often driven more by donor interests than by those of local political elites (Sørensen 2013).

Based on purely economistic principles, remittance data suggests that migrants – despite the global financial crisis – continue to provide critical financial support to millions of households across Latin America. After the historic high of nearly USD 65 billion in 2008 and the 15 % drop due to the global financial crisis in 2009, Latin

America received a total of USD 61.3 billion in remittances in 2012. The share of remittances from Europe, in particular that from Spain, has started to fall since 2009, a decline that has been countered by a growth in remittances sent from the United States. Economic uncertainty and high unemployment rates among Latin American migrants in Southern Europe continue to affect the level of remittances that migrants are able to mobilize, affecting in particular the Andean region, while improved economic conditions in the United States are believed to explain the 'back-on-track' increases in remittances to, for example, Central America (Maldonado and Hayem 2013).

12.4 Settlement: The Relationship Between Migration and Development

Governments and international organizations construct policy norms and strategies based on a variety of social, economic, and political considerations. When the migration-development debate entered international policy discussion tables in the early 2000s, it did so on the basis of three developments: a spectacular surge in global remittances (that caught the eye of the World Bank and other global financial institutions), a simultaneous decrease in international budgets for development assistance (pressuring international institutions to look for development finance elsewhere), and increased preoccupations with migration pressure on welfare budgets in migrant receiving countries in the global North.[4] The hard-working migrant, often marginalized in both home and host countries, emerged in the disguise of the 'migrant superhero' (Sørensen 2011), and became celebrated as the new development-kid on the block. How did this transformation occur? To address this rather paradoxical situation, let's turn to the trajectory of the migration-development policy discourse.

The relationship between migration and development can broadly be divided into two strands: One that focuses on development through economic growth and one that from a human development and human rights perspective finds that migration only is likely to foster development when inequality between and within nations is the end result. Despite the lack of consensus on how development is to be understood, in particular whether redistributional justice forms part of the package, migration has by 2014 become firmly established on the global development policy agenda. A common critique of this agenda is that it is driven by the policy interests of Northern governments and international organizations, and that Southern

---

[4] In the early 2000s, remittances constituted double the size of Official Development Assistance (ODA) and had by 2013 risen to triple the size. The growing influence of migrant social networks and the overall volume of financial resources flowing through these networks appeared to target the poor at least as well as ODA (which not in itself is an indicator of success), and to contribute to offset the progressive fragmentation of international responses to development and humanitarian crises.

discussion partners rarely have power to influence the setting of principles and priorities but merely are offered to be partners in implementation (Castles and Delgado Wise 2008; Delgado Wise and Covarrubias 2009). However, as increasing numbers of developing countries have begun to see remittances from their long-distance nationals as a significant resource on which to base national development strategies, the critique should also be directed southwards to Latin American countries, where levels of both income and consumption inequality despite rising remittance transfers remain high (Phillips 2009; Bastia 2011).

From an economic development perspective the range of impacts migration can have on development in migrant-sending countries is often summed up by reference to the '3 Rs' of Recruitment, Remittances and Returns. Recruitment refers to the importance of assessing who migrates, if they are low skilled and unemployed rather than highly educated and needed on the local labor market (contribute to brain-drain). Remittances refer to financial transfers sent by migrants, their volume and impact on local spending and investment. Returns refer to whether returning migrants bring new technologies and acquired skills, whether they remain to foster development in the country of origin, return to retire, or continue to circulate. The relationship between the three 'Rs' varies which is why the link between migration and development remains uncertain and unsettled (Papademetriou and Martin 1991; Martin et al 2006).

Another letter combination highlighting the relation between transnationalism and economic development is provided by the additional '5 Ts'. Here it is suggested that migrant mobility contributes to foster growth in the areas of Transportation (migrant demand for travel services), Tourism (migrant spending during occasional home visits), Telecommunication (the phone calls exchanged between migrants and their loved ones left behind), Trade (migrant consumption of 'nostalgic' home country goods that may eventually introduce these products to a larger market of consumers), and Transfer services (of remittances and Home-Town Association donations) (Orozco 2005). The economic influence of the transnationalization of Dominican lives and livelihoods during the 1980s and 1990s provides a good example of developmental effects beyond the mere transfer of remittances.

Despite the economic downturn of the global economy, a recent World Bank report concludes that remittances have reduced the share of poor people in developing countries. Cross-country analysis shows significant poverty reduction effects of remittances, e.g. that a 10 % increase in per capita official remittances may lead to a 3.5 % decline in the share of poor people. Remittances are associated with increased household investments in education, entrepreneurship, and health that all are expected to have a high social return in most circumstances. Pointing to studies based on household surveys in El Salvador it is found that children of remittance recipient households have a lower school drop-out ratio and that these households spend more on private tuition for their children. Children in remittance receiving households may have higher birth weight, reflecting that remittances enable households to afford better health care. In other cases remittances provide capital to small, credit-constrained entrepreneurs (World Bank 2013).

Based on such assessments the International Organization for Migration's (IOM) most recent report finds supportive evidence that human mobility substantially contributes to progress for achieving most of the Millennium Development Goals (MDGs) (Laczko and Brian 2013). However, a critical human development perspective may find that even when remittances have a positive effect on poverty reduction and economic growth, the impact is often modest, the redistributive effect may be lacking, and in the cases where remittances continue to flow during economic crisis, their steady flow cannot substitute for sound public policies (Blossier 2010). There is therefore good reason for critically questioning the monetarizing and instrumentalizing bias surrounding the production of knowledge about remittances. As coined by José Luís Rocha, too much focus on the financial aspects of remittances easily ignores the human development aspects of the social and patriarchal relationships remittances destroy or build, the family micro-policy they determine, and the state reduction they encourage, thereby sidestepping any mention of the political and socioeconomic conflicts of the societies where the remittances end up (Rocha 2008). Additionally, critical analysis of policy discourse may reveal how remittance debates more often than not reflect a sending-state interest in capturing and utilizing this source of foreign currency, pretty much in the same way as a too narrow focus on risk and vulnerability echoes receiving states' efforts to control or manage migration (Hernández-León 2008).

In a global context of state withdrawal from providing public services, policy attempts to govern mobility for the benefit of development could be seen as reluctance to seriously approach global inequality and change status quo.

As access to mobility (and protection of continued mobility opportunities) is a fundamental premise for nurturing the development potential of migration (Sørensen et al. 2002), it should not require much mathematical skills to figure out that changes in mobility flows will have an effect on individual migrants, their families, and, indeed, on entire communities. And the collateral consequences of massive return are indeed causing serious problems in many Latin American migrant sending countries, first and foremost through the matter of lost remittances. For families that have come to depend on remittances, deportation can be a financial catastrophe. In particular in those instances where migration is based on debt and the loans have not been repaid. In situations where economic recession is accompanied by mass-deportations – or conflict resolution by large scale repatriation – remittances not only diminish, but more pressure on scarce or unevenly distributed resources almost certainly will occur, raising the potential for social and political instability.

So, with due respect for migration's complex and multidirectional relationship to development, I suggest that the three Rs of recruitment, remittances and return are evaluated against changes in mobility patterns and migration control dynamics following the global financial crisis. Crisis rhetoric –whether related to economic downturn, unmanaged migration or border security – appears to justify harsher mobility policy discourses and stricter migration control measures. In the United States as well as in the European Union migration management is targeting irregular migrants and instituting new forms of governing movement and people hereby increasing migrant vulnerability. To circumvent new state processes of governing mobility, migrants have come to rely on new recruitment processes, remittances are increasingly spent on repaying debts financing undocumented travel arrangements, and increasingly return is occurring in the form of deportation. These competing trends suggest adding what I term the three Ds of Danger, Debt and Deportation to the analysis of migration's developmental effect on Latin America.

12.5   Involuntary Homecoming: On Dangers, Debt and Deportations

Europe's economic crisis is said to reverse migration between Europe and Latin America which according to some sources once again has become a major destination for young, jobless Europeans. To escape the Great European Recession, the Portuguese go to Brazil, the Spanish to Argentina, Chile and Uruguay. Mexico is another popular destination for these so-called European migrants, who nevertheless often are Europeans with dual nationality and descendants of former Latin American migrants to Europe (Córdova Alcaraz 2012). For example, in 2011 only 62,000 of the 500,000 emigrant leaving Spain were born there, whereas at least 100,000 were Latin Americans from primarily Ecuador, Bolivia, Colombia, Argentine, Paraguay and Peru (Laczko and Brian 2013).

But the reverse flow cannot be attributed to migratory processes' reversible character only (Durand and Massey 2010). From 2008 to the present, more than 1.9 million people have been deported from the United States, the overwhelming majority of Latin American (Mexican and Central American) origin.[5] In 2013, ICE carried out a total of 368,644 'removals' of which 235,093 were deported upon being apprehended along the border while attempting to enter the United States; the remaining 133,551 involved individuals apprehended in the interior of the country (ICE 2014). Whereas the total represented a 10 % drop from the previous year (and was the first time deportation rates fell since President Obama took office in 2008), some nationalities experienced considerable increase in their deportation rates. The number of deported Guatemalans, for example, grew from approximately 30,000 in 2011, 45,000 in 2012, to almost 48,000 in 2013. Hondurans experienced a similar growth, from approximately 22,000 in 2011, 32,000 in 2012 to 37,000 in 2013.[6]

Deportations from the United States began several years prior to the economic crisis and should perhaps from a strictly legal standpoint be attributed to the Illegal Immigration Reform and Immigrant Responsibility Act (IIRIRA) signed into law in

---

[5] The great majority or 65 % of the total number of deported migrants from the U. S. in 2013 were Mexicans, followed by Guatemala, Honduras, El Salvador, the Dominican Republic, Ecuador, Brazil and Colombia.

[6] For deportation from the U.S., see https://www.ice.gov/removal-statistics/

1996, and to the securitization of migration policy following the terrorist attack in 2001. In the case of Europe, deportation is more directly attributable to the conjunction of the economic crisis and stricter European Union border control following the implementation of the 2008 EU Return Directive.[7] When originally agreed upon, Spanish Vice President Fernandez de la Vega assured Latin American migrants and authorities that the Directive would not lead to deportation as Spanish migration norms would give preferential treatment to Latin-Americans. But already in 2010, Spain deported around 30,000 undocumented Latin American migrants while around 7,500 were refused admission in Madrid's Barajas Airport.[8] The following year the level of deportation and border apprehension increased 4 %.[9] In addition to high unemployment rates fear of deportation provided yet another push for some Latin American migrants in Spain to leave on their own account. Among the circumstances mentioned "fear of immigration measures that might be taken by the new centre-right People's Party (PP) government" has been mentioned.[10]

Since Dominicans and other Latin American migrants began to direct their hopes of better futures to the United States, Spain, and other prospering economies in the global north, transnational resilience has diverted into increased vulnerability for those who didn't manage to cross or legalize their migration status before a dramatic intensification and diversification of migration control strategies were introduced, rendering the developmentalization of migration policy discourse somewhat redundant. This vulnerability is further exacerbated by exposure to danger, debt and deportation.

Restrictive migration control policies constitute a key factor in increasing the risk associated with migration. By severely limiting access to regular forms of migration, prospective migrants are forced into the arms of recruiters operating at various levels of (in)formality and (il)legality. Social network driven coyote or migrant smuggling arrangements have increasingly been taken over by organized criminal networks that now control many of the undocumented routes towards the United States and, even if to a lesser extent, towards Europe. The dangers migrants face en route include extortion, sexual violence, kidnapping, abuse of authority,

---

[7] DIRECTIVE 2008/115/EC OF THE EUROPEAN PARLIAMENT AND OF THE COUNCIL of 16 December 2008 on common standards and procedures in Member States for returning illegally staying third-country nationals.

[8] Some variation in approach between Northern and Eastern Europe on the one hand, and southern Europe on the other, can be observed. In Northern Europe deportation on the whole is increasing, while in Southern European frontier states, such as Spain (but also Malta, Cyprus, Italy and Greece), greater emphasis is placed on removing people before they arrive (militarization of maritime borders, but also deportation upon arrival in airports).

[9] Spanish deportation and border apprehension numbers stem from media coverage, e.g. http://comunicacionpopular.com.ar/7-800-deportados-desde-espana-en-2011/ and www.taringa.net/posts/noticias/6719193/Espana-expilsa-30mil-inmigrantes-por-ano.html (both accessed during February 2014).

[10] See http://www.migrantesecuador.org/index.php/noticias/espana/9096

detention and extortion by authorities as well as private agents (security companies, transportation companies, organized crime and gang members). The ransom demanded for letting free kidnapped migrants range between USD 1,000 and 5,000 (Córdova Alcaraz 2012). Organized crime has in several instances been found to act in complicity with government agencies at points of arrival and departure. In Guatemala and Peru, for example, migration authorities are believed to be among the most corrupt state actors making huge profits on migrant extortion and smuggling. Corrupt migration officials are allegedly playing an integral part by, in the words of Isabel Rosales Sandoval "greasing the wheels of the migration industry through corruption (Rosales Sandoval 2013: 215). In Peru widespread corruption within the General Directorate for Migration and Naturalization has played a similar role (Berg and Tamagno 2013).

The hardening of US and European immigration policies has elevated the power of Northern governments to arrest, detain, and ultimately deport undocumented migrants. As discussed above, this has led to increased deportation, in the US case strategically referred to as removals. Behind the mere numbers, the deportees consist of a diverse population of migrants, spanning settled migrants who have lived and worked for years abroad to new arrivals apprehended during a first attempted unauthorized entry. The increase in deportation has led migration scholars to focus attention on deportation, deportability and deportees (see e.g. De Genova and Peutz 2010; Juby and Kaplan 2011; Golash-Boza and Hondagneu-Sotelo 2013). In these studies deportation is examined as an increasingly global mechanism of state control, deportability (the protracted possibility of being deported) as the real effect of internalized migration policies and practices, and deportees as members of a new global diaspora consisting of "people who had to leave one home only to be forcibly removed, often years later, from another" (Kanstroom 2012: ix). Some attention has been paid to the effects of mass deportations on the migrants sending countries, for example by Hagan et al. (2011) who indicates that deportation produces several negative effects. These include first the termination of the ability to send remittances upon deportation, second the additional pressures on local labor markets with high unemployment rates, and third the exportation of gang affiliation, adding yet another level of social problems to poor and overburdened communities.

The costs involved and debts incurred to finance mobility across ever more policed borders are seldom taken into account in analyses of migration's effect on home country economies. However, migration is increasingly a process that runs on debt, with migrants and families indebting themselves in ways that many are unable to repay, resulting in the loss of mortgaged homes and productive assets. This is in particular the case for marginalized sectors of Latin America's population who embark on migration without access to pre-recession transnational social networks. While studying a migrant-sending highland community in northern Guatemala, David Stoll found that 75 % of the surveyed migrants households in lack of access to other means had lend money on property titles. In a context where many get by on USD 1,500 a year, the average debt reported by migrant households amounted to USD 16,000. In this particular case migrants were being pulled by promises of higher wages and pushed by early access to micro credit that became invested in undocumented journeys to the US (Stoll 2010). Studying similar processes in both Guatemala and Honduras I have met several undocumented migrants who in lack of other opportunities took loans with local loan sharks, at times involved with larger organized criminal networks, capable and willing to threaten those unable to pay in order to get the rest under their control (Sørensen 2011, 2013). Similar patterns are reported elsewhere in Latin America. In Ecuador unscrupulous loan sharks have for years charged exorbitant interest fees for the loans migrants take to pay human smugglers for their passage (Wells 2013). Criticizing the migration-development parlor of international institutions and home governments, Stoll asks if migration in reality sucks more value from the sending communities than it returns? I for my part insist that remittance statistics seriously suffers from over-reporting by neither subtracting the money used to repay the cost of the journey nor the reverse money flows sent by families to migrants in prolonged situations of unemployment or transferred to pay the ransom for those abducted on the way.

Deportation policy undermines long-standing family reunification principles and poses dire social, economic and psychological costs for deportees and their families (Hagan et al. 2008). The threat of deportation is particularly poignant for families of mixed status (Brabeck et al. 2011), who in the incidence of deportation of one or more family members become subjected to the disruption of family ties, now in the opposite direction. In the case of the Dominican Republic, Kanstroom (2012) has pointed to the fact that hardly any attention has been paid to the sending countries that must process and repatriate ever-increasing numbers of new diasporas of deportees, who often have stronger ties to their former communities abroad than to those to which they are forcibly removed.

Turning our gaze to the effects of deportation on migrant-sending countries, deported Latin American migrants often arrive from countries that have embraced migration-development rhetoric and implemented out-reach programs to incorporate their citizens abroad, but lack effective state programs for reception and integration of deported nationals. To the deported migrant, deportation represents a personal and familial catastrophe. To the migrant sending state, the deportee represents a distortion of the migration-development logic. Stripped of his or her remittance capacity, the "migrant hero" of the remittance dependent nation so to speak becomes "deportee trash" overnight (Sørensen 2011). The disposability of deportees is nowhere as apparent as in the deportee reception areas of the International Airports in countries such as the Dominican Republic, Guatemala and Honduras where deported migrants in the best of cases are treated as vulnerable nationals in need of charitable assistance (a phone call, a bus ride, a health check), in other cases as criminals not worthy of national incorporation. When such programs exist, they are generally financed by foreign donors, not national budgets.

Brotherton and Barrios (2011) describe the experience of social displacement and stigmatization that deported Dominican migrants face when touching ground on the island, often after many years abroad, as being essentially removed for a third time from a settled environment. The first displacement was their initial migration, often decided by their parents. The second was their apprehension and detention in the United States, and the third their forcible repatriation to the Dominican Republic. In the case of Central Americans, but also pertaining to e.g. Peruvians and Colombians, the displacement logic may be linked to historical experiences of being forcibly displaced by civil war, either internally or to neighboring countries. When I in Guatemala in 2012 interviewed deportees after a larger immigration raid in Postville Iowa, many compared their apprehension, detention and deportation to what happened to them or fellow villagers during the Guatemalan civil war. Just like then, people were forcibly dislocated, just like then some disappeared along the way. Comparing across cases, however, both Dominican and Central American deportees experienced to return to situations circumscribed by a lack of rights, a lack of access to work and educational opportunities, and a lack of safety and security. They had embarked on migration after restrictive migration policies were introduced, arrived to the U.S. or Europe just as the financial crisis sat in, and contrary to a positive recruitment-remittances-return path followed by earlier migrants, their vulnerability had been exacerbated by the dangers related to having to travel in undocumented and dangerous ways, facilitated by indebting themselves and their families, and, upon a deported return, finding themselves further dislocated from the promise of development through migration.

12.6   Concluding Remarks

> Who wants yet another confirmation that those transnational spaces are not what they once were and that the balance of class forces in the wake of neoliberal political, economic and criminal justice doctrines and in the midst of the world's crisis-ridden financialization have ensured that their capacity to labor has become obsolete? (Brotherton and Barrios 2011: 297).

As the global economy undergoes profound restructuring, migration policy regimes aspire to ever stricter control measures, and undocumented migration become criminalized I note that not only migratory processes, but also social progress obtained through migration, are reversible. The contradiction between the promises of overcoming poverty and solving national development problems by remittances and how difficult an endeavor migration has become to large segments of Latin American populations reflects the tension between neoliberal development discourse (based on free mobility of capital and goods) and migration policy (based on control of human mobility).

In parallel with the Great Recession, new migration management objectives have been put in place. These encompass "the double aspiration of strictly controlling human mobility" while organizing it in "ways that make it compatible with a number of other objectives pursued by both state and non-state actors", such as e.g. the recruitment of workers or the development of migrant producing countries (Pecoud 2013: 1–2). The disciplining of mobility is international in scope and involves agreements between states on migration related topics, such as a willingness to take back deported migration (readmission agreements) in exchange for concessions in other areas such as development aid, preferential trade arrangements or quotas for circular migration and temporary labor migration programs (TLMPs). In Latin America – as in other migrant-sending regions – migration-development policy discourse is contributing to the disciplining of both migrants and migrant sending states. The normative rationale goes as follows: Migrants should only travel with permission, be hard-working, send remittances, invest productively and return with savings large enough to provide for themselves and their families. Migrant-sending states should ensure that only those permitted mobility are allowed to leave the country and accept that circular or temporary migration are what allow migrant-receiving states to regulate their labor markets in tune with shifting economic situations. While migrant-sending Latin American governments throughout the 1990s and early 2000s had some success in subjecting their trans-national populations to transnational governmentality by promising the incorporation of migrants living abroad into the national polity (Baker-Cristales 2008), the neglect experienced by other migrants stepping off the deportation flights in the countries they supposedly 'belong to' somehow subverts the myth of transnational inclusion. The limits to trans-territorial nation-state building become apparent when the agenda for neoliberal, transnational governmentality (understood as restrictive migration policy and rigid enforcement action) is firmly set by migrant-receiving states in North America and Europe. Under such conditions, the effect of migration on development may rest less on Latin American states' willingness to commodify their population (as migrant workers) and more on their ability to stall the deportations (Sørensen 2014).

In contrast to the constant collection and discussion of data on remittances, international organizations and fora for discussing the entanglement of migration and development have been relatively reluctant to quantify and qualify the human costs of deportations for the migrants involved as well as the societal costs for migrant-sending countries experiencing high deportation rates. Some concern has been raised. During the Global Forum on Migration and Development (GFMD) in Manila in 2008, for example, the institutionalization of TLMPs was criticized for creating a second class of marginalized workers, allowing employers to exploit migrant workers, and create a situation in which migrants bear the costs of international migration. It was mentioned that "developmental impacts" of migration should be measured according to 4 Rs (and not only 3), adding (migrants') rights to recruitment, remittances and returns.[11] Rights were understood as rights to human development. As discussed throughout this chapter, however, a human development perspective would maintain that development through migration only is likely to occur as long as migrants are secured the right to mobility. Therefore, policy discussions around the effects of migration on development will need to address the new realities of tightened migration control regimes and the effects of Danger, Debt and Deportation on migrant sending developing countries.

---

[11] See GFMD Roundtable Discussion at www.gfmd.org/documents/.../gfmd_manila08_csd_Session_2-1_en.pdf

Discussing these issues in a Latin American context I cannot but end this chapter by relating remittances to other money flows and potentially productive labor to unproductive activities. In the first case, and relating to Central America only, USAid provided approximately $243 million in development assistance to Central America in 2011. ICE spent $132.36 million on removal flights in 2010 and had spent $73.22 million through May 31, 2011. The same year the US Department of Homeland Security spent approximately $1 billion on apprehending, detaining and deporting 76,000 Central American migrants.[12] One can only imagine the 'developmental effect' these enormous sums could have had, had they been invested in the creation of decent employment in the countries of origin. In the second case, and of relevance to both receiving and sending countries, one could consider the number of potentially productive labor hours lost in unproductive activities such as deporting undocumented migrants and in the incommensurable cost of the lives lost at the borders dividing the 'developing' and the 'developed' world. Considering the range of issues confronting present-day migrants should remind us all that although neoliberalism in principle allows for the exercise of migrant entrepreneurship (as happened with Dominican transnationals in the 1980s and 1990s), the current limitations put on human mobility reverses taken-for-granted paths of the migration-development nexus, and, in addition, creates further global inequalities that not only are unsustainable but also contradictory to all that policy talk about ending global poverty by supporting democratization and respecting human rights.

References

Baker-Cristales, B. (2008). Magical pursuits: Legitimacy and representation in a transnational political field. *American Anthropologist, 110*(3), 349–359.

Basch, L., Glick Schiller, N., & Szanton Blanc, C. (1992). Transnationalism: A new analytical framework for understanding migration. In L. Basch, N. Glick Schiller, & N. C. Szanton Blanc (Eds.), *Toward a transnational perspective on migration: Race, class, ethnicity and nationalism reconsidered* (pp. 1–24). New York: New York Academy of Sciences.

Basch, L., Glick Schiller, N., & Szanton Blanc, C. (1994). *Nations unbound: Transnational projects, postcolonial predicaments and deterritorialized nation states*. Pennsylvania: Gordon and Breach.

Bastia, T. (2011). Should I stay or should I go? Return migration in times of crisis. *Journal of International Development, 23*, 583–595.

Bauman, Z. (2004). *Wasted lives: Modernity and its outcasts*. Cambridge: Polity Press/Blackwell.

Berg, U. D., & Tamagno, C. (2013). Migration brokers and document fixers: The making of migrant subjects in urban Peru. In T. Gammeltoft-Hansen & N. N. Sørensen (Eds.), *The migration industry and the commercialization of international migration* (pp. 190–214). London: Routledge.

---

[12] For US spending on deportation, see http://timesfreepress.com/site/between-two-worlds/depor tation/php; for similar deportation spending calculations, see http://www.irr.org.uk/pdf2/ERA_ BriefingPaper4.pdf

Blossier, F. (2010). Migradollars and economic development: Characterizing the impact of remittances on Latin America. Council of Hemisphere Affairs. http://www.coha.org/migradollars-and-economic-development/. Accessed 28 Mar 2014.

Brabeck, K. M., Lykes, M. L. B., & Hershberg, R. (2011). Framing immigration to and deportation from the United States: Central American immigrants make meaning of their experiences. *Community, Work, & Family, 13*(3), 275–296.

Brotherton, D. C., & Barrios, L. (2011). *Banished to the homeland: Dominican deportees and their stories of exile*. New York: Columbia University Press.

Camus, M. (2008). *La sorpresita del Norte: Migración internacional y comunidad en Huehuetenango*. Ciudad de Guatemala: INCEDES.

Castles, S., & Delgado Weis, R. (2008). *Migration and development: Perspectives from the south*. Geneva: International Organization for Migration.

Córdova Alcaraz, R. (2012). *Rutas y dinámicas migratorias entre los países de América Latina y el Caribe (ALC), y entre ALC y la Unión Europea*. Geneva: International Organization for Migration.

De Genova, N., & Peutz, N. (2010). *The deportation regime: Sovereignty, space, and the freedom of movement*. Durham: Duke University Press.

Delgado Wise, R., & Márquez Covarrubias, H. (2009). Understanding the relationship between migration and development: Toward a new theoretical approach. *Social Analysis, 53*(3), 85–103.

Durand, J., & Massey, D. (2010). New world orders: Continuities and changes in Latin American migration. *Annals of the American Academy of Political and Social Sciences, 630,* 20.

Glick Schiller, N., & Faist, T. (2009). Introduction: Migration, development, and social transformation. *Social Analysis, 53*(3), 1–13.

Golash-Boza, T., & Hondagneu-Sotelo, P. (2013). Latino immigrant men and the deportation crisis: A gendered racial removal program. *Latino Studies, 11*(3), 271–292.

Guarnizo, L. E., & Días, L. M. (1999). Transnational migration: A view from Colombia. *Ethnic and Racial Studies, 22,* 397–421.

Guarnizo, L. E., & Smith, M. P. (1998). The locations of transnationalism. In M. P. Smith & L. E. Guarnizo (Eds.), *Transnationalism from below* (pp. 3–34). New Brunswick: Transaction Publishers.

Hagan, J., Erschbach, K., & Rodriguez, N. (2008). U.S. deportation policy, family separation, and circular migration. *International Migration Review, 42*(1), 64–88.

Hagan, J., Rodriguez, N., & Castro, B. (2011). Social effects of mass deportation by the United States government 2000–10. *Ethnic and Racial Studies, 34*(8), 1374–1391.

Hernández-León, R. (2008). *Metropolitan migrants – The migration of urban Mexicans to the United States*. Berkeley: University of California Press.

ICE – U.S. Immigration and Customs Enforcement. (2014). FY 2014 ICE immigration removals. http://www.ice.gov/removal-statistics.

Juby, C., & Kaplan, L. E. (2011). Postville: The effects of an immigration raid. *Families in Society: The Journal of Contemporary Social Services, 92*(2), 147–153.

Kanstroom, D. (2012). *Aftermath: Deportation law and the new American diaspora*. New York: Oxford University Press.

Kearney, M. (1995). The local and the global: The anthropology of globalization and transnationalism. *Annual Review of Anthropology, 24,* 547–567.

Krohn-Hansen, C. (2013). *Making New York Dominican: Small businesses, politics, and everyday life*. Philadelphia: University of Pennsylvania Press.

Kyle, D. (2000). *Transnational peasants: Migrations, ethnicity, and networks in Andean Ecuador*. Baltimore: Johns Hopkins University Press.

Laczko, F., & Brian, T. (2013). Introduction. In F. Laczko & L. J. Lönnback (Eds.), *Migration and the United Nations post 2015 development agenda*. Geneva: International Organization for Migration.

Levitt, P., & Glick Schiller, N. (2004). Conceptualizing simultaneity: A transnational social field perspective on society. *International Migration Review, 38*(3), 1002–1039.

Maldonado, R., & Hayem, M. L. (2013). *Remittances to Latin America and the Caribbean 2012: Differing behavior across sub-regions*. Washington, DC: Multilateral Investment Fund/Inter-American Development Bank.

Martin, P., Martin, S. F., & Weil, P. (2006). *Managing migration: The promise of cooperation*. Oxford: Lexington Books.

Mata-Codesal, D. (2013). Linking social and financial remittances in the realms of financial know-how and education in rural Ecuador. *Migration Letters, 10*(1), 23–32.

Morehouse, C., & Blomfield, M. (2011). *Irregular migration in Europe*. Washington, DC: The Migration Policy Institute.

Olwig, K. F., & Sørensen, N. N. (2002). Introduction. In N. N. Sørensen & K. F. Olwig (Eds.), *Work and migration: Life and livelihoods in a globalizing world* (pp. 1–20). London: Routledge.

Orozco, M., & World Bank. (2005). Transnationalism and development: Trends and opportunities in Latin America. In *Remittances: Development impact and future prospects* (pp. 307–330). Washington, DC: World Bank.

Orozco, M., & Yansura, J. (2013). *Migration and development in Central America: Perceptions, policies, and further opportunities*. Washington, DC: Inter-American Dialogue Working Paper.

Paerregaard, K. (2008). *Peruvians dispersed: A global ethnography of migration*. Larham: Lexington Books.

Papademetriou, D., & Martin, P. (1991). *The unsettled relationship: Labor migration and economic development*. Westport: Greenwood Press.

Pécoud, A. (2013). Introduction: Disciplining the transnational mobility of people. In M. Geiger & A. Pécoud (Eds.), *Disciplining the transnational mobility of people* (pp. 1–14). Basingstoke: Macmillan.

Phillips, N. (2009). Migration as development strategy? The new political economy of dispossession and inequality in the Americas. *Review of International Political Economy, 16*(2), 231–259.

Portes, A., & Guarnizo, L.-E. (1991). Tropical capitalists: US-bound immigration and small enterprise development in the Dominican Republic. In S. Díaz-Briquets & S. Weintraub (Eds.), *Migration, remittances, and small business development* (pp. 37–59). Boulder: Westview Press.

Portes, A., Guarnizo, L. E., & Landolt, P. (1999). The study of transnationalism: Pitfalls and promise of an emergent research field. *Ethnic and Racial Studies, 22*(2), 217–237.

Robertson, W. I. (2003). *Transnational conflicts: Central America, social change and globalization*. London/New York: Verso.

Robertson, W. I. (2008). *Latin America and global capitalism: A globalization perspective*. Baltimore: Johns Hopkins University Press.

Rocha, J. L. (2008). *Centroamericanos – redefiniendo las fronteras*. Managua: Impresiones Helios.

Rosales Sandoval, I. (2013). Public officials and the migration industry in Guatemala: Greasing the wheels of a corrupt machine. In T. Gammeltoft-Hansen & N. N. Sørensen (Eds.), *The migration industry and the commercialization of international migration* (pp. 215–237). London: Routledge.

Rouse, R. (1992). Making sense of settlement: Class transformation, cultural struggle, and transnationalism among Mexican migrants in the United States. In N. Glick Schiller, L. Basch, & C. Szanton Blanc (Eds.), *Toward a transnational perspective on migration: Race, class, ethnicity, and nationalism reconsidered* (Annals of the New York Academy of Sciences 645, pp. 22–55). New York: New York Academy of Sciences.

Smith, M. P. (1994). Can you imagine? Transnational migration and the globalization of grassroots politics. *Social Text, 39*, 15–33.

Smith, M. P. (2000). *Transnational urbanism: Locating globalization*. New York: Blackwell.

Sørensen, N. N. (1994). Roots, routes and transnational attractions: Dominican migration, gender and cultural change. *The European Journal of Development Research, 6*(2), 104–118.

Sørensen, N. N. (1998). Narrating identity across Dominican worlds. *Comparative Urban and Community Research, 6,* 241–269.

Sørensen, N. N. (2004). Globalisación, género y migración transnacional: El caso de la diáspora dominicana. In N. Escriva & A. N. Ribas (Eds.), *Migración y Desarrollo* (pp. 87–109). Córdoba: Consejo Superior de Investigaciones Científicas.

Sørensen, N. N. (2011). The rise and fall of the 'Migrant Superhero and the New 'Deportee Trash': Contemporary strain on mobile livelihoods in the central American region. *Borderlines – Journal of the Latino Research Center, 5,* 90–120.

Sørensen, N. N. (2013). Migration between social and criminal networks: Jumping the remains of the Honduran migration train. In T. Gammeltoft-Hansen & N. N. Sørensen (Eds.), *The migration industry and the commercialization of international migration* (pp. 238–261). London: Routledge.

Sørensen, N. N. (2014). Central American migration, remittances and transnational development. In D. Sánchez-Ancochea & S. Martí i Puig (Eds.), *Handbook of Central American governance* (pp. 45–58). London: Routledge.

Sørensen, N. N., & Gammeltoft-Hansen, T. (2013). Introduction. In T. Gammeltoft-Hansen & N. N. Sørensen (Eds.), *The migration industry and the commercialization of international migration* (pp. 1–23). London: Routledge.

Sørensen, N. N., & Guarnizo, L. E. (2007). Transnational family life across the Atlantic: The experience of Colombian and Dominican migrants in Europe. In N. N. Sørensen (Ed.), *Living across worlds: Diaspora, development and transnational engagement* (pp. 151–176). Geneva: International Organization for Migration.

Sørensen, N. N., & Stepputat, F. (2001). Narrations of authority and mobility. *Identities, 8*(3), 313–342.

Sørensen, N. N., Van Hear, N., & Engberg-Pedersen, P. (2002). The migration-development Nexus: Evidence and policy options. *International Migration, 40*(5), 49–74.

Stoll, D. (2010). From wage migration to debt migration? Easy credit, failure in El Norte, and foreclosure in a bubble economy of the western Guatemalan Highlands. *Latin American Perspectives, 37*(1), 123–142.

United Nations. (2013). *International migration in 2013: Migrants by origin and destination.* (Population Facts No. 2013/3) United Nations, Department of Economic and Social Affairs, Population Division.

United Nations Development Programme. (2005). *Informe sobre desarrollo humano El Salvador 2005: Una Mirada al Nuevo nosotros. El impacto de las migraciones.* San Salvador: UNDP.

Wells, M. (2013). Ecuador tackles loan sharking that funds human smuggling. Insight Crime. http://www.insightcrime.org/news-briefs/ecuador-cracks-down-on-the-loans-that-fund-human-smuggling. Accessed 20 Feb 2014.

World Bank. (2013). Migration and development brief 20. http://siteresources.worldbank.org/INTPROSPECTS/Resources/334934-1110315015165/MigrationandDevelopmentBrief20.pdf. Accessed 20 Apr 2013.

Chapter 13
Increasing Vulnerability and the Limits of Resilience Among Latin American Immigrants

María Aysa-Lastra

Articles in this volume focus on the effects of the Great Recession on Latin American immigrants, and identify changes in labor market conditions, effects of implementing punitive immigration laws and policies, trends in perceptions towards immigrants during the last economic downturn, and changing conditions in the countries of origin. The title of this concluding article describes a recurrent argument in the chapters of this volume: Latino immigrant vulnerability increased as a result of the Great Recession. Specifically, this drastic economic downturn exacerbated the vulnerability of Latino immigrants that was already underway due to long term trajectories in three core areas: deterioration of working conditions for Latino migrants in general, but particularly for unskilled and unauthorized migrants; intensification of law enforcement towards immigrants; and at the intersection of these two longstanding trends, the resulting racialization and discrimination of immigrants, particularly in the US. In the case of Spain, we also observe deterioration of working conditions simultaneously with very high unemployment rates.

In the US Latino immigrants -particularly those perceived as undocumented- are increasingly seen as socially undesirable subjects due to the implementation of punitive state immigration laws (Chap. 8). The discourse created around these state laws amplified immigrants' visibility and criminalized their presence in the US (Flores-Yeffal et al. 2011). In Spain immigrants appear to be more integrated (Chap. 7), but still the majority of them have suffered downward occupation mobility (Aysa-Lastra and Cachón 2013) and some have been criminalized (Aysa-Lastra forthcoming). In these two contexts, a large number of Latino immigrants are positioned at the lowest ranks of the occupational scale. Their labor in these occupations is vital for supporting the wants and employment trends of the highly skilled, and, middle and upper classes in aging capitalist societies (see Chap. 10).

M. Aysa-Lastra (✉)
Department of Sociology and Anthropology, Winthrop University, Rock Hill, SC, USA
e-mail: aysalastram@winthrop.edu

© Springer International Publishing Switzerland 2015
M. Aysa-Lastra, L. Cachón (eds.), *Immigrant Vulnerability and Resilience*,
International Perspectives on Migration 11, DOI 10.1007/978-3-319-14797-0_13

255

Immigrants have responded to their increasing vulnerability with resilient practices identified in the chapters of this volume. They frequently accept lower quality jobs, often with lower wages and poor working conditions; gain employment for other household members, particularly women, in sectors that were less affected by the Great Recession; temporarily diminish their financial commitments to their families in origin countries (Chap. 11); and, return to their countries of origin after long periods of unemployment or migrate to third countries. However, in a neoliberal and modern era, the exercise of individual agency through a creative process in the search for "basic trust", understood as the reduction or elimination of potential events which could cause alarm and create fear (Giddens 1991: 127), is curtailed by the state and its implementation of punitive policies (Foucault 1995) or by the unanticipated consequences of globalization (Stiglitz 2012). According to Giddens, modernity and globalization produce difference, exclusion and marginalization through the differential access to forms of self-actualization and empowerment. These mechanisms of suppression and disempowerment of the self can deprive individuals, in this case vulnerable immigrants, from the opportunity to creatively and reflexively engage in the construction of their identity. Giddens's argument is clear "the poor are more or less completely excluded from the possibility of making lifestyle choices" (1991: 6). We all have the capacity to make decisions, even under conditions of severe material constraint, but no one can exercise agency in immigrant detention centers.

The harsh conditions of the labor market, the punitive policies implemented by the state towards unauthorized migrants and the resulting racialization, discrimination and criminalization of immigrants are in fact the mechanisms of suppression and disempowerment that Giddens refers to. These mechanisms limit (but not eliminate) unauthorized immigrants' range of options, and push them to hide within their own host communities. They become "invisible subjects" living in constant fear of deportation and minimizing their contact with local authorities (see Chap. 8, Aysa forthcoming). Moreover, many detained and deported immigrants have been kept in detention centers, in conditions similar to those of criminals, although they committed no crimes. Consequently, their arrival to their origin communities results in their criminalization and complicates their reintegration (see Chap. 12).

In order to bring together the findings offered in this volume, this concluding chapter is divided into two main parts. First, I describe potential factors responsible for the observed immigrant vulnerability during and after the Great Recession and contrast contexts of reception for Latino immigrants. In the second part, I provide examples of how immigrants responded to their increased vulnerability, what we have referred throughout the volume as immigrant resilience, and explain how the implementation of immigration policies in the US and a difficult economic environment in Spain have limited their resilient strategies. In this second part, I also consider changes in immigrant choices and strategies, return migration (particularly from Mexico to the US and from Spain to the Andean region) and forced return migration (or deportations) and its effects. To close the volume, I identify areas of further research to continue the exploration of Latino immigration using a transatlantic comparative perspective.

13.1   Increasing Vulnerability: Bad Jobs, Racialization, and Criminalization

Globalization has increased inequalities and decreased economic security. As a result, there is a growing polarization in the labor market, and a decline in human security. Human security is understood as the absence of, or freedom from, any threat to the core values of human dignity such as physical survival, well-being, and identity (Commission on Human Security 2003). Therefore, there are two polarizing forces at play for those on the move: (a) increasing competition and dynamism for highly skilled immigrants, and (b) an increasing number of unskilled workers who cross international borders. Consequently, immigrants, particularly unskilled workers will be placed in social categories that "correspond" to their class, race and ethnicity, gender and legal statuses, and these social positions are likely to reinforce their vulnerability. As defined in Chap. 1, the vulnerability of a person or group, such as immigrants, is determined by the absolute or relative deprivation of symbolic, social, emotional, or material resources or the difficulty or impossibility to use them in a specific historical context due to institutional, political, economic, social, or cultural constraints.

The vast literature on immigrant integration suggests that as immigrants spend more time in their destination communities, they become more acculturated, enhance their integration, and reduce their vulnerability. However, theories of segmented assimilation show that this segmented process traps some immigrants in the lower social tiers (Portes and Zhou 1993; Haller et al. 2011), and theories of replenished ethnicity (Jimenez 2008) proposed that the continued influx of a sizable immigrant population sharpens intergroup boundaries and animates expectations about ethnic authenticity. Moreover, the emerging literature on the effects of increasing legislation against immigrants shows that the rise in unauthorized Latino migration to the US-fueled by increasing demand of unskilled workers after 1965, and the discourse generated by some politicians and journalists framed Latino immigrants as dangerous subjects threatening the host society. Therefore, Latino immigrants have been subjected to "rising hostility, official exclusion and heightened repression" (Massey and Pren 2012: 15; Ngai 2003).

In Europe, particularly in Spain, the guiding principles for immigration law have centered on immigrant integration and multiculturalism. The six immigrant exceptional regularization processes introduced since 1986, as well as a continuing process of permanent individual regularization by *arraigo* or length of residence, have benefited 1,162,979 immigrants (Cachón 2009: 195–196). In addition, Latino immigrants have been awarded particular concessions such as a reduction in the timeframe for naturalization in comparison to other groups (2 years for Latin American immigrants, vs. 10 years for nationals of other countries). Furthermore, the cultural and linguistic proximity of Latin America to Spain, and the experience of millions of Spanish nationals as emigrants in Latin American countries during and after the Spanish civil war, have facilitated the integration of Latino immigrants in Spain. However, the sustained and very high levels of unemployment have severely affected their quality of life, limited their opportunities, and even altered their life projects. Many immigrants have returned to their countries of origin or migrated to third countries.

13.1.1 A Jobless Recovery in a Segregated Labor Market

Chapters included in Part I of this volume provide clear evidence of the subordinated position of immigrants in segregated (and bifurcated) labor markets, in which we find the "good" jobs that allow skilled workers to advance positions in their careers as they build and consolidate their patrimony over time; and the "bad" jobs -those low paid employments in which workers are deprived from benefits and promotions and in which redundancies are common (Kalleberg 2013).

Although US employment recovered to pre-recession levels by June 2014, several years after the recession was over according to GDP growth, we have witnessed a jobless recovery (Coibion et al. 2013). A similar pattern was observed after the European crisis of the 1980s and it is very likely to be observed once again, and more vividly, in Southern Europe countries. In Spain, the economically active population has decreased and the unemployment rate is (artificially) decreasing. In this scenario of discouraged workers, employment will last many years before reaching levels equal to those registered before the recession (Cachón 2014).

The comparative analysis of employment developed by Cachon and Aysa (Chap. 2) shows that in both countries, Latino immigrant employment has become more vulnerable than native employment during the Great Recession. This higher vulnerability is due to immigrant employment's higher sensitivity to changes in the economic cycle. This higher sensitivity is explained by several factors: immigrants' overrepresentation in sectors most affected by economic crises (e.g. construction); their overrepresentation in temporary and non-tenure jobs; selective and discriminatory layoffs; participation in the informal economy; overrepresentation among the young population and among those with lower educational level; institutional factors, including additional requirements often linked to jobs to sustain legal status (for the case of the US, an authorized minority); additional demands from their families in countries of origin (e.g. the need to send remittances to sustain their families); differences in access to social protection (Amuedo-Dorantes et al. 2013); and, in the case of the US punitive immigrant legislation against employers of undocumented immigrants (Massey and Gentsch 2014).

At the beginning of the economic downturn, unemployment rates were higher among Latinos immigrants than among natives. As the recession progressed, we found different trends in the US and in Spain (Chap. 3). In the US, we identified trends indicating resilience to unemployment among Latino immigrants. After 2009, estimated Latino immigrant unemployment rates were lower than the rates for natives *ceteris paribus*. Latino immigrants were more flexible in the quality and geographical location of their jobs (Cadena and Kovak 2013). We also observed a deterioration in the quality of jobs held by Latino immigrants in the US: Latino immigrants real median weekly wages for full time employment in the tax year 2012 decreased; the poverty rate for Latino immigrants before the crisis was three times that of natives, and it has increased since 2007; part-time employment for economic reasons grew during the Great Recession especially among Latino immigrants; and a larger proportion of Latino immigrants compared to natives worked part-time despite wanting a full time job. In Spain, the deep and long employment crisis has profoundly affected Latino immigrants and their increased vulnerability is reflected in very high unemployment rates. One common trend in both countries is the relative lower proportion of long term unemployment among Latinos. However, these trends are not homogenous by gender.

Parella (Chap. 4) using an intersectional approach, found that employment losses are more prevalent among traditionally male occupations than among female occupations which are concentrated in domestic work and care sectors, often under informal employment arrangements. Moreover, other indicators such as wages revealed that Latin Americans immigrants earned the lowest wages before and during the crisis. In Spain the gender gap in pay has been considerably reduced for Latin Americans.

Immigrant vulnerability can be partially explained by immigrants' differential levels of education when compared to natives, but if ethnicity, class and the immigrant condition are barriers to immigrants' integration and social mobility, then we should observe smaller gaps between highly skilled immigrants and native populations. In addition, skill level should serve as a premium against unemployment and immigrant vulnerability during economic downturns (Orrenius and Zavodny 2009). Following this argument, Bradatan and Kollouj (Chap. 5) found that the 2008 economic crisis had a stronger effect on the unemployment rate of highly skilled Latin American immigrants than on US or Spanish natives, despite natives' maintaining a high level of labor force participation during that period. In other words, these highly skilled immigrants continuously look for jobs despite the difficulties of a shrinking labor market. The effect of the crisis on employment for highly skilled migrants was most notable in Spain. Regardless of skill level the foreign born were the first to lose their jobs. However, possessing high level skills served as a shield against very high unemployment among this group in comparison to unskilled workers and particularly to unskilled Latino immigrants.

Analyses in this first part of the volume indicate that the Great Recession not only increased the vulnerability of unskilled male immigrants, but also that immigrant women and highly skilled immigrants also faced the consequences of the downturn. Although the structure and demand generated by a labor market are fundamental features of international migration (Chap. 10), there are other fundamental elements like immigration policy and migration social capital. In the US, the continuous implementation of anti-immigrant legislation at the federal, state and local level has imposed several barriers to immigrants, and especially to undocumented immigrants. Menjivar and Enchautegui (Chap. 6) analyzed the labor market performance of unauthorized immigrants during the Great Recession focusing on the confluence of stricter law enforcement, criminalization of immigrant workers and limited economic opportunity. In addition to declines in the quality of immigrants' jobs they uncover exacerbated undergroundness and vulnerability during the economic downturn. In the next section, I describe some elements of the evolution of immigration policies in the US and Spain.

13.1.2 Receiving or Rejecting Latino Labor Migrants

According to Castells (1999) even in a global economy governed by neoliberal principles, labor mobility is limited by institutions, cultures, borders, politics and xenophobia; and these elements have feed-back effects among them. Immigration policy (particularly towards immigrants from Latin America) are at opposite ends of the spectrum in the US and Spain. The US has intensified the implementation of law enforcement efforts whereas Spain, before the Great Recession, designed and implemented immigration policies and laws intended to foster the economic and social integration of immigrants.

The US has a long history of restrictive and conditional immigration policy, from the Naturalization Act of 1790, to the National Origins Act of 1927, the Mexican Repatriation during the Great Depression (Hoffman 1974), and the Bracero Program (1942–1964). However, during the civil rights era and in an effort to de-racialize federal policies (Massey and Pren 2012) the US implemented the Immigration and Nationality Act of 1965 -which after being amended in 1976 and 1978- imposed per-country limitations on immigration for all countries. Since then, the US has implemented legislation to curb unauthorized migration and secure America's borders (e.g. Immigration Reform and Control Act, the Antiterrorism and Effective Death Penalty Act, the Illegal Immigrant Reform and Immigrant Responsibility Act, the Uniting and Strengthening America by Providing Appropriate Tools Required to Intercept and Obstruct Terrorism Act). Recently, US officials have discussed increasing the number of immigrant visas for highly skilled workers, particularly in science, technology, engineering and math (STEM), to enhance America's competitiveness in the globalized market.

Discussions on the immigration reform at the legislative level and discourse in the media, as well as the economic pulse of the US economy, have resulted in what Golash-Boza and Hondagneu-Sotelo (2013) called "a gendered racial removal program," which is instrumented by substantially increasing border control budgets, maintaining large and permanent detention and removal operations predominantly targeting male migrants, and designing state legislation to promote interventions that "make life so unpleasant" for noncitizen immigrants, that they voluntarily leave the US regardless of their economic, social, and cultural ties -the so called "self-deportation" policies (Pedroza 2013). These practices have reduced immigrants' trust in the legitimate authority of the State (Brotherton et al. 2013; Roy 2013), blocked any possibility of the integration of immigrants at the margins of American Society (Menjivar and Abrego 2012), and separated thousands of immigrant and mixed status families, who will only be temporarily deterred from joining their relatives in US territory (Hagan et al. 2008). In addition, the difficulty to travel has accelerated the north bound migration of thousands of children and youth, evidenced by the largest registered flow of unaccompanied minors to the US (about 47,000) (Krogstad and Gonzalez-Barrera 2014). The racial frames imposed on Latinos (Brown 2013) have fostered an environment of widespread discrimination and oppression against them in the US (Flores-Yeffal et al. 2011) that has resulted in increasing criminalization of immigrants (Ackerman and Furman 2014), not only while in the US but also as deportees in their countries of origin.

In Europe, despite several examples of xenophobia against immigrants (Cachon 2011), integration and immigration directives led by the European Commission (e.g. Common Basic Principles agreed in 2004, the 2005 Common Agenda for Integration, the 2009 Stockholm Programme and the Europe 2020 Strategy), have aimed at integrating legal migrants and EU citizens. However, the most recent strategies do not clearly set specific provisions for unauthorized immigrants, other than the emphasis on "security" of the European space.

The 11 Common Basic Principles of 2004 (European Commission 2004) set the agenda for immigrant integration policies at the national level. The first principle states that "Integration is a dynamic, two-way process of mutual accommodation by all immigrants and residents of Member States". However, other principles refer to the immigrant's responsibility to gain basic knowledge of host society's language, history and institution as conditions for integration, as well as the visible contributions of his/her employment. This is what Joppke (2007) has called "repressive liberalism". His analysis of obligatory civic integration courses and tests for newcomers implemented in Netherlands (which in the past embraced a multicultural model), France (previously implemented an assimilationist model) and Germany (which for decades was an example of a segregationist model) unveils that these countries adopted the liberal European standards and relied on migrants' 'self-sufficiency' and 'autonomy' making migrants independent of the state. Therefore, implementations of various immigrant integration programs had diverse outcomes across the region. In 2011, a new legal provision in the "Treaty concerning EU support to the promotion of integration of third-country nationals residing legally in Member States" (European Commission 2011) recognizes the changing demographic, social, economic and political context in Europe and recommended actions in three main areas: immigrant integration through participation; more action at local level; and, involvement of countries of origin.

In the European Union context, Spain (and to some extent Italy with the Turco-Napolitano Law of 1998) was a pioneer in setting a multicultural an integrationist immigration policy, which was created and implemented with the participation of the immigrant community through immigrant organizations. For example, in 2007 the Spanish government approved the Strategic Plan for Citizenship and Integration. This program included recommendations on 10 areas deemed strategic for immigrant integration: education, social services, housing, reception, employment, equality of treatment, gender perspective, immigrants' participation and sensitization of the Spanish society towards the immigration phenomenon, and co-development of the sending countries. The efforts towards immigrant integration resulted in the top-bottom approach to immigrant organizations and their transformation.

Cebolla-Boado and Lopez-Sala (Chap. 9) described the mortality of these organizations as well as the effects of funding cuts. They concluded that the economic slowdown provoked a change in the implementation of integration policy at the national level.

Before the economic meltdown, between 2002 and 2011 Spain issued 665,761 citizenships through naturalization (Ministry of Labor and Social Security 2013). This is both the result of extraordinary regularization programs and the implementation of an integrationist policy at the period of highest immigration to Spain. During the Great Recession, no changes have been made to Spain's immigration policy, only changes in the resources dedicated to accomplish the policy's stated goals, which have primarily affected immigrants' access to social and health care services.

The previous paragraphs describe the different orientations of contemporary immigrant legislation in the US and Spain. The Great Recession and its impact on employment and the subsequent implementation of conservative policies to control public debt in Spain limited the Spanish government's capacity to continue its progressive immigration policy. In the US, the effects of the Great Recession amplified the anti-immigrant sentiment produced by restrictive contemporary immigration laws.

13.2   The Limits of Latino Immigrants' Resilience

In our introductory chapter, we define resilience as an act of resistance within a "field of possibilities" delimited by the agent's position in the social structure. The exercise of human agency and immigrants' acts of resistance are not only delimited, but also limited by immigration law and law enforcement practices as well as by high levels of unemployment, especially of long term unemployment.

In the US, anti-immigration policies and law enforcement efforts at national, state, and local levels have reinforced the racialization of unauthorized immigrants. Conley (Chap. 8) describes how Latino immigrants in Alabama, a state that implemented the most punitive and restrictionist immigration law in the US (HB 56: the Beason-Hammon Alabama Taxpayer and Citizen Protection Act), adapted their daily routines to the restrictions imposed by the law. Latino immigrants feared interacting with government agencies for any purpose (from provision of utilities, to schooling for kids and reporting victims of crime) and were subject to racial profiling.

Anti-immigrant laws implemented in various states, particularly HB56, have been an unprecedented test for the anti-immigration movement. Only 3 years after their implementation in 2011, and in the midst of the recovery from the Great Recession, many elements of HB56, and Arizona's controversial SB1070 have proven to be unconstitutional, thus becoming costly mistakes for government agencies. Many Latino immigrants stayed in Alabama during this process, but according to population estimates based on 1-year estimates from the American

Community Survey (for years 2010, 2011, 2012) some foreign born Latino non-citizens who left the state after implementation of HB56 might have not returned as of 2012.

There are no cases of state level anti-immigrant policies in Spain. However, there are few instances where municipal authorities temporarily prevented immigrants from registering in the municipal records, limiting their access to social services. In order to compare differences in natives' perceptions towards immigrants in both countries, Cea D'Ancona and Valles Martínez (Chap. 7) analyze data from opinion surveys on the topic. Their study shows, that although ethnic discrimination is present in both countries, the acceptance of Latino immigrants is higher in Spain than in the US. This difference seems to be explained by the perceptions that Spanish natives have on Latino immigrants' social integration as well as common culture and historical ties. However, there are variations among Latinos based on ethnicity. Indigenous Latin American immigrants and those perceived as poor are not as well accepted. The study concluded that ethnic discrimination, then, is confounded with economic discrimination or class-based racism. As in the case of Latino racialization described by Conley (Chap. 8), phenotype (and particularly skin color) is a marker for origin and implicitly for class. The crisis itself has not affected the specific perception of Latin American immigrants in Spain, and their return to origin countries might have alleviated any fear about competition in a weak labor market. One common trend in both countries is that xenophobia increases in areas where immigrants are perceived as a cultural threat, particularly if their group size increases rapidly, as in the case of many new destinations in the US (Massey and Sanchez 2010).

In the analysis of the effects of the Great Recession on Latino immigrants in the US and Spain I find two scenarios: the US labor market demands labor migration but the US government limits immigrant's chances of succeeding; and the Spanish immigration policy aims to integrate immigrants but the Spanish labor market is not demanding the labor of a large immigrant population and several more years will pass before the Spanish labor demand returns to pre-recession levels. Both of these scenarios are problematic and consequential for immigrants. In the next section, I present data on voluntary and forced return migration from both countries.

13.2.1 Searching for a Better Future: Here or Elsewhere?

Since the late 2000s we have observed changes in the trends of Latino migration. These declining trends were even more pronounced during the Great Recession. During the late 2000s Latino migration decelerated first in the US and in the early 2010s in Spain. The slowdown of Latino immigration to the US is caused by two forces. Some Latino immigrants, predominantly Mexicans, are returning home and relatively fewer Latino immigrants are traveling to the US. In the case of Spain, there are an increasing number of South Americans, particularly Ecuadorian and Colombians returning to their home countries. The immigration flow is changing, not only in magnitude and direction but also in its composition. Immigration flows are increasingly feminized. Durand and Aysa (Chap. 10) analyzed structural factors and immigration trends in Latin America and noted that changes in demographic pressures on the labor markets have receded. Although the conditions in the region have improved during the last decade, there are still countries with low levels of development or where insecurity and crime are of concern.

Because the US does not collect population records, return migration can be analyzed by examining data from the origin countries. Ramirez Garcia and Meza Gonzalez (2012) used data from the 2000 and 2010 Mexican censuses to estimate Mexican born immigrant stock in the US. According to their estimations, the annual average net migration flow between 1995 and 2000 was of 241,830 migrants, and for the period 2005–2010 it declined to 36,539 migrants. In addition, return migrants (as defined above) went from 260,650 between 1995 and 2000, to 307,783 between 2005 and 2010.

Although the Mexican case is frequently studied, data from US decennial census indicate that similar trends are observed for a variety of Latin American countries. Table 13.1 shows US immigration growth rates for intercensal periods between 1960 and 2010. The average immigration growth rate between 2000 and 2010 (about 32 %) is significantly lower than for the previous decennial period (about 91 %). For all countries, but Cuba and Argentina, the rates of growth between 2000

Table 13.1 Decennial US immigration growth rates from selected Latin American countries, 1960–2010

Country	1960–1970	1970–1980	1980–1990	1990–2000	2000–2010
Latin America	98.61	142.38	92.29	91.33	31.93
Cuba	454.70	38.44	21.25	18.42	26.58
Dominican Republic	415.26	176.26	105.65	97.69	27.85
Haiti	481.94	229.68	143.95	86.04	40.03
Mexico	31.92	189.48	95.43	113.53	27.61
El Salvador	149.08	500.92	392.80	75.61	48.54
Guatemala	222.54	263.41	257.90	112.93	72.85
Honduras	193.99	104.80	178.19	159.68	84.75
Nicaragua	70.20	173.90	281.88	30.64	12.37
Argentina	170.24	53.76	34.37	35.28	36.99
Bolivia	216.97	110.54	116.36	70.20	48.09
Colombia	404.99	125.86	99.38	78.20	24.85
Ecuador	378.01	134.92	66.40	108.37	48.40
Peru	205.03	156.18	159.84	92.92	54.05
Venezuela	65.64	193.28	26.56	154.12	71.95

Sources: US Census Bureau, 2006–2011 American Community Surveys (ACS), Table B05006 "Place of birth for the foreign-born population"; Decennial Census 2000, Summary file 3, Table QT-P15. "Region and country or area of birth of the foreign-born population: 2000"; Gibson and Lennon (1999). Own estimations

and 2010 are lower than between 1990 and 2000. Those countries with low levels of development or experiencing periods of political instability are still sending a substantial number of immigrants to the US (e.g. Haiti, El Salvador, Guatemala, Honduras, Bolivia, Ecuador, Peru and Venezuela).

While municipal residential records are available in Spain, their accuracy is questionable. When compared to immigration data from countries of destination for Spanish origin migrants, the research literature recognizes that Spanish municipal residential records underestimate return migration (Cachon 2014). Although return migration data is underestimated, if we assume that this underestimation is uniform over time, then variations in the data refer to real trends in net migration. Table 13.2 shows net migration statistics from municipal residential records by Spanish citizenship and country of birth. Estimations for 2012 indicate a negative net migration of 6,534 persons; 56,392 Spanish citizens left Spain and the largest groups were born in Spain, Ecuador, Venezuela, Morocco, and Colombia.

For non-Spanish citizens trends were different: 336,110 immigrants arrived to Spain and 320,657 left the country. Morocco is a country with a circular flow of migrants. People from Ecuador, Bolivia, Argentina, and Colombia have left Spain in large numbers. However, Cubans immigrants (Spanish citizens and non-citizens alike) continue to arrive, as well as immigrants from the Dominican Republic.

Trends of out-migration accelerated in 2013, as presented in Table 13.2. Spain lost 111,153 persons: 33 % were Spanish citizens (of whom 78 % were born in Spain) and 67 % were Spanish non-citizens. The largest emigration is of persons born in other countries of the European Union, followed by persons born in Ecuador (39 % Spanish citizens; 61 % Spanish non-citizens), Bolivia (3 % Spanish citizens; 97 % Spanish non-citizens), Colombia (65 % Spanish citizens; 35 % Spanish non-citizens) and Argentina (91 % Spanish citizens; 9 % Spanish non-citizens). Net immigration from Cuba and the Dominican Republic is still substantial even when large contingents of Latin American immigrants are leaving Spain.

Even as a significant number of immigrants who arrived during the Spanish immigration boom are returning to their countries of origin or to other countries, the data show diverse patterns. There is a sustained circular migration between Morocco and Spain, a constant net immigration from Cuba and the Dominican Republic, and return migration to South America. In the case of Cuban immigrants a large percentage is composed of descendants of Spanish citizenships who benefited from the Historic Memory Law (Izquierdo 2011). The case of the Dominican Republic might be explained by the consolidation of migrant social capital through networks resilient to changes in the economic cycle. There is also a constant and positive net migration of people from China.

As mentioned earlier one of the guiding principles of Spanish immigration policy was to lead co-development programs with sending countries. Spain signed and funded several bi-national agreements and programs with Morocco in 1999; Colombia, Ecuador and Dominican Republic in 2001; Romania and Poland in 2002; and Bulgaria and Guinea Bissau in 2003. It has been common among European countries to sign bi-national agreements to regulate migration (Geronimi et al. 2004). The efficiency of these agreements is questionable. The majority of

Table 13.2 International migration statistics from municipal residential records by Spanish nationality and country of birth (2013)

Country of birth	Immigration			Emigration			Net migration		
	Total	Spanish citizens	Spanish non-citizens	Total	Spanish citizens	Spanish non-citizens	Total	Spanish citizens	Spanish non-citizens
TOTAL	342,390	35,354	307,036	453,543	72,449	381,094	−111,153	−37,095	−74,058
Europe	145,213	20,887	124,326	223,066	49,780	173,286	−77,853	−28,893	−48,960
European Union	125,151	20,321	104,830	207,705	49,114	158,591	−82,554	−28,793	−53,761
Spain	26,541	18,197	8,344	63,668	47,278	16,390	−37,127	−29,081	−8,046
Romania	28,782	15	28,767	58,429	15	58,414	−29,647	0	−29,647
Africa	56,377	1,154	55,223	59,118	2,879	56,239	−2,741	−1,725	−1,016
Morocco	32,294	614	31,680	34,210	2,160	32,050	−1,916	−1,546	−370
America	102,376	12,301	90,075	140,711	19,149	121,562	−38,335	−6,848	−31,487
Argentina	7,003	1,106	5,897	12,317	1,586	10,731	−5,314	−480	−4,834
Bolivia	5,543	185	5,358	14,765	444	14,321	−9,222	−259	−8,963
Colombia	11,807	784	11,023	17,295	2,682	14,613	−5,488	−1,898	−3,590
Cuba	8,741	3,147	5,594	3,555	977	2,578	5,186	2,170	3,016
Ecuador	8,293	1,346	6,947	23,170	7,124	16,046	−14,877	−5,778	−9,099
Dominican Republic	9,907	704	9,203	5,475	790	4,685	4,432	−86	4,518
Venezuela	7,674	2,165	5,509	7,555	2,241	5,314	119	−76	195
Asia	37,787	942	36,845	30,179	596	29,583	7,608	346	7,262
China	12,943	269	12,674	9,611	72	9,539	3,332	197	3,135

Source: Instituto Nacional de Estadística (2014), own estimations

return migrants do not participate in the programs created as laid out in the agreements. The bi-national agreements signed between Spain and Colombia, and Spain and Ecuador deserve special attention because Ecuadorians and Colombians are the two largest groups of Latin American immigrants in Spain. Both agreements included provisions on return migration. Article 12 in both agreements establishes that both countries will design assistance programs for voluntary return and that these programs should support reintegration through the development of projects that recognize work experience acquired abroad; the promotion of small business; and, the creation of bi-national companies. As described in Chap. 10, Colombia has created a framework for migrant return. Due to the importance of international migration for Ecuador, the country created an emigrant-dedicated Ministry, the Secretaria Nacional del Migrante, which carries out the program "Bienvenidos a casa". This plan is in line with the binational agreement previously described and, as many other programs in the region [e.g. "Programa Paisano" (Mexico) or "Colombia Nos Une"], is aimed at connecting with immigrants and increasing their national identification (Delano 2011; Boccagni and Lagomarsino 2011). It is still too early to evaluate the success or failure of these programs on return migrant integration to communities of origin.

13.2.2 Forced Return Migration

The bi-national cooperation agreements and the reintegration programs designed by the countries of origin for voluntary return migrants are a stark contrast to the forced return migration campaign implemented through enforcement and removal operations in the US. According to the data published by the Department of Homeland Security 5,573,641 immigrants were returned or removed from the US (DHS 2013) between 2007 and 2012. Returned aliens are those who left without an order of removal, and removed aliens are those who received an order of removal. Among those removed, there are aliens who had criminal records, and those without criminal records. Table 13.3 shows estimated removal and returned alien rate, which is the number of removals and returned aliens per 1,000 persons born in the same country of origin and residing in the US in 2012. If we rank the countries by this rate, then we observe that the highest number of deportees net of the size of the migration flow per country is led by Honduras, and followed by Guatemala, Mexico, and Colombia. These countries are above the national average rate of 15 deportees per 1,000 foreign born persons from the same country living in the US. Moreover, if we compare the number of returned aliens with the number of removed aliens, we observe a different pattern by country. Immigrants born in Colombia are more often given the opportunity to return to their countries of origin without a deportation order. However, aliens from Honduras, Guatemala and Mexico are more frequently removed from the US territory. More than half of Latin American non-immigrant nationals who are removed from the US do not have criminal records.

Table 13.3 Alien return and removal statistics, United States, 2013

Region and country of nationality	Foreign born population (thousands)	Return	Removal		Alien return and removal rate[a]
			Criminal	Non-criminal	
Total	40,824	229,968	199,445	219,939	15.9
Africa	1,724	1,708	656	656	1.8
Asia	11,932	46,293	1,428	2,328	4.2
Europe	4,809	13,270	1,251	1,340	3.3
Americas	22,120	167,952	195,909	215,532	26.2
Oceania	240	608	189	65	3.6
Selected LACC countries					
Argentina	176	62	109	99	1.5
Bolivia	72	83	92	53	3.2
Brazil	326	520	421	1,835	8.5
Colombia	677	11,775	1,043	456	19.6
Cuba	1,114	87	49	7	0.1
Dominican Republic	957	24	2,168	665	3.0
Ecuador	421	761	702	1,018	5.9
El Salvador	1,272	297	8,640	10,037	14.9
Guatemala	859	22	13,459	25,218	45.1
Haiti	606	88	558	125	1.3
Honduras	522	163	13,785	17,730	60.7
Mexico	11,563	18	151,018	155,852	26.5
Nicaragua	258	35	725	648	5.5

Source: Yearbook of immigration statistics: 2012 (DHS 2013); Migration Policy Institute (2012).
[a]Returned and removed aliens per 1,000 persons born in the same country of origin residing in the US in 2012

According to official statistics, the numbers of returned and removed aliens have not increased on an annual basis during the Obama Administration (DHS 2013); however, the proportion of persons who have received deportation orders, and have therefore been criminalized without committing a criminal offense, has increased. Sorensen (Chap. 12) analyzes how the intensification and diversification of migration control in an era of security, and particularly exacerbated during the Great Recession, threaten to undo the link between migration and development. The migration-development link was built via immigrants' agency and transnationalism over time, through three main mechanisms: recruitment, remittances and circularity. Currently, migratory experiences are instead painful realities that encompass irregularity, danger, debt and deportation.

Although deportations from Spain are rare, the Spanish government has enforced measures aimed at ordering the transit of persons, particularly from

Latin America, with an instrument called "*Carta de Invitacion*" (letter of invitation) in which a relative or a friend sponsors a visit to Spain for up to 3 months for non-tourists. This document is issued by police departments. The case of the controversial fences in Ceuta and Melilla for immigrants coming from Africa and the Middle East and their increasing criminalization, is also of great concern, particularly when immigrants are sent back to their countries of origin without due process.

The comparison of the American and Spanish contemporary labor markets and policies towards immigrants as well as observed patterns of voluntary and forced return show two very different scenarios for Latin American migrants and none of them ideal even from a neoliberal perspective. In the US anti-immigrant laws have resulted in an unwelcoming context for Latino immigrants, and in Spain the very high unemployment rate is pushing immigrants to third countries or to their home countries.

13.3   The Road Ahead

As comparative social scientists our goal is to understand, describe and explain why social processes take diverse forms across social contexts and identify how globalized processes are localized. This volume focuses on one of the largest international migration flows to their main destinations, the US and Spain. These host countries offer radically different contexts of reception and both were heavily affected by the last global economic crisis. The diverse chapters included in the volume illuminate how Latino immigrant employment was affected during and after the economic crisis, and how immigration policy has shaped the conditions for immigrants in both contexts. Immigrants have responded by generating resilient strategies to their increasing vulnerability, including returning to their home countries, and potentially maintaining those social bridges they built during their trip. However, those detained and forcibly returned to their countries of origin, possess fewer and limited social and economic resources and are likely to experience the negative effects of their criminalization. For them the prospects of successful reintegration in their own communities are bleak.

The vast literature on international migration, offers several examples of international comparative research that have enriched our understanding at the micro, meso and macro levels of analysis. Together, the chapters in this volume aim to advance research conceptualizing migration as a complex, dynamic, and multidirectional social process in which immigrants as agents make decisions, not only to migrate to a definite destination, but also to consecutively adapt to changing environments and migrate to multiple communities or return to their home countries. These decisions are based on their social position and conditions in the community of origin, their moral codes and values, their effective and perceived social support, their perception on the opportunities of employment (and for some, professional advancement), their knowledge about the regulations they are subject to, as well as their perception on enforcement mechanisms. It is a fascinating opportunity and a moral duty for social scientists to continue working towards the understanding of how human agency is shaped in a globalized world ruled by neoliberal principles but limited by the state.

References

Ackerman, A. R., & Furman, R. (2014). *The criminalization of immigration. Contexts and consequences*. Durham: Carolina Academic.

American Community Survey. (2012). U.S. Census Bureau https://www.census.gov/acs. Accessed 23 June 2014.

Amuedo-Dorantes, C., Puttitanun, T., & Martinez-Donate, A. P. (2013). How do tougher immigration measures affect unauthorized immigrants? *Demography, 50*, 1067–1091.

Aysa-Lastra, M. (forthcoming). Immigrants' experiences with law enforcement authorities in Spain. In R. Furman, & A. R. Ackerman (Eds.), *The immigrant other: Lived experiences in a transnational world*. New York: Columbia University Press.

Aysa-Lastra, M., & Cachón, L. (2013). Segmented occupational mobility: The case of non-EU immigrants in Spain. *Revista Española de Investigaciones Sociológicas, 144*, 23–47.

Boccagni, P., & Lagomarsino, F. (2011). Migration and the global crisis: New prospects for return? The case of Ecuadorians in Europe. *Bulletin of Latin American Research, 30*(3), 282–297.

Brotherton, D. C., Stageman, L. C., & Leyro, S. P. (2013). *Outside justice. Immigration and the criminalizing impact of changing policy and practice*. New York: Springer.

Brown, H. E. (2013). Race, legality, and the social policy consequences of anti immigration mobilization. *American Sociological Review, 78*(2), 290–314.

Cachón, L. (2009). *La "España inmigrante": marco discriminatorio, mercado de trabajo y políticas de integración*. Barcelona: Anthropos.

Cachon, L. (2011). *Inmigracion y conflictos en Europa. Aprender para una mejor convivencia*. Barcelona: Editorial Hacer.

Cachón, L. (2014). La nueva emigración desde España y Cataluña en la Gran Recesion. Unas reflexiones provisionales. In E. Sanchez-Montijano (Ed.), *L'emigració a Catalunya, España i Unió Europea*. Barcelona: CIDOB.

Cadena, B. C., & Kovak, B. K. (2013). Immigrants equilibrate local labor markets: Evidence from the great recession. National Bureau of Economic Research working paper 19272.

Castells, M. (1999). *The information age: Economy, society and culture*. London: Wiley-Blackwell.

Coibion, O., Gorodnichenko, Y., & Koustas, D. (2013). Amerisclerosis? The puzzle of rising U.S. unemployment persistence. National Bureau of Economic Research working paper 19600.

Commission on Human Security. (2003). *Human security now*. New York: United Nations.

Delano, A. (2011). *Mexico and its diaspora in the United States: Policies of emigration since 1848*. New York: Cambridge University Press.

Department of Homeland Security (DHS). (2013). 2012 yearbook of immigration statistics. http://www.dhs.gov/yearbook-immigration-statistics-2012-enforcement-actions. Accessed 14 June 2014.

European Commission. (2004). Common basic principles. http://ec.europa.eu/ewsi/en/EU_actions_integration.cfm. Accessed 14 June 2014.

European Commission. (2011). European agenda for the integration of third-country nationals. http://eur-lex.europa.eu/legal-content/EN/ALL/?uri=CELEX:52011DC0455. Accessed 14 June 2014.

Flores-Yeffal, N. Y., Vidales, G., & Plemons, A. (2011). The Latino cyber-moral panic process in the United States. *Information, Communication and Society, 14*(4), 568–589.

Foucault, M. (1995). *Discipline and punish: The birth of the prison.* New York: Vintage Books.
Geronimi, E., Cachón, L., & Texidó, E. (2004). *Acuerdos bilaterales de migración de mano de obra: Estudio de casos* (Studies on international migration 66). Ginebra: International Labor Organization.
Gibson, C., & Lennon, E. (1999). *Historical census statistics on the foreign-born population of the United States: 1850 to 1990* (Working Paper No. 29), US Census Bureau.
Giddens, A. (1991). *Modernity and self-identity: Self and society in the late modern age.* Cambridge: Polity Press.
Golash-Boza, T., & Hondagneu-Sotelo, P. (2013). Latino immigrant men and the deportation crisis: A gendered racial removal program. *Latino Studies, 11*(3), 271–292.
Hagan, J., Eschbach, K., & Rodriguez, N. (2008). U.S. deportation policy, family separation, and circular migration. *International Migration Review, 42*(1), 64–88.
Haller, W., Portes, A., & Lynch, S. M. (2011). Dreams fulfilled, dreams shattered: Determinants of segmented assimilation in the second generation. *Social Forces, 89*(3), 733–762.
Hoffman, A. (1974). *Unwanted Mexican Americans in the great depression: Repatriation pressures, 1929–1939.* Tucson: University of Arizona Press.
Instituto Nacional de Estadistica. (2014). Estadisticas de Variaciones Residenciales. http://www.ine.es. Accessed 14 June 2014.
Izquierdo, A. (2011). *La migracion de la memoria historica.* Barcelona: Bellaterra.
Jimenez, T. R. (2008). Mexican immigrant replenishment and the continuing significance of ethnicity and race. *American Journal of Sociology, 113*(6), 1527–67.
Joppke, C. (2007). Beyond national models: Civic integration policies for immigrants in Western Europe. *West European Politics, 30*(1), 1–22.
Kalleberg, A. L. (2013). *Good jobs, bad jobs: The rise of polarized and precarious employment systems in the United States 1970s to 2000s.* New York: Russell Sage.
Krogstad, J. M., & Gonzalez-Barrera, A. (2014). Number of Latino children caught trying to enter U.S. nearly doubles in less than a year. Pew Research Center. http://www.pewresearch.org. Accessed 14 June 2014.
Massey, D. S., & Gentsch, K. (2014). Undocumented migration to the United States and the wages of Mexican immigrants. *International Migration Review, 48*(2), 482–499.
Massey, D. S., & Pren, K. A. (2012). Origins of the New Latino underclass. *Race and Social Problems, 4*, 5–17.
Massey, D. S., & Sanchez-R, M. (2010). *Brokered boundaries: Creating immigrant identity in anti-immigrant times.* New York: Russell Sage.
Menjivar, C., & Abrego, L. (2012). Legal violence: Immigration law and the lives of Central American immigrants. *The American Journal of Sociology, 117*, 1380–1421.
Ministry of Labor and Social Security. (2013). Observatorio Permanente de la Inmigracion. Concesiones de nacionalidad española por residencia. http://extranjeros.empleo.gob.es/es/Estadisticas/operaciones/concesiones/index.html. Accessed 16 June 2014.
Migration Policy Institute. (2012). Foreign born population by country of birth. http://www.migrationpolicy.org/programs/data-hub/us-immigration-trends. Accessed 14 May 2014.
Ngai, M. M. (2003). *Impossible subjects.* Princeton: Princeton University Press.
Orrenius, P., & Zavodny, M. (2009). Tied to the business cycle: How immigrants fare in good and bad economic times. Migration Policy Institute. www.migrationpolicy.org. Accessed 7 May 2014.
Pedroza, J. M. (2013). Removal roulette: Secure communities and immigration enforcement in the United States (2008–2012). In D. C. Brotherton, L. C. Stageman, & S. P. Leyro (Eds.), *Outside justice. Immigration and the criminalizing impact of changing policy and practice* (pp. 45–68). New York: Springer.
Portes, A., & Zhou, M. (1993). The new second generation: Segmented assimilation and its variants. *Annals of the American Academy of Political and Social Sciences, 530*, 74–96.

Ramirez Garcia, T., & Meza Gonzalez, L. (2012). Emigracion Mexico-Estados Unidos: Balance Antes y Despues de la Recesion Economica Estadounidense. In *CONAPO. La Situacion Demografica de Mexico* (pp. 241–259). Mexico City: Consejo Nacional de Poblacion.

Roy, E. (2013). Deciding to cross: Norms and economics of unauthorized migration. *American Sociological Review, 78*(4), 574–603.

Stiglitz, J. E. (2012). *The price of inequality: How today's divided society endangers our future.* London: W. W. Norton.